THE 50 GREATEST PHOTO OPPORTUNITIES IN SAN FRANCISCO

Matthew Bamberg

Course Technology PTR

A part of Cengage Learning

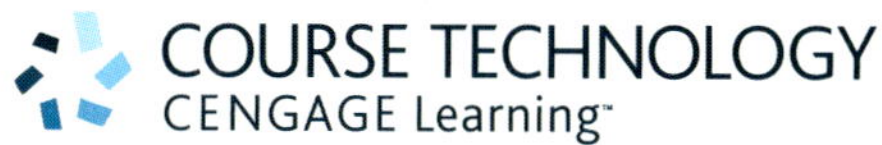

Australia, Brazil, Japan, Korea, Mexico, Singapore, Spain, United Kingdom, United States

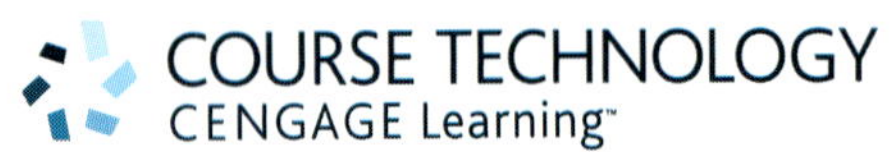

The 50 Greatest Photo Opportunities in San Francisco
Matthew Bamberg

Publisher and General Manager, Course Technology PTR:
Stacy L. Hiquet

Associate Director of Marketing:
Sarah Panella

Manager of Editorial Services:
Heather Talbot

Marketing Manager:
Jordan Casey

Executive Editor:
Kevin Harreld

Project Editor/Copy Editor:
Cathleen D. Small

Technical Reviewer:
Monica Stevenson

Editorial Services Coordinator:
Jen Blaney

Interior Layout Tech:
Bill Hartman

Cover Designer:
Mike Tanamachi

Indexer:
Larry Sweazy

Proofreader:
Kim V. Benbow

Library of Congress Control Number: 2008931090

ISBN-13: 978-1-59863-800-4

ISBN-10: 1-59863-800-9

Course Technology, a part of Cengage Learning
20 Channel Center Street
Boston, MA 02210
USA

Cengage Learning is a leading provider of customized learning solutions with office locations around the globe, including Singapore, the United Kingdom, Australia, Mexico, Brazil, and Japan. Locate your local office at: **international.cengage.com/region**.

Cengage Learning products are represented in Canada by Nelson Education, Ltd.

For your lifelong learning solutions, visit **courseptr.com**.

Visit our corporate Web site at **cengage.com**.

Printed in the United States of America
1 2 3 4 5 6 7 11 10 09

For Alan and Alicia

Acknowledgments

The field work in San Francisco for this book wouldn't have been possible without Fred Rimando and Bill Tarquino, who took the time to scout out photo locations all over the city as well as assist me in setting up shoots, even in remote places deep in the night. Ramiro Ortega and Todd Larson did a great job of sorting through the hundreds of photos I shot, helping me to choose the best ones to put in the book.

On the writing end, first and foremost I'd like to thank Cathleen Small for the best editing around. I'd like to acknowledge Amadou Diallo for critiquing my photos and offering keen advice on technical issues, and my agent, Carole McClendon, for having the faith in me that I could do the job.

About the Series Editor

Amadou Diallo is a New York City–based photographer, author, and educator whose passion for travel photography has taken him around the world. His words and images have been featured in national magazines and have graced some of the most popular photography-related sites on the Web. His fine art photography has been exhibited in galleries nationwide and is in a growing number of private collections. He is on the faculty at New York's renowned International Center of Photography. For information about his photography and workshops, please visit www.diallophotography.com. Amadou lives in Fort Greene, Brooklyn.

About the Author

Matthew Bamberg began his career in the arts as a graduate student at San Francisco State University in 1992. His work in the visual and media arts included video production and software applications. He completed his master's degree in creative arts in 1997.

After being a public school teacher for 14 years in the 1980s and 1990s, Bamberg became a writer. He began to photograph for the articles he was writing while working for the *Desert Sun* newspaper and *Palm Springs Life* magazine in California.

Bamberg's experience with cameras goes back to 1998, when he started shooting from different locations around the world. He began selling his photographs first at consignment stores, then at galleries and other retail venues in Southern California. His catalog of photography consists of thousands of photographs from his travels in Myanmar, Cambodia, Vietnam, Argentina, Uruguay, Canada, Morocco, Russia, the Baltic states, and countries throughout Europe. Those photos are soon to be published in his upcoming book, *101 Quick and Easy Secrets to Create Winning Photographs* (Course Technology PTR, 2009).

Bamberg began shooting with a Canon Rebel G film camera and worked his way up first to various point-and-shoot digital models, then to the Canon 350D (Rebel XT). Today, Bamberg shoots with a variety of cameras and lenses, including the Canon 5D with various L-series lens attachments.

Bamberg's first book was published in late 2005. In an effort to increase sales of the book, He worked with the publisher to start a blog, The Digital Traveler (digitalartphotographyfordummies.blogspot.com). The blog has become a popular forum where people can get photography tips as well as travel recommendations for places of interest for photographers.

Aside from writing about f/stops, shutter speeds, and the fabulous job the digital camera manufacturers have done that permits photographers to take almost noiseless pictures in the dark at high ISO speeds, Matt has written content and provided photographs for articles on Homestore.com, America Online, and The Weather Channel. In addition to writing photography books, Bamberg is an adjunct professor at National University and a trainer at College of the Desert.

Contents

CHAPTER 3 Events 117

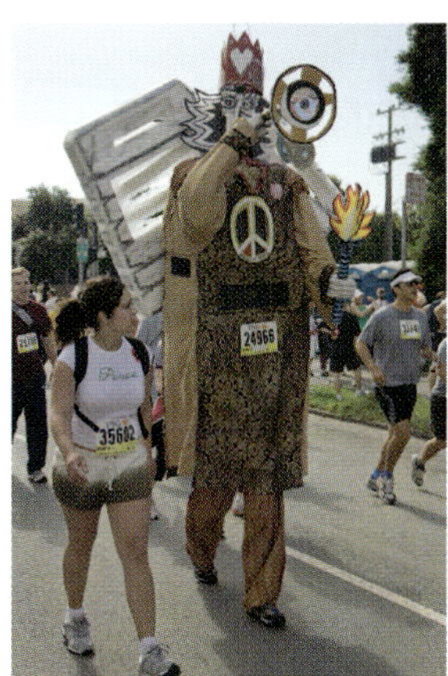

CHAPTER 4 Urban Oasis 143

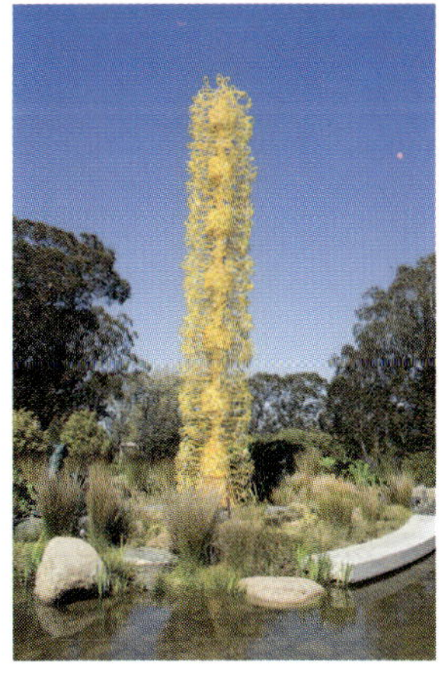

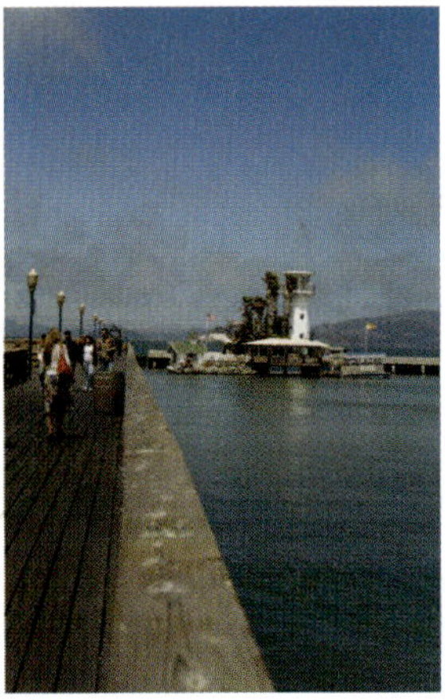

Introduction

This book is one in a series of travel guides written for photographers. If your photographic ambitions begin and end with a cell phone camera, this book may offer little beyond pleasing images. But if photography plays a large role in your travel plans, this book is equal parts photo essay and how-to guide for capturing some amazing shots on your trip. Have you ever seen a published photograph and wondered just how it was created? Well, this is your chance to go behind the scenes as I walk you through all the steps necessary to re-create what's in the book. You'll come away with professional-quality images that will have friends and family marveling at your vacation photos.

Great Travel Photos

Taking a vacation snapshot is easy; just press the shutter button. Creating a memorable photograph of your travels is another thing entirely. Thumb through any magazine of travel photos, and you'll find that the best contain three basic elements: a compelling subject, an interesting vantage point, and appealing light.

Pros may make it look easy, but the truth is that long before the camera comes out of the bag, a good deal of research and planning are required to combine these three factors in a single image. While on assignment, a travel photographer may spend days choosing subjects, exploring different vantage points, and waiting for the right weather before getting the shot that's finally published. For amateur shutterbugs in an unfamiliar city with only a limited amount of time to photograph, such in-depth preparation is rarely possible. The result? Disappointing photos.

This book helps you make the most of your photography in San Francisco by presenting 50 of the best photo opportunities the City by the Bay has to offer. I'll show you exactly where to find the most interesting and least obstructed views, give you the best times of day to shoot, and guide you through the steps I used to photograph the images in these pages. Think of this book as your personal assistant. The research, location scouting, and planning have already been done, allowing you to dedicate your time to capturing stunning photographs of the city.

San Francisco

San Francisco is an international tourist destination well known for its cable cars, bridges, Chinatown neighborhood, and Victorians. Its funky, offbeat neighborhoods have become settings for popular TV shows, novels, and movies. Over the course of one day, you could shoot hundreds of photographs because the city is filled with interesting architecture, lively street life, secluded getaways, and breathtaking views. This book aims to assist you in shooting a select group of compelling photographs of popular tourist destinations, as well as off-the-beaten-path hideaways. The choice of 50 photo ops in a city filled with a multitude of sights was a challenge. If I've missed one of your favorites, please know that some of mine didn't make the list either.

The shots in this book aim not only to help you learn traditional photography skills, such as f/stops and shutter speeds, but also to acquire some important rules for taking pictures. Of course, after you know the rules, feel free to break away from emulating the photos in this book and add your own personal touches.

There are a few websites that give you some great information about what's going on in the city—sanfrancisco.com, sfbg.com (*San Francisco Bay Guardian*'s website), and sfgate.com (*San Francisco Chronicle*'s website). You'll find that the public transportation system, called Muni, is the best way to get around. You can plan a trip by clicking Plan a Trip at sfmuni.com. For detailed maps of the city, go to maps.google.com, click Change Default Location, and type in **San Francisco**.

How This Book Is Organized

Each chapter covers a particular theme, with photo opportunities arranged in alphabetical order. At the start of each photo opportunity you will see weather icons like those shown below, followed by the best times of day to shoot. Taken together, this information helps you plan your daily itinerary based on optimal photographic conditions.

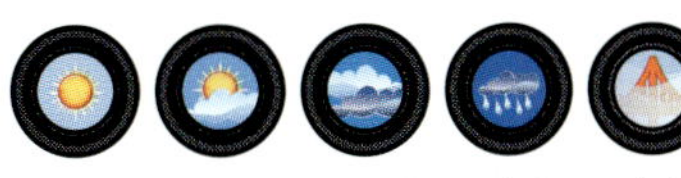

These icons indicate, from left to right, sunny, partly cloudy, overcast, rainy, and foggy conditions.

Accompanying text gives a brief overview of the history and significance of what's being photographed. Next, two shots for each photo opportunity are paired with detailed information showing you step by step how to get an identical shot. A photo caption provides lens and exposure information, as well as the time of day the image was photographed. You'll also find travel directions and admission information.

Will My Photos Look Like Yours?

With this book you'll learn where to go, what to shoot, and how to photograph it for professional-looking results. But snapping the shutter is, in many ways, only the start to making a great picture. The skills involved in transferring high-quality images to your computer, making adjustments for contrast, color, and saturation, and then printing them are thoroughly covered in numerous books on digital photography. The focus of this book is on everything that happens up until the shutter button is pressed.

The appeal of a book like this is that you learn in great detail how to compose shots identical to those of a professional photographer. But please don't stop there. Everyone has his or her own way of seeing, and you may find that a different angle, time of day, or weather condition makes a more compelling statement about your personal experience in San Francisco.

I've identified 50 interesting subjects to photograph, and I'll show you how I went about doing it. Whether you choose to duplicate every shot in the book or use these images to spark your own creative take on the city, my goal is for you to enjoy photographing this town as much as I do.

Photo Gear

The desire to capture professional-quality images doesn't mean you have to own the most expensive equipment. But you will need the flexibility that a single lens reflex (SLR) camera/lens system offers to duplicate the images between these covers. In many instances, a tripod will be required for a sharp image. I promise to keep the tech jargon to a minimum, but you should be familiar with terms such as aperture, shutter speed, depth of field, and focal length to get the most out of the sections describing how I set up each shot. These images were shot with a digital camera, but the concepts and techniques apply equally to film shooters.

Cameras and Lenses

While I'm out shooting or giving photography seminars, many people ask me about the photography equipment I use. I use a wide range of professional and semi-professional equipment. Some of it I'd recommend to people, and some of it I'd advise against purchasing. I use two cameras: a Canon EOS 5D and a Canon Digital Rebel X. I usually have a Canon 24-105mm f/4L IS lens on the 5D and a Tamron f/3.5-f/6.3 28-300mm on the Rebel XT. When I want wider angles, I opt for my Sigma 17-35mm f/2.8-f/4 lens. I can recommend steves-digicams.com and dpreview.com for finding the reviews about cameras and lenses. Flash and flash units aren't covered in this edition as ambient light is the only light necessary to take the photos in this book.

Digital Cameras and Focal Length

Unlike in the film days, when all SLR cameras used the same size of film, today's digital models vary in the size of the sensor that records the image. With an identical lens, two different cameras can provide different angles of view based solely on the physical dimensions of their sensors. On a full-frame sensor—one that measures 24x36mm—a 50mm lens is considered a standard view. But put that same lens on a camera with a smaller sensor, and a significant portion of the image is cropped off. To achieve a comparable view, you need to use a wider focal length. Table I.1 shows approximate focal length equivalents between a full-frame sensor and two reduced-sized sensors. For simplicity's sake, all lens focal lengths listed in this book will correspond to their full-frame equivalents. If the dimensions of your camera's sensor are smaller than the 24x36mm film standard, you'll need to use a wider lens to achieve the same field of view.

TABLE I.1 APPROXIMATE FOCAL LENGTH EQUIVALENTS

To match the coverage of a full frame sensor at...	A 1.5x crop sensor needs a lens at...	A 2x crop sensor needs a lens at...
20mm	12mm	10mm
50mm	35mm	25mm
85mm	55mm	42mm
100mm	70mm	50mm
200mm	135mm	100mm

Equipment Rental

If you're in San Francisco and you find it necessary to rent camera equipment, there are three businesses that have a full line of rental equipment. Adolph Gasser Photography (gassers.com) is located downtown. Pro Camera Rental and Supply (procamerarental.com) is located in Potrero Hill. Calumet Photographic (calumetphoto.com) is located in the South of Market neighborhood.

OK. Enough about gear. Let's get to the photos.

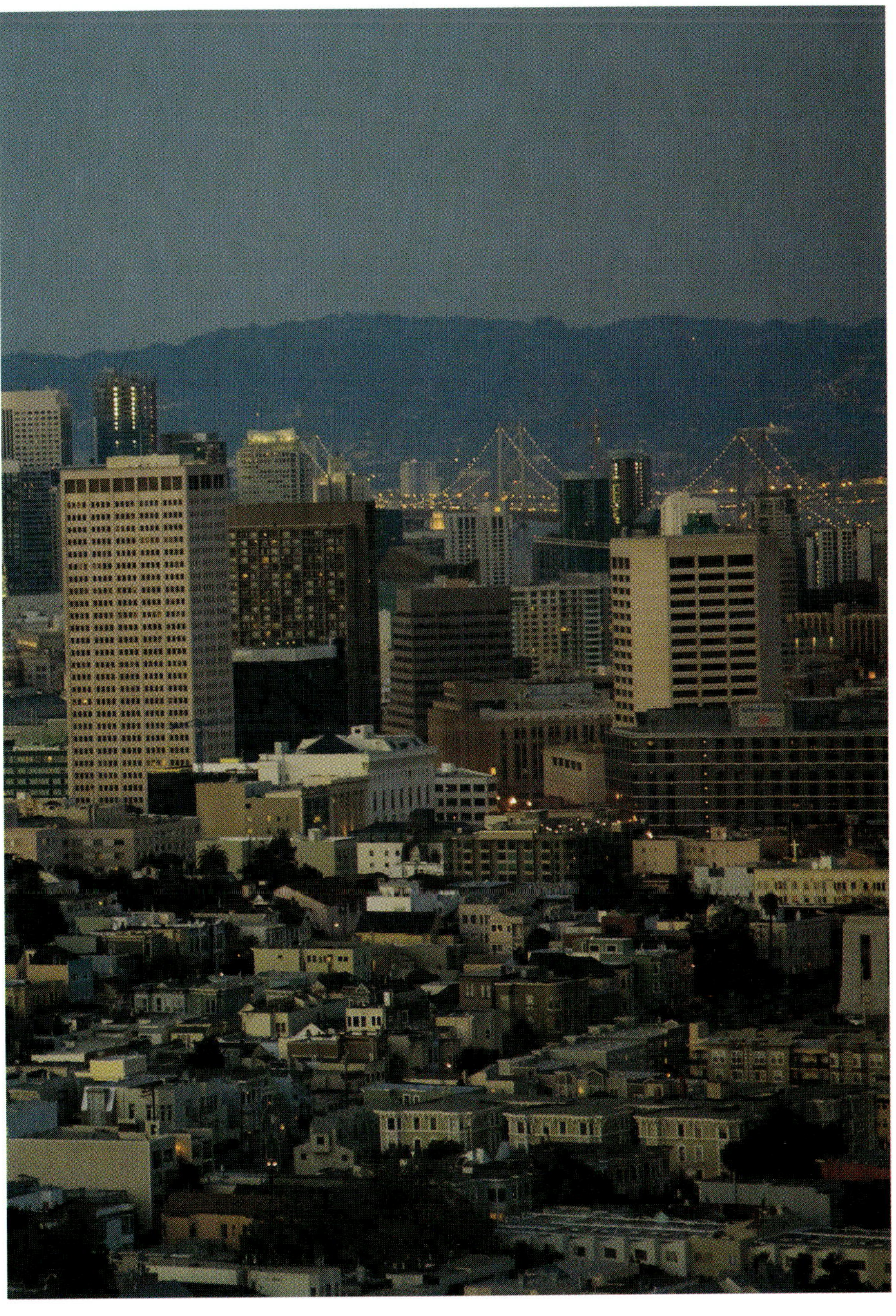

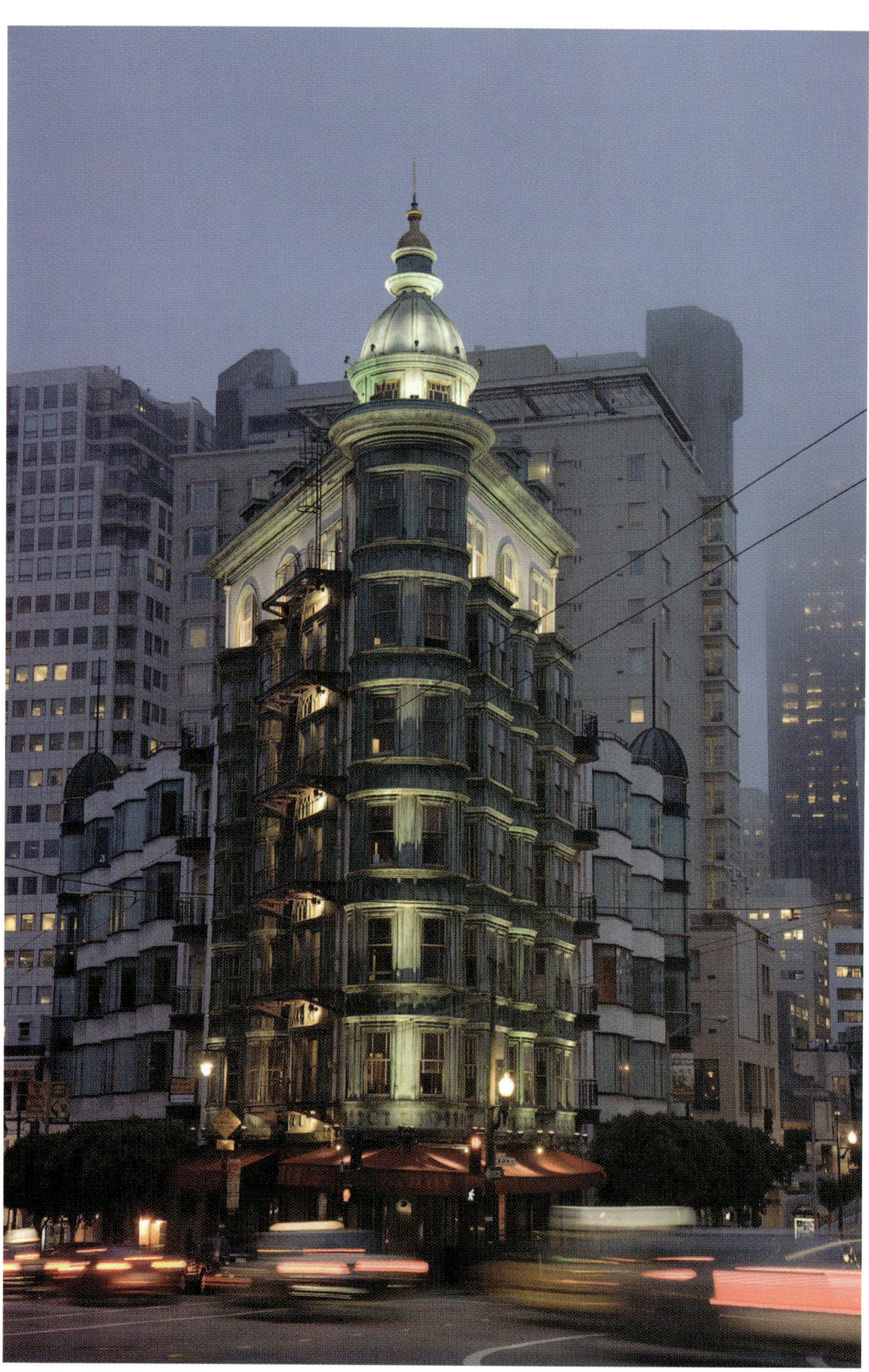

Columbus Tower.

Chapter 1

Architecture

San Francisco began as a small outpost during the Gold Rush in the mid-1800s. By the early 20th century, the bustling town of colorful Victorians and brick buildings had blossomed into an important port on the West Coast. The 1906 earthquake and fire changed all that, but the city endured and rebuilt. Today it's a booming city of the digital age, filled with skyscrapers, bridges, grand movie palaces, and Victorian houses. In this chapter, we'll explore the architectural masterpieces that grace the rolling hills of one of the most beautiful cities in the world.

Shooting Like a Pro

San Francisco's architecture is a grand display of eclectic design, which can be captured in small parts or on a broad scale. The bits of architectural detail are the easiest to capture. A sculptural work engraved into a building comes to life when shot with a telephoto lens. Telephoto lenses have the ability to bring items that are far away up close, which results in a tight focus, or narrow angle of view, on selected architectural details. There is a plethora of works on all types of buildings, from turn-of-the-last-century Victorians in the neighborhoods to grand neoclassical structures downtown. More complicated to photograph are entire buildings because of the tendency for parallel vertical lines formed from various vertical elements in the composition to converge or lean inward when you point your camera upward. To avoid converging lines—such as building edges and columns that lean into each other—you need to step back a few meters or more so you can keep the upward tilt of your camera to a minimum to bring the lines to a parallel configuration.

Overhead wires, which provide electricity needed to run streetcars throughout the city, are common, as are ubiquitous power lines. Sometimes they can be included in the shot as part of the city's character; other times, they are distracting obstructions. The overhead wires for streetcars are most distracting when included in the frame with power lines because power lines tend to be bunched up as they approach an edifice.

Particularly challenging is when the best shot comes from the middle of the street. In San Francisco, sometimes it's possible to photograph from the middle of the street because there are islands used for bus and streetcar stops (or vegetation) that offer good vantage points for taking a picture. On many of these islands, there's even plenty of room to set up a tripod.

Finally, it's always a good idea to scout out different vantage points before you shoot. Sometimes a good shot of a building might come a few blocks away from where the building is located.

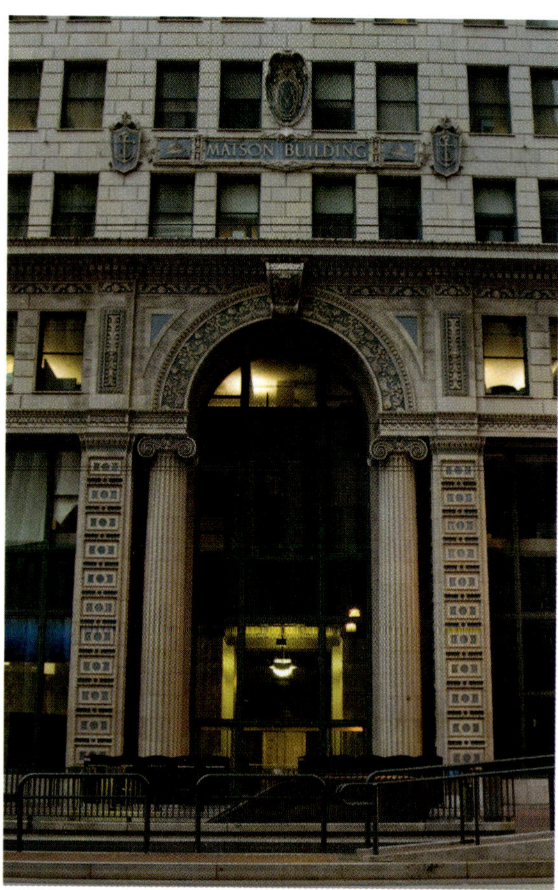

Matson Building near the Embarcadero.

The Gear

While a telephoto lens is good for architectural details on buildings, a wide-angle lens is best for capturing large parts of a building or an entire building. Wide-angle lenses are also good for shooting rows of Victorians, such as those that line Alamo Square. There's less chance of you having to tilt your camera upward, which can cause your photograph to contain a building that looks like it is falling over.

You can, however, use this effect and use the converging lines that result when you photograph the building up close to create drama, as shown in the image of the ghost sign and high rise near North Beach. But most of the time, you'll want to keep the vertical lines that appear as part of a building straight up and down, as in the shot of the Matson Building.

You can determine whether you have a wide-angle lens or a telephoto lens by looking at the focal length of the lens. Some lenses have only one focal length, which means they are not adjustable. Zoom lenses, on the other hand, have a range of focal lengths that can be adjusted. Wide-angle lenses have small focal lengths. For the purposes of photographing pictures in this book, lenses with focal lengths from 17–22mm on a full-frame camera (a camera with a sensor that measures the same as a film frame, or 24×36 mm) will do for most situations, though there are times when you may need to go with a focal lengths as small as 14mm. You can get wide-angle zoom lenses for a good price both on the ground and online. A good range for a wide-angle zoom lens is 17–35mm.

Finally, don't forget to use a tripod with a bubble level to ensure that both horizontal and vertical axes of your frame are straight.

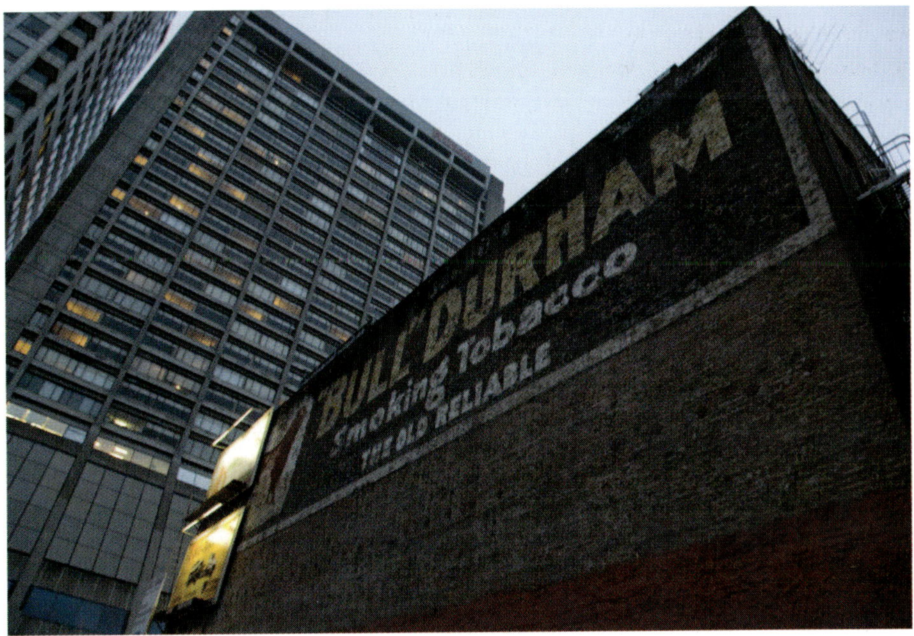

Ghost sign and high rise juxtaposed near North Beach.

The Plan

The best conditions for achieving a high-quality photo require you to shoot when the sky turns navy blue, which occurs about a half-hour after sunset. In the summer, the sun sets well after 8:00 p.m. so you can set up a tripod on almost any street after 8:00 to get in some primetime shooting as the sky turns navy blue.

In the winter the sun sets early, so you'll have to do most of your shooting during the day. Light is softer on winter days, making for some nice pictures of high-rise domes and above-the-street shots.

In the shopping areas of Powell Street and Union Square, shoot at dawn because there is heavy traffic during the day, which can leave your shots clogged with people. If you want people in your architecture shots, shoot on the weekends, because that's when the shopping areas are most crowded. With the exception of Christmas, crowds tend to thin out during fall and winter, which is the off-season.

Detail shots of Victorians work great when the sun is shining directly on the part of the building you are photographing. If you frame your image so the sky is in the background, make sure the sun is behind you so the sky will show up blue, as in this Victorian detail shot.

Finally, don't forget San Francisco's stunning views. If you're up high, take a picture. On any given walk up a hill or from most high rises, you're likely to encounter a breathtaking view, as shown in this shot from Coit Tower.

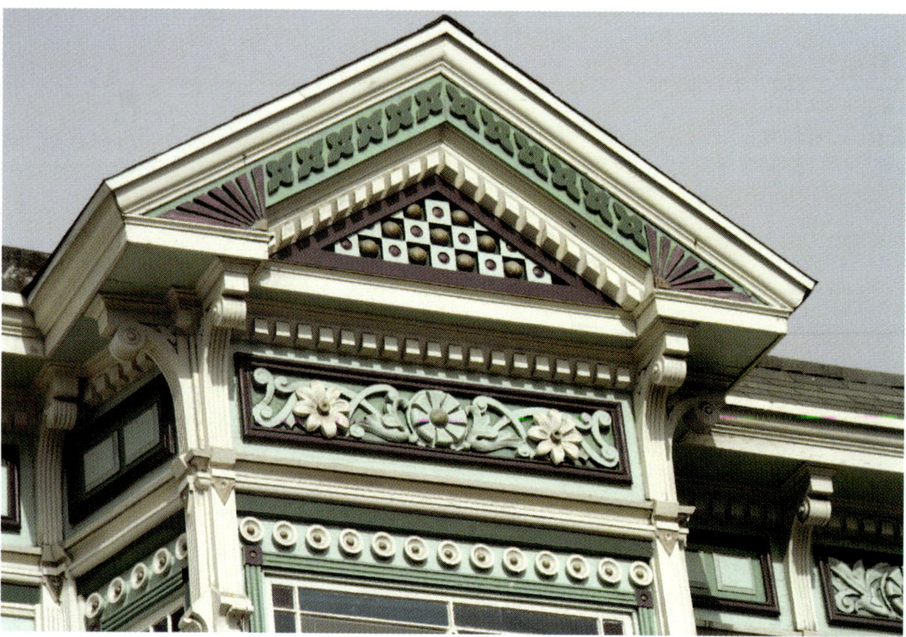

Victorian detail.

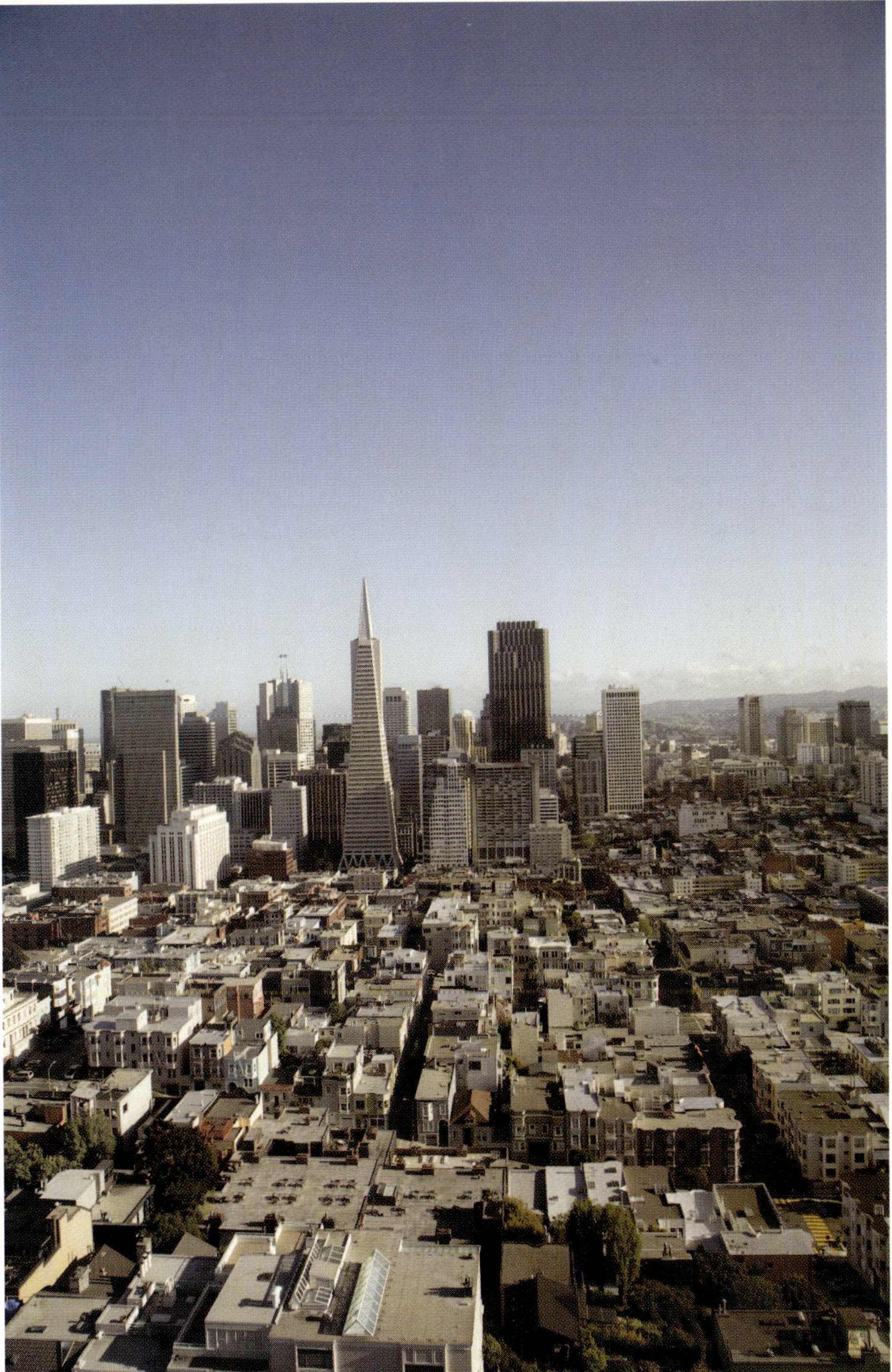

View from Coit Tower.

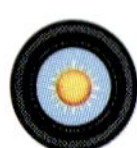 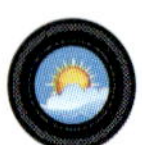 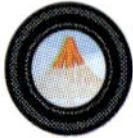

When to shoot: morning, afternoon, evening

Golden Gate Bridge

The Golden Gate Bridge opened in 1937. It's a suspension bridge with an Art Deco design. The bridge isn't gold per se, but a red-orange, which is an international maritime color. The sleek towers with repeated arched openings rise 500 feet.

Joseph Strauss, the chief engineer of the bridge, worked with engineers and architects to build it. The shape of the bridge towers and the Art Deco design were the brainchild of Irving Marrow. Also on board for the project were Charles Alton Ellis and Leon Moisseiff, who worked together to produce the structural design, a thin roadway that flexed with weight and wind by transferring stress to the overhead cables.

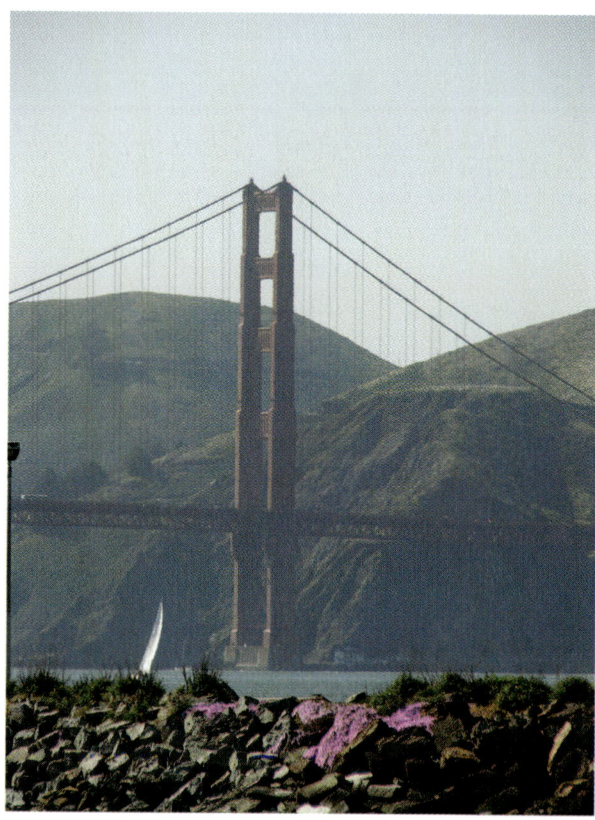

Golden Gate Bridge view in spring from the Marina Green.

The 1.7-mile-long bridge that spans the bay from San Francisco to Marin County can be photographed from many locations throughout the city and from the Marin Headlands to the north.

Located at the entrance to the San Francisco Bay, the area around the bridge has its own microclimate. Fog can move into the bridge at any time in spring and summer, and rain falls frequently in the winter, so dress appropriately. The best time to photograph the bridge during the day is in winter before or after a storm has passed. You'll get the clearest sky during these times with less light dispersion, which can happen when either fog or smog is nearby. The Bay Area experiences a short Indian summer when skies are clear and the weather is hot. You'd think that this would be ideal weather for photographing the bridge, but it isn't always because pollution comes with wind from an easterly direction. Finally, the entrance to the bay is a wind tunnel, which can hamper nighttime photography. During a stiff wind, your camera can shake even if it's on a tripod. However, there are many places at the tourist stop on the San Francisco side of the bridge where you can find a break from the wind.

The Shot

This shows the bridge on a May evening during dusk. You get to the spot by walking downhill (west) from the large tourist lookout near the main parking lot. After you walk downhill, you'll see a large fence. In front of the fence is a sizable graveled area where you can set up shop. In that area, you'll notice a floodlight blasting light toward the bridge. Position yourself so that your back is facing the floodlight with your lens aiming toward the bridge. You'll have to wait about 20 minutes after the sun has gone down for the lights on the bridge towers to go on. You'll need those lights to bring out the red in the towers. Exposures need not run more than 10 seconds, as there's lots of light coming from the west, even an hour or two after the sun has gone down. As far as composition is concerned, the photograph follows the rule of thirds for balance. The bridge moves along a plane into the photo one-third the way up, ending in rustic Marin County (to the north). The horizon sits at the lower third of the frame, so that the land and sea occupy one-third of the area below the horizon, and the sky with its golden color occupies the top two-thirds of the photograph.

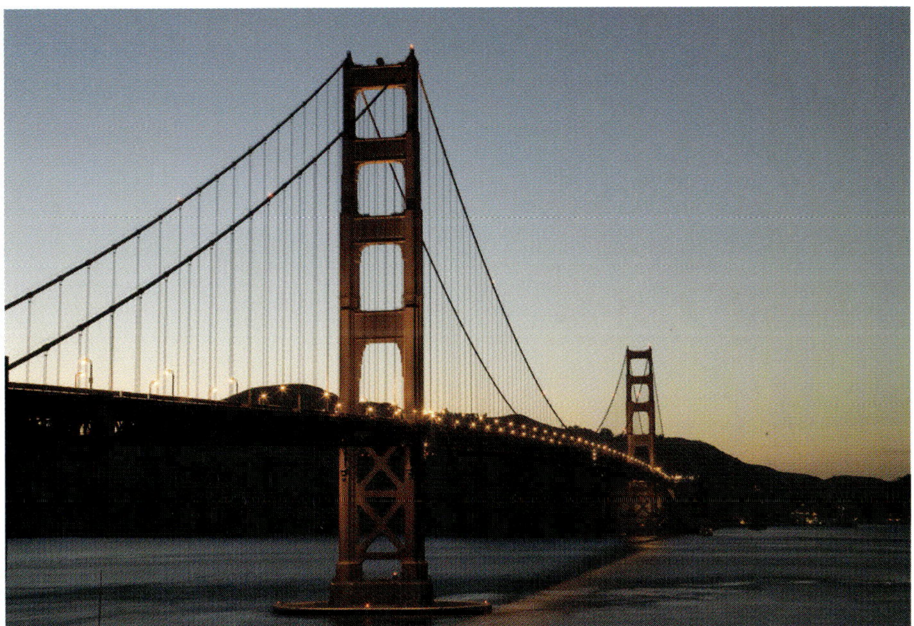

Focal length 55mm; ISO 200; aperture f/20; shutter speed 10 seconds; May 7:15 p.m.

The Shot

There's a footpath that winds down to Fort Point (the westernmost end of a series of parks with bay and bridge views that extends more than three miles east to Fisherman's Wharf) so that you can get pictures from various levels below the bridge. The path begins as a paved area just south of the southeast parking lot of the Golden Gate Bridge. This shot shows the bridge as seen from a point near the beginning of the footpath. I caught the activity that occurs under and around the bridge—sailboats, freighters, and cruise ships pass through daily. There's a fence along the footpath, but it's not high enough to keep you from taking a great picture of the bridge. The best time to shoot from here is during spring and summer because the sun will be behind you (to the southwest) so that blue sky sits in the northeast.

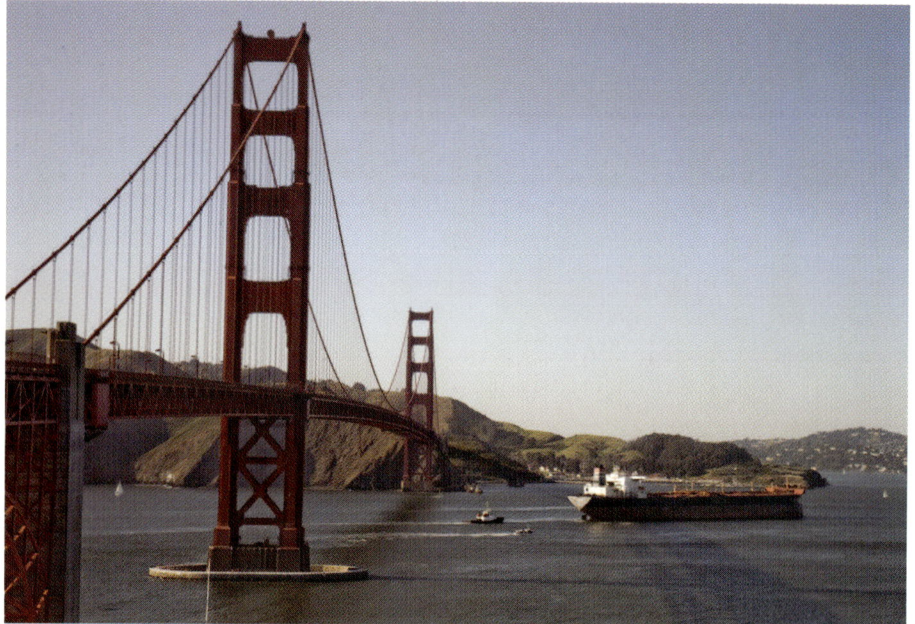

Focal length 58mm; ISO 200; aperture f/22; shutter speed 1/60; May 5:30 p.m.

GOLDEN GATE BRIDGE VIEWS FROM AROUND THE TOWN

There are great shots of the Golden Gate Bridge from Fort Mason, Marina Green, Aquatic Park, and Crissy Field. In these areas mornings are best to shoot so that the sun is behind you (in the east), so you'll get blue sky in the west. If you shoot to the west in afternoon, you'll get whiteout from the blazing afternoon sun. If it's foggy, however, and the fog is low so that some of the bridge shows, you can get some unique shots

If you're photographing from Lincoln Park, China Beach, or Baker Beach, you can shoot in the afternoon in spring in summer because you'll be shooting to the north-east as the sun goes down in the southwest.

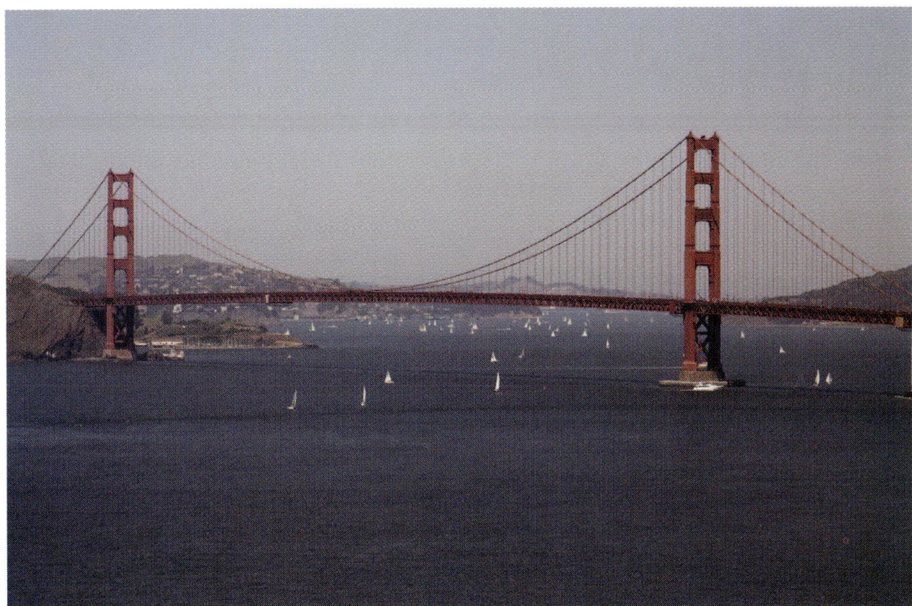

View of the Golden Gate Bridge from Lincoln Park.

Getting There

If you're taking mass transit, from downtown catch the 38 Geary on Market Street to Geary Blvd and Park Presidio Blvd. Transfer to the 28 19th Ave, which will take you to the Golden Gate Bridge.

If you're driving, from San Francisco, the South Bay, or the East Bay, take Highway 101 North to the last San Francisco exit (Golden Gate National Recreation Area View Area exit) just before the Toll Plaza. At the stop sign, turn left into the southeast parking lot.

From North Bay, take 101 South across the Golden Gate Bridge. Have exact change ready to pay the (currently) $5 toll, collected southbound only. Take the far-right toll lane #1 and make an immediate right, exiting the highway just past the Toll Plaza. Make an immediate right onto the roadway passing underneath the Toll Plaza and directly into the southeast parking lot.

From the southeast parking lot, to get to where this shot was taken, go to the lookout that's up the ramp from the parking lot. Go down the steps to the asphalt path. Take that path about 100 feet until it ends in a graveled area.

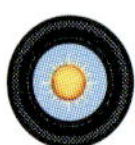 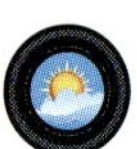 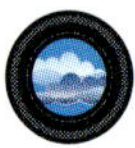 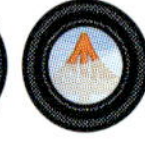

When to shoot: morning, afternoon, evening

City Hall

City Hall, designed by Arthur Brown of the firm Bakewell and Brown, opened in 1915. The Beaux-Arts style architecture of the building combines Greek and Roman designs with features popular during the Renaissance. Many sculptural ornaments are common in Beaux-Arts architecture. You can get great photographs by using a zoom lens to isolate and frame any of the ornamental details on the building. City Hall also has a dome, which is similar to that of the Church of St. Louis des Invalides in Paris. It is the fifth largest dome in the world. It rises over a foot higher than the United States Capitol dome.

The Shot

City Hall is one of those types of buildings that you can photograph at just about any time. It features views both at the main entrance on Polk Street (between Grove and McAllister) and at the back entrance on Van Ness. The former has the sun shining on it during the morning, and the latter does during the afternoon. Of special interest, though, is a photograph at dusk when the fog rolls in, creating light that is subtle and nuanced. The light dispersed by the fog makes the architecture look mysterious not only because of the fog, but also due to the trees being cut bare and leading into the classical architecture. The pathway of trees leading to City Hall in the plaza east of it begins near Larkin Street, which runs north to south. By walking south in the plaza, you can frame the shot so the first group of trees moves diagonally into the first third of the frame of the photograph. Photographer beware! It can get very chilly photographing in these conditions. Since the light was low and the conditions were windy, I used a high ISO to photograph the building. By using a high ISO, you can prevent blur from camera shake.

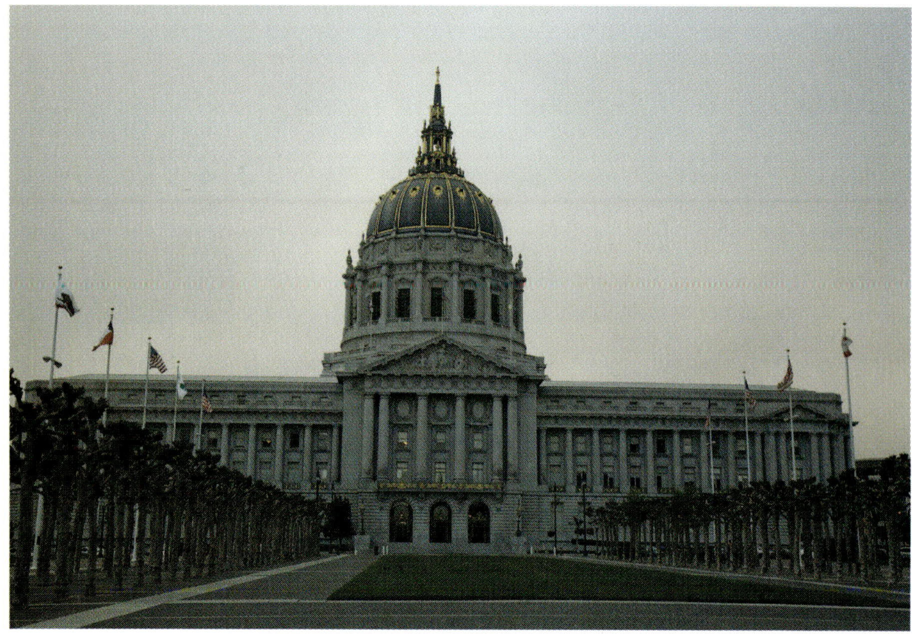

Focal length 45mm; ISO 800; aperture f/11; shutter speed 1/250; April 6:00 p.m.

The Shot

The dome is also one of those any-time shots. The dome is the same regardless of whether you shoot it from the west side of the building on Van Ness or the east side of the building at Polk Street. There's nothing like capturing a dome with golden metal sculptural work on a sunny day. The sun has the metal sparkling. To get the sparkle, shoot from Larkin Street in the morning and from Van Ness in the afternoon. The sky will be a deeper blue above and behind the dome if you shoot in the morning from Larkin Street because you'll be aiming your camera at the part of the sky that is over the Pacific Ocean, where there is no smog.

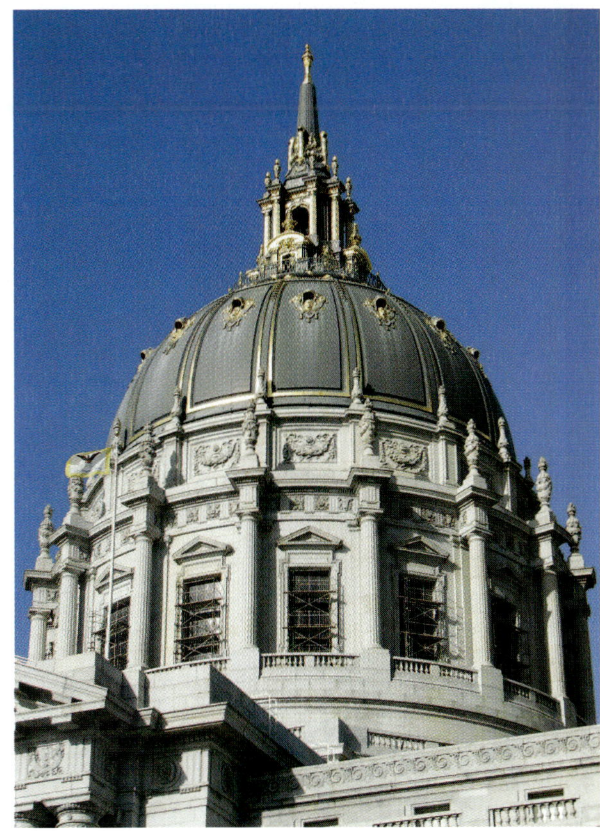

Focal length 76mm; ISO 100; aperture f/4.5; shutter speed 1/1000; April 2:00 p.m.

Getting There

If you're taking mass transit, from downtown take the Muni Metro J, K, L, or M line to Civic Center.

If you're driving, from the South Bay, take 101 North to the101-N/Duboce Ave/Mission St exit. Keep right at the fork in the ramp. Turn right onto Mission Street. Turn slightly left onto Van Ness Avenue. Turn right onto McAllister and right onto Dr. Carlton B. Goodlett Place.

From the East Bay, take 80 West to the 9th St/Civic Center exit. Keep right at the fork in the ramp. Turn left on Harrison Street and right on 9th Street. Turn slightly left onto Hayes Street, then right onto Van Ness Avenue. Turn right onto McAllister and right onto Dr. Carlton B. Goodlett Place.

From the North Bay, take 101 South and exit at Lombard Street. Turn right on Van Ness Avenue and left on McAllister. Make a right onto Dr. Carlton B. Goodlett Place.

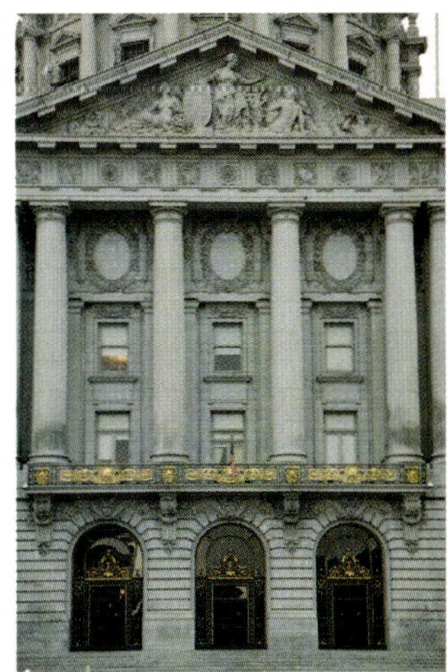

The façade of City Hall.

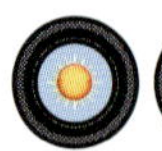 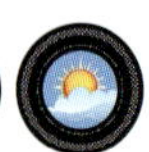

When to shoot: morning, afternoon, evening

Victorians

During Queen Victoria's reign in Britain, a style of architecture that included elaborate ornamentation on buildings, which could be produced efficiently, became commonplace first in Britain, then in the United States. A Victorian building boom in San Francisco from 1870 to 1915 came about as part of increased manufacturing of materials and goods. The homes were made from redwood, a rot- and termite-resistant and pliable wood, which came from trees that grew in abundance in Northern California. Mass-produced nails and wood cuttings to build the homes were made in large numbers at factories and were easily transported by the new railroads.

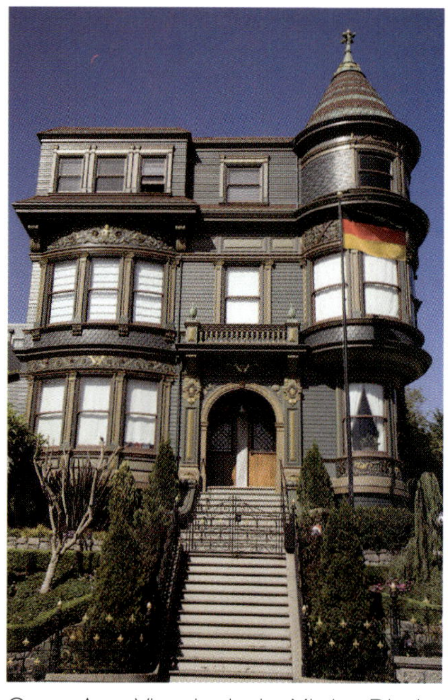

Queen Anne Victorian in the Mission District.

Because a variety of cultures immigrated to San Francisco, many different types of Victorians were built. There are Gothic, Italianate, Stick House, Queen Anne, and French styles, each style influenced by the culture of the people who built it.

Some Victorians look similar because they were built from prefabricated design plans and decorated with woodcarvings that could be ordered from factories and delivered by mail. The similarities among homes, often attached to each other along a block, make for interesting repetition of shapes and forms when photographed together. Such is the case with a group of homes called the "Painted Ladies" in the Alamo Square historical neighborhood. The homes were originally painted gray and black, but have been restored over the last few decades and painted in a variety of colors, which makes them popular to photograph.

The Shot

Cow Hallow, a section of the city uphill from the Fisherman's Wharf area, is a district with many notable Victorians. The advantage here is you get spectacular views of the bay behind them. If you walk along Broadway in Cow Hollow, some of the streets running north to the bay come with good views. One in particular is on the northeast corner of Divisadero and Broadway, where there's a Victorian you can frame in the foreground with the bay in the background. Often, there's fog in the bay that really adds another dimension to the picture.

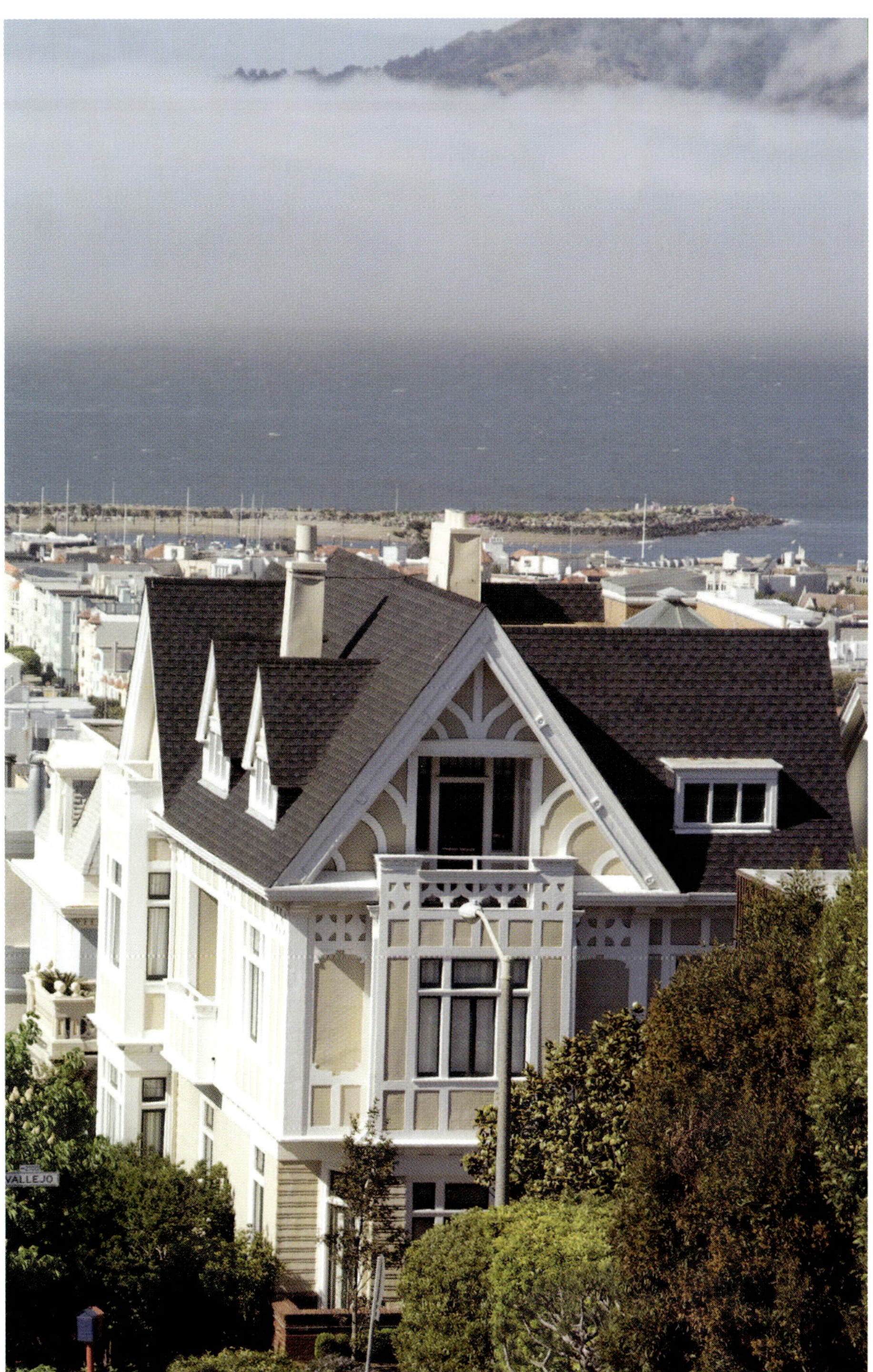

Focal length 163mm; ISO 200; aperture f/10; shutter speed 1/400; April 5:20 p.m.

The Shot

The "Painted Ladies" are best photographed during the late afternoon when the sun is hitting their façades. If it's foggy downtown, wait for a day when the fog hasn't gone that far

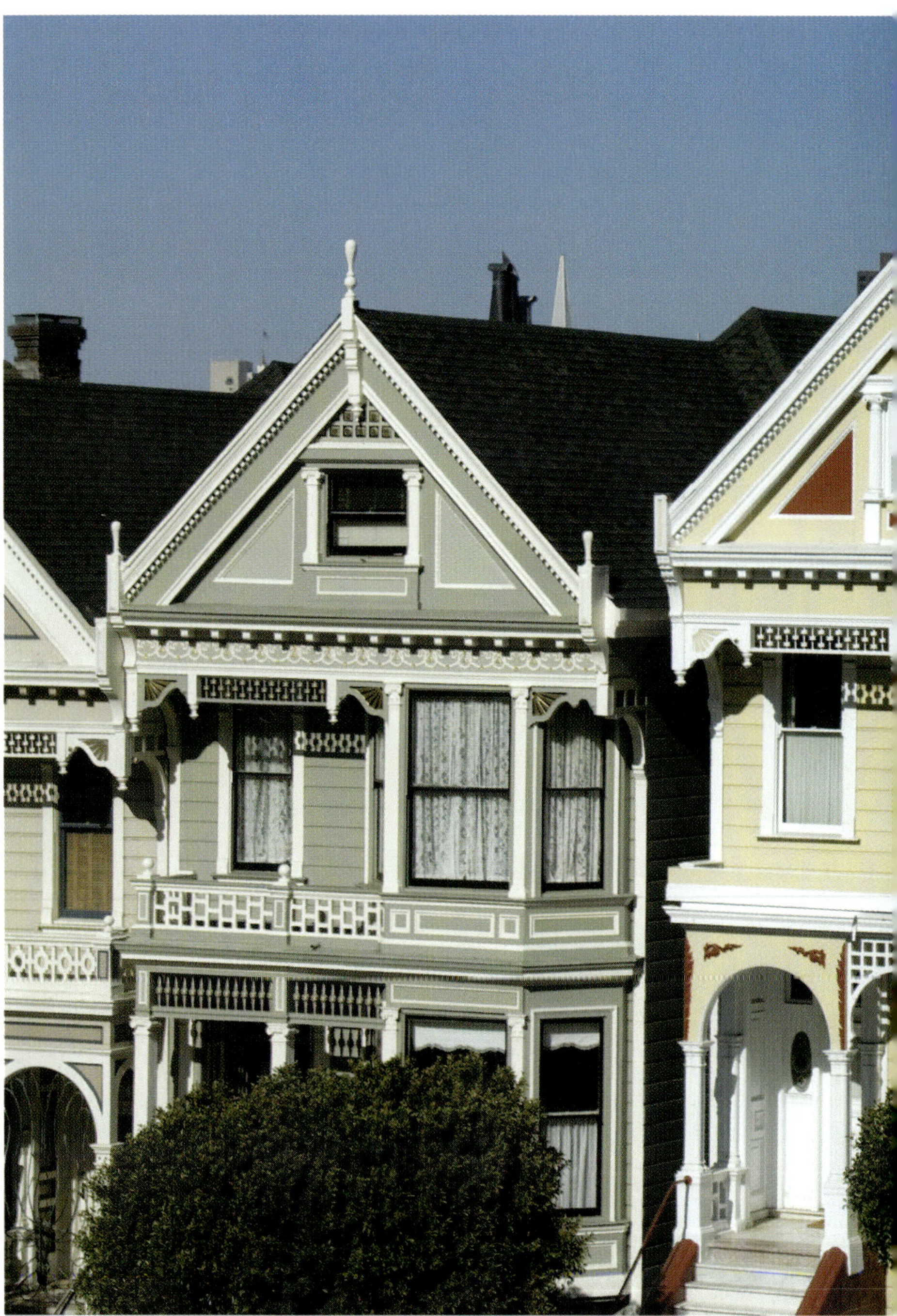

east. To photograph the Victorians without the view behind them, walk up the stairs, then partway up the hill just to the southwest of Fulton and Steiner. Frame your shot with just three Victorians and no view above to emphasize the architecture.

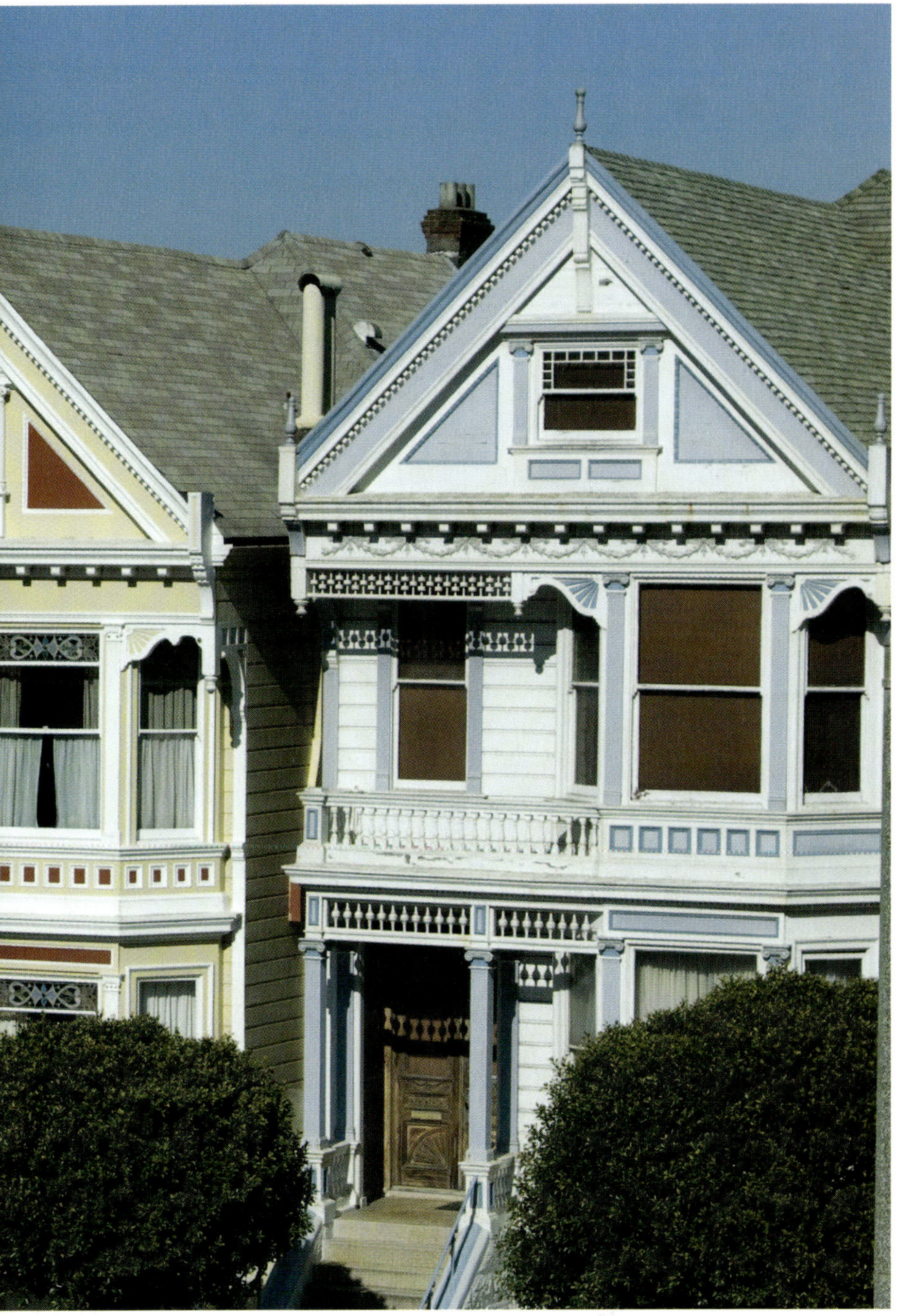

Focal length 55mm; ISO 200; aperture f/11; shutter speed 1/500; April 4:15 p.m.

A CITY OF VICTORIANS

San Francisco's first Victorians were built just after the Civil War. Victorians are concentrated in neighborhoods such as Noe Valley, the Castro, Pacific Heights, Cow Hollow, Hayes Valley, Haight-Ashbury, the Mission, and Potrero Hill. Many Victorians are city, state, and/or national landmarks.

Two Victorians are open to the public. Both are furnished in period furniture and can be viewed inside and out.

The Haas-Lilienthal House at 2007 Franklin Street is a Queen Anne–style Victorian that is open regularly as a museum. It was built in 1886. For hours the house is open, call (415) 441-3004.

The Colonial Dames Octagon House, built in Cow Hollow 1861, at 2645 Gough Street (at Union) is open for tours. For more information, call (415) 441-7512.

The Victorians with the least amount of obstructions in front of their façades are listed here. Each is a city, state, and/or national monument. Some are private residences. Do not disturb the occupants.

- A stick-style residence, the Charles Dietle House, built in 1885, at 294 Page Street at Laguna.
- Parisian-style flats built in 1910 in Haight-Ashbury at 1677–81 Haight St.
- Classic Revival Apartments in the Western Addition, built in 1904, at 91 Central Avenue.
- A Second Empire–style Victorian is the Western Addition apartment house at 1347 McAllister Street.
- Clunie House in Haight-Ashbury, built in 1897, at 301 Lyon Street (at Fell).
- A Queen Anne, the Atherton House, in Pacific Heights, built in 1881, at 1990 California Street (at Octavia).
- A Queen Anne, the Belden House, in Pacific Heights, built in 1889, at 2004–2010 Gough Street (between Clay and Washington).
- Belle Epoque Apartments in Pacific Heights, built in 1915, at 2415–17 Franklin Street.
- Italianate Manor Victorian in Pacific Heights, built in 1865, at 2727 Pierce Street between Vallejo and Green.
- Queen Anne, the Chambers Mansion in Pacific Heights, built 1887, at 2220 Sacramento Street (between Laguna and Buchanan).
- Classic Revival Victorian, the Queen House, in Pacific Heights, built in 1895, at 2212 Sacramento Street (between Laguna and Buchanan).
- Chambord Apartments in Nob Hill, built in 1921, at 1298 Sacramento Street (at Jones).
- Koshland House in Presidio Heights, built in 1904, at 3800 Washington Street (at Maple).
- Mish House in Haight-Ashbury, built in 1885, at 1153 Oak St (between Divisadero and Broderick).
- A Queen Anne, the Edward Coleman House in Pacific Heights, built in 1895, at 1701 California Street.

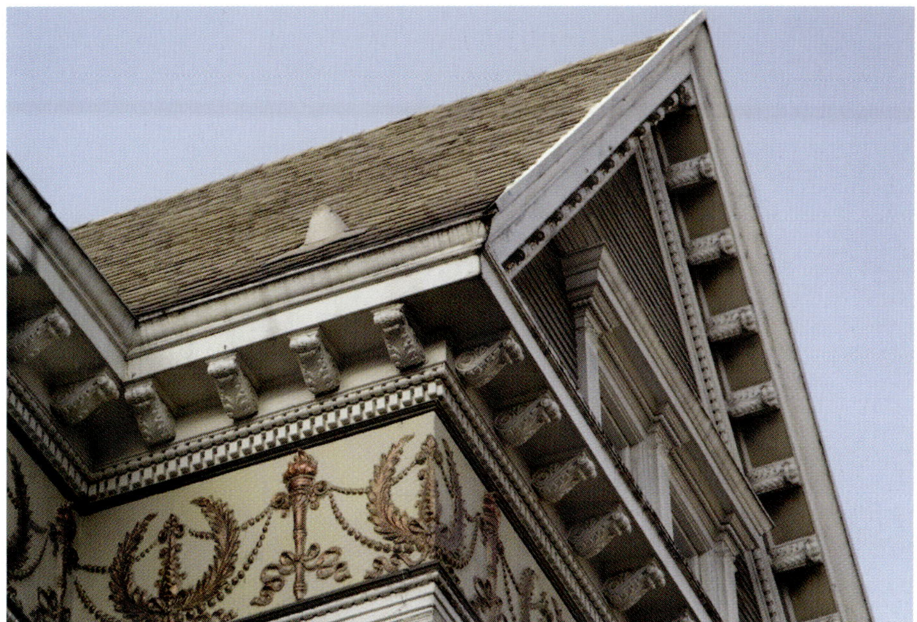

Architectural detail on Edward Coleman House.

Getting There

To get to the Painted Ladies using mass transit, from downtown take the 21 bus. You can catch the bus from various stops on Market Street. Get off at Steiner.

If you're driving from the South Bay, take 101 North to the101-N/Duboce Ave/Mission St exit. Keep right at the fork in the ramp. Turn right onto Mission St. Turn slightly left onto Van Ness Ave. Turn left on Hayes to Steiner.

From East Bay, take 80 West to the 9th St/Civic Center exit. Keep right at the fork in the ramp. Turn left on Harrison Street and right on 9th Street. Turn slightly left onto Hayes Street. Take Hayes Street to Steiner Street.

From North Bay, take 101 South and exit at Lombard Street. Turn right on Van Ness Avenue and right on Hayes to Steiner.

To get to Cow Hollow using mass transit, from downtown, catch the K, L, or M Muni Metro train. Get off at Castro Street and transfer to the 24 Divisadero bus. Get off at Broadway.

If you're driving from the South Bay, take 101 North until it ends on Octavia Boulevard. Turn left at Fell, right on Fillmore, and left on Broadway to Divisadero.

From the East Bay, take 80 West to 101 North, then follow the South Bay directions from Octavia.

From the North Bay, take 101 South to Lombard and turn right at Divisadero to Broadway.

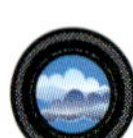 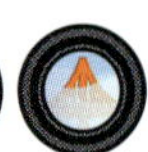

When to shoot: morning, afternoon

Auto Row

A strip along Van Ness came to be known as Auto Row in the 1920s, with giant, grand showrooms for the new cars coming to market.

Over the years, the number of car dealerships on Van Ness has dwindled. There are two historic buildings that housed car dealerships in the early part of the 20th century. One is Don Lee Cadillac, which has been restored carefully and now is the Kabuki Theater. The other is Earle C. Anthony Packard, which is now British Motors. Nowhere is intricate architecture displayed better than on the old Cadillac dealership on Van Ness. Built in 1921, the Don Lee Building was restored and converted to a movie theater more than 10 years ago. This building was designed by Charles Peter Weeks and William P. Day, who are also well known for designing the Mark Hopkins and Sir Francis Drake hotels. The queen of the Van Ness Avenue automobile palaces is the old Packard dealership, which was built in 1927. The red marble columns in front have been painted gray. (Sometimes people do awful things to buildings!) The interior contains an elaborate coffered ceiling. The building was designed by Bernard Maybeck.

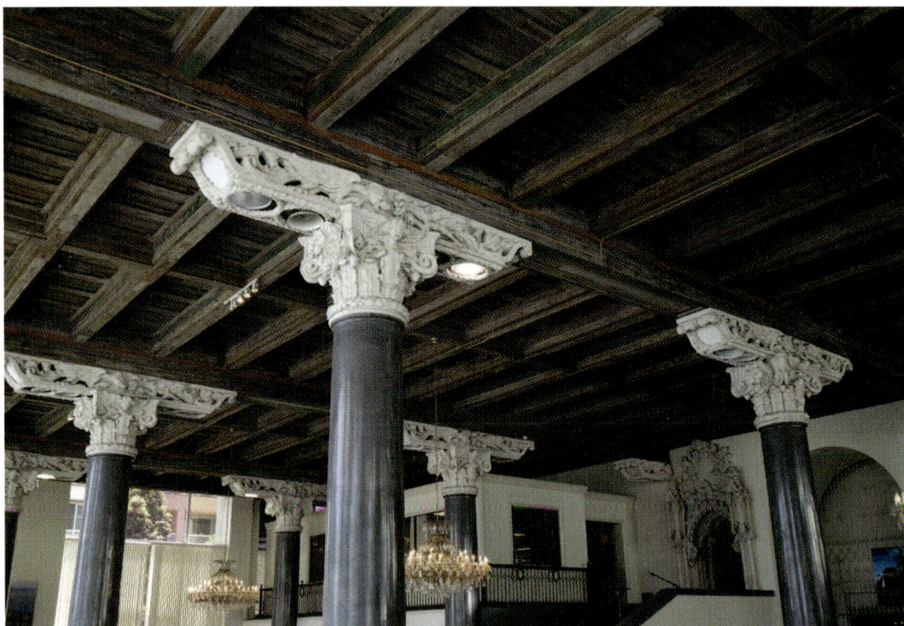

The interior of British Motors (the old Packard dealership).

The Shot

This shot details the sculptural ornamentation on the façade of the Don Lee Cadillac Building. If you try to shoot the ornament from below the building, tilting your camera up at the ornament, you'll get severe lens distortion. Better to take the shot from across the street so that the scene of the two men with wheels on either side of an emblem would have no lens distortion. A foggy afternoon is perfect for this ornament-like object because the fog disperses the light from the sun, which at that time of day shines directly on the building's façade. If you have direct sunlight on the ornament, you'll get shadows over the word "Cadillac."

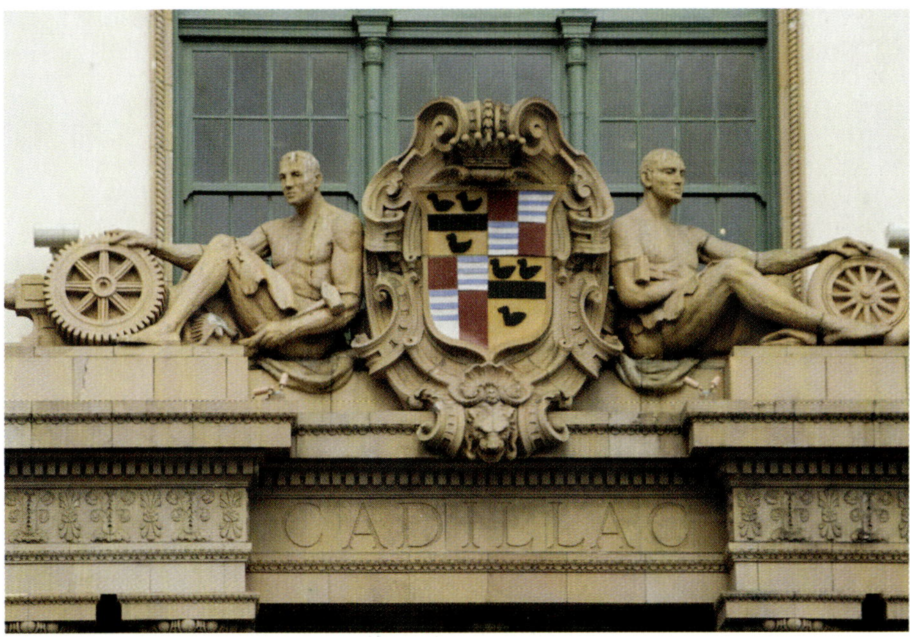

Focal length 188mm; ISO 200; aperture f/6.3; shutter speed 1/640; June 3:30 p.m.

The Shot

The midday light spreads over the columns, which are gray, but there's red marble underneath that. The image also details the floor-to-ceiling glass, which is there so that customers can see the cars in the showroom. In the picture, though, you get an interesting reflection of the surrounding buildings. The drama of the image is enhanced by the use of an 18mm focal length. All columns lead to the detailed sculptured work at the top. If you look closely, the two sets of converging columns and the area of glass are the three major areas of the photo. The diagonal lines in the image give the architecture a sense of strength and power.

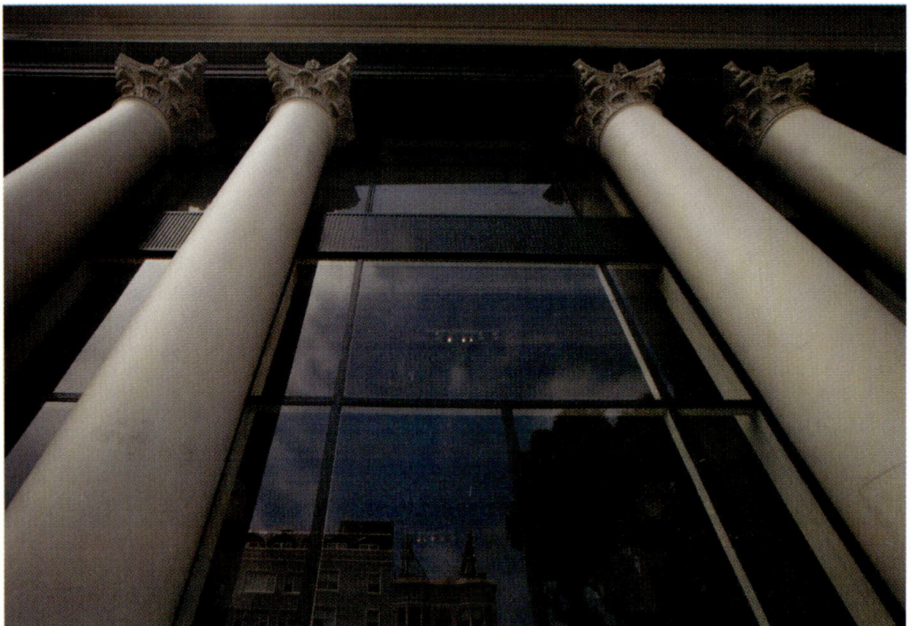

Focal length 18mm; ISO 200; aperture f/8; shutter speed 1/200; May12:00 noon

Getting There

British Motors, which is at 901 Van Ness at Ellis, is on the west side of the street. The Kabuki Theater, which is at 1000 Van Ness, is on the east side of the street. Each site is one block from the other.

To get to Van Ness using mass transit, from downtown, take the Muni Metro J, K, L, or M line to Van Ness, then transfer to the 47 Van Ness bus. Get off at Ellis for British Motors and O'Farrell for the Kabuki Theater.

If you're driving to Van Ness from the South Bay, take 101 North to the101-N/Duboce Ave/Mission St exit. Keep right at the fork in the ramp. Turn right onto Mission Street. Turn slightly left onto Van Ness Avenue. Drive to Ellis, then O'Farrell.

From the East Bay, take 80 West to the 9th St/Civic Center exit. Keep right at the fork in the ramp. Turn left on Harrison Street and right on 9th St. Turn slightly left onto Hayes Street, then right onto Van Ness Avenue. Drive to Ellis, then O'Farrell.

From the North Bay, take 101 South and exit at Lombard Street. Turn right on Van Ness Avenue. Drive to O'Farrell, then Ellis.

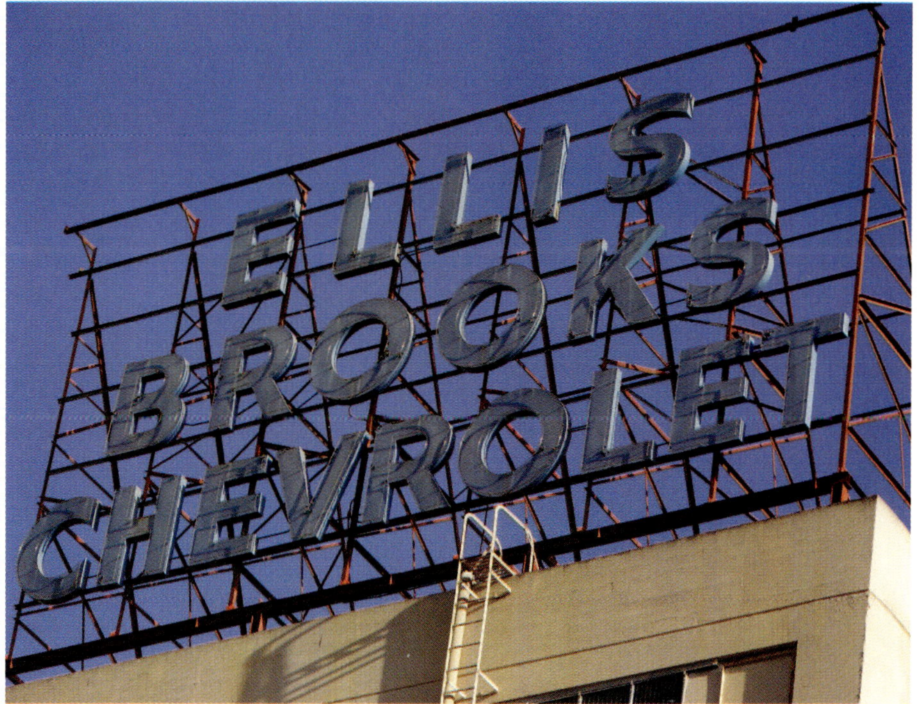

The grand sign indicates you're on Van Ness Avenue's Auto Row.

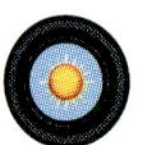 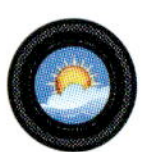

When to shoot: morning, afternoon

AT&T Park

AT&T Park is an open-air ballpark, home to the San Francisco Giants of Major League Baseball. It opened in 2000. One of the reasons the park was built (other than it being close to downtown) is that the park that preceded it, Candlestick Park, was located at a spot where the wind howled and the fog often poured in during game time. The new park alleviates that somewhat, although no matter what you do in San Francisco, there will always be wind when the fog comes rolling in. In front of the park are statues of Willie Mays and Juan Marichal. If you're lucky enough to attend a game, choose a seat high up, where you get views not only of the scoreboard, giant glove, and Coke bottle (bubbles come out from it when the Giants hit a homerun), but also of the bay behind. For information about tickets and game schedules, go to the San Francisco Giants website at http://sanfrancisco.giants.mlb.com. For photo ops inside the park, you have to go to a game; no one is allowed in the park when a game is not being played.

The Shot

The best shots of the outside of the park come from the 3rd St Bridge, just a short walk south from the front entrance of the park. The park almost looks like a boat when framed with a wide-angle lens from the bridge. Frame the shot so that the bleachers are in the left third of the frame, and the empty space (where the field is) falls about a third of the frame from the rightmost side of the image. This shot really only works in the afternoon on a sunny day because the sun will be behind you, leaving the entire sky a deep blue. It's the deep blue that makes the picture.

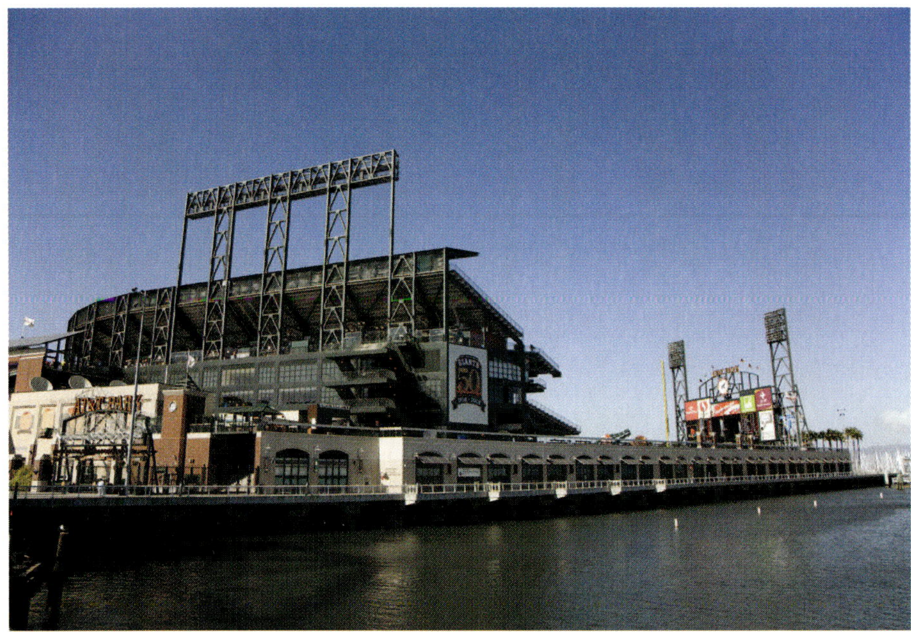

Focal length 24mm; ISO 200; aperture f/4; shutter speed 1/2000; April 2:30 p.m.

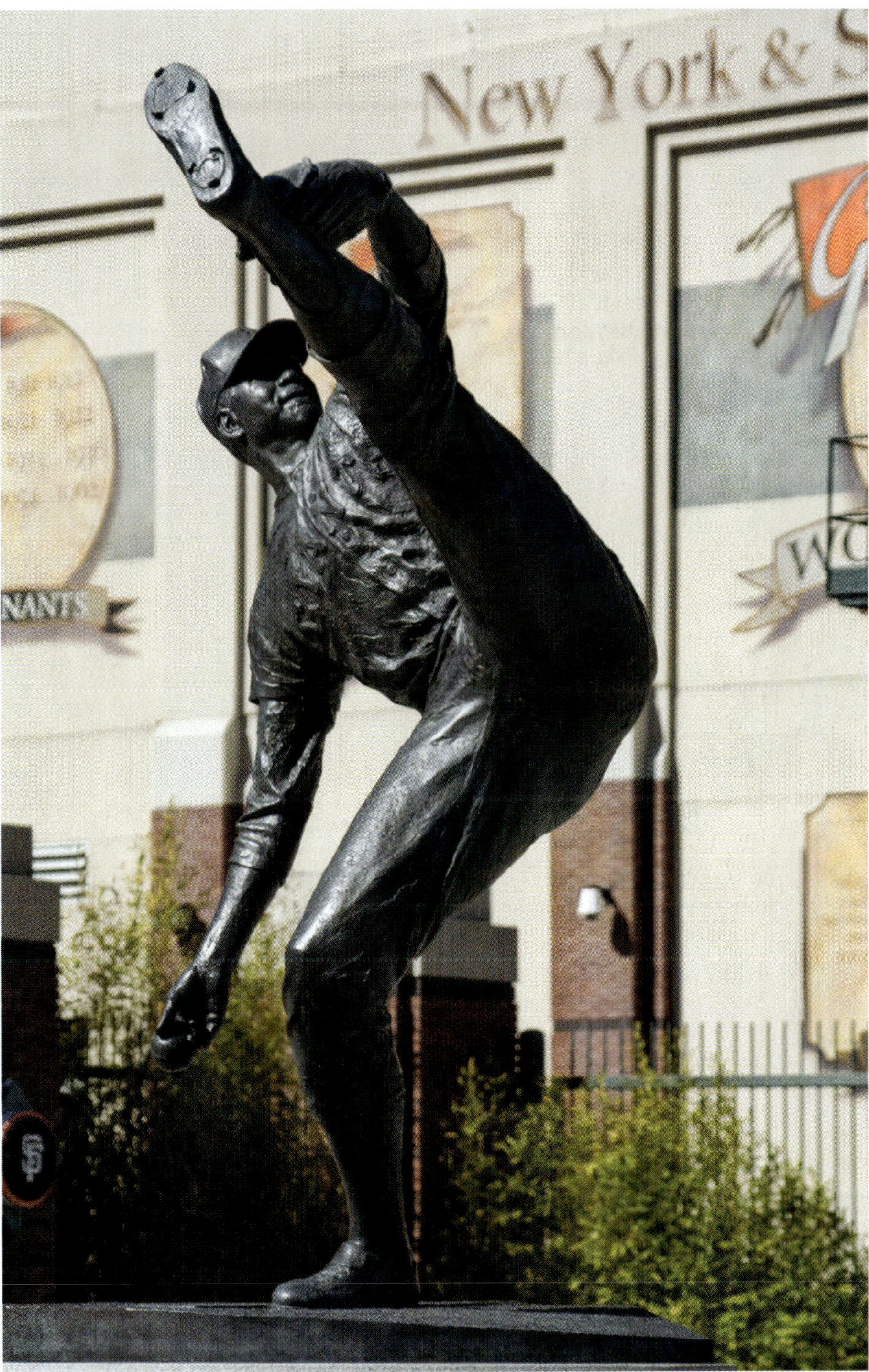

Juan Marichal statue.

The Shot

The scoreboard is filled with bright colors. To frame it, leave blue sky on either side of it. You can leave the pair of giant lights to illustrate how massive the structure is. If you just frame the scoreboard tightly, you won't really be able to tell how huge the structure is. As far as the camera shake that can happen when you're using a telephoto lens, you have to hold very still. To do that, you have to wait for a break in traffic that is crossing the bridge because it does shake a bit when vehicles go over it.

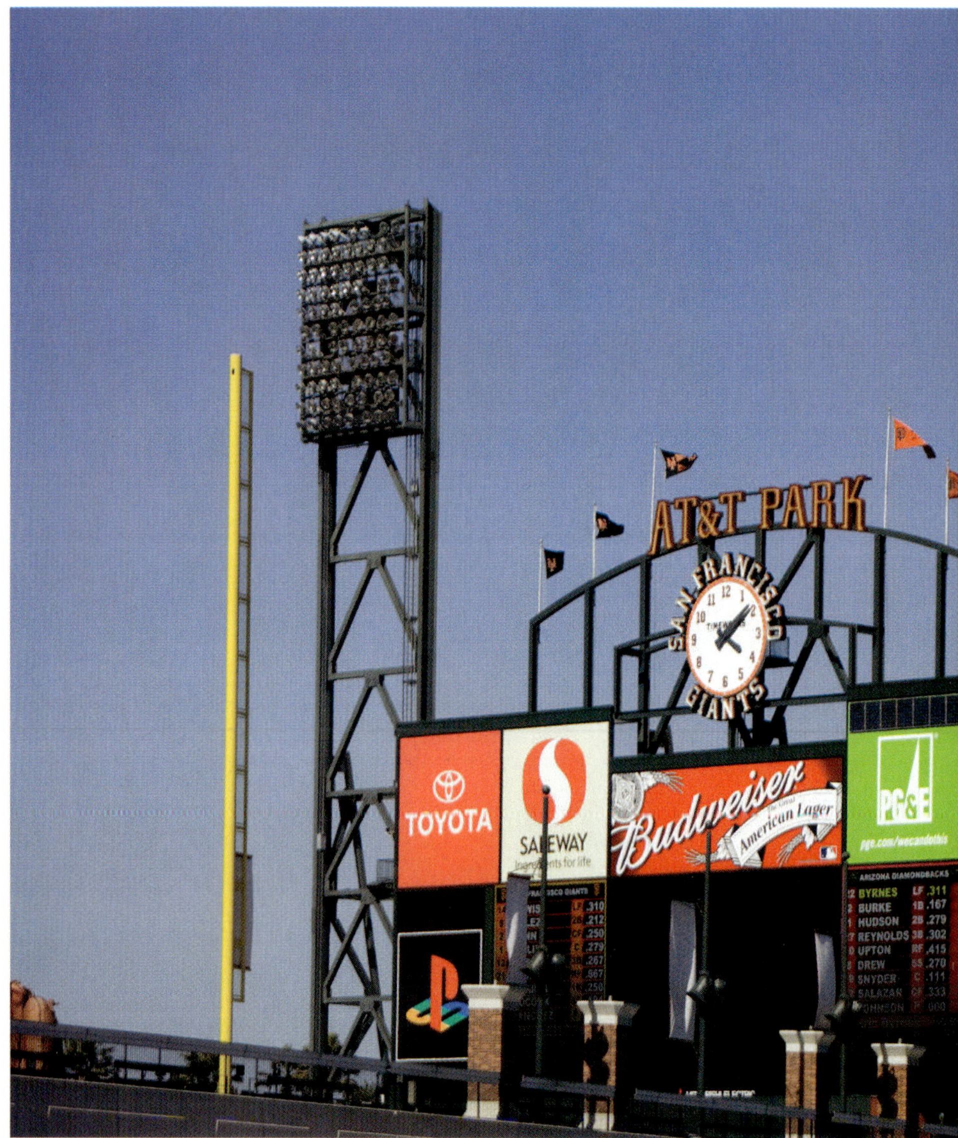

Focal length 115mm; ISO 200; aperture f/5; shutter speed 1/200; April 2:30 p.m.

Getting There

To get there using mass transit, from the Embarcadero or Montgomery station downtown, take the Muni Metro N or T line inbound and get off at the Second and King stop, which is right next to the ballpark. Muni buses 10, 30, 45, and 47 also stop within one block of the ballpark.

If you're driving from the Peninsula/South Bay, take I-280 North (or 101 North to 280 North) to the Mariposa Street exit. Turn right on Mariposa Street, then left on Third Street to get to the parking lots.

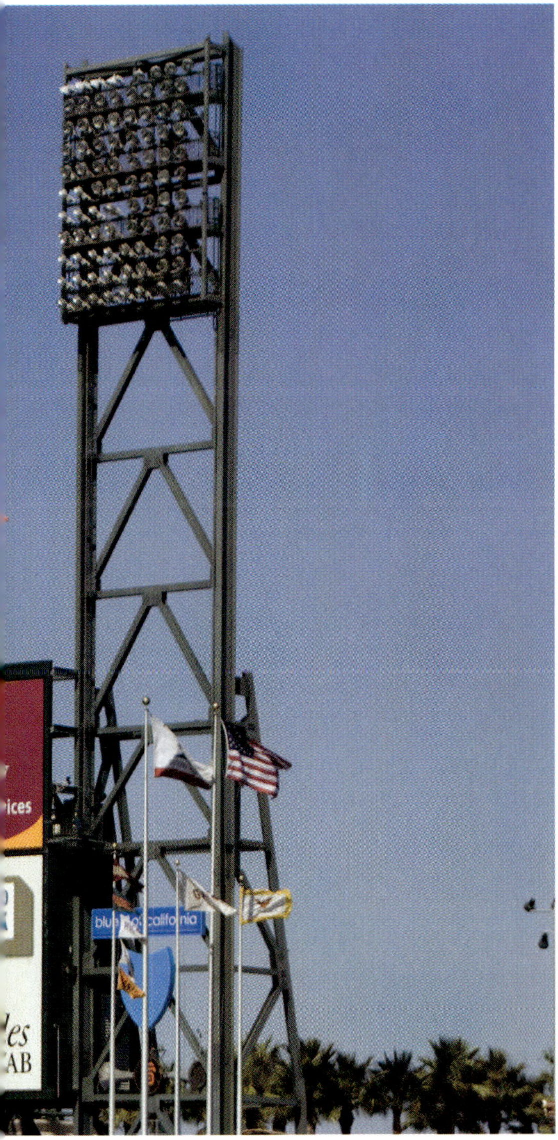

From the East Bay, take 80 West/Bay Bridge to the Fifth Street exit. Exit onto Harrison Street. Turn left onto 6th Street and continue onto 280 South. Take the 18th Street exit and turn left. Continue over the freeway and make a left at 3rd Street. Continue on 3rd Street to the parking lots.

From the North Bay, take 101 South/Golden Gate Bridge to the Marina Boulevard exit. Continue on Marina Boulevard past Fort Mason and turn left onto Bay Street. Turn right onto the Embarcadero. Continue on the Embarcadero under the Bay Bridge until it turns into King Street. Turn left onto 3rd Street (the ballpark is on your left) and continue across the bridge to the parking lots.

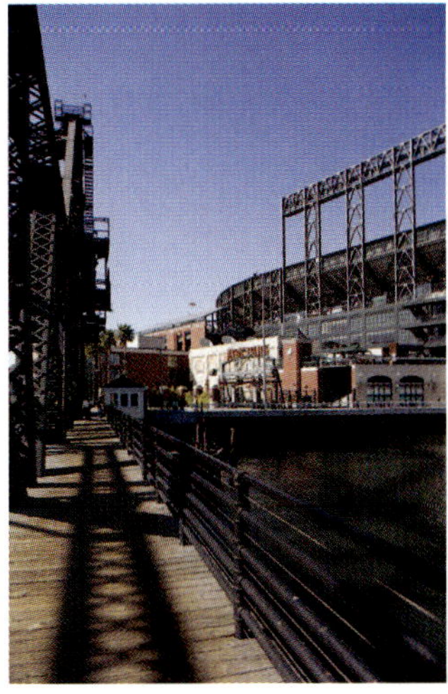

The guardrail and wooden walkway on the bridge reach toward the park.

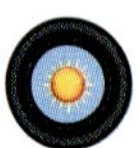 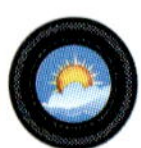

When to shoot: morning, afternoon, evening

Ferry Building

The design of the Ferry Building tower combines elements of the Campanile in the Piazza San Marco (Italy) and the 12th-century Giralda Tower in Seville (Spain). The Ferry Building opened in 1898, quickly becoming the center of travel for commuters from other parts of the bay and train travel from the east. At one time, before the Bay Bridge was built, it was the second busiest ferry terminal in the world.

A. Page Brown designed the building, which has a 240-foot clock tower that has survived two earthquakes, one in 1906 and the other in 1989. The 660-foot structure was one of the first steel-frame buildings in San Francisco.

The Shot

This shot shows the clock tower and one of the Embarcadero towers framed together. It was taken from behind the Ferry Building. You can get there by cutting across the building (walk east inside it) and exiting the back door. Walk east on the large pier area behind the building until you see the clock tower and the Embarcadero together in the skyline. Frame the shot vertically so you can include only those two pieces of architecture. You can always crop the photo later if you have too much background.

THE INS AND OUTS OF EXPOSURE COMPENSATION

Exposure compensation allows you to automatically underexpose or overexpose what the camera has determined as optimal exposure. The exposure compensation values (EV values) can range from –2 to 0 to underexpose and from 0 to +2 to overexpose. On most dSLR cameras, you have a choice of incrementing the numbers between these values by 1/2 or 1/3. There are a number of ways you can enhance your image quality by using exposure compensation. You can use it to enhance color, to lengthen shutter speeds, and to make your photos lighter. When you set your EV value down to –1/2 or –1, you can get color on sunlit surfaces to deepen, as shown in this image of a peaked roof. When you want to blur people to show their movement during the day, you can set your EV value to –2 to begin with a dark image and then take a series of pictures, increasing your shutter speed each time until you get the right exposure (and moving people or objects blurred). The last way you might use exposure compensation is to brighten objects by setting EV values above 0.

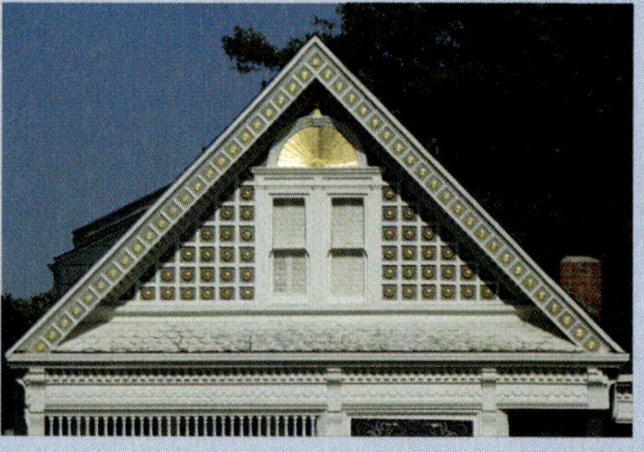

Deepen colors by lowering exposure compensation.

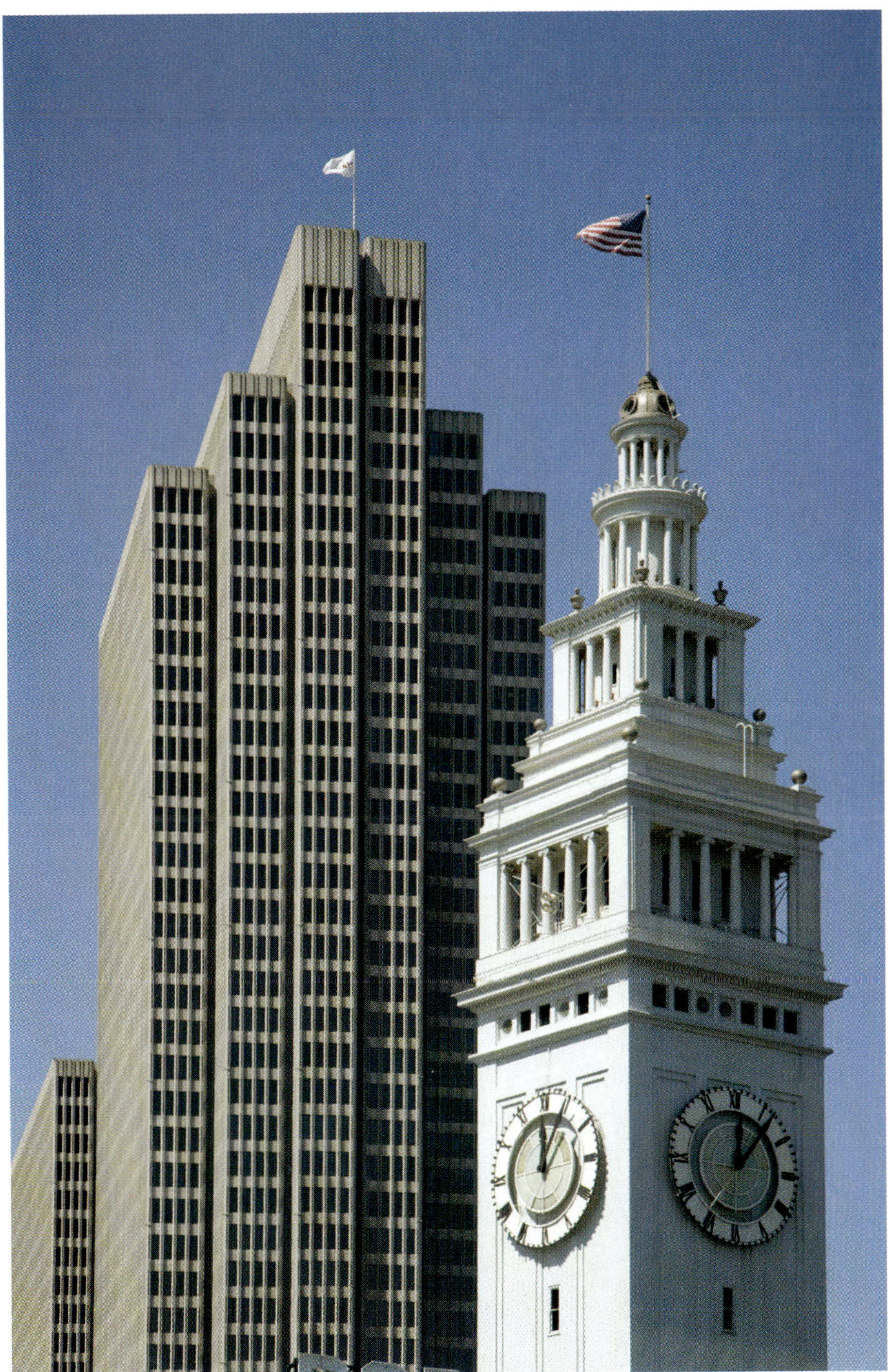

Focal length 105mm; ISO 200; aperture f/9; shutter speed 1/500; April 2:30 p.m.

The Shot

You can get an image of the Ferry Building with interesting traffic patterns (when the picture is taken at slow shutter speeds) at a bus-stop island just northwest of Main Street, near the Embarcadero Hyatt Regency. There's plenty of room for a tripod on the island. Other transit-stop islands on Market Street (to the northwest) have street signs obstructing the view of the Ferry Building. The transit wires that show up in the picture, while not pretty to some, are what San Francisco's Market Street is all about. (Streetcars zip up and down the roadway, running along the wires.) If you're going to photograph at the hour when the sky turns navy blue, it helps to lower your exposure compensation a few stops so that you can leave the shutter open longer, not only to get the great blue color in the sky, but also to get the star effect with the light from the lamps that line the street. The star effect is enhanced by using more narrow apertures, as it's caused by diffracting light within the lens when the shutter stays open for a long time.

The best thing about this corner is that you can pick up all kinds of special effects from the passing traffic, to the bus that skirts right near you (like the one you see on the left side of the image), to red and white streaks from accelerating cars. This type of imagery symbolizes the feeling that all traffic in San Francisco leads to the Ferry Building, which, at one point in the city's history, was just the case.

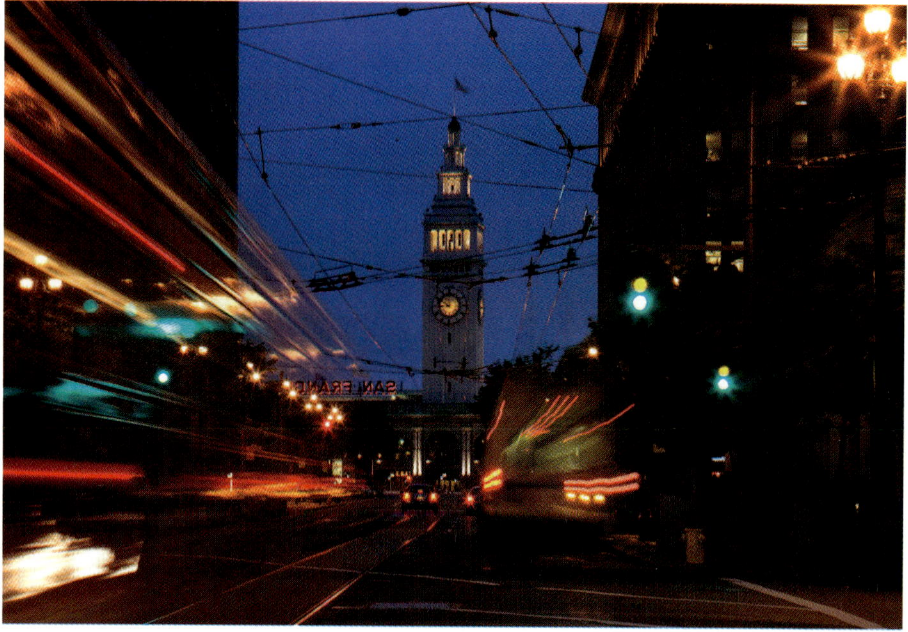

Focal length 75mm; ISO 200; aperture f/22; 3.2 seconds; June 9:00 p.m.

Getting There

To get there using mass transit, you can take BART or Muni. The Ferry Building is across the street from the Embarcadero BART and Muni station. The Embarcadero is the last downtown stop and is accessible to trains that come from and go to various points in the city, including the K, L, M, N, and J trains that travel underground. The F train (vintage street cars) stops directly in front of the Ferry Building. Buses go all over the city.

The Ferry Building is just east of the Embarcadero (which is the street that runs along the bay). If you're driving, from the South Bay, take 101 North to 280 North. Exit at King Street, which turns into the Embarcadero.

From the East Bay, take 80 West and exit at Fremont Street. Make a left at Folsom and a left at the Embarcadero.

From the North Bay, take 101 South to Lombard. Make a slight left on Lombard, a left at Van Ness, a right at Bay, and a right at the Embarcadero. Make U-turn at Howard Street because you'll overshoot the Ferry Building by a couple of blocks.

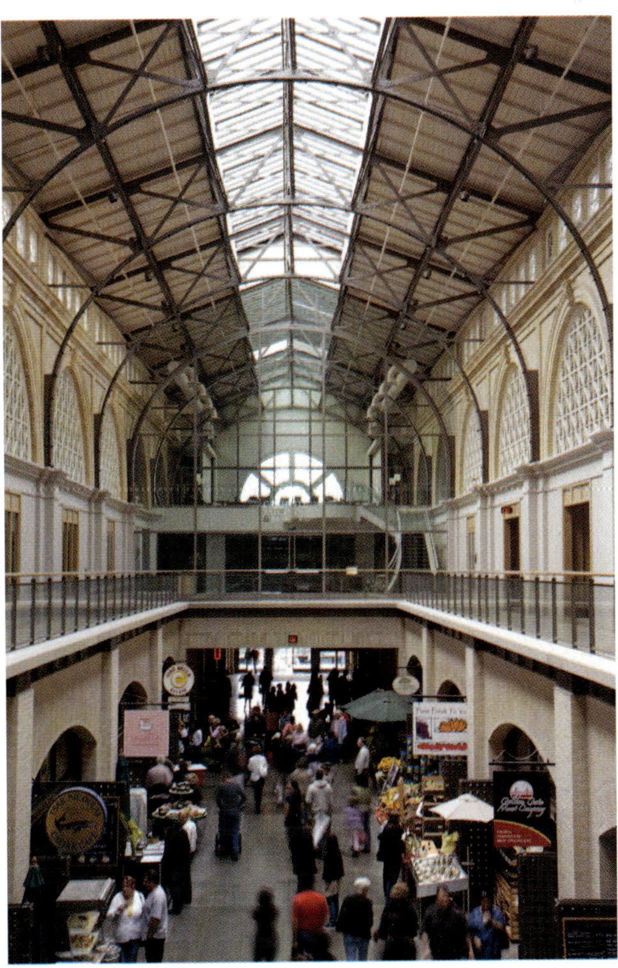

Inside the Ferry Building.

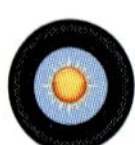 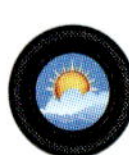

When to shoot: morning, afternoon

Powell Street Architecture

You can't help but notice the cable cars at the Powell Street turnaround. Often overlooked, however, are the inside and outside of the buildings that rise above. I take note of two here: the old Emporium department store and the Flood Building. Each contains different architectural elements—one on the inside of the building and the other on the outside—as well as different stories that tell the history of the area.

Emporium Dome

The Emporium dome used to be a part of the inside of the Emporium department store, which was built in 1896. It was restored and left intact, so it's now a part of the Westfield San Francisco Centre. There are 900 lights encased in the ribs of the dome

The Flood Building

The Flood Building is one of the world's prime pieces of real estate. Built in 1904, the Classic Revival structure designed by architect Albert Pissis was, at one point in history, destined for the wrecking ball. Woolworths was going to replace the building with a three-story modern structure. All were evicted from the building, and just before it was about to be torn down, Washington D.C. intervened. The government needed an office building in San Francisco for the Korean War. They moved in under eminent domain. The building has stood ever since.

The Shot

While the front of the Flood Building offers a unique view of architecture that curves around a corner, the back of the building is a better photo op. In the front there are endless obstructions in the way of a good shot—transit wires, trees, and vehicles. If you walk north on Powell one block past the cable car turnaround (located where Powell ends at Market), you'll see the heavy architectural detail that graces the back of the building. Walk across the street diagonally so you end up on the northwest corner of Powell and Ellis. You'll be at a good angle to shoot where the building comes together on the southeast corner. If you line up the alignment grid in the viewfinder of your camera so that the vertical line where the two sides of the building meet is straight, you'll get a good shot. Include a bit of sky at the top. To get the sky blue, shoot in the afternoon in summer, when the fog has burned off.

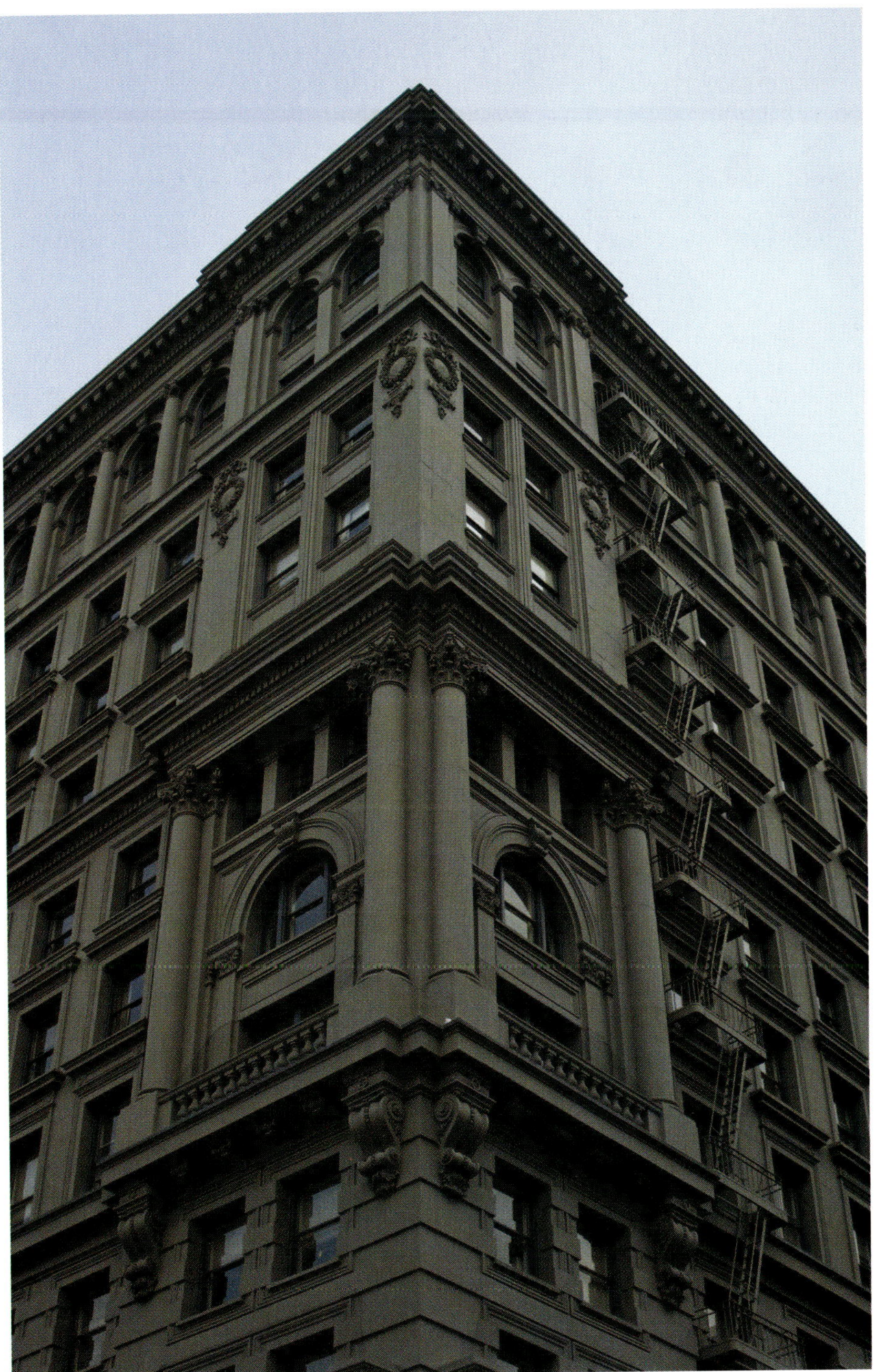

Focal length 28mm; ISO 200; aperture f/6.3; shutter speed 1/250; June 1:35 p.m.

The Shot

If you walk across the street from the cable car turnaround to the Westfield San Francisco Centre entrance and take the elevator to the fourth floor, you'll be on your way to the most comfortable photo shoot ever. The old Emporium department store dome sits below a lobby of comfortable couches. Just lay back and shoot away any time of day! Try different apertures in Av mode to see the effects you can get from the backlit situation. If you're shooting with a camera that does not have a wide angle, experiment with getting different quadrants of the circle inside the frame, not only centering it in the middle.

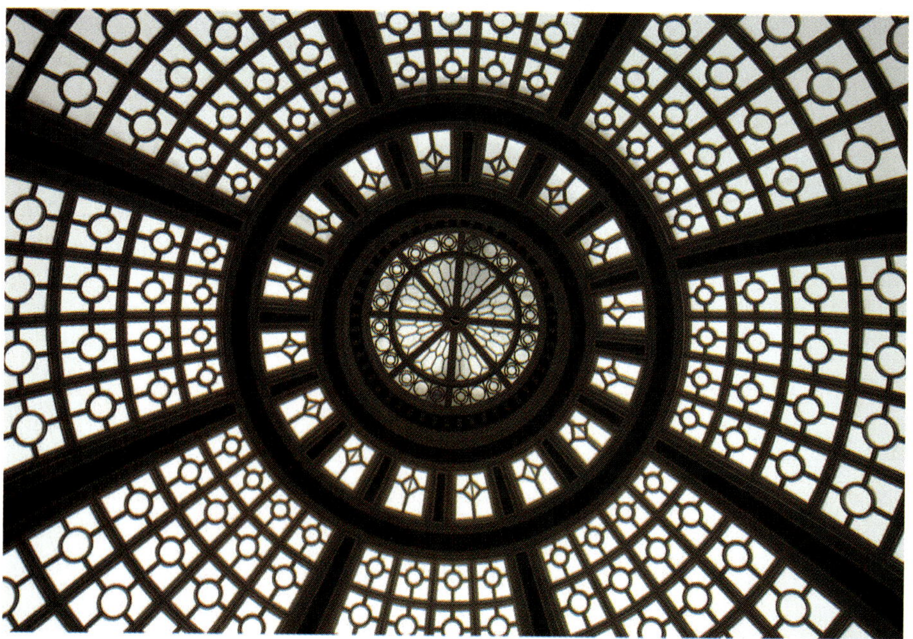

Focal length 35mm; ISO 200; aperture f/7.1; shutter speed 1/500; May 12:00 noon

APERTURE AND SHUTTER PRIORITY

You may notice the letters Av (or A) and Tv (or S) on the top dial of your dSLR camera. Whether Av or A and Tv or S is used depends on your camera's manufacturer. When you set your camera's dial to Av (or A), you are setting the aperture priority mode, and when you set it to Tv (or S), you are setting the shutter priority mode. When you set your camera to Av (or A), it allows you to choose a specific aperture (with numbers that increase as the aperture narrows—2.8, 4, 5.6...22, for example), and the shutter speed will change according to what the camera calibrates for that aperture. When you set your camera to Tv (or S), it allows you to choose a specific shutter speed (say, 1/4000 second to 30 seconds), and the aperture is determined by the camera.

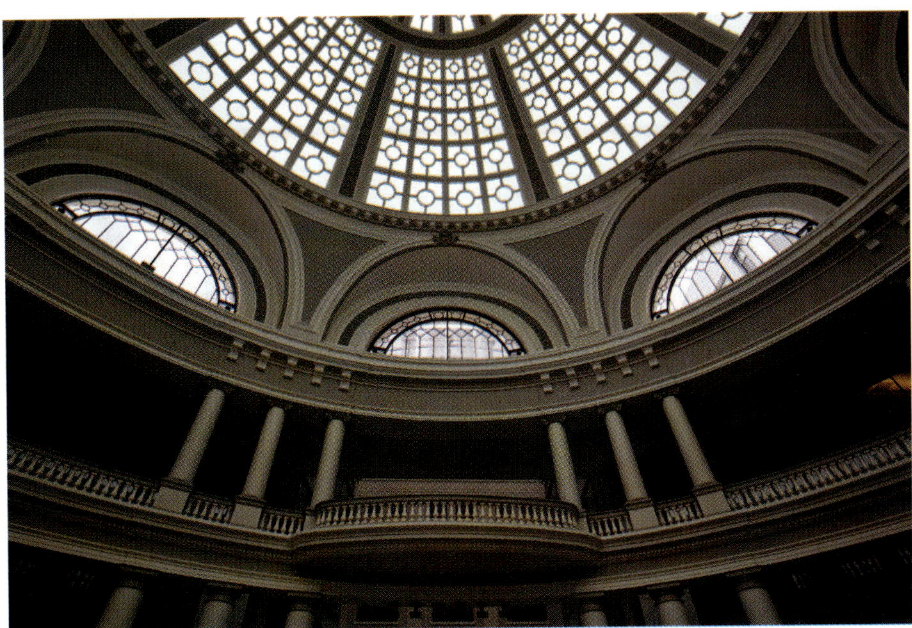

Sculptural detail around the Emporium dome.

Getting There

To get there using mass transit, the Powell Street station is one of the main stations in the city. You can take Muni Metro train K, L, M, or N to Montgomery Street, Embarcadero, or AT&T park or outbound to other areas of the city. The buses on Market Street go all over the city.

If you're driving from the South Bay, take 101 North to 280 North into San Francisco. Exit at 6th Street and take a right on Market Street. The Powell Street station is 1-1/2 blocks up on the left.

From North Bay, take 101 South and exit at Lombard Street. Turn right on Van Ness Avenue and left on Bush Street. Turn right on Jones Street and then left on O'Farrell. Turn right on Market Street. Go 1-1/2 blocks, and the Powell Street station is on the left.

From the East Bay, take 80 West and exit at 5th Street. Take a right at Market. The Powell Street station is in the middle of the block on the left.

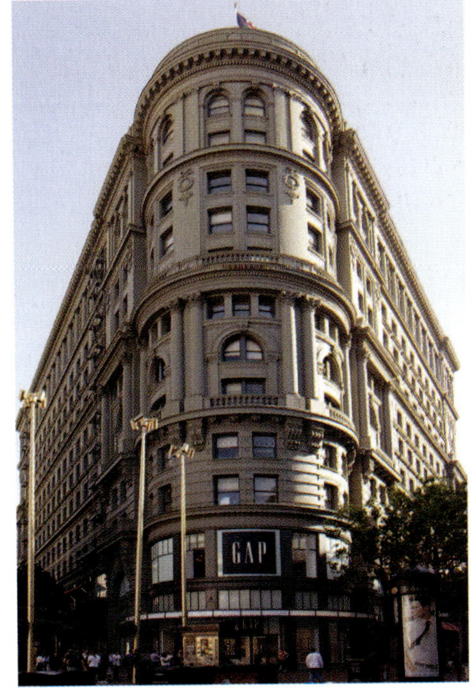

Front of the Flood Building.

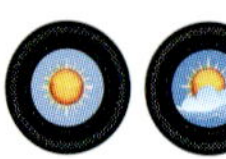
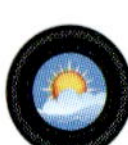

When to shoot: clear night

Bay Bridge

Unlike the Golden Gate Bridge, where you can walk across on a walkway, the Bay Bridge is for vehicular traffic only. The bridge has two decks. The top deck takes traffic west from Oakland to San Francisco, and the bottom deck takes traffic east from San Francisco to Oakland.

The Bay Bridge opened in 1936, six months before the Golden Gate Bridge. Back then, the bridge had a railroad on the lower deck. In 1959, the railroad was replaced with five lanes to carry traffic.

Two major spans connect each shore (Oakland and San Francisco) with Yerba Buena Island. The East Bay structures (which span from Yerba Buena Island to Oakland) are scheduled to be replaced by an entirely new crossing now under construction. The western span is the most interesting because it's a suspension bridge more than 9,000 feet in length and 220 feet above the water. More than 250,000 vehicles cross the bridge daily.

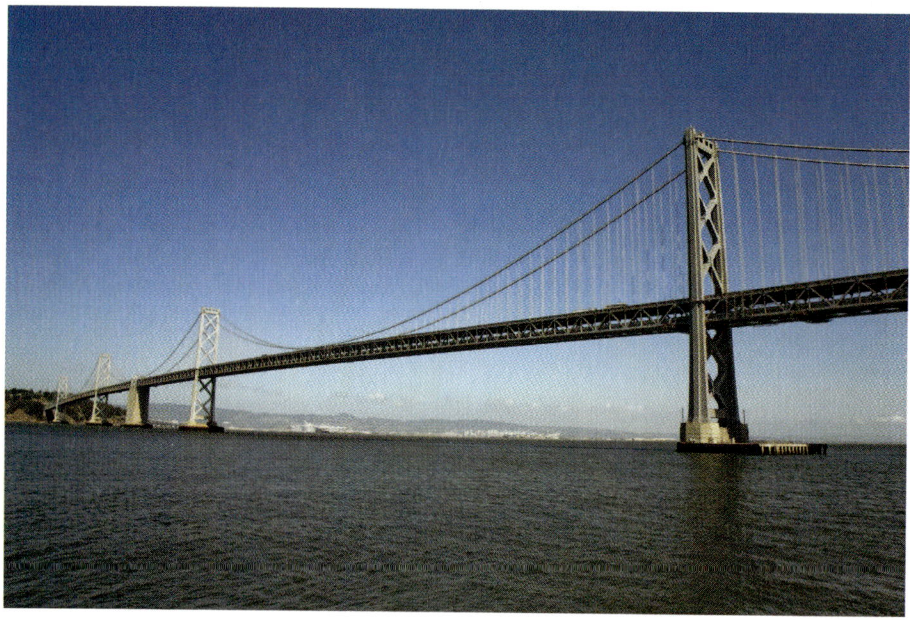

Bridge during the afternoon.

The Shot

I shot the bridge on a night with calm seas, which doesn't happen all that often. The smooth surface of the water caused the lights to be reflected with little distortion. This is one of those shots where you can get good results with long exposures because of a dearth of light emanating from the bridge. The part of the bridge that's photographed here is the span that runs from Yerba Buena Island to San Francisco. I framed the shot so that it contains the eastern end of this part of the span so as to avoid the bright lights that appear behind the bridge at mid-span. These lights were very bright—bright enough to cause whiteout at the exposure I chose for the shot. You can see the beginning of these lights on the right side of the frame. Another way to avoid whiteout from the East Bay lights is to shoot the entire span with a wide-angle lens so that the lit area will take up less room in the frame.

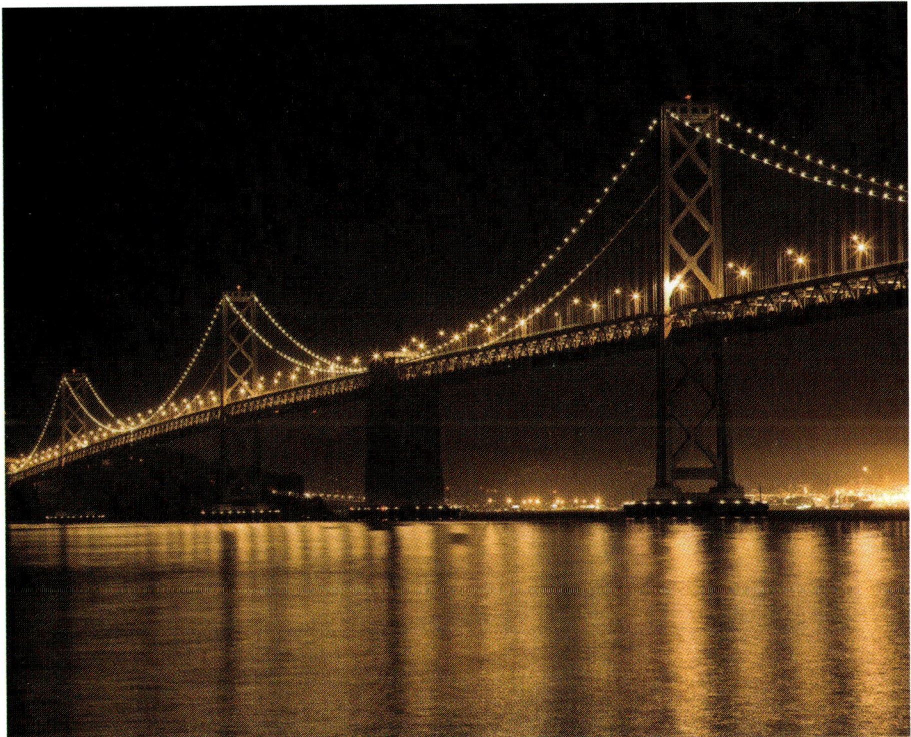

Focal length 75mm; ISO 200; aperture f/11; 20 seconds; April 10:00 p.m.

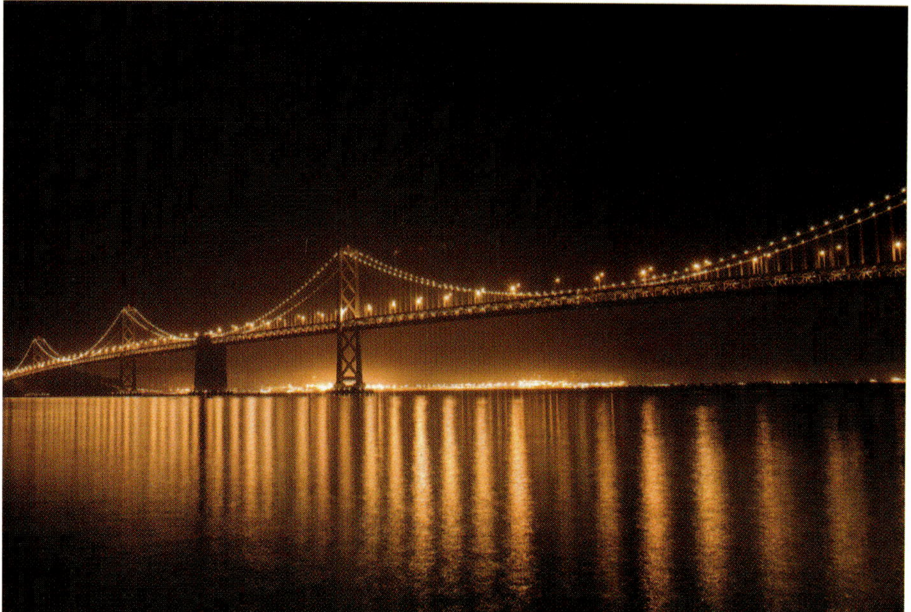

Wide-angle view of the Bay Bridge.

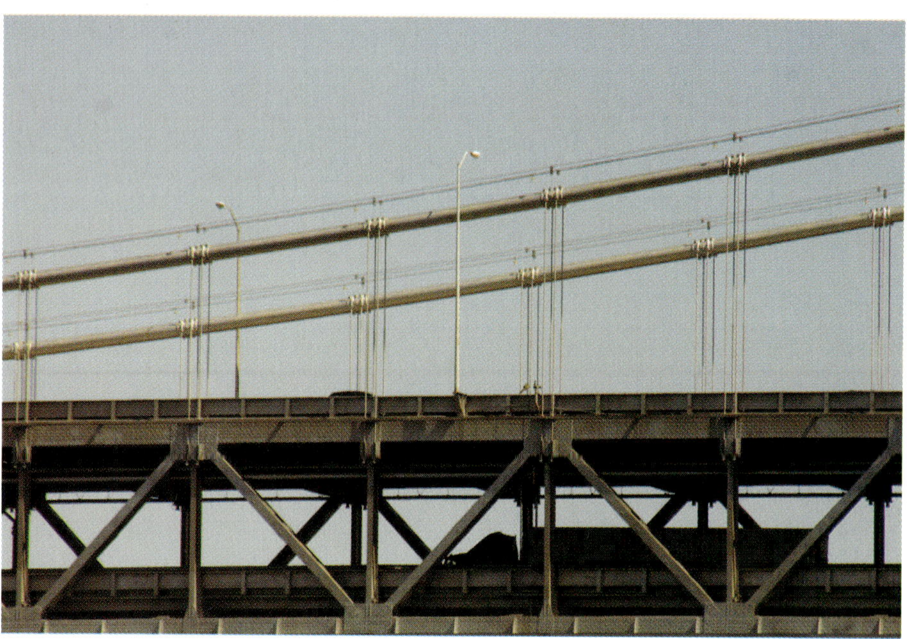

Close-up of steel that makes up the bridge.

The Shot

I turned my tripod around to capture part of the span so one of the towers rises up in an almost-vertical position, giving a majestic, powerful look to it. The shot was framed so that you can see some of the geometric design of the tower. I also looked at the rise and fall of the top cables (which are lit) so that the eye flows across the frame from left to right, going up on the left side and going down on the right.

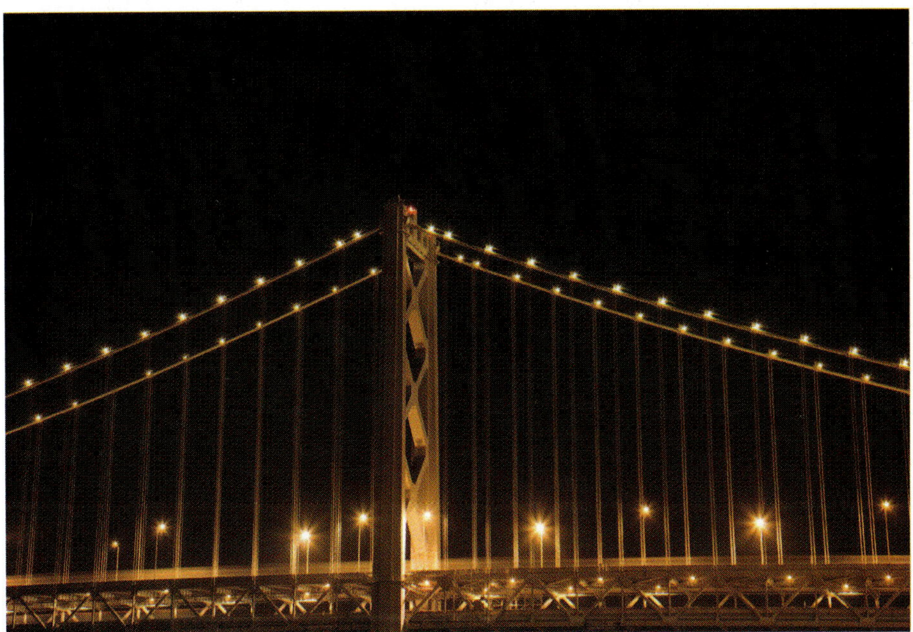

Focal length 108mm; ISO 200; aperture f/7.1; shutter speed 20 seconds; April 10:45 p.m.

Getting There

To get there using mass transit, the Bay Bridge views are near the Embarcadero BART and Muni station in downtown San Francisco, from which you can catch the J, K, L, M, N, and T trains to various points around the city. BART runs to various stops in the city also, most notably to the 16th and 24th St Stations in the Mission District. The station is within walking distance of Rincon Park on the waterfront. To get to a good spot to photograph, walk northeast on Market Street from the Embarcadero station to the Ferry Building, then take a right and walk southeast along the Embarcadero until the park spreads out a bit into the bay. You can photograph anywhere from where Mission Street ends to where the Bay Bridge begins.

If you're driving, the views are just to the southeast of the Ferry Building. To get to the Bay Bridge photo ops, see the directions to the Ferry Building earlier in this chapter.

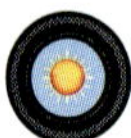

When to shoot: morning, early afternoon

Legion of Honor

The Beaux-Arts building that is known as the Legion of Honor is located on a greenbelt known as Lincoln Park. The site overlooks the Pacific Ocean and the Golden Gate Bridge. Constructed in 1924, the building is a three-quarter-scale adaptation of the 18th-century Palais de la Légion d'honneur in Paris. Inside the building is a museum that houses ancient and European art. The museum was built to honor soldiers who died in World War I. Built in 1924, the museum is known for the statue of Rodin's "Thinker" that is displayed in its Court of Honor.

The Shot

The Legion of Honor is close to the ocean so that during the summer it's often covered in fog, which makes for a bad shot because of the white sky you get under those conditions. The best sky for this photo is a clear blue one, because that color contrasts the off-white color of the structure. If you get clouds in behind the building, they'll draw attention away from the clean horizontal and vertical lines that comprise the building's architecture. You get a full view of the courtyard that includes columns on either side of the main entrance using a wide-angle lens, giving the image depth. The architectural elements of the building cast light in different directions and patterns, offering a multitude of interesting shadows.

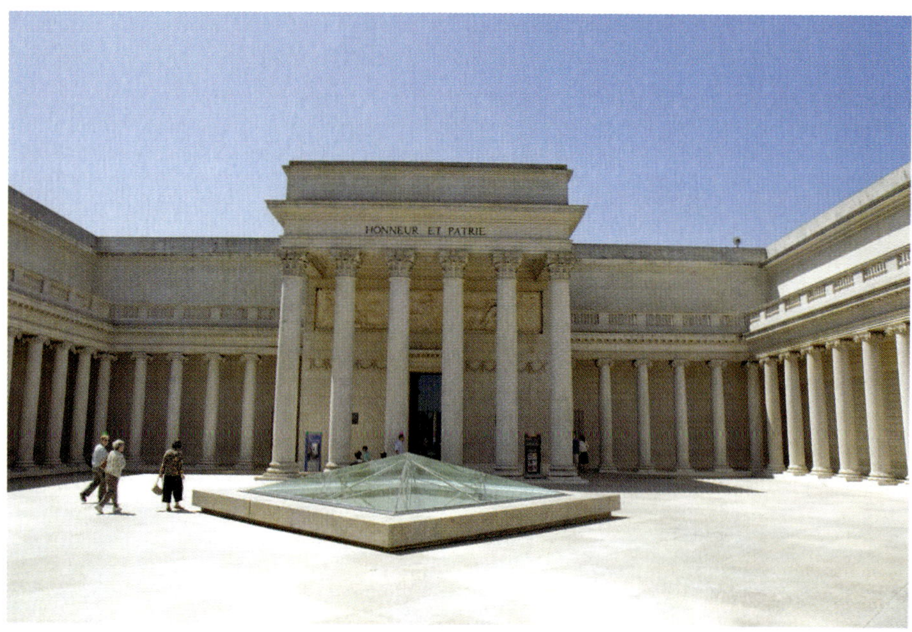

Focal length 24mm; ISO 200; aperture f/10; shutter speed 1/250; April 12:30 p.m.

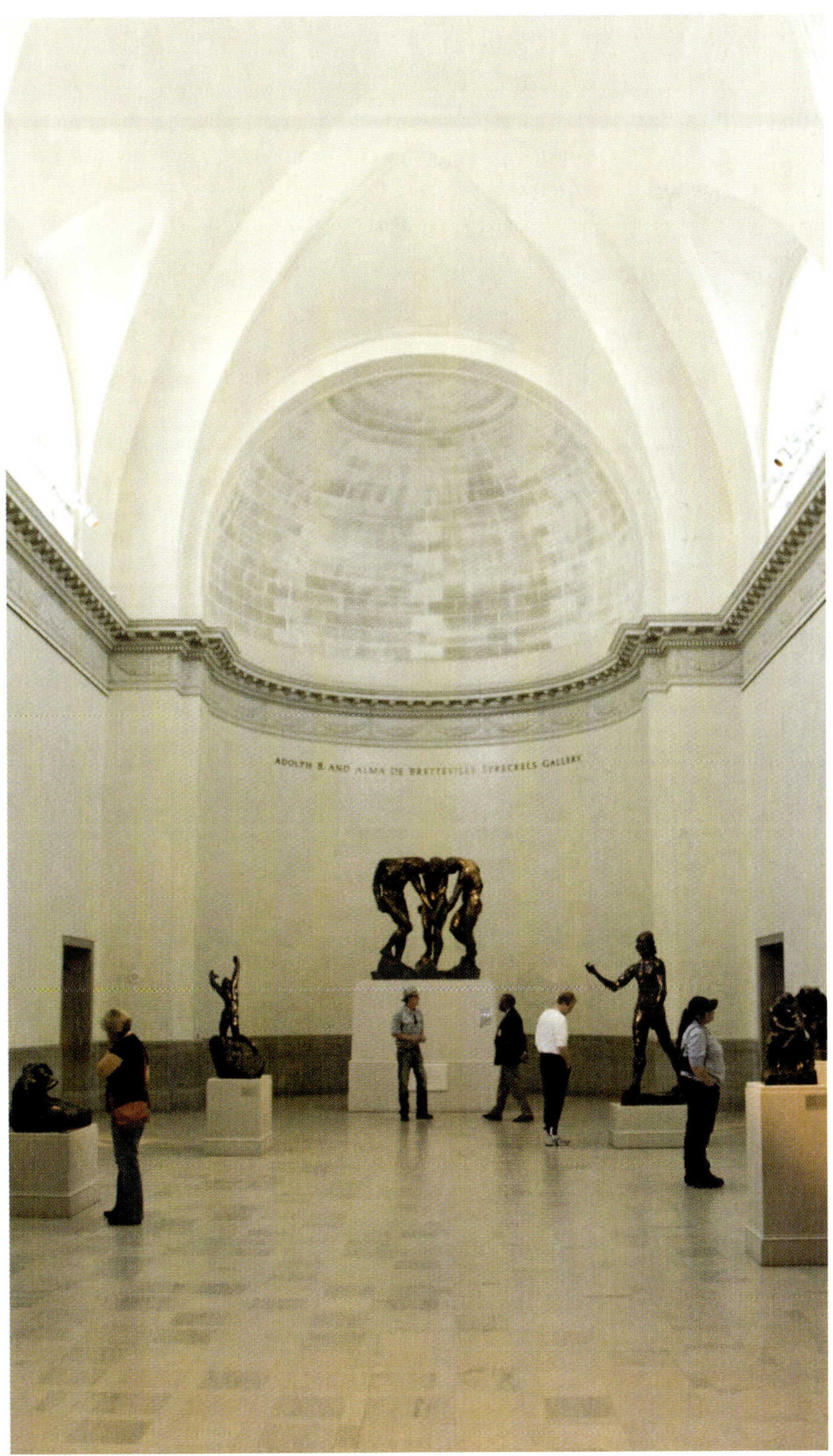

Inside the museum shows skylights and high ceilings.

The Shot

I waited for the person walking through the hallway in the background to reach the first third of the frame so as to get that subject to be a prominent part of the picture. That person is an important part of the framing because that's where the eye ends up as a result of following the lines of the columns. Notice, too, how the curvature of the lens makes the foreground columns appear rounded as a group. You usually wouldn't want that kind of distortion in a photograph, but in this case it works well to enhance the depth of the shot.

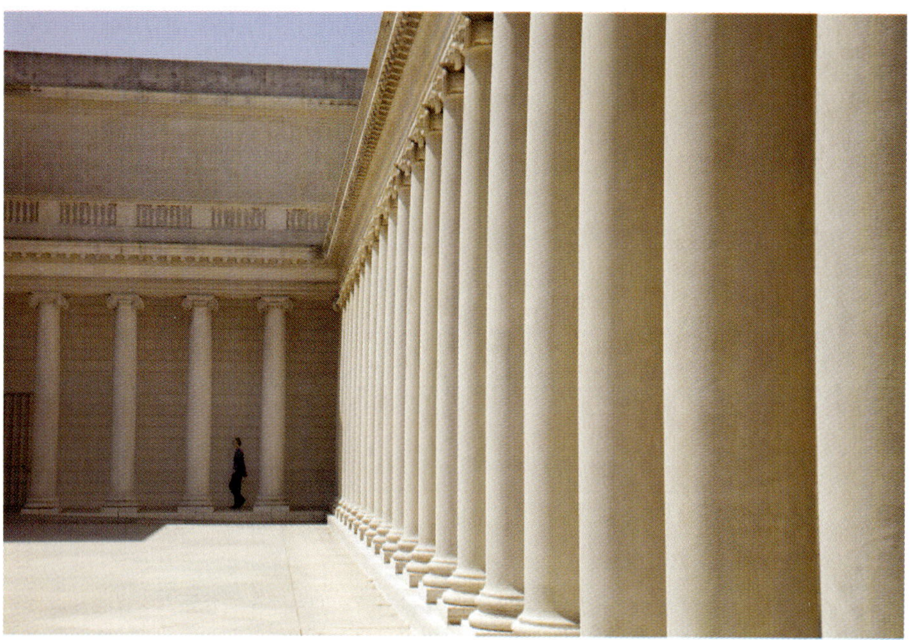

Focal length 60mm; ISO 200; aperture f/5; shutter speed 1/250; April 1:00 p.m

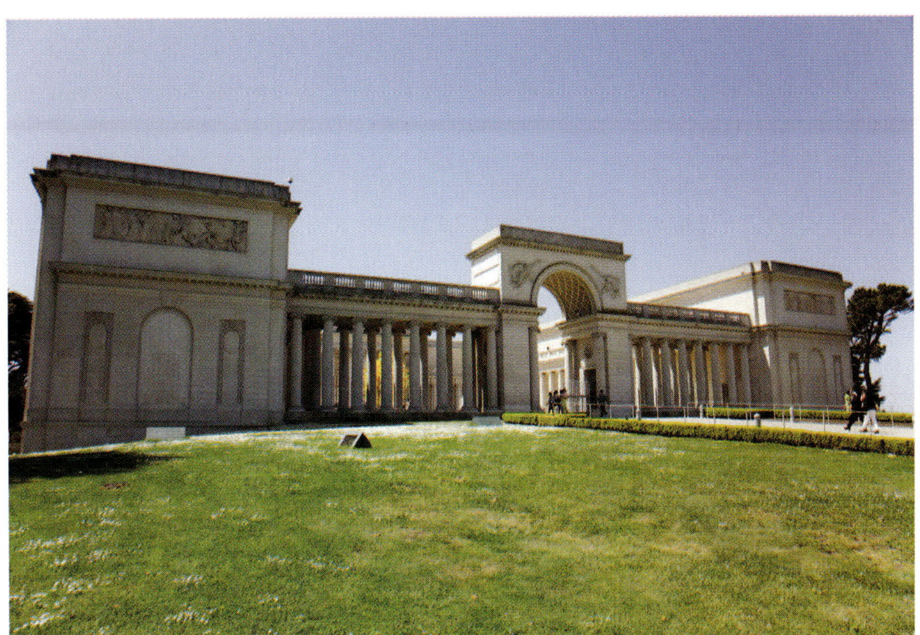

In spring, flowers (small daisies) bloom on the lawn of the Legion of Honor.

Getting There

The Legion of Honor is located at Lincoln Park, at 34th Avenue and Clement Street, in an area known as Land's End.

To get there using mass transit, from downtown, catch the 2 Clement or the 38 Geary on Market or the 1 at Howard and Main.

If you're driving, from the North Bay/Golden Gate Bridge, take the 19th Ave/Park Presidio exit immediately after exiting the Toll Plaza. Take Park Presidio south to Geary Street. Turn right (west) on Geary. Take Geary to 34th Avenue. Turn right (north) on 34th Avenue into Lincoln Park. The museum is just past the golf course.

From the South Bay, take 280 North/19th Avenue north into Golden Gate Park. Stay left after crossing Lincoln Avenue into the park. Bear left onto 25th Avenue. Take 25th Avenue north to Clement Street. Turn left (west) on Clement Street and right on 34th Avenue. The museum is just past the golf course

From the East Bay/Bay Bridge, take I-80 West to the 9th St. exit. Stay on 9th Street until it turns into Hayes. Continue on Hayes to Franklin Street. Turn right on Franklin. Then turn left onto Geary Street and take it to 34th Avenue. Go right on 34th Avenue to museum, which is just past the golf course.

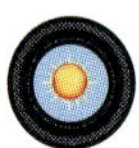
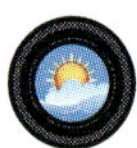

When to shoot: late afternoon, early evening

Financial District Banks

Filled with contemporary and historical architecture, the Financial District of San Francisco is a photographer's paradise. The district encompasses an area bound by the Embarcadero and Market, 3rd Street, Kearny, and Washington Streets. The area was the center of European and American settlement during Spanish and later Mexican rule. Following American annexation and the California Gold Rush, the area boomed, and the bay shoreline, which originally ended at Battery Street, was filled in and extended to the Embarcadero. Gold Rush wealth and business made San Francisco the financial capital of the West Coast as many banks and businesses set up in the neighborhood. The West Coast's first and only skyscrapers at the time were built in the area along Market Street. To get a view from above, you can go to the 17th-floor rooftop park at 343 Sansome Street.

Two bank buildings are of significant architectural interest—the first is the Humboldt Bank Building. When it was built in 1908, the Humboldt Bank Building was thought of as an architectural masterpiece. Today it's no longer a bank, but it remains occupied as offices. The building is constructed with granite, marble, and tile over a concrete and steel frame. It's topped with a wedding cake–style dome. The other notable building, the Bank of America Center, was built in 1969 and is the second tallest building in San Francisco. (The Transamerica Pyramid is the tallest.) Designed with thousands of bay windows, the building is 52 stories high.

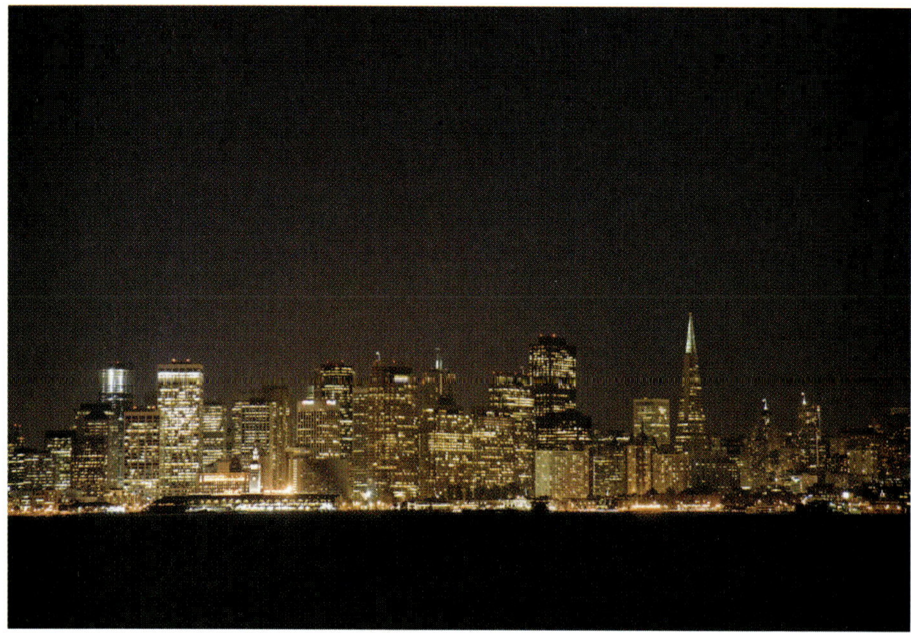

SF skyline, which includes the Financial District as seen from Treasure Island.

The Shot

The Bank of America Center can be photographed any time because it wraps around a city block in all directions. The photo op shows it photographed from behind the main entrance of the building at Pine and Kearney Streets. This is the best spot to photograph the building in the afternoon because the sun is behind you, giving the frame a deep blue sky as well as offering ample light on the building itself. In the morning, it's best photographed from the front on California Street. The sun's reflection on the building creates an interesting pattern of light that extends outward from the center of the high rise.

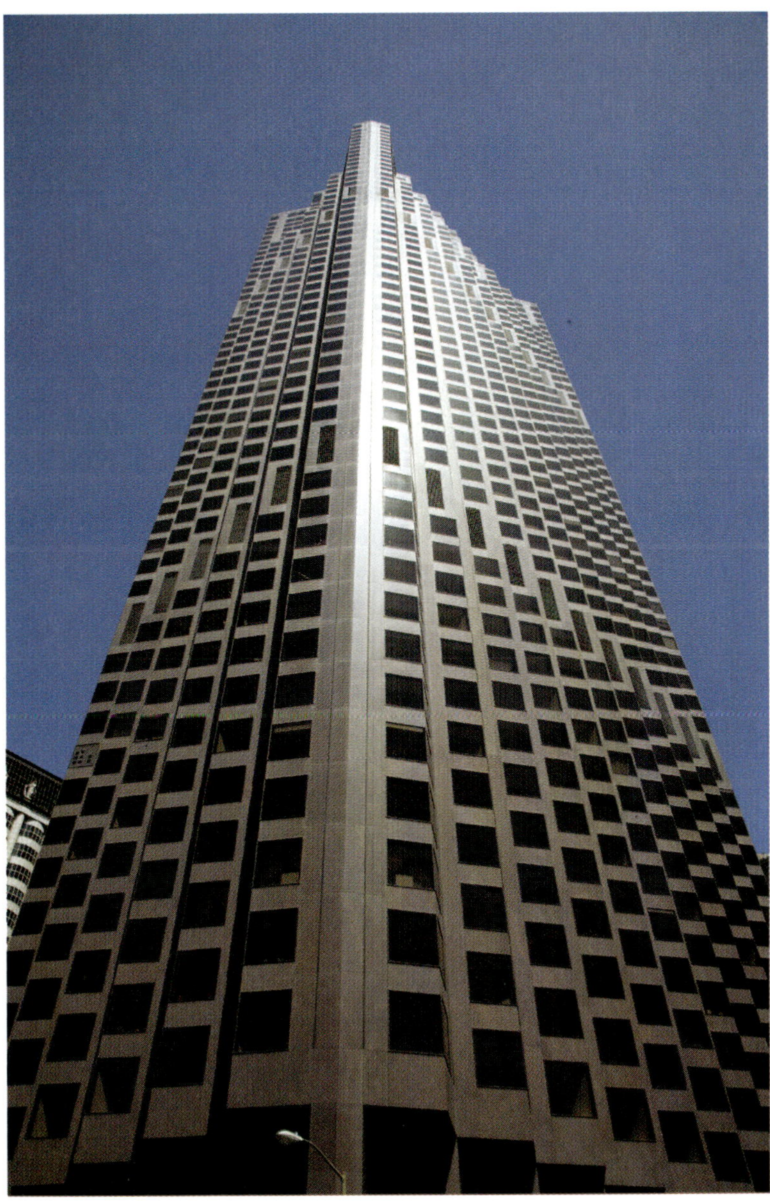

Focal length 24mm; ISO 200; aperture f/18; shutter speed 1/100; April 1:00 p.m.

The Shot

To get a clear shot of the Humboldt Bank Building dome, walk southwest on Market from the Montgomery Street station and stand in front of 595 Market Street. The best time for the shot is from morning to midday. Fog in late spring and summer can be a factor, as shown in the image. I had to stand around and wait for the fog to break up a bit before I could take the picture so I could get some blue sky in the frame. The fog mixed with blue sky creates an interesting effect, with good contrast between the background elements and the building. You can get a sharp shot without a tripod if you shoot in Av mode with your aperture set to its widest value. In setting your aperture wide, your camera will automatically set the fastest shutter speed possible for a good exposure.

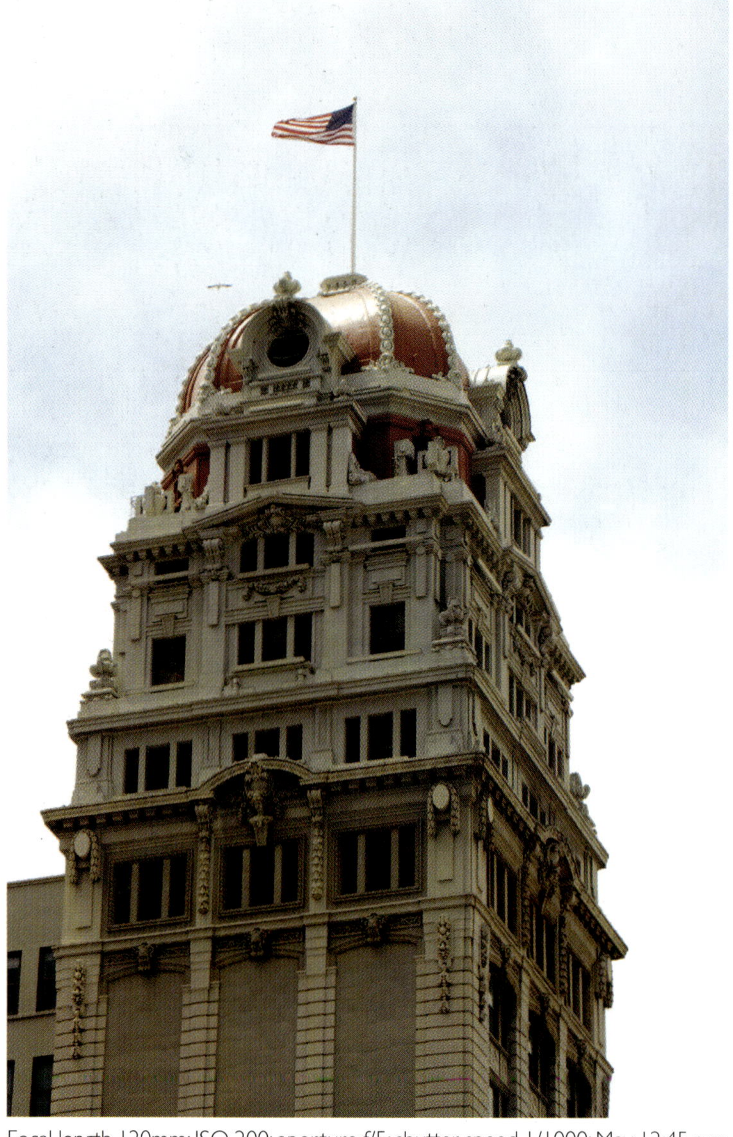

Focal length 120mm; ISO 200; aperture f/5; shutter speed 1/1000; May 12:45 p.m.

Getting There

To get there using mass transit, the Montgomery Street station serves the Financial District. You can take Muni Metro trains K, L, M, and N to various points around the city. The buses on Market Street also go all over the city.

If you're driving, from the South Bay, take 101 North to 280 North into San Francisco. Exit at 6th Street and make a right on Market Street. The Montgomery Street station is four blocks northeast on Market Street.

From North Bay, take 101 South and exit at Lombard Street. Turn right on Van Ness Avenue and left on Bush Street. Turn right on Jones Street and then left on O'Farrell. Turn right on Market Street. The Montgomery Street station is four blocks northeast on Market Street.

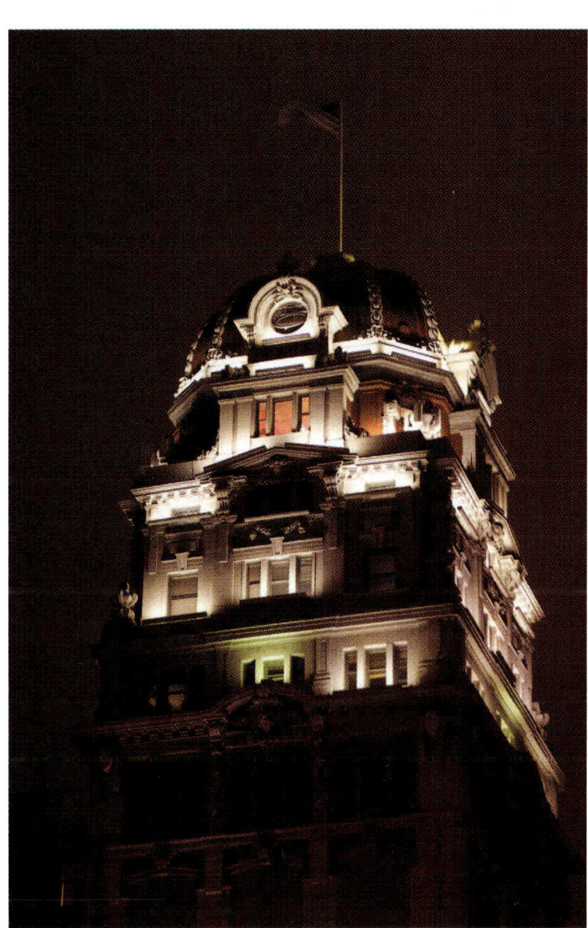

Humboldt Building at night.

From the East Bay, take 80 West and exit at 5th Street. Make a right at Market. The Montgomery Street Station is three blocks northeast on Market Street.

The Humboldt Bank Building is at 785 Market Street, two blocks southwest of the Montgomery Street station at 4th Street. To get to the Bank of America Center from the Montgomery Street station, walk three blocks north on Montgomery Street to Pine Street. The building is between Pine and California Streets at 555 California.

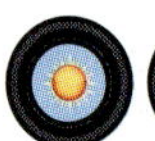 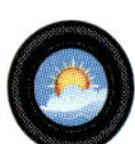

When to shoot: afternoon, before dawn, after dusk

Movie Palaces

There's nothing like photographing the marquee of a movie palace. Two theaters in San Francisco have some great neon—the Castro and the Roxie. Timothy L. Pflueger designed the Castro Theatre. It is one of the few remaining movie palaces in the nation from the 1920s that is still in operation. Pflueger chose an exterior design reminiscent of a Mexican cathedral. The oldest continuously operating movie theater in San Francisco is the Roxie, which opened as the C. H. Brown Theater in 1909. The neon signs to both theaters have recently been replaced.

The Shot

During the day the Castro Theatre is best caught in the afternoon, because that's when the sun is shining directly on the building. If you're shooting in auto mode, be careful of over exposure, as that can happen when a bright sun is shining on an almost-white surface. To prevent overexposure (darken your photo), you can lower your exposure compensation a couple of spots in the minus column. Remember, it's always better to underexpose than to overexpose because underexposure can be fixed easily in an image processing program.

At night there are two ways to catch the theater, marquee, and sign or just the sign. One way is to use a tripod and shoot in auto mode at a normal ISO (say, 200). The other is to increase the ISO above 800 and handhold your camera to shoot. There's much less chance of blur at 800 ISO than at 200 ISO. You can do this in P mode on a dSLR camera or auto mode on a point-and-shoot. I find that I get good photos of lit neon or plastic-backlit signs without a tripod when I set my camera to Av mode with an f-stop from f/4 to f/8.

To get to the exact location of the shot, cross the street from the theater and walk a little downhill (south) toward the corner of Castro and 18th. Set up a tripod right near the parked cars. There's a little extra room there for one. Make sure that there are no wires within your view of the theater. If there are, you've walked too far south.

I like to take a series of shots with a tripod and use Av mode with a small aperture to get everything in the shot sharp. This is a hectic neighborhood, so you'll want to be as efficient as possible. This shot is best about 45 minutes after the sun sets. There's about a 20-minute window when the sky goes navy blue, and this is what you want to catch over the building. One good thing about the fog is that it doesn't prevent the sky turning navy blue; the sky turns navy blue in spite of it.

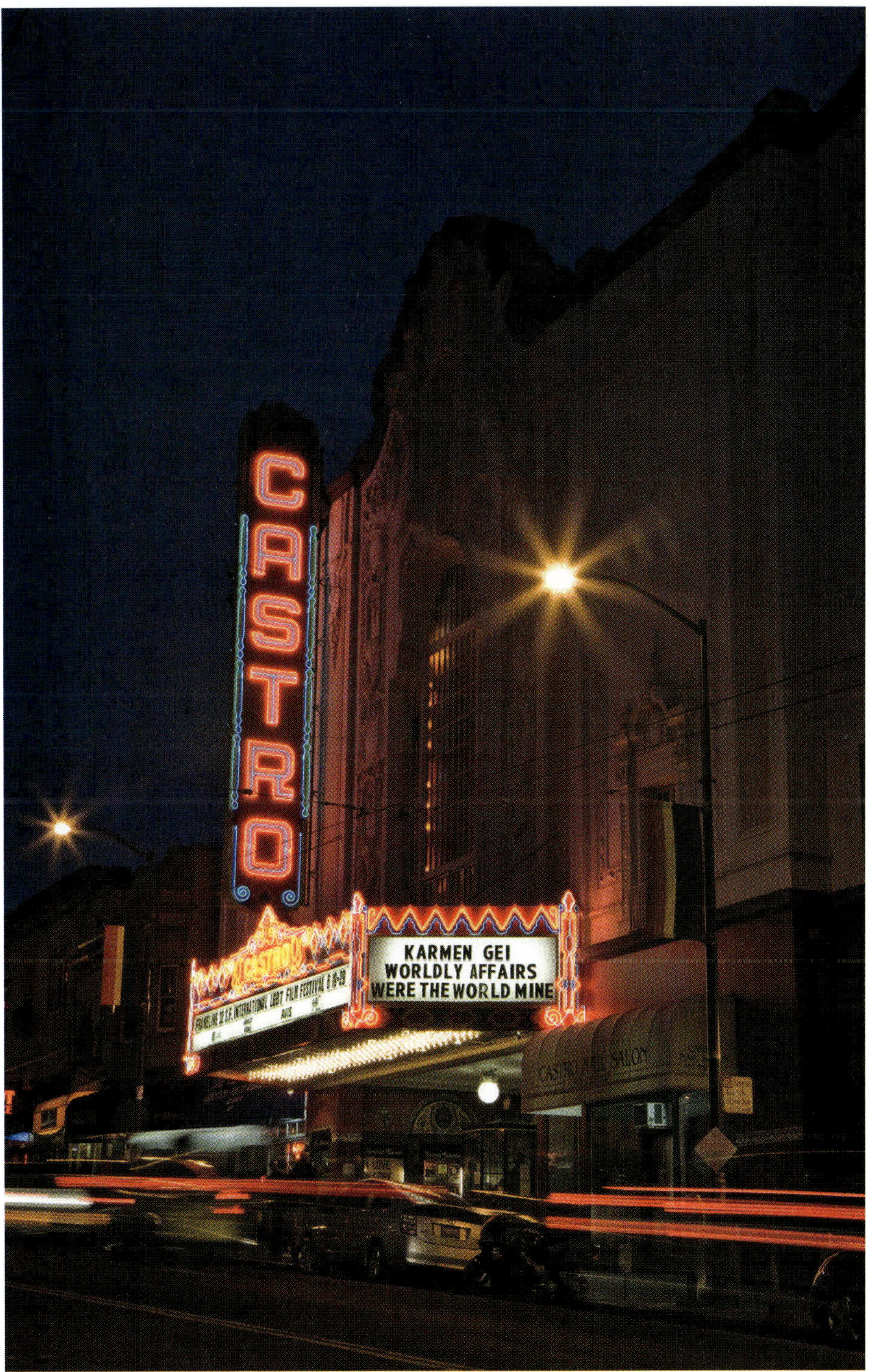

Focal length 50mm; ISO 200; aperture f/16; 2 seconds; June 9:00 p.m.

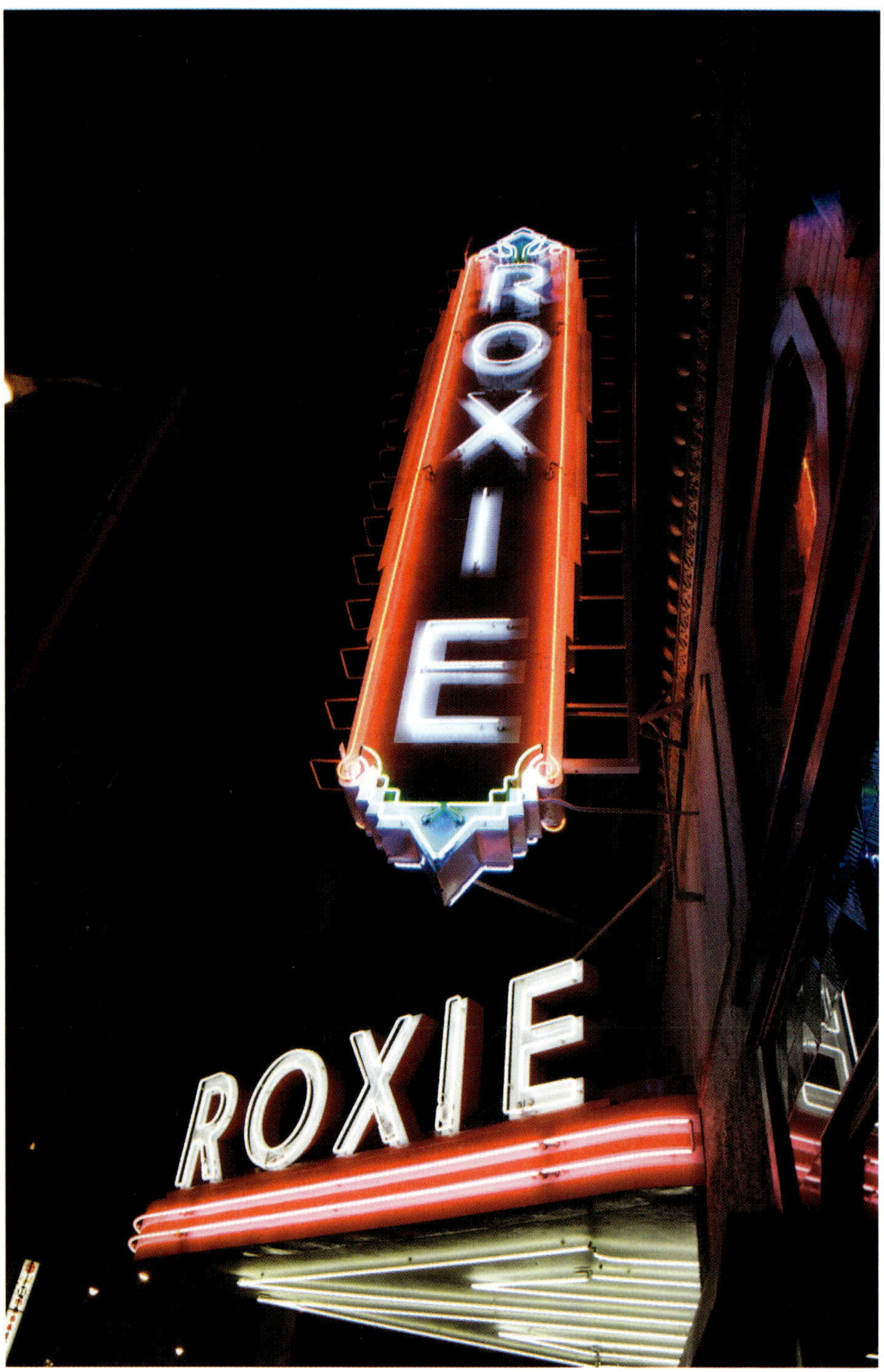

Focal length 24mm; ISO 200; aperture f/8; shutter speed 1/10; April 10:00 p.m.

The Shot

You can get a good shot of the Roxie neon from across the street. Zoom in a bit so you don't get the streetlight in the frame. You can get this shot without a tripod at 800 ISO because of the ample light that comes from the sign. Just keep your body and hands as still as you can. I also choose f/8 in Av mode, letting the camera decide on the shutter speed for this and all signs, because I find that light neither blasts with overexposure nor darkens with underexposure. I find, though, that this setting doesn't work with all cameras. Some do well with the neon when you put the flash on; others do well at larger apertures—say, f/4.

This sign is brand new, but you'd never know that at night because of its Art Deco lighting design. During the day, it's apparent that the sign hasn't a scratch on it.

Getting There

To get there using mass transit, take the K, L, or M underground Muni train from downtown to the Castro Street station. You can also take any of the vintage streetcars (F-Market) you see on Market Street. They all drop you off at Castro and Market, near the theater.

If you're driving, from the South Bay, take 101 North to the Cesar Chavez exit. Make a left on Cesar Chavez, a right on Mission, and a left on 18th. Take 18th to Castro and make a right. The movie theater is on the right at the end of the block.

From the East Bay, take I-80 West to 101 North until it ends at Market Street. Take a left on Market Street and go to Castro. The movie theater is on the left.

From the North Bay, take 101 South. Make a slight left to exit on Lombard Street, and then make a right on Van Ness. Make a right on Otis to Mission, a right on 18th, and a right on Castro. The movie theater is on the right at the end of the block.

The Roxie is at 3125 16th Street, just 1-1/2 blocks west of the Mission and 16th BART station between Valencia and Guerrero. Drive to the Roxie from the Castro by going south on Castro, left on 18th, and left on Valencia to 16th.

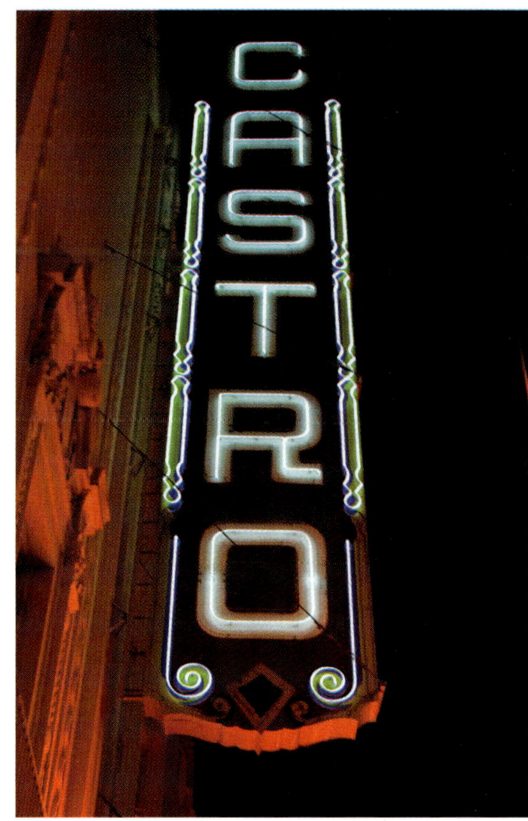

Theater sign caught when the blinking lights shine in blue.

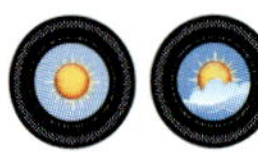

When to shoot: morning, afternoon

Modern San Francisco

It wasn't only the North Beach beats and the Haight-Ashbury hippies who started new fads in the middle of the 20th century. During the '50s and '60s, architects all over the world were streamlining new structures, taking away many of the decorative elements that existed in earlier eras. San Francisco wasn't left out when the world went modern. The new architectural era brought modular structures with repeating geometrical patterns in a new movement of minimalism. Two great examples of mid-century modern San Francisco dot the skyline with streamlined sophistication. The first—the Transamerica Building—is a work of geometrical modern design, and the second—St. Mary's Cathedral—is a symbol of the modern design movement in church building.

Completed in 1972, the 853-foot Transamerica Building has 48 floors and was constructed with white quartz aggregate by the architectural firm of William L. Pereira & Associates. Unlike high rises with four rectangular faces that climb to the sky, the Transamerica Building rises up in a pyramid shape so that more sun hits the street because there's less building at the top from which to cast shadows down below. You can go up to the 27th floor for views from the Transamerica Building. There are views of this building from many vantage points all over the city.

Next, climb up to anyplace where the city's skyline comes into view, and you'll find a structure that's as ubiquitous as the Transamerica Building rising above the city—a towering modern symbol of San Francisco, the giant concrete cross that makes up St. Mary's Cathedral. Built in 1971, this piece of programmatic architecture is built of reinforced concrete that flows outward from top to bottom into the shape of a cross.

The Shot

You can get a nice morning view of San Francisco's most notable building from the south side of Clay Street, just east of where it meets Montgomery. The building is structured so that a good shot of a sun-soaked surface can be found at any time during a sunny or partly cloudy/foggy day. To get a blue sky as part of your shot, make sure you shoot so that the sun is behind you (your camera is not pointing into the sun). There's a redwood-tree park next door to the building. The trees you see in front of the building extend from there to the park next door, making for a rather rustic setting for a downtown area. In this shot the sun hits the TA Building from the southeast so that the light on the surface is rather bright. You can lower your exposure compensation by one or two stops to enhance the details of the geometric patterns that surround the windows, especially the rows of semicircles under the line of windows on each floor.

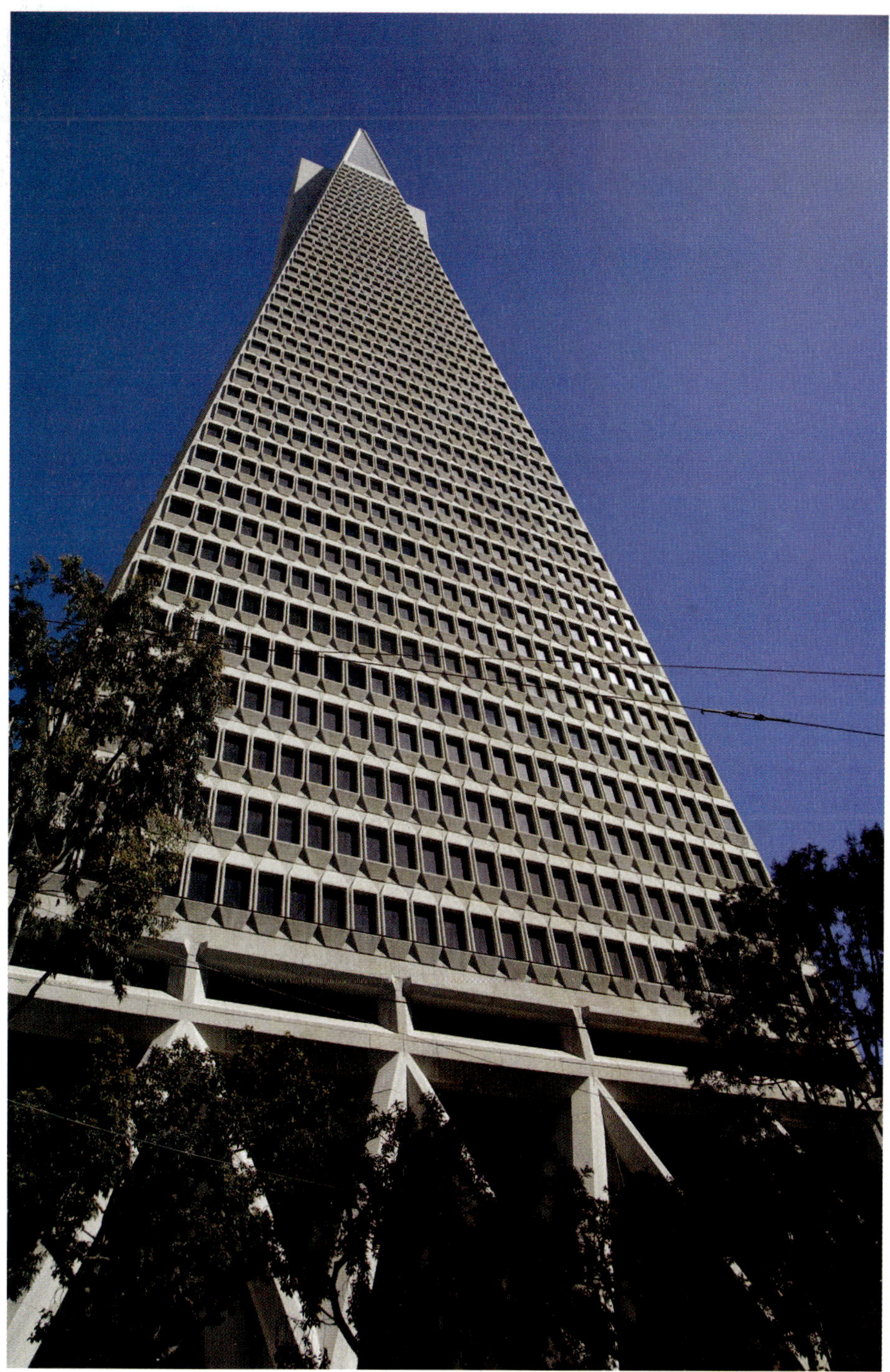

Focal length 24mm; ISO 200; aperture f/7.1; 1/500; May 11:00 a.m.

The Shot

The best time to photograph St. Mary's is in the early morning or late afternoon. You'll get blue sky in the background at these times, while at noon you'll get whiteout in your sky. The concrete surface also has a better cast of white when it's directly in the sunlight. The church looks like an optical illusion, but if you look hard enough, you can see the cross at the top of what look like concrete flaps, which is what they really turn out to be after you go a quarter of the way around the church to the façade that faces west. A pair of flaps (there's one on the east side, also) makes the vertical and horizontal axes of a huge cross that's enhanced with a dark, elongated rectangle that sets up the vertical axis of the cross. By not including this demarcation in the photo, you enhance the minimalism in the photo, photographing according to a plan in which less is more—a phrase coined by designer Ludwig Mies van der Rohe in the middle of the 20th century.

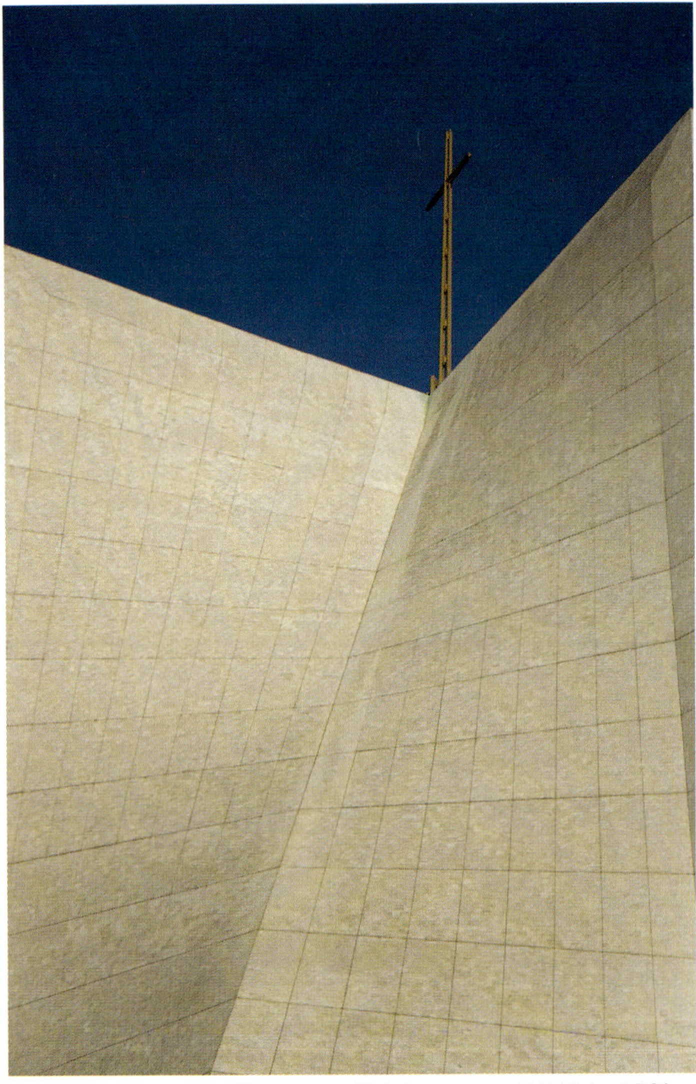

Focal length 70mm; ISO 200; aperture f/5.6; shutter speed 1/800; April 5:30 p.m.

Getting There

The Transamerica Building is at 600 Montgomery Street. To get there using mass transit, from the Montgomery Street BART/Muni station, walk seven blocks north on Montgomery Street to Clay Street. The TA building's south face can be seen from Clay Street.

If you're driving, from the South Bay, take 101 North. Take a slight right when you get to the sign saying Oakland/I-80/Bay Bridge/Seventh St/US-101 N, then take the 4th Street exit. Make a slight left at Bryant Street, then a left at 3rd Street, which will change to Kearny Street. Turn right at Clay Street and left at Sansome to Montgomery.

From the East Bay, take 80 West to 101 North. Take the 4th Street exit, then follow the directions from the South Bay.

From the North Bay, take 101 South to Lombard Street. Take a left on Van Ness, a right at Bay, a right at Columbus, and a right at Montgomery.

Located at the corner of Gough and Geary Streets, St. Mary's Cathedral is at 1111 Gough Street at Geary Street. You can catch the 38 Geary or 38 Geary Limited from Sutter and Market downtown. Get off at Geary and Van Ness and walk two blocks west to Gough. The church is on the left side of the street.

If you're driving, from the South Bay, take 101 North to Exit 434A. Merge onto Mission Street/US-101 North toward the Golden Gate Bridge. Take a slight left on Van Ness Avenue and turn left at Geary.

From the East Bay, take 80 West to 101 North, then follow the directions from the South Bay.

From the North Bay, take 101 South to Lombard Street. Turn right on Gough and take it to Geary.

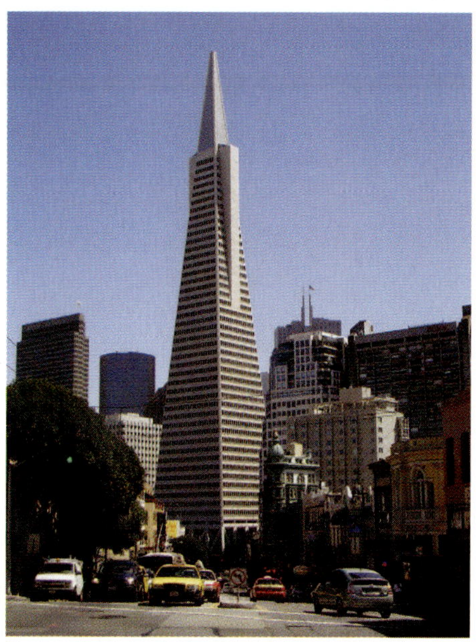

Transamerica Building as seen from Broadway and Columbus.

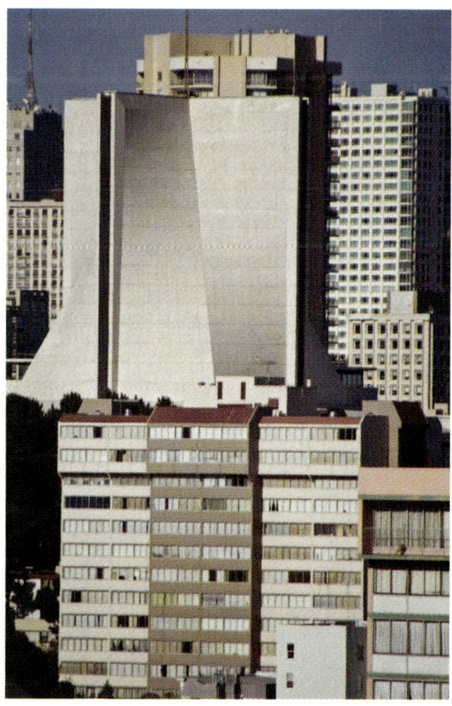

St. Mary's Cathedral on the San Francisco skyline.

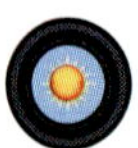 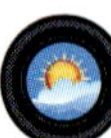 When to shoot: morning

Mission Dolores

The church, Mission Dolores Basilica, and the mission, Misión San Francisco de Asís, together are referred to as Mission Dolores.

California has a long history of Catholicism, which extends from the time the missionaries from the Old World came to convert the native people to Catholicism. Mission Dolores has always had a central place in the religious, civic, and cultural life of San Francisco. Misión San Francisco de Asís was founded June 29, 1776, under the direction of Father Junipero Serra and is both the oldest original intact mission in California and the oldest building in San Francisco. It was completed in 1791 and was the first church in the area. It's one of a string of missions that extend up and down the California coast. Many of the artifacts, both inside and outside, are original and make for great photographs. Next to Misión San Francisco de Asís, Mission Dolores Basilica, a Spanish Baroque structure, was completed in 1918. Behind Misión San Francisco de Asís is a graveyard.

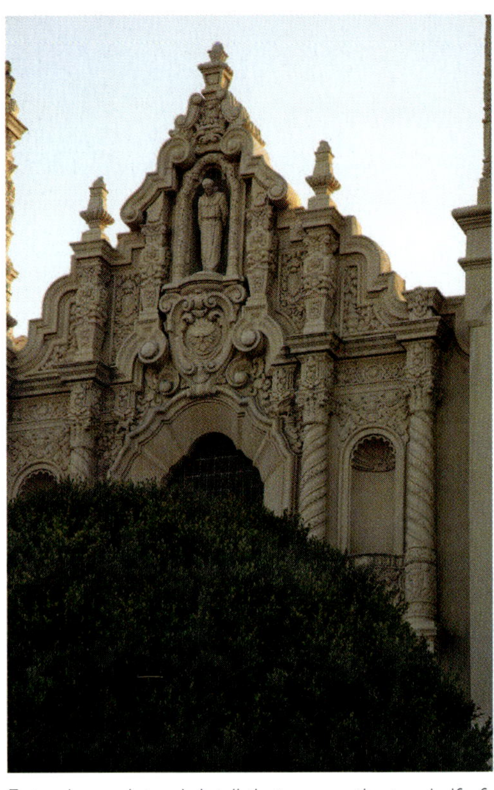

Extensive sculptural detail that covers the top half of the Basilica.

In the front wall (fachada) of the mission are three niches containing the three original bells brought up from Mexico in the 1790s. The names of the bells, from south to north, are San Martin, San Francisco, and San Jose. The central bell is in its original wooden stocks, secured by rawhide. Many of the roof tiles are the originals made on site in 1794. Mission Dolores is particularly famed for its artwork.

The Shot

The early-morning shot of the mission was taken with a wide angle on the sidewalk to the side of the building, near the front of the Basilica. In capturing the side, you can see the rough whitewashed surface of construction materials—adobe, brick, wood, stone, and tile—which is common on many of the California missions. Also present in the framing are the eaves of the roof, which are constructed from planks of wood. To prevent whiteout from the combination of sun shining on the building and its white surface reflecting it, lower your exposure compensation a stop or two

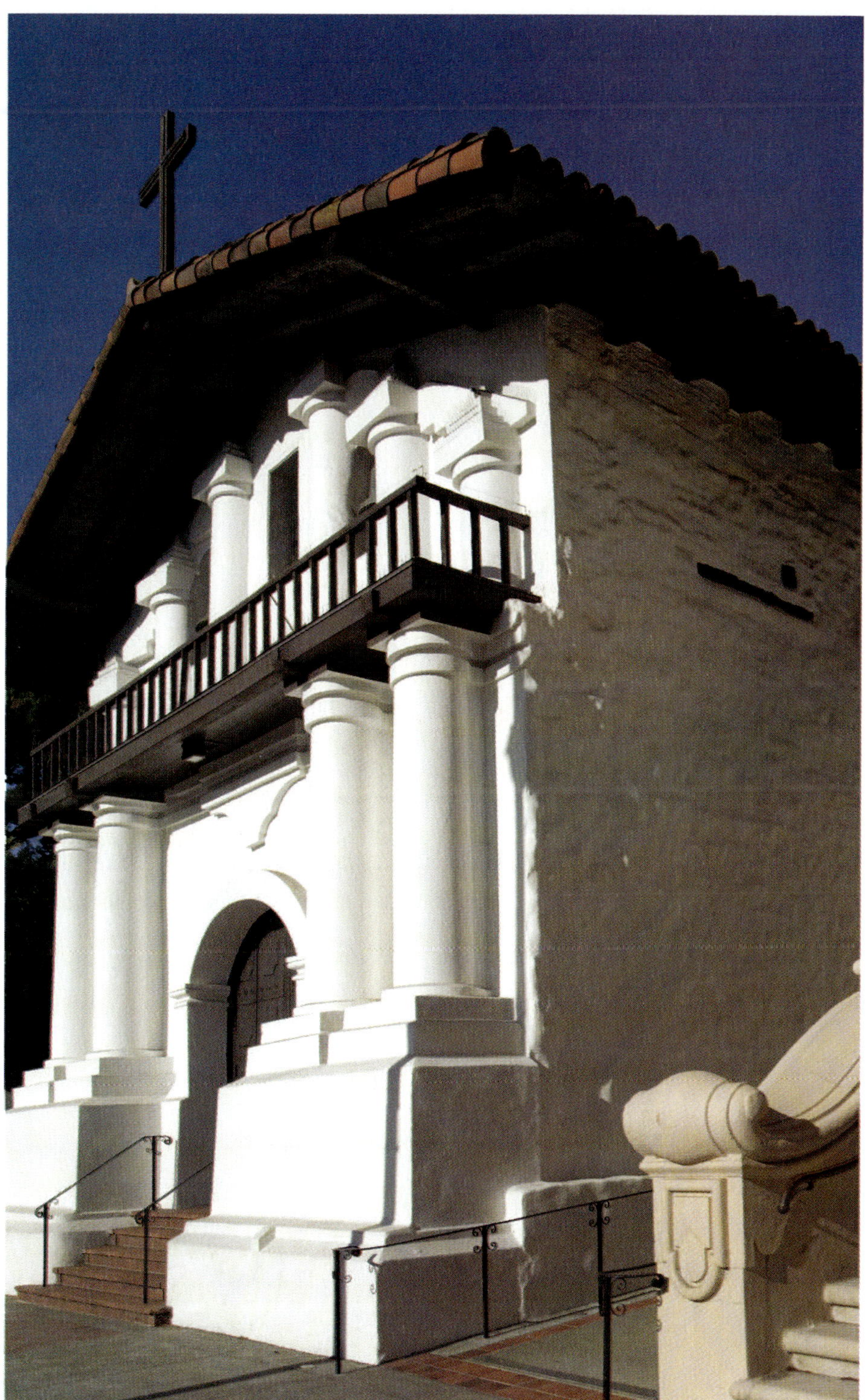

Focal length 18mm; ISO 200; aperture f/5; shutter speed 1/1000; May 7:30 a.m.

The Shot

Something as simple as a window in a mission building can be captivating. The recessed nature of the window adds depth, and the yellow light in the room adds mystery. Usually painted or stained-glass windows are easy to shoot without a tripod because of ample light coming through from outside; however, this window's lack of bright light calls for a higher ISO speed, which is what I used so that the image wouldn't be blurred.

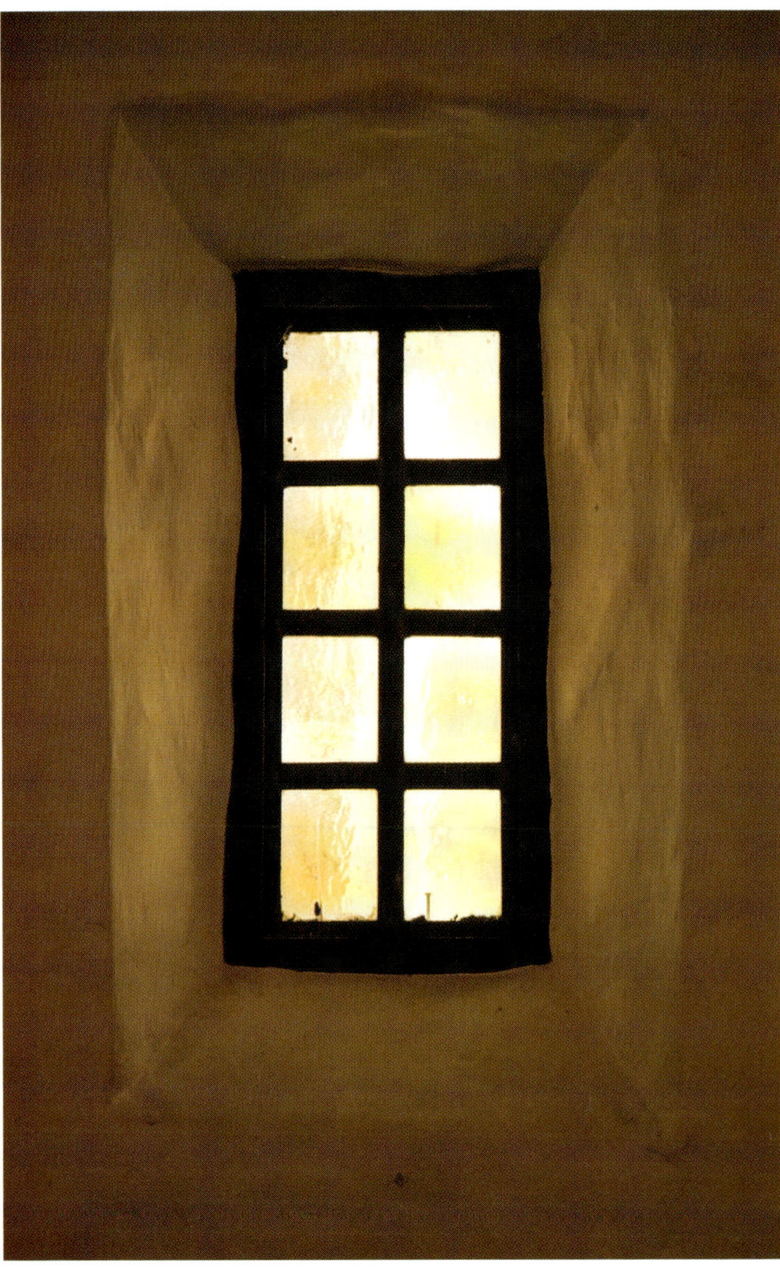

Focal length 90mm; ISO 1000; aperture f/4; shutter speed 1/80; April 3:00 p.m.

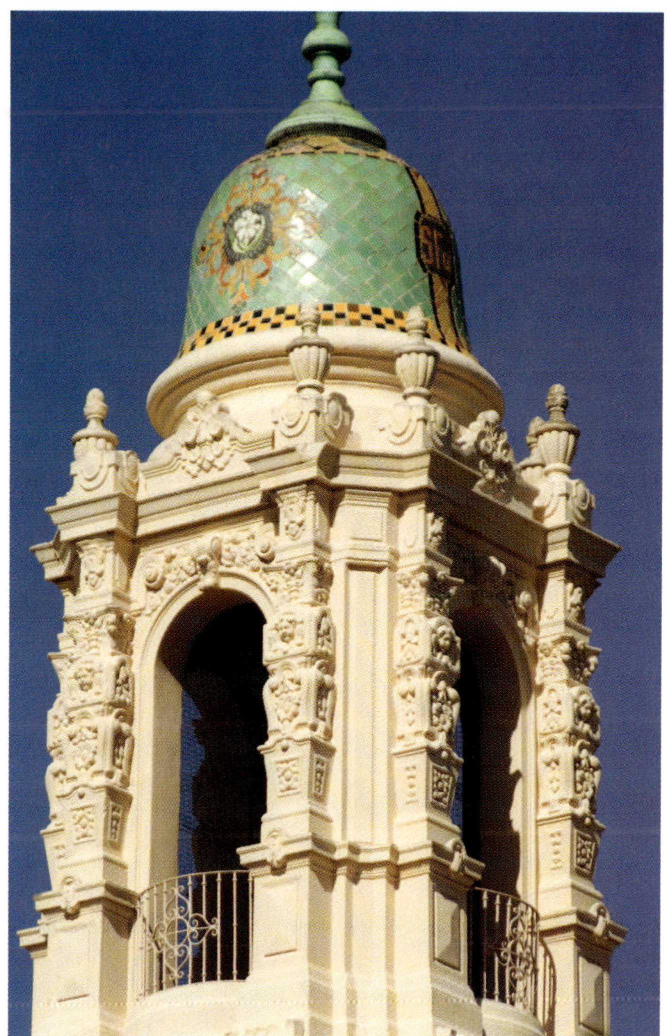

One of the spires of the Basilica.

Getting There

Mission Dolores is at 3321 16th Street between Dolores and Guerrero.

To get there using mass transit, from downtown take the J Church to 16th and Church. Walk 1-1/2 blocks east, and Mission Dolores is on the left.

If you're driving, from the South Bay, take 101 North to the Cesar Chavez exit. Make a left on Cesar Chavez, a right on Guerrero, and a left on 16th.

From the East Bay, take 80 West to 101 North until it ends at Market Street. Make a right on Market, a right on Valencia, and a right on 16th.

From the North Bay, take 101 South. Make a slight left to exit on Lombard Street, a right on Van Ness, a right on Otis to Mission, and a right on 16th.

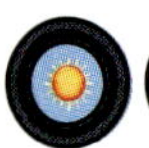 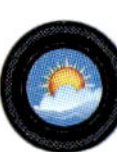

When to shoot: morning, afternoon, evening

Chinatown

The boundaries of Chinatown are much the same today as they were in 1880—from California to Broadway and Kearny to Stockton. The street running through the heart of Chinatown was Calle de la Fundacion (Foundation Street). It was then called Dupont, and it was finally named Grant Avenue to honor General Ulysses S. Grant, head of the Union Army during the Civil War and president of the United States.

All of Chinatown had to be rebuilt after the 1906 earthquake destroyed it. From 1906 to 1929, many Edwardian buildings went up, and then later they were decorated to look Chinese, or *chinoiserie.*

While you're walking up and down Grant Street, if you look up at the balconies, you'll see Edwardians built from 1909 to 1929 that are painted bright colors. There used to be many more than the few you see today, but they were torn down because, believe it or not, Chinatown has not been declared a historic district by any government entity. A pair of pagodas at California and Grant and the Chinese Telephone Exchange (now United Commercial Bank) are two of many colorful Chinese architecture monuments in Chinatown. Sing Chong and the other pagoda, Sing Fat (on the southwest corner), were built in 1908. Built in 1909, the Chinese Telephone Exchange was the first building to set the style for the new Chinatown after the 1906 earthquake. The building stands out from the rest by its peaked roofs and pagoda style. The building was an office for telephone operators who spoke five Chinese dialects.

The Shot

The partial skyline at the gateway to Chinatown with a pagoda placed prominently and interesting simple skyscrapers in the background makes for an interesting perspective detailing old and new San Francisco. On the left of the frame is Sing Chong, one of two pagodas at the intersection of California and Grant. I stood up the hill on the south side of California Street to take the picture. I positioned myself uphill at a point where I could get modern buildings in the background to contrast with the older buildings (Sing Chong and Old St. Mary's Church) in the foreground. To soften the focus in the background, I used a lower f/stop and set my focus points on the foreground building. In doing so, the foreground really stands out.

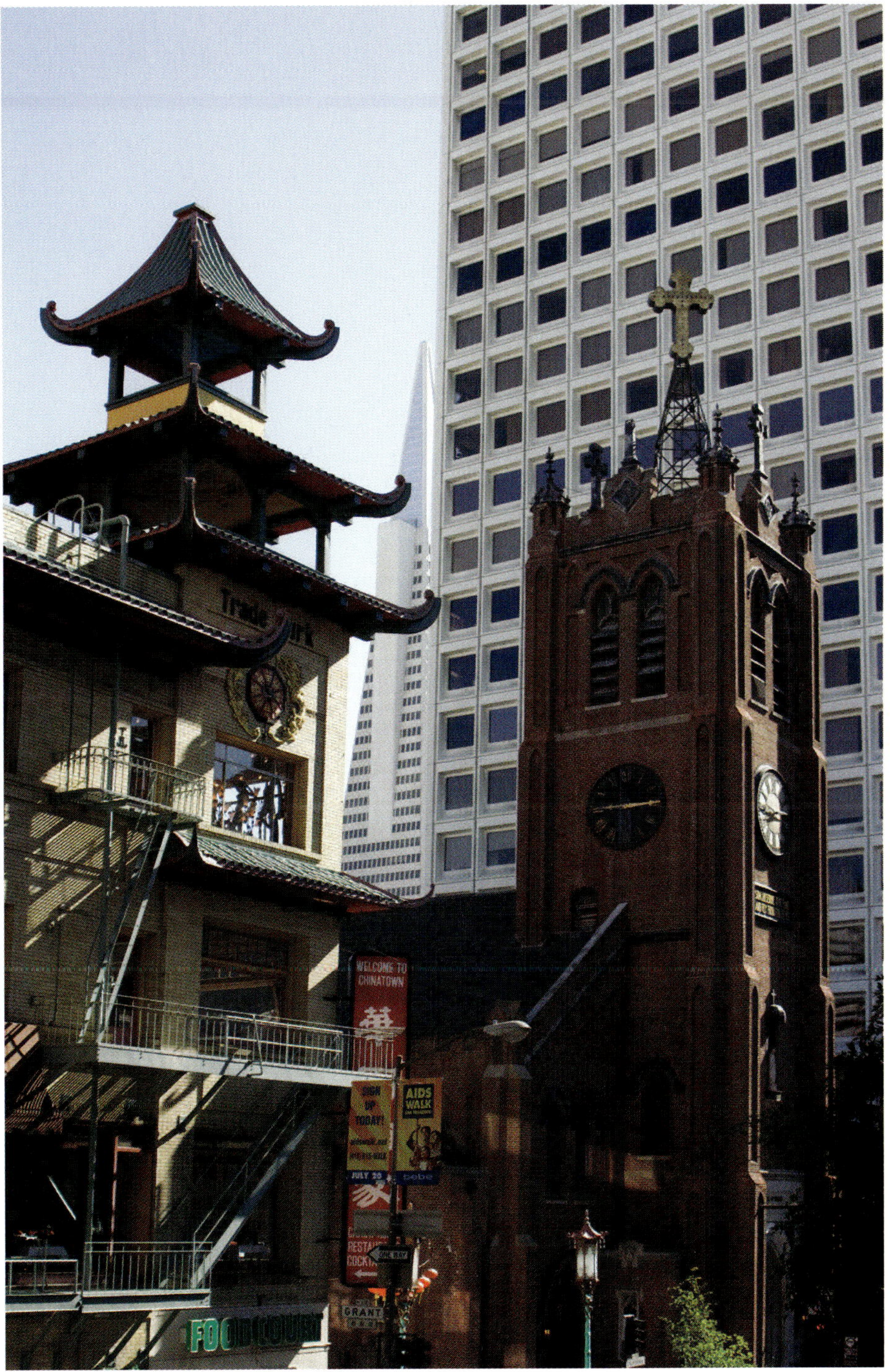

Focal length 28mm; ISO 200; aperture f/6.3; shutter speed 1/320; May 10:15 a.m.

The Shot

I gave the picture of the Chinese Telephone Exchange some depth by including a small part of the side of the building in the frame. I took the picture from a point across the street and a few steps west of the building. The building rarely gets any sun because it's enclosed by three walls and faces north, but because of its bright colors, it photographs well in the shade. To prevent converging lines, I used a wide-angle lens and stepped into a doorway across the street to set myself back from the building.

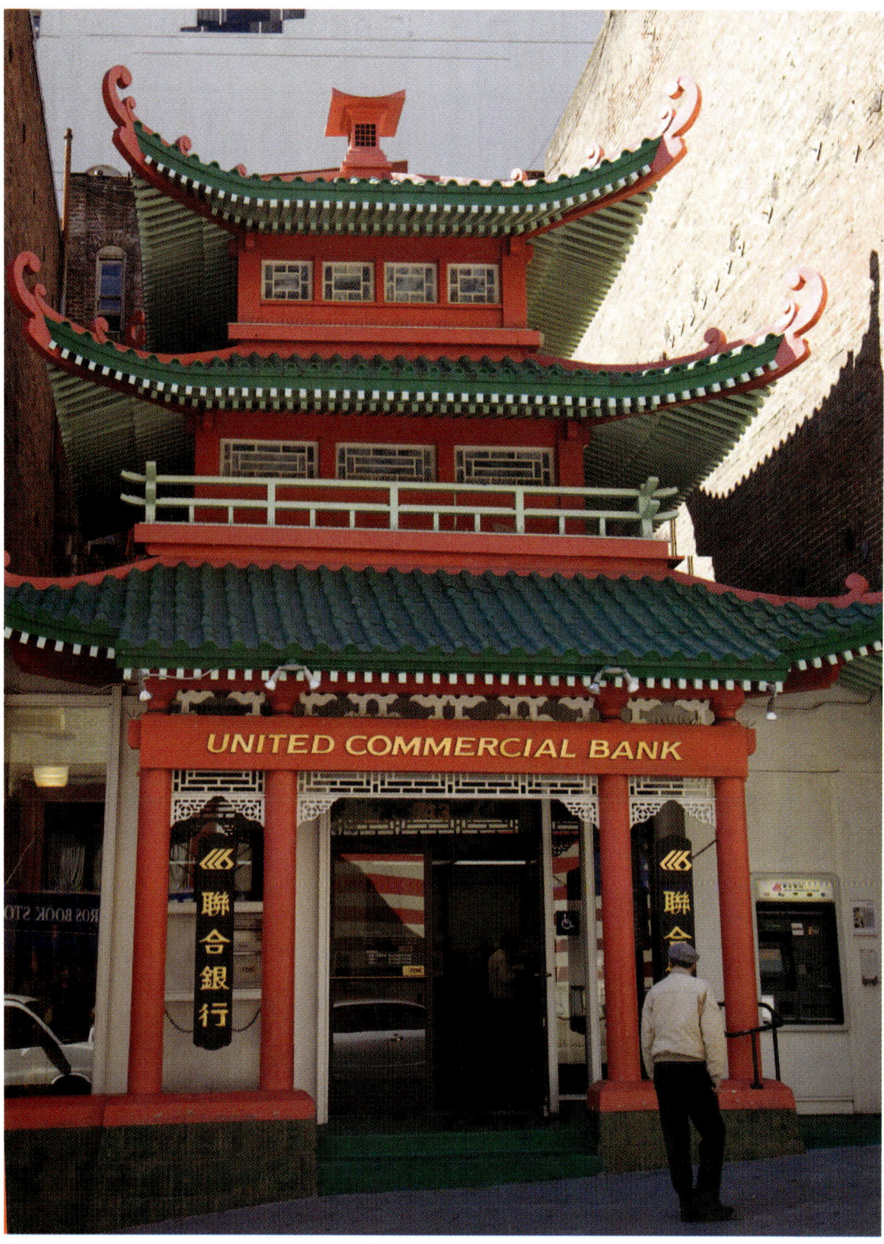

Focal length 40mm; ISO 100; aperture f/5.6; shutter speed 1/125; May 11:30 a.m.

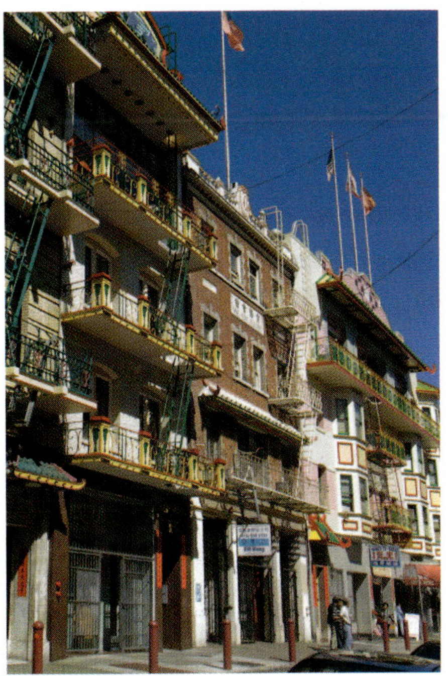

Row of buildings on the west side of Waverly Place in Chinatown.

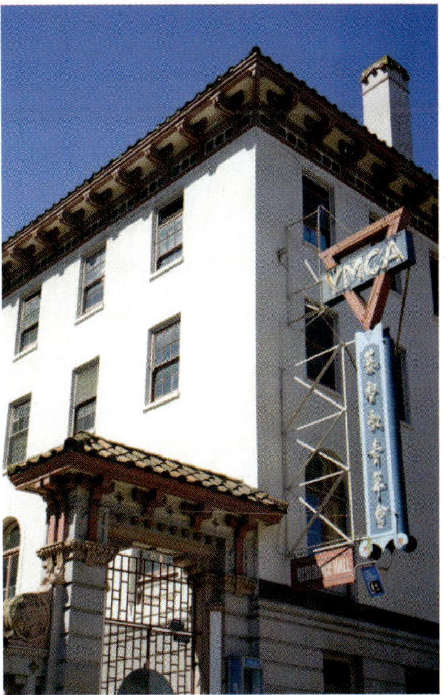

Classical Chinese architecture of the Chinatown YMCA.

Getting There

Grant and California is a good place to start a photography tour of Chinatown. Directions to this point are given below.

To get there using mass transit, take the 30 Stockton bus from downtown (4th and Market) to Stockton (one block west of Grant) and California. Or, you can catch the 1 California Bus from downtown (at Main and Howard) to Sacramento (one block north of California) and Grant.

If you're driving, from the South Bay, take 101 North. Exit at 4th Street and take a slight left at Bryant and a left at 3rd, which turns into Kearny (after you cross Market). Take a left at Pine and a right on Grant to California.

From the North Bay, take 101 South to Lombard. Take a right at Van Ness, a left at Broadway, a right on Stockton, a right on Sacramento, a left at Joice, and a left on California.

From the North Bay, take 80 West to Fremont Street. Take a left at Fremont, which turns into Front Street. Take a left on Pine and a right on Grant.

To get to the Chinese Telephone Exchange (United Commercial Bank), walk four blocks north on Grant and take a right on Washington. The building is just on the right, on the south side of Washington Street.

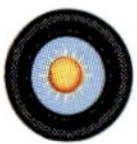 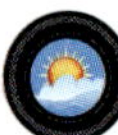

When to shoot: morning, early afternoon

Palace of Fine Arts

In 1915, San Francisco hosted the Panama-Pacific International Exposition (the World's Fair). It was nine years after the 1906 earthquake, and the city wanted to show the world that it had recovered. The fair lasted nine months, celebrating the relatively new National Park system and the opening of the Panama Canal. The Palace of Fine Arts was built for the Exposition, and Fort Mason bordered the Exposition grounds.

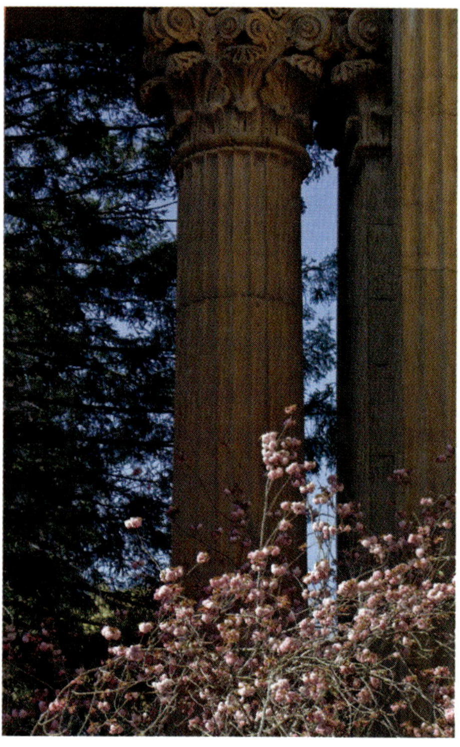

Front view of figures on the edge of the rotunda.

Originally designed by Bernard Maybeck and built in 1915, the Palace rotunda was demolished and reconstructed in the mid-1960s. Thirty Corinthian columns were reconstructed in the 1970s and frame a wide walkway. They, too, are replicas of original columns that were part of the Exposition site. Ulric Ellerhusen sculpted the weeping figures at the top of each column. These figures are unusual in that their backs face you, so you can only see a bit of the back of their heads. Some speculate that they were intended to express contemplation; others think it's the melancholy of life without art. As of this writing, the Palace rotunda is currently covered in scaffolding due to its renovation. That work will be complete by Spring 2009.

The Shot

The Palace of Fine Arts is unique in that you can go to one spot to take beautiful afternoon photographs and another for morning photographs. In the morning there are great photo ops of the lagoon and the colonnades that line it. They face east so that the sun is behind you, giving a deep blue sky in the background when you take a picture of them as they gracefully stand above the water. On the other hand, if you take a short hike around to the back of the colonnades, to where you have a clear, up-close view of the weeping figures at the tops of the them, the sun (if it is not blocked by fog) will come blazing through the sides and above the figures so that you'll have a blazing white background. So what's the solution? You have to go back to the spot in the afternoon when the sun is behind you. That's exactly what I had to do when I took my picture of the figures. I arrived at the spot in the morning when I could take a good picture of the lagoon, but I couldn't get a good image of the weeping figures, so I had to come back in the afternoon to take the pictures of the sculpted ladies with their heads between their arms, weeping away.

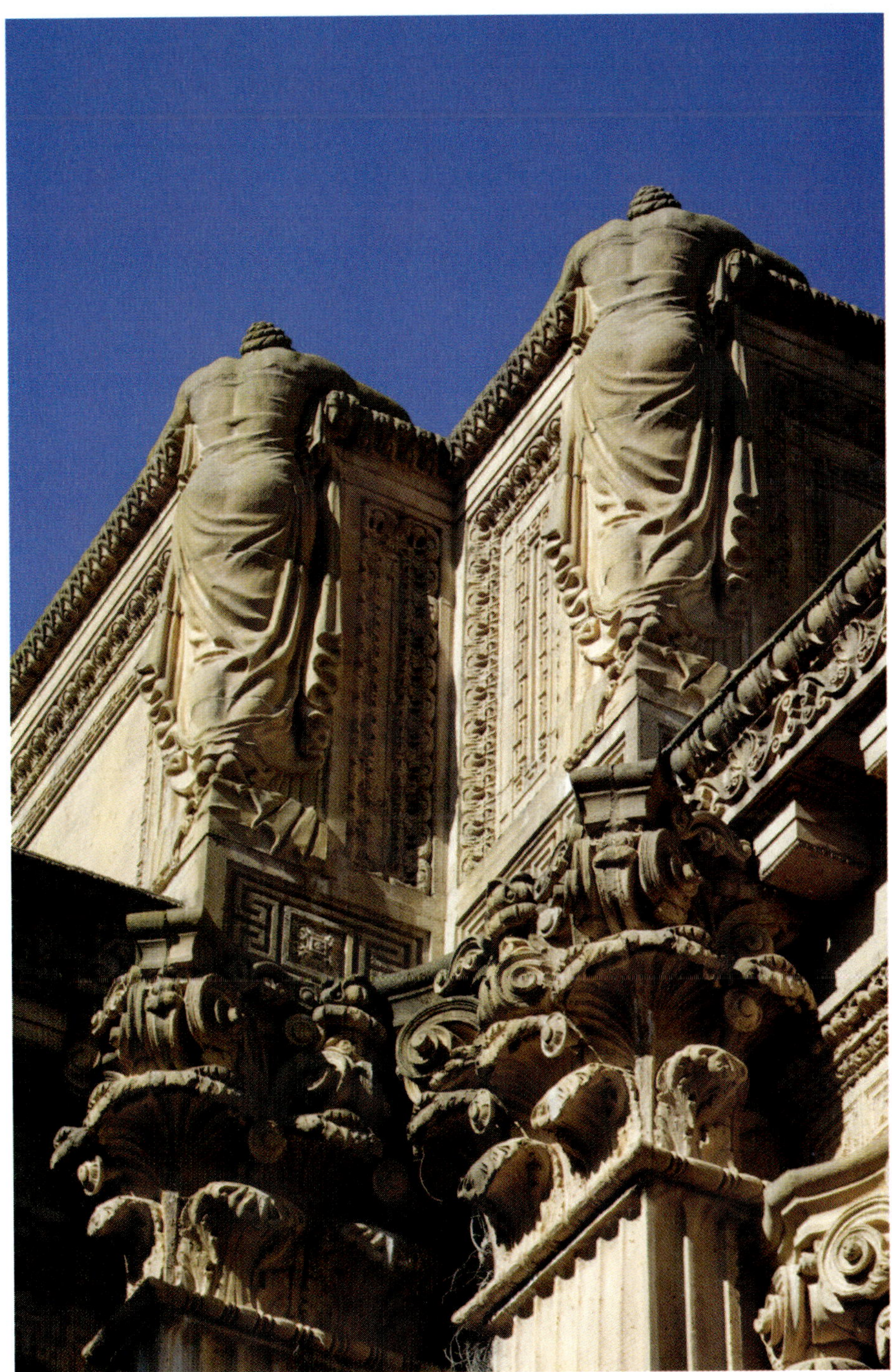

Focal length 105mm; ISO 200; aperture f/4.5; shutter speed 1/1000; April 3:00 p.m.

The Shot

This image is also on the other side of the lagoon, where the shot is best taken in the afternoon when the sun is behind you and when light illuminates the colonnades. I framed the image using the Rule of Thirds because the right third of the frame positions two columns in the foreground, and the remaining two thirds show the shot's perspective as the colonnades move to the background. To get to the shot from the lagoon, walk north along the footpath until you arrive at the southernmost of the Palace's colonnades. Take a picture from a point just where you see only the colonnades to avoid converging lines.

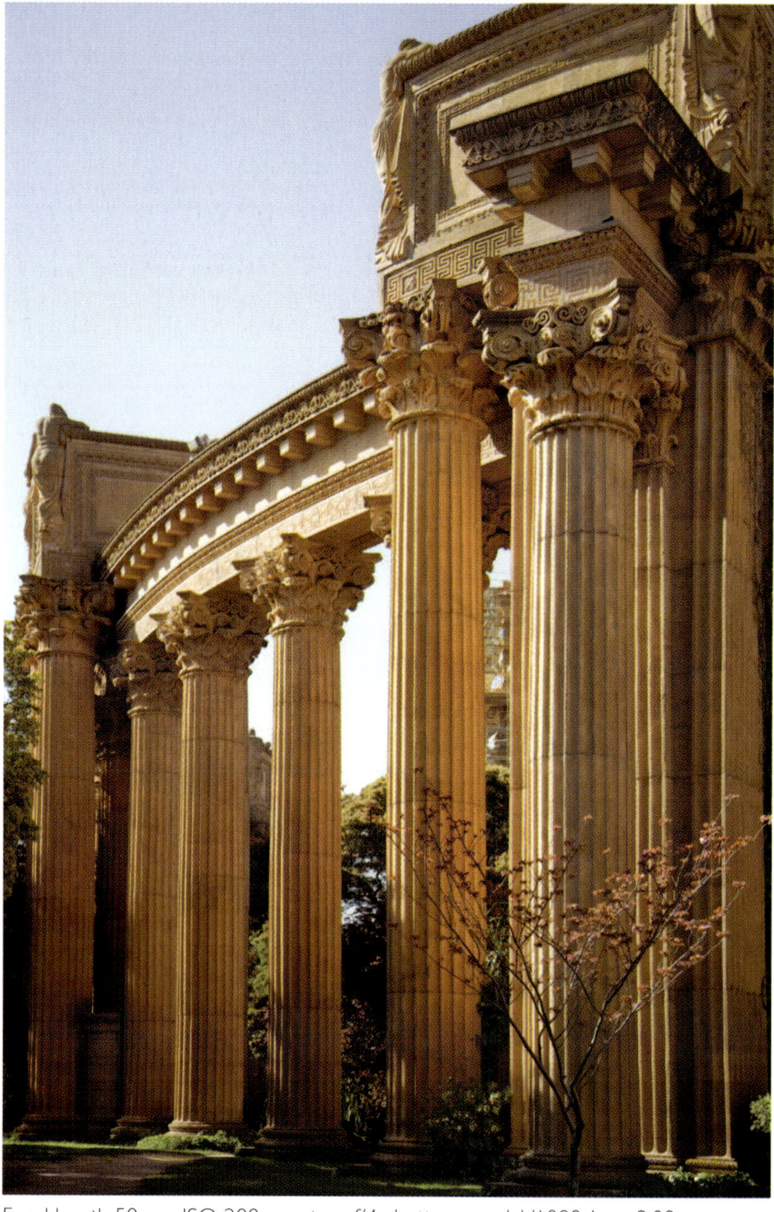

Focal length 50mm; ISO 200; aperture f/4; shutter speed 1/1000; June 3:00 p.m.

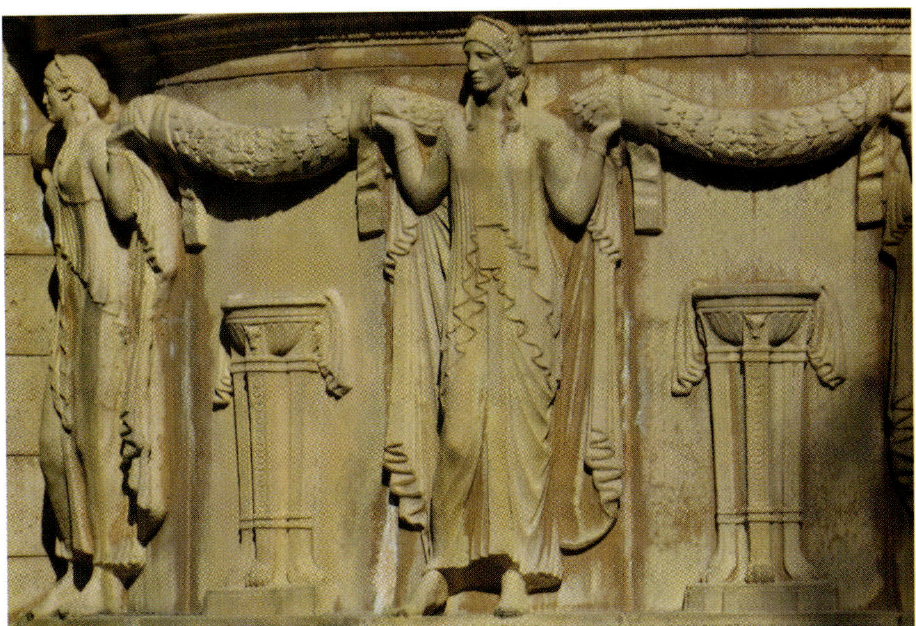

Column in spring with blooming tree.

Getting There

The Palace of Fine Arts is at 3301 Lyon Street.

To get there using mass transit, from downtown (4th and Market), take the 30 Stockton to Broderick Street and Beach Street. Walk one block west to Baker, and you'll see the Palace of Fine Arts across the street.

If you're driving, from the North Bay, take 101 South to the Marina exit. Take a right at Lyon Street. This will take you to the parking lot.

From the East Bay, take 80 West to the 9th Street exit. Turn right on 9th, left on Hayes Street, right on Franklin Street, and left on Lombard. Follow Lombard and turn right on Lyon Street. Go one block and turn left into the parking lot.

From the South Bay, take 101 North and exit at 9th Street, then follow the East Bay directions from 9th.

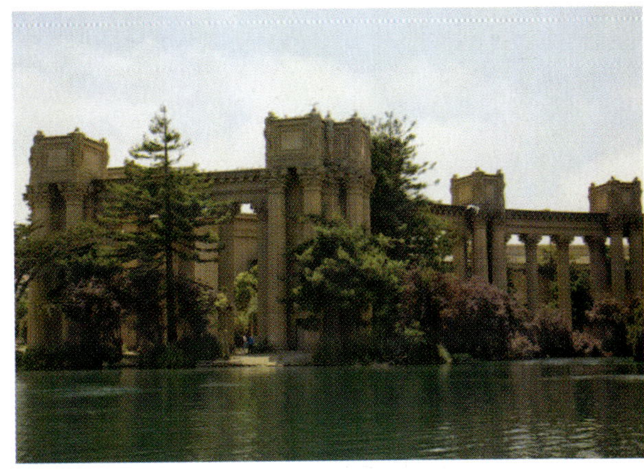

Colonnades as seen from lagoon.

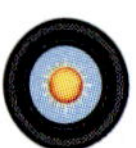 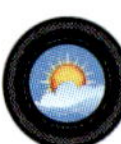 When to shoot: afternoon, evening

Coit Tower

Built in 1933, Coit Tower graces the San Francisco skyline from the top of Telegraph Hill. Lillie Hitchcock-Coit, a philanthropist and honorary firefighter, left a small fortune to the city of San Francisco. The money was used to build the 210-foot Art Deco–style tower.

Forty-five artists hired under the Public Works of Art Project during the Great Depression painted the murals inside Coit Tower. The murals are intact and are quite an experience to see and photograph. The artists were from CSFA (*California School of Fine Arts*) and included Maxine Albro, Victor Arnautoff, Ray Bertrand, Rinaldo Cuneo, Mallette Dean, Parker Hall, Edith Hamlin, George Harris, Robert B. Howard, Otis Oldfield, and Frede Vidar.

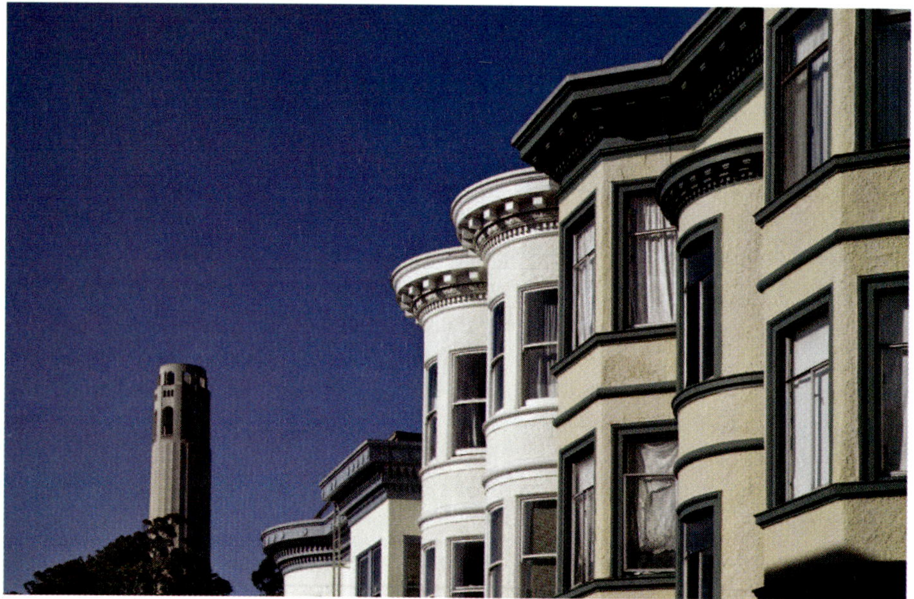

Entrance to the Humanities and Social Sciences Library.

The Shot

The front of the tower at sunset is a good time to photograph Coit Tower because the sun shines on the face and the sky is blue in back. Getting this shot is a bit tricky because there are many trees near the tower. For this reason, zoom in as close as you can to the tower so that it is cropped tightly, without any tree branches in the background. Another alternative is to frame just the top of the tower in a shot.

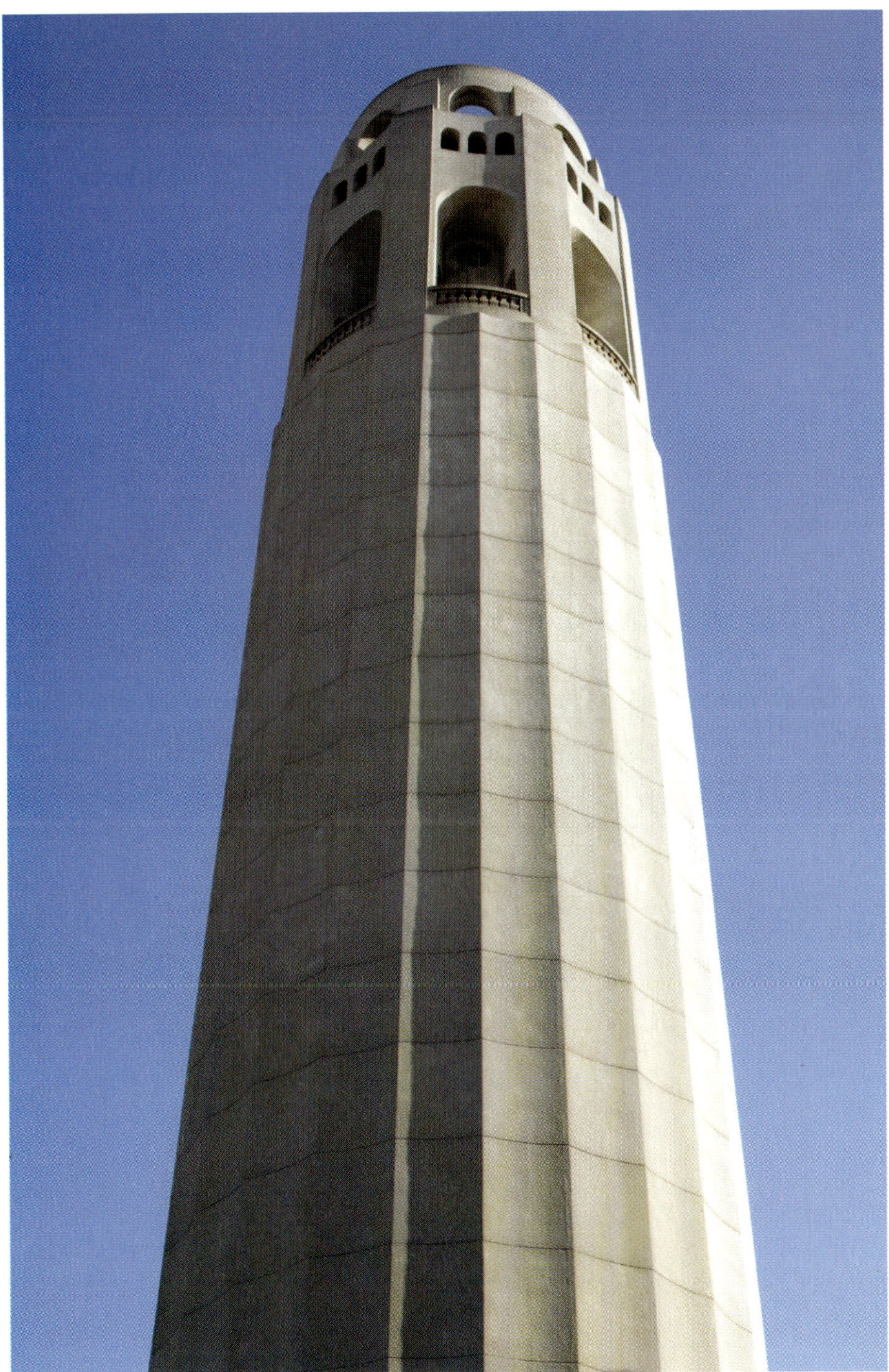

Focal length 40mm; ISO 200; aperture f/10; shutter speed 1/250; April 5:00 p.m.

The Shot

Whether inside or outside, photographing murals is easier than taking other photos because you're only working with two dimensions (a flat surface). You don't have to worry about focal length, and noise is usually at a minimum because of the deep colors you're working with. Because the inside of the tower where the murals are painted is poorly lit, you can use a high ISO speed (I used ISO 1000 with excellent results) to get a clear shot of the art works. You can deepen the colors of murals using a vibrance slider in Camera Raw format or the hue/saturation tools in image processing programs such as Photoshop. Many digital cameras also have saturation options so that you can edit images in-camera. Again, because murals are two-dimensional, they respond especially well to tweaking in or out of the camera.

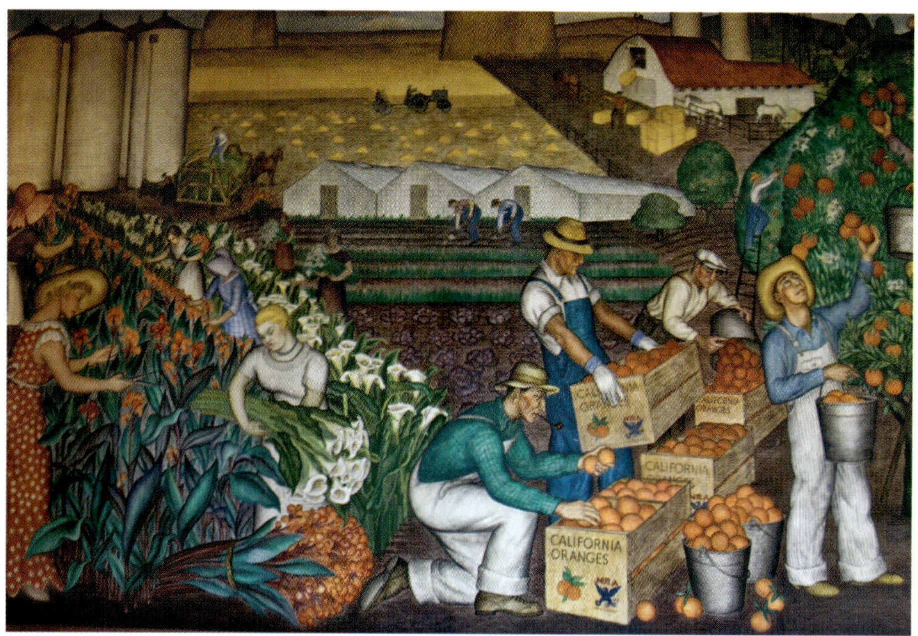

Focal length 24mm; ISO 1000; aperture f/4; shutter speed 1/30; April 5:00 p.m.

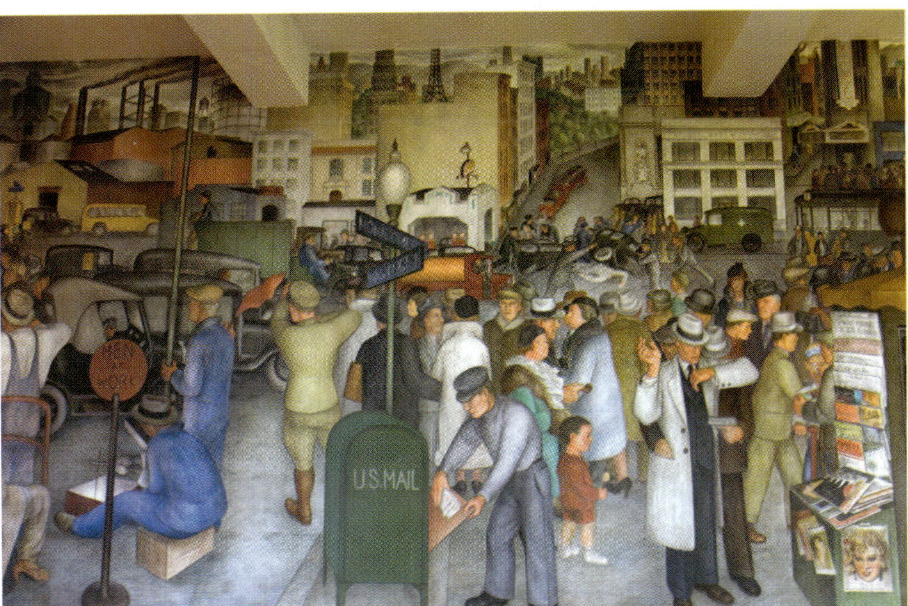

Another mural inside Coit Tower.

Getting There

To get there using mass transit, from the Embarcadero downtown (in front of the Ferry Building), you can take the F Market to Fisherman's Wharf and then the 39 Coit to Coit Tower.

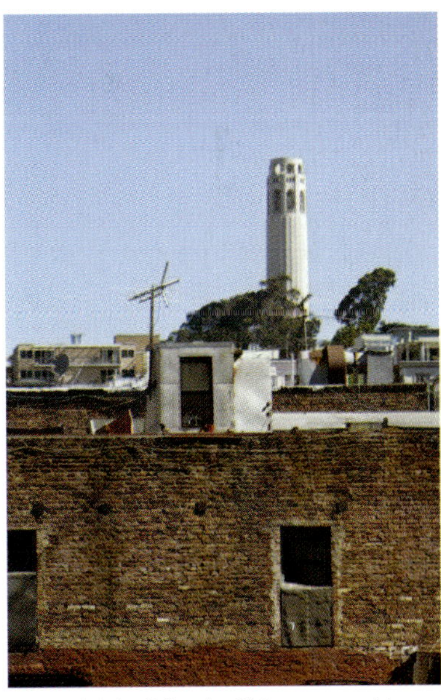
Old brick building in Chinatown with Coit Tower in the background.

If you're driving, from the South Bay, take 101 North to 280 North toward the Port of San Francisco. Exit onto King Street, which turns into the Embarcadero. Turn left on Bay Street, left on Stockton, and left on Lombard. Lombard turns right and becomes Telegraph Hill Boulevard, which Coit Tower is on.

From the East Bay, take 80 West to the Fremont Street exit. Keep right and follow the signs for Folsom Street. Turn left on Folsom and left at the Embarcadero, and then follow the South Bay directions from the Embarcadero.

From the North Bay, take 101 South to San Francisco. Make a slight left at Lombard Street. Turn left at Van Ness, right on Bay Street, right on Stockton, and left on Lombard, which becomes Telegraph Hill Boulevard, where you'll find Coit Tower.

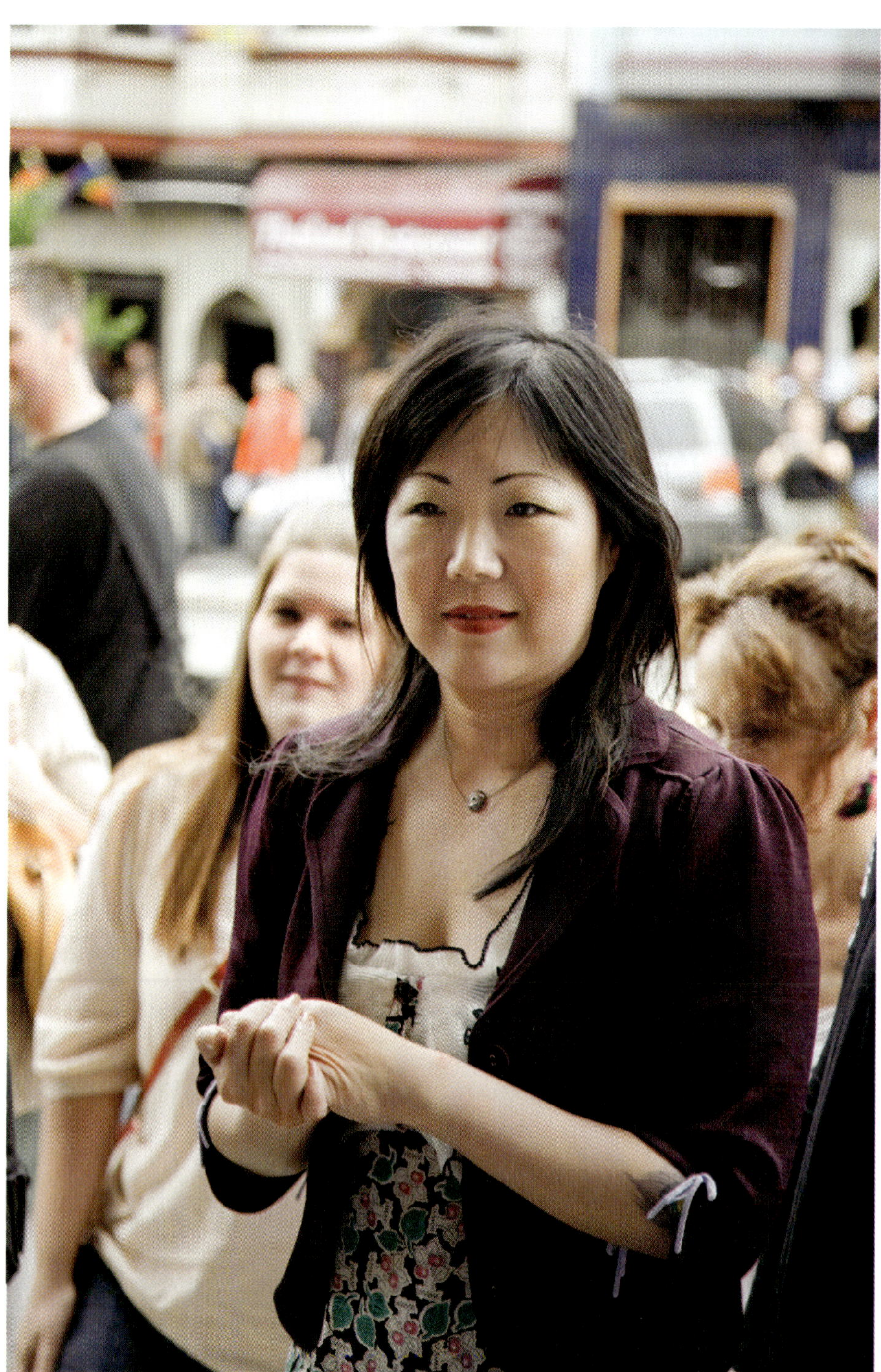

Margaret Cho, a well-known San Francisco star, at a gay film festival opening.

Chapter 2

City Life

The true measure of any city is its people. Due to its long and continuing tradition of embracing diverse cultures, San Francisco delivers. Each neighborhood of the city dances to the beat of its own unique flavor and often to a different drum. From hippies of the Haight to the urban hipsters of Union Street, this chapter seeks to show you how to find scenes, subjects, and objects that represent everything that is San Francisco.

San Francisco city life hums day and night, from people doing gymnastics moves in the morning at Portsmouth Square to the North Beach lights blinking into the night. Unlike other cities in the United States where people drive from place to place, most people who live in the city use the vast mass transportation system that runs from the bay to the ocean on every major street. The system consists of electric buses, subway trains, motor buses, streetcars, and "little cable cars that climb halfway to the stars." The cable cars and streetcars are colorful and are beautiful to photograph.

No city in the United States has a street scene as diverse as that in San Francisco. On any given day, you can catch mimes who can be mistaken for robots, women who follow the Japanese trend of dressing up like little girls, superheroes in tights, and Uncle Sam belting out his voice through a loudspeaker. You can also find businesspeople in the Financial District, art shoppers on Union Street, tourists on Powell Street, lovers in the Haight, cable-car operators pulling brakes, protesters at BART stations, vintage streetcars along the Embarcadero, and so much more. Whether city life is mundane or has produced a miracle, you'll need to have your camera with you at every minute to catch the expected and its counterpart, the surprise.

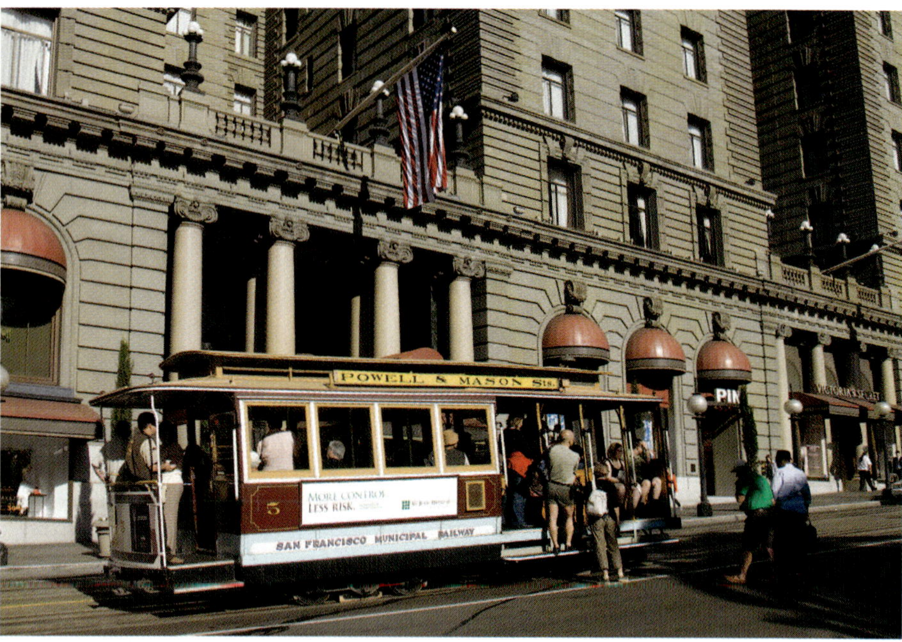

Cable car in front of the St. Francis Hotel.

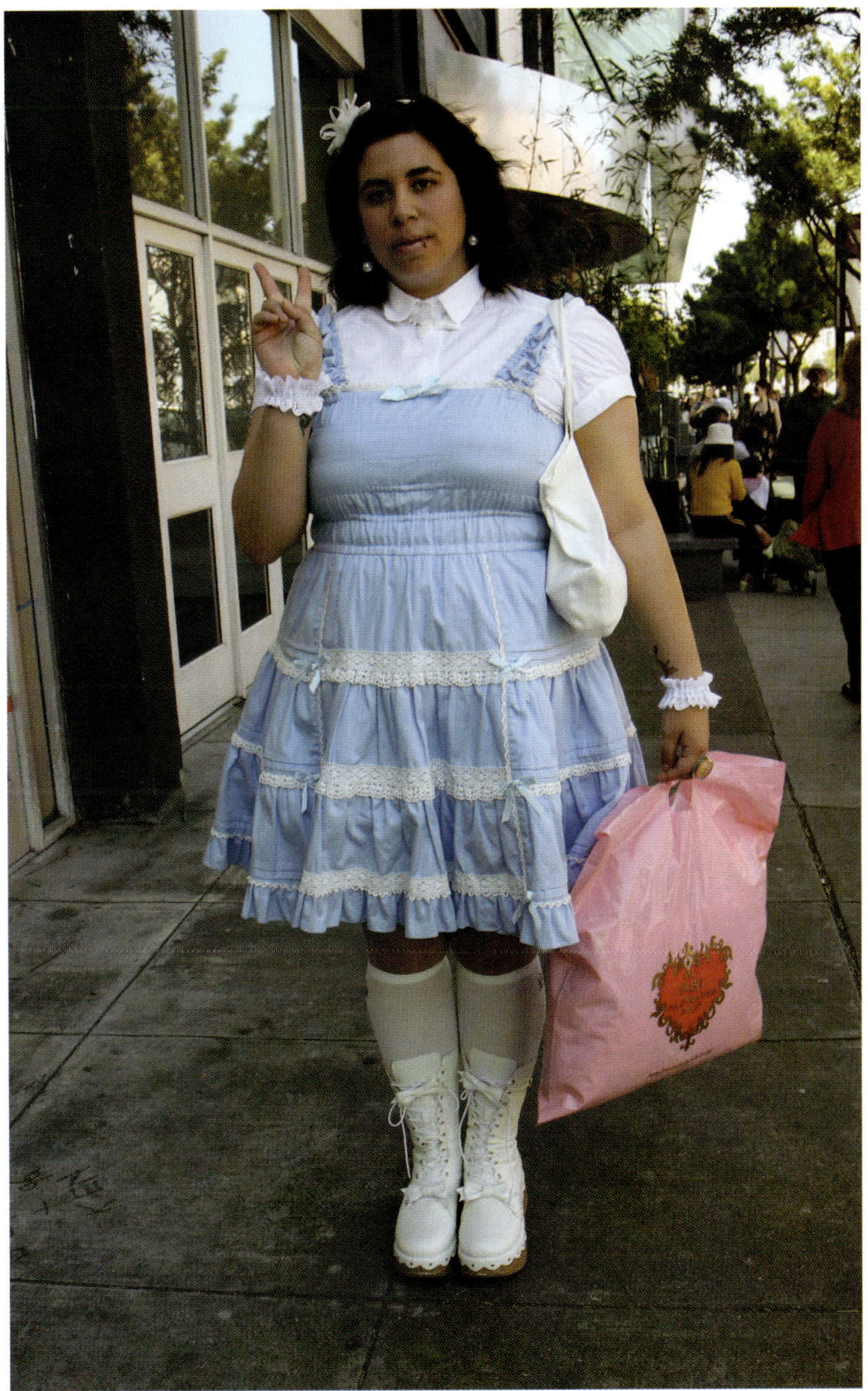

Woman dressed as a little girl.

Shooting Like a Pro

San Francisco city life is all about narrative, the art of telling a story. It's no wonder Armistead Maupin wrote *Tales of the City*, a series of novels that tell the wild stories of San Franciscans in the '70s. When you can spot a story happening or you can create one with your lens, you're on your way to shooting like a pro. The production of a narrative photograph can be as simple as photographing people getting off a crowded vintage streetcar or as complex as framing a protest march so that viewers know what all the fuss is about.

Capturing movement is one of the first things that comes to mind when you're thinking about professional photography and storytelling. From the movement of dance to that of traffic trails, you can measure distance with respect to time or how fast a movement is taking place by intentional blur you produce in your subjects and/or objects when you shoot with a tripod at longer shutter speeds. Remember, too, that creating movement of subjects using blur is good, but only if your background is sharp—except when you're panning a shot, and in that case, your subject is sharp and your background is blurred.

The Gear

The most important thing to remember when photographing city life is to have your camera with you at all times. You never know what's going to happen on any San Francisco street the minute you leave your home or your hotel room. You might catch a gypsy out on the street, for example. To shoot city life like a pro, you have to be versatile, working with both telephoto and wide-angle focal lengths. The L-series Canon 24-105mm lens is a good choice for street photography.

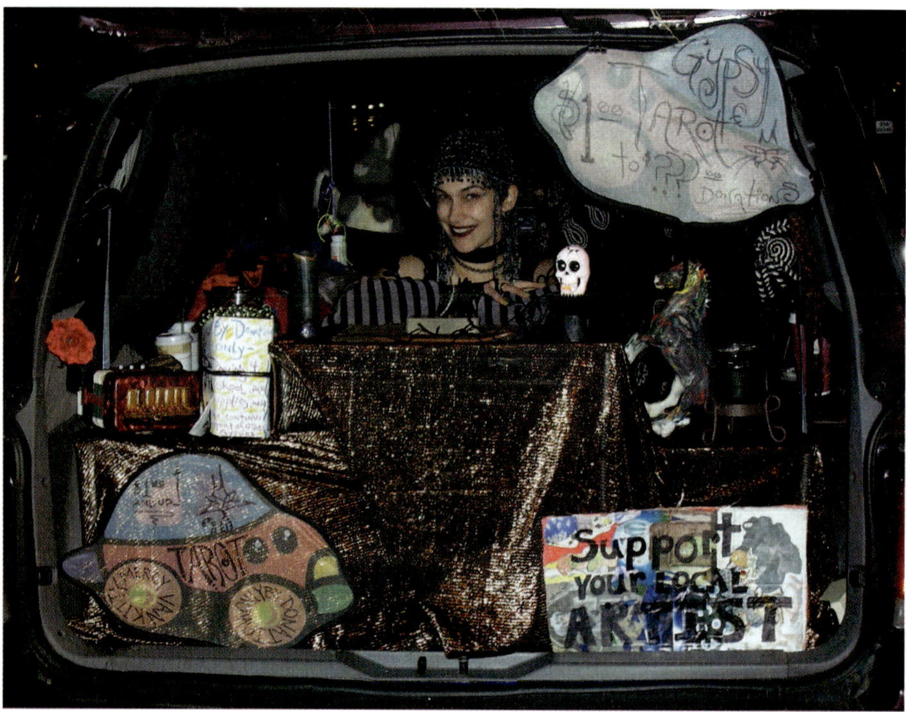

A self-proclaimed gypsy is in the business of reading Tarot cards.

When you want to capture movement, you can carry a tripod with you. A lightweight one with a carrying handle can do the trick. If you know your camera and can tweak ISO speeds quickly as well as have a steady hand, you can survive without a tripod and still record movement with sharp backgrounds. Using a tree or pole to brace yourself helps, too. You can also find a place to set your camera down so that it doesn't move. Finally, use your camera's timer so that you don't get blur from camera shake. When you set the self-timer on your camera, it will delay taking a picture for a specified number of seconds (on most cameras you can set it for two or ten seconds) after you have pressed the shutter release button. If you don't set the timer, the shutter opens while your finger is still in the process of pressing the shutter release button so that you risk blur from camera shake.

The Plan

The time of year, the day of the week, and the time of day play large parts in getting good photographs of people in the city. During April and October, there's a better chance of days without fog and rain. On those days the streets are filled with performance artists and musicians who are not shy in front of the camera. On weekends and at rush hour, there are more people on the streets than there are at other times and days. In summer there's often heavy fog that clears the streets of people because it gets very cold. If you're going to sell your photographs, it's a good idea to carry model release forms for people to sign. (See the sidebar entitled "Getting a Release" later in this chapter.) Finally, it's best to ride mass transportation to get around, for two reasons: You won't have to worry about parking, and you'll get some great photo ops at the stations and on the buses, streetcars, and subway trains while you're riding them.

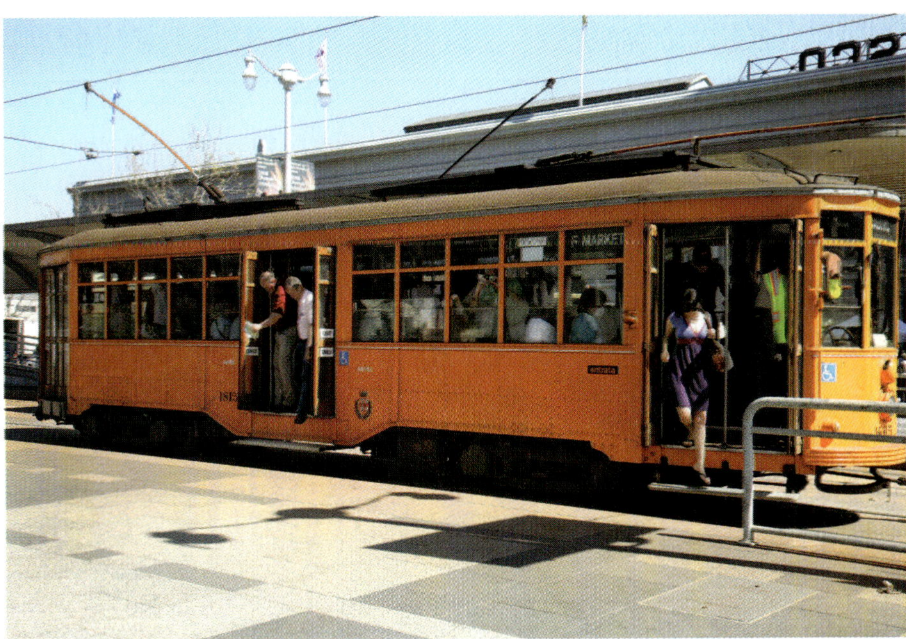

People getting off a vintage streetcar.

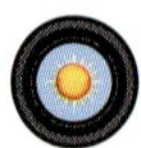 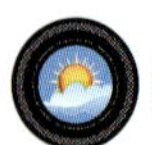 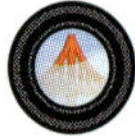

When to shoot: afternoon, evening, night

North Beach History

No neighborhood in San Francisco has been bawdy and offbeat for as long as North Beach has. The area began as a Barbary Coast neighborhood in the mid-1800s. The neighborhood was a gateway for people from around the world who wanted to get rich by finding the gold in the Mother Lode. Miners and sailors invaded the neighborhood, making it a bustling zone of bars and brothels. Much of it stayed, but it mellowed throughout the years, becoming a zone of popular restaurants, cafes, and nightclubs. Today the neighborhood is known as North Beach, the most densely populated in San Francisco.

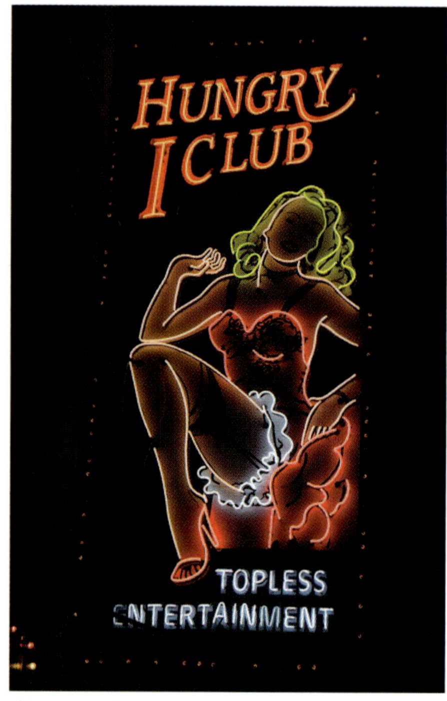

Close up of North Beach neon.

For decades, North Beach has been a predominately Italian neighborhood with some of the finest Italian food on the West Coast. Cafes abound, the most famous being the Caffé Trieste, a gathering place for the Beat Generation's greatest writers. Imagine Francis Ford Coppola typing on a yellow typewriter while men in berets and dark turtlenecks milled about. It wasn't only writers who came to Trieste—Pavarotti sang here, and Joe Rosenthal, the photographer who shot the two men raising the flag at Iwo Jima, sipped his coffee here. The writers still come, and the place hasn't changed all that much over the years, making photographs of the place a narrative of nostalgia.

The Shot

Caffé Trieste is *the* North Beach hangout and has been for decades. Its facade symbolizes the Beat Generation people who sipped coffee here—Jack Kerouac and Alan Ginsberg, to name a couple. I had to be quick with this shot to get the man with the cane in the frame. For this reason, I used a large aperture in Av mode so that the camera automatically calculated a fast shutter speed and he would be in sharp focus. When I use a wide aperture, I have to remember to be careful to focus on my subject because the depth of field will be shallow. Before the man passed, I was in the process of taking multiple shots of the cafe. He just happened to walk by as I was shooting. His look makes the image feel as if it was taken in another time. I like that both men in the picture are wearing hats and that the man sitting is playing with a digital camera, which keeps the viewer studying the picture to figure out all that is happening there—a pleasant combination of the present and the past.

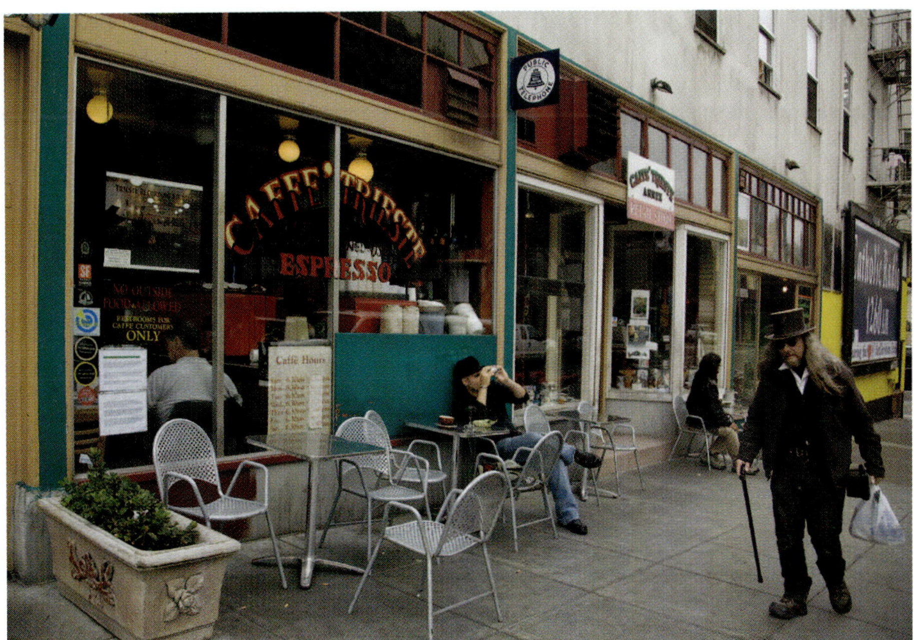

Focal length 24mm; ISO 200; aperture f/4; shutter speed 1/1000; August 11:48 a.m.

PHOTOGRAPHY'S GOLDEN RULE: THE RULE OF THIRDS

If there were a Golden Rule in photography, it would be the Rule of Thirds. It's the tried-and-true way to make your frame's composition easy to look at.

All you have to do is think of your frame in terms of it being divided into thirds in a number of ways: from top to bottom, from left to right, and sometimes diagonally. These divisions act as guidelines for arranging the contents of your image.

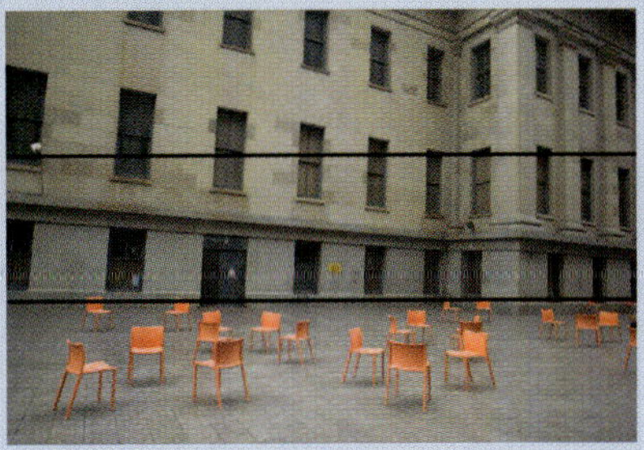

Chairs lie in an area at the bottom third of the frame.

One example of how the Rule of Thirds works is illustrated in the image of the orange chairs, shown here. The chairs lie in the lower third in the frame, filling up the area below the line that marks the bottom third of the frame, thus following the Rule of Thirds. The remaining two-thirds of the frame are occupied by the drab gray building. It's lucky those orange chairs are in the bottom third of the frame, because they offer high contrast to the plain building that occupies the top two-thirds of the frame.

Now that you know the Rule of Thirds (if you didn't know it already), you'll be prepared to break it when you feel the artistic need.

The Shot

This shot is best from the curb in front of the Garden of Eden nightclub at 529 Broadway. It shows that trails from the passing vehicles combined with nightclub signs add a sense of slick movement to the image. Because there is quite a bit of light emitted from the signs, I set the EV compensation all the way down (to –2 EV) in order to get a good set of trails and not to blast out the white light on the signs. The shot is a waiting game of getting just the right amount of traffic passing by to get a good set of trails. Notice, too, that I've followed the Rule of Thirds, incorporating the buildings in the right two-thirds of the frame. The trails ultimately lead to nowhere but the dark, leaving the viewer with his own thoughts about passing this neighborhood.

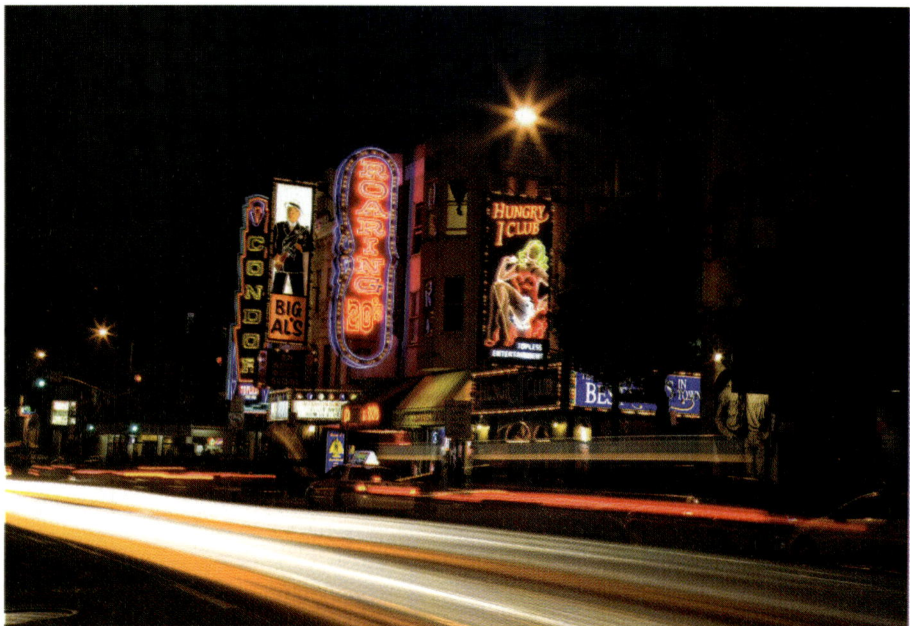

Focal length 55mm; ISO 200; aperture f/22; shutter speed 2.5 seconds; May 8:24 p.m.

Getting There

If you're taking mass transit, take the 30 Stockton from downtown (4th and Market) and get off at Grant and Columbus. Walk a few steps north to Broadway.

If you're driving, from the South Bay, take 101 North. Take exit 434A, then take a slight left on S. Van Ness Avenue. Take a right on Broadway to Columbus.

From the East Bay, take 80 West and exit at Fremont Street. Turn left on Folsom, left on the Embarcadero, and left on Broadway to Columbus.

From the North Bay, take 101 South to Lombard Street. Take a right at Van Ness and a left at Broadway to Columbus.

The nightclub signs are east of the Broadway and Columbus intersection (on Broadway). Walk east half a block on the south side of Broadway. The clubs will be across the street from there.

The Caffé Trieste is at 601 Vallejo Street. From Grant and Broadway, walk north on Grant toward Fresno Street, then make a left at Vallejo.

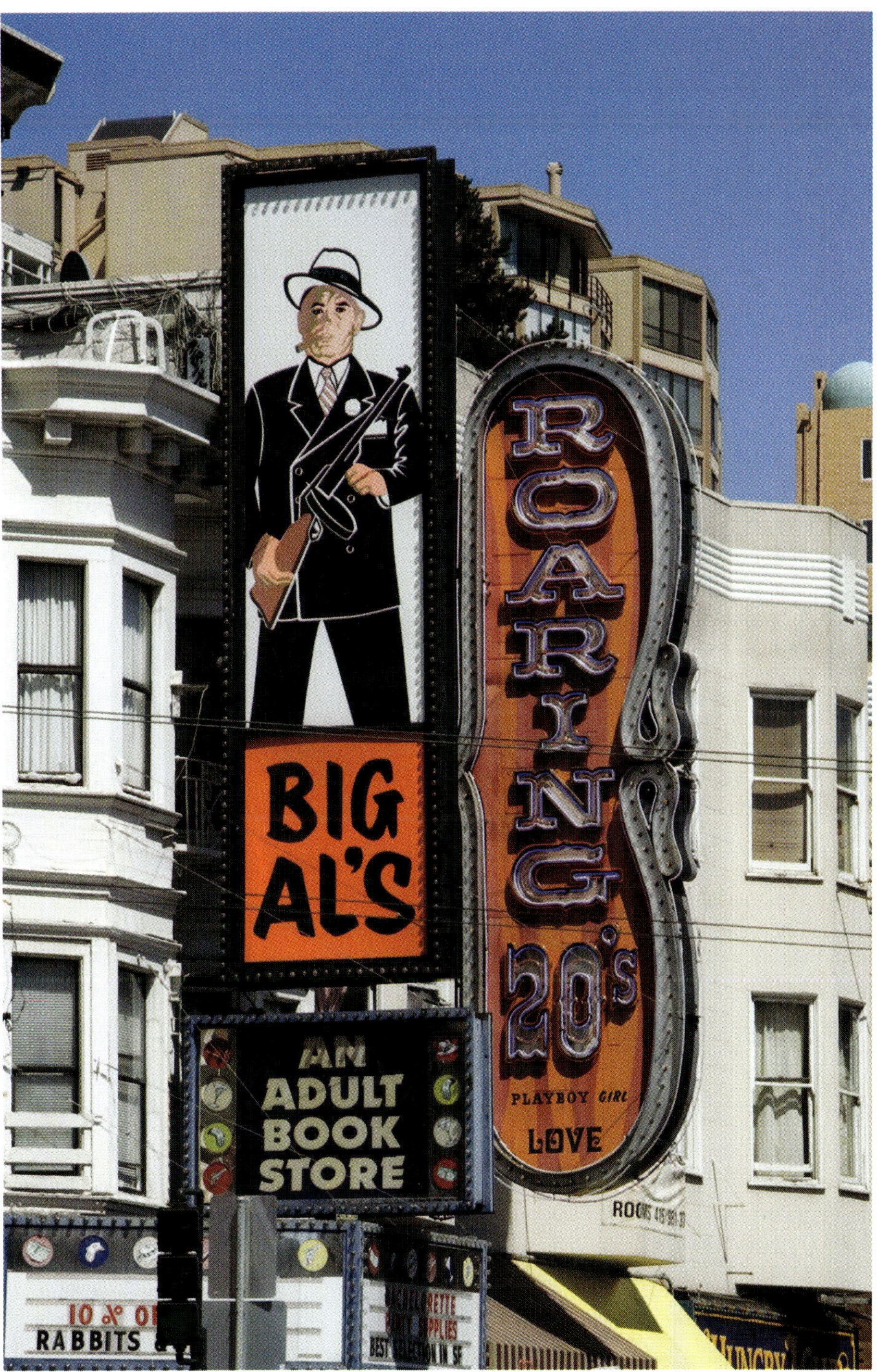

Big Al's and Roaring 20s signs during the day.

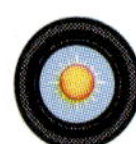 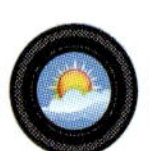 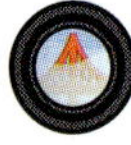

When to shoot: morning, afternoon, evening

Haight-Ashbury

No place in the world identifies more with the '60s than Haight Street and the Haight-Ashbury neighborhood. The center of the neighborhood is, you guessed it, at Haight and Ashbury Streets. When photographing here, it's almost essential to look for blasts from the past, anything from the go-go boots and other clothing items that many on the street wear, to the psychedelic murals of color that cover storefronts and walls throughout the neighborhood. Don't forget the current trends either, from shops that pierce and tattoo to upscale restaurants and bars.

There's a plethora of history in the Haight (as it's fondly called) that's worth noting as you go around seeking photo ops. Before the Summer of Love in 1967, hipsters called "Beats" lived in North Beach. That neighborhood became crowded, leaving the poets, artists, and anti-establishment crowd with no place to live. At the time the Haight was dilapidated as people flocked to the Bay Area suburbs. The Victorians were left empty as property values plummeted. Cheap housing brought hippies first, and their culture of colorful rebellion spread shortly thereafter.

"Cheap" is no longer a word that describes the Haight, as it's probably one of the priciest neighborhoods in the country. However, the hippie culture never went away completely, and independent storeowners keep it alive with the offbeat, from old-fashioned head shops, which sell "smoking" accessories, to recycled clothing stores that sell lots of tie-dyed T-shirts and old jeans. Each store has a niche (as do many of the people who pass by), and whatever it may be at the moment, you'll surely find an interesting narrative for your photographs about how life has evolved from the '60s to today.

The Shot

The legs coming out of the window is one of many humorous photo ops in the Haight. The photo is on the north side of Haight, just to the west of Ashbury. The image was shot with a zoom lens just southeast of where the subject was located. (I crossed the street to Haight's south side and walked a little east from there.) The most important factor in creating a tight concept is including only the legs and heels in the frame. (There's a Haight-Ashbury sign right next to the legs.) I used Av (Aperture Priority) mode to shoot it, setting the aperture just a bit smaller (larger f/stop) than I would have if I were shooting a portrait, in which case I would want a blurred background. In this case, though, I want sharper focus on the background, which includes the back portion of the legs and the details of the Victorian. I also had to be careful not to make my aperture too small because when you shoot in Av mode, the camera will make the shutter speed a bit longer so that there's a chance of blur from camera shake. If I had a tripod, I could have shot using a very small aperture (large f/stop such as f/18) for a sharp picture with details throughout.

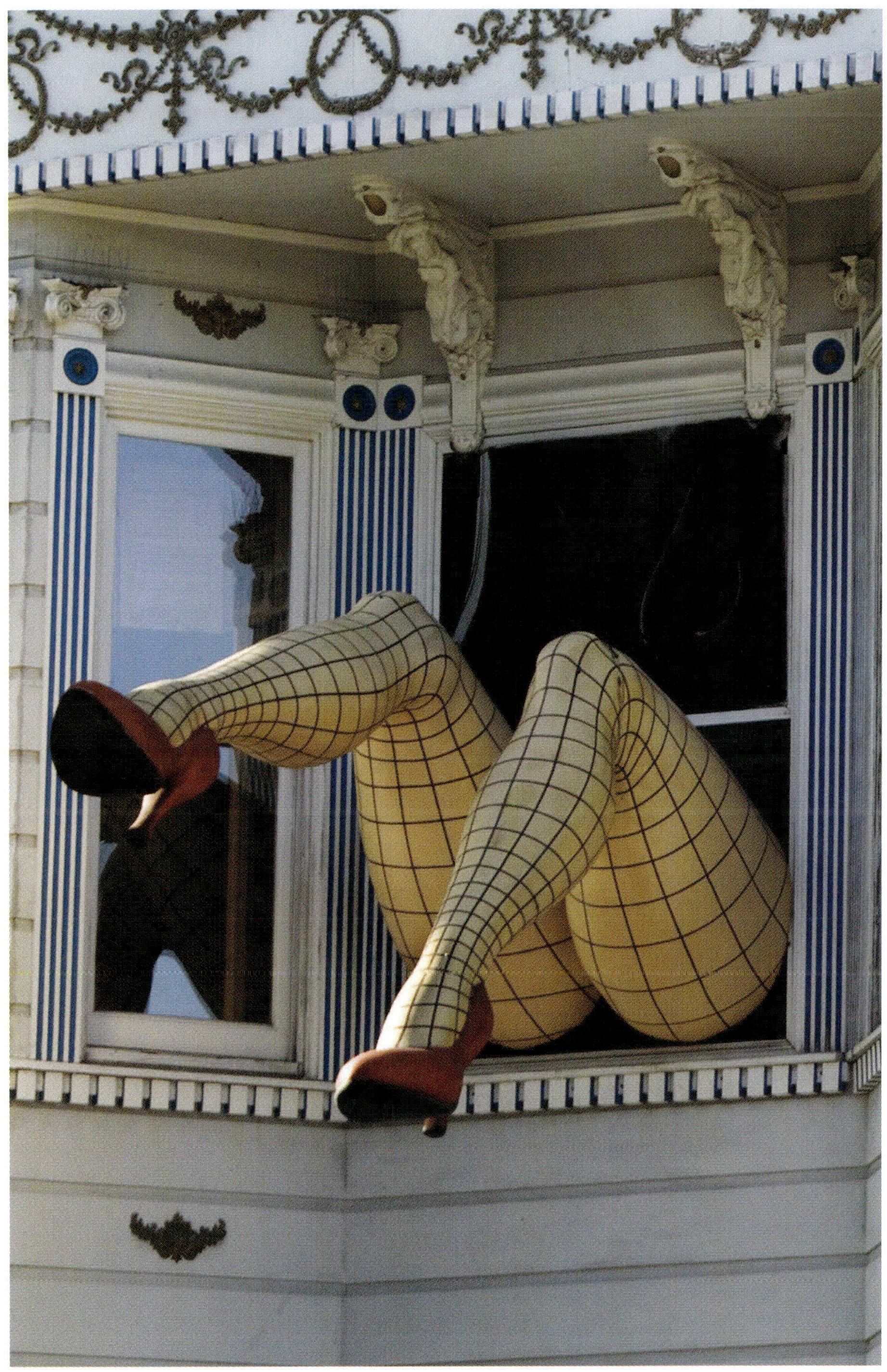

Focal length 109mm; ISO 200; aperture f/6.3; shutter speed 1/160; April 4:07 p.m.

SAN FRANCISCO THROUGH A CANDID LENS

I have a couple of rules for taking candid pictures that I tend to live by when I'm out on the streets. I like to profess them to all who'll listen:

- Carry a camera with you at all times.
- In San Francisco, expect the weird, wild, and wonderful to show its face any time. Keep your aperture open wide—that is, have your camera set to Av mode with the aperture set to the lowest possible value for the focal length at which you're shooting. When you shoot at a large aperture (f/stops of f/2.8 to f/5.6), you're less likely to get blur from camera shake. Cameras set fast shutter speeds when set to wide apertures in Av mode. When the shutter opens and closes at anywhere from 1/8000 to 1/500 seconds, as it's likely to when set at a low f/stop on a sunny day, a sharp shot is more likely to result. All this changes at night, when you need a camera with a flash set to auto mode.
- Don't be afraid to ask for permission.
- If someone is wearing an outfit that immediately catches attention or is performing an acrobatic stunt in public, he probably won't mind having his picture taken. If he wants money, give it to him. He has to make a living, too. When you take a picture of someone in an unusual outfit, have him do something more than just pose for the shot. If you're photographing someone dressed like Little Bo Peep, have her find her sheep. Take a dozen shots and pick the best one.
- If you take just one or two shots on a cloudy day, in the shade or inside a building there's a chance for blur. When you're working quickly, your hands shake more. Having a set of shots from which to choose gives you a better chance at getting one sharp image. Remember, the advantage of digital is you can always throw away the images you don't like. When I shot in film, the cost of developing the photos made it prohibitive to shoot as many images as I liked.

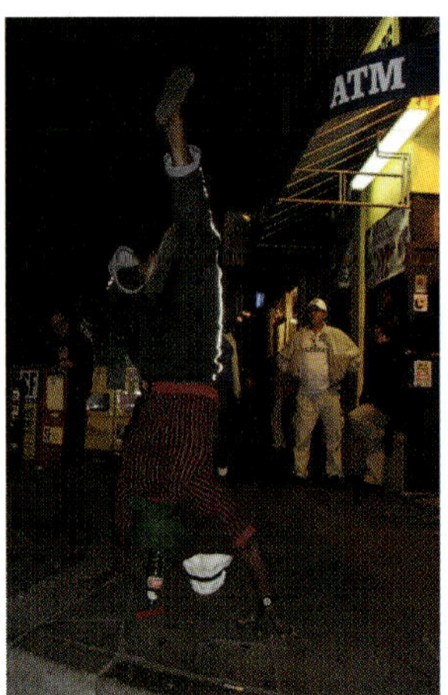

Man in the Mission performs a headstand on a Coke bottle.

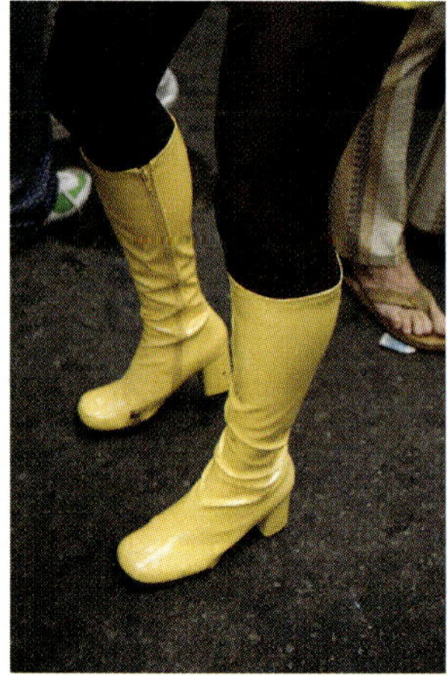
Go-go boots never go out of style in the Haight.

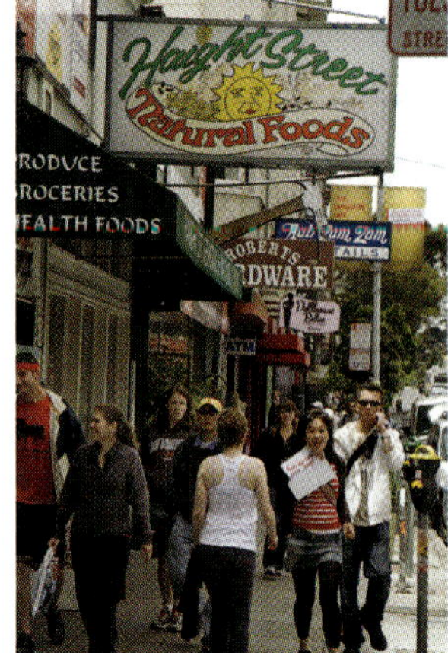

Fog in the Haight softens shadows.

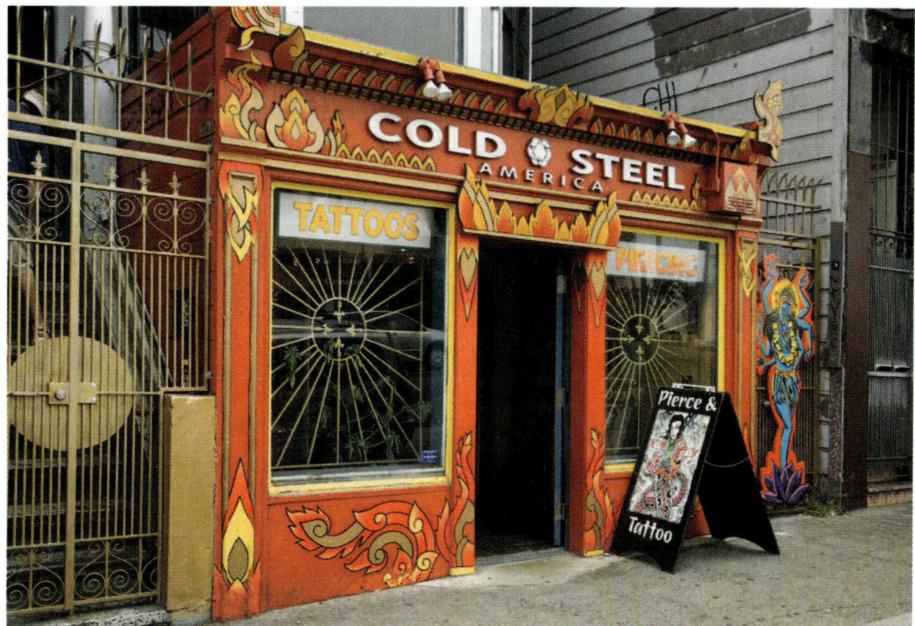

Focal length 35mm; ISO 400; aperture f/7.1; shutter speed 1/400; May 4:18 p.m.

The Shot

The most striking part of this image is its red color. The afternoon light had dispersed with the light layer of fog that had rolled in just before the picture was taken. To take advantage of this almost-perfect lighting scenario, I lowered my EV value by one stop, thus saturating the colors even more. Another aspect of this picture is the steel gates on either side of the building, which match the building's message of "Cold Steel." Normally, the fold-out sign on the sidewalk would have been an obstruction in this photo, but by placing it a third from the end of the frame, it works to add some depth to the shot.

Getting There

To get there using mass transit, from downtown, take the 7 Haight. Get off at Haight and Ashbury. The Haight Street commercial district runs from Haight and Masonic (one block east of Ashbury) west to the foot of Golden Gate Park at Haight and Stanyan.

If you're driving, from the South Bay, take 101 North until it ends on Octavia Boulevard. Turn left at Fell, left on Masonic, and right on Haight to Ashbury.

From the East Bay, take 80 West to 101 North, then follow the South Bay directions from Octavia.

From the North Bay, take 101 South to Lombard, turn right at Divisadero, and turn right on Haight to Ashbury.

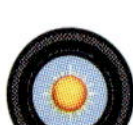 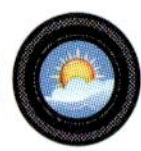

When to shoot: morning, afternoon, evening

Embarcadero

For decades the Embarcadero neighborhood was forgotten—an unsightly collection of abandoned structures along a scenic waterfront. The deterioration began after the Bay Bridge was built, causing ferry traffic to decline. Worse still was a freeway that was constructed along the waterfront, which had traffic speeding by the empty buildings. All that ended after the Loma Prieta earthquake in 1989, when the freeway was damaged. The city tore it down, and major gentrification of the area began.

Lots of development had occurred in the area—a plaza, four high rises, and a hotel—in the '70s and '80s, but none of it brought people to gather in the neighborhood because of the noise from the freeway nearby. The Vaillancourt Fountain, a massive collection of intertwined rectangular, concrete tubes, was meant to match the freeway by which it was built. It was to be a centerpiece of the Justin Herman Plaza. Today, the fountain is still a prominent public work of art seen as an eyesore to some and as an ingenious sculpture to others.

The Shot

This street performer has been around San Francisco for years. Three years before I wrote this book, I photographed him on Union Square, so you're sure to run into him somewhere. In this shot the performer has placed himself in a part of the Ferry Building that looks futuristic, one that nearly matches the costume that he wears. Another aspect of this photo—one where I got lucky—was that I didn't get blown highlights where the part of the suit reflected the sun. Blown highlights occur when a part (often small) of an image is pure white. The sensor managed to pick up a shade of off white, for which I was thankful because blown highlights are a photographer's nightmare. Especially impressive in the setting is the text "ERECTED," which sits clearly in the background—a word that matches the subject's stance. The illusion of this figure is that it has been erected permanently, which is the idea behind the performance-art aspect of the piece—the robot comes alive, albeit in a mechanical sort of way, when money is put in the basket in front of it.

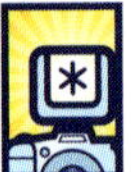

You can set your camera on a large personal item, such as a backpack, to get a shot at an angle when you don't have a tripod available or when you're in a place where you can't use one. Just set your camera's self-timer before you press the shutter release and make sure that the personal item is on a stable surface.

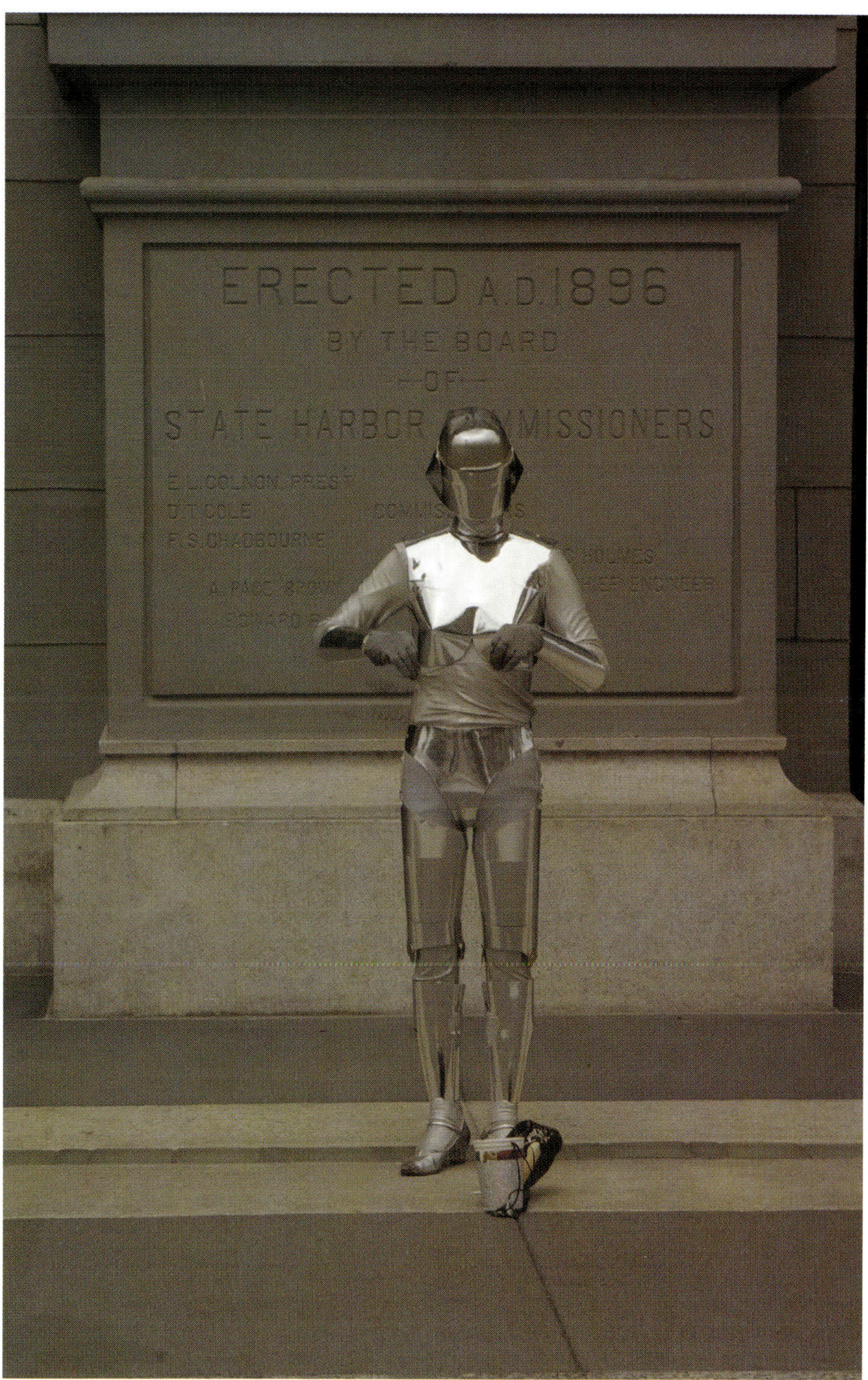

Focal length 58mm; ISO 400; aperture f/14; shutter speed 1/250; July 5:15 p.m.

The Shot

One of San Francisco's biggest industries is tourism. Catering to tourists is a big part of city life, and nowhere is this more evident than at a hotel reception desk. In this shot I used my favorite trick, shooting a classy photo without a tripod at a low ISO speed. When you use a low ISO speed there's much less chance of getting noise, leaving you with a very sharp photo, especially if your camera is either on a stable surface or on a tripod. I was working in a great space in the west side of the lobby in front of the front desk of the hotel. I set the backpack and camera on a wall that was just about at eye level, making it easy to look through the camera before shooting. I set the camera's timer and took a series of several shots. I then looked at the shots and adjusted the camera so that the front desk appeared at the bottom of the frame.

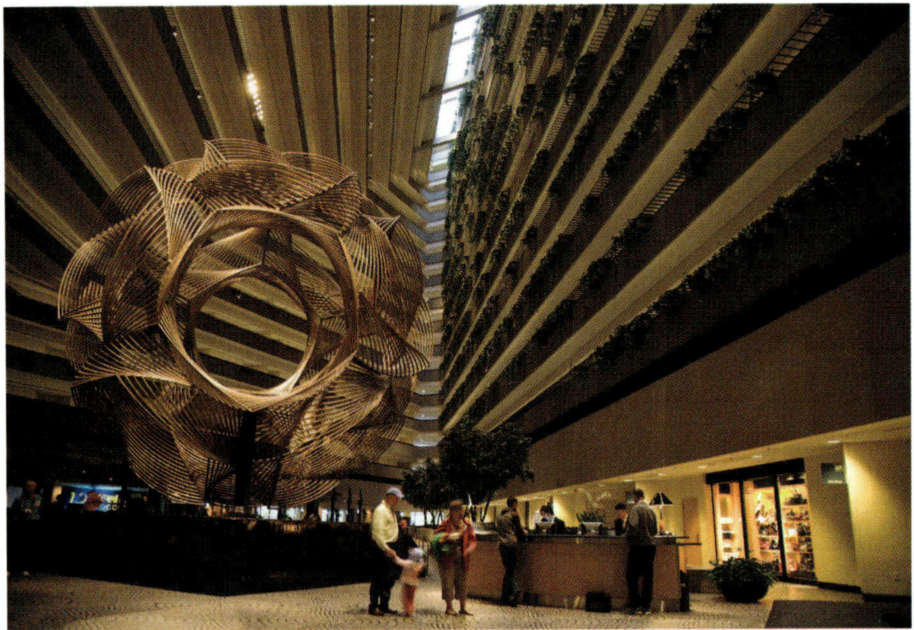

Focal length 24mm; ISO 200; aperture f/4; shutter speed .6 seconds; July 8:30 p.m.

Getting There

To get there using mass transit, the center of the Embarcadero is Justin Herman Plaza, which is a short walk from the Ferry Building. The Embarcadero is the last downtown stop and is accessible to trains that come from and go to various points in the city, including the K, L, M, N, and J trains that travel underground. The F train (vintage streetcars) stops directly in front of the Ferry Building. Buses on the ground go all over the city.

If you're driving, the Ferry Building is just east of the Embarcadero (which is the street that runs along the bay).

From the South Bay, take 101 North to 280 North. Exit at King Street, which turns into the Embarcadero.

From the East Bay, take 80 West, exit at Fremont Street, turn left at Folsom, and turn left at the Embarcadero.

From the North Bay, take 101 South to Lombard. Make a slight left on Lombard, a left at Van Ness, a right at Bay, and a right at the Embarcadero. Make a U-turn at Howard Street, because you'll overshoot the Ferry Building by a couple of blocks.

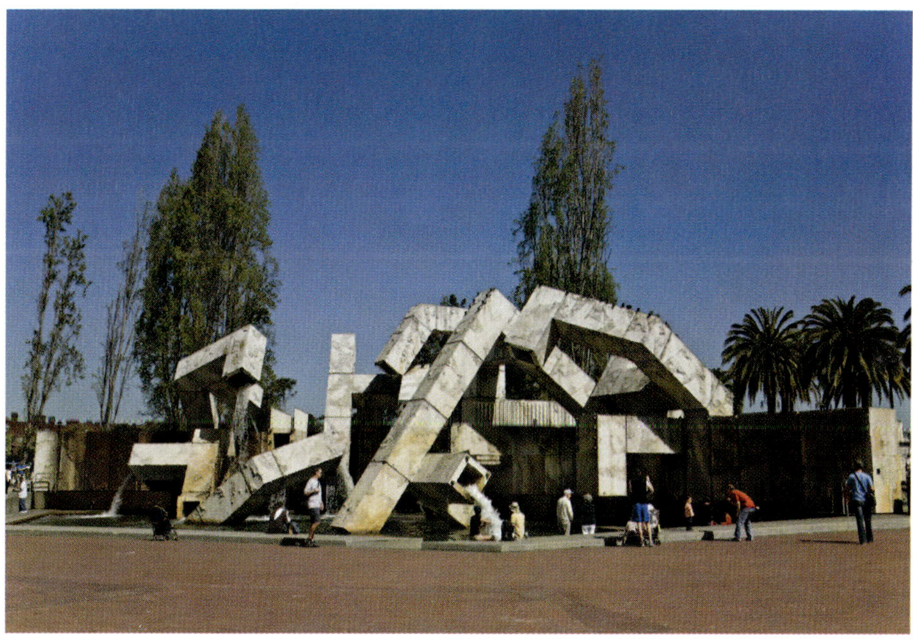

Vaillancourt Fountain has been a controversial structure.

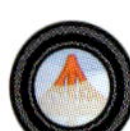

When to shoot: morning, afternoon, evening

Cable Cars

After seeing horses and a carriage slide to their deaths on a sharp incline, Andrew Hallidie, a wire manufacturer, had a new idea—a cable-car system for the steep hills of the city. In 1873, he tested his first cable car at the top of Nob Hill. Cable-car lines were then built all over the city. After the Great Earthquake in 1906, some of the cable-car lines were changed to streetcars. The difference between a cable car and a streetcar is that cable cars run on rails with a space between them where the cable pulls them, and streetcars run on overhead electric wires.

Shots of the cable cars are perfect for having your photos tell a story because of the process involved in getting them (the shots?) to move. Operators manually control everything right there in front of you, from releasing a huge brake inside to pushing the car around outside at the Powell Street cable car turntable. The turntable is actually a round structure in the road upon which the cable car is placed and turned around.

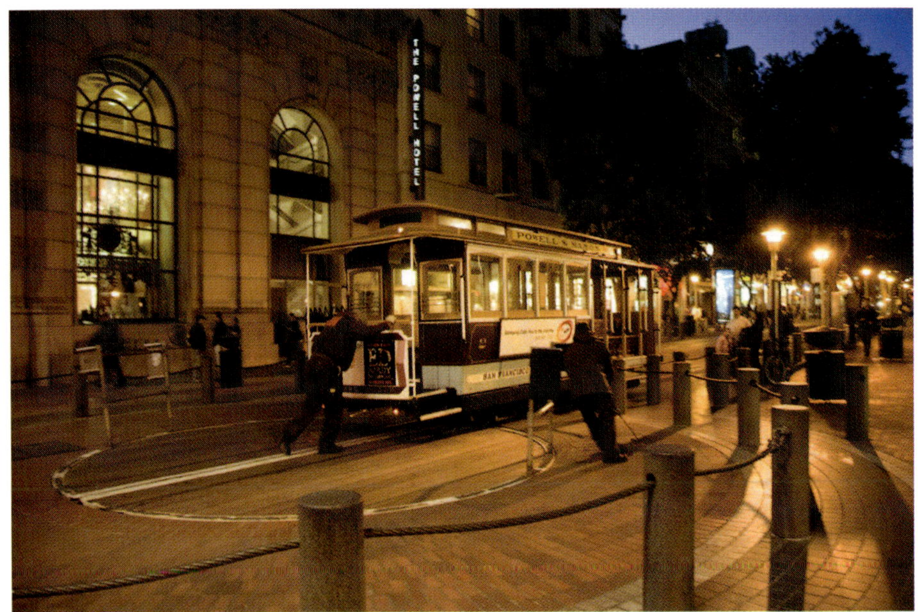

Cable-car operators turn the car manually at the Powell Street turnaround.

The Shot

In this shot I wanted to capture a mini-narrative that shows people getting on the cable car while the operator is getting the car ready to go (see the left of the image). I knew I wanted to blur the people but not the cable car itself, to show the people in action as they boarded the car. I found the perfect vantage point among a group of trees—away from the crowd but with a clear view of the cable car—that stands on the west side of the cable car turnaround on Powell Street, so I set up my tripod. I found that taking the picture with a shutter speed around 1/20 second would be a good place to start after pressing the shutter release button half way down in Av mode to see what the camera calculated for shutter speeds at various apertures. Next, I guess-timated a somewhat slower shutter speed (1/13) than the camera calculated, a little slower than what would be recommended for shooting without a tripod at a 24mm focal length. I could have taken this picture without a tripod if I could've kept my body still by bracing it against a tree. My guess of shutter speed was perfect for the amount of light that was available on that foggy afternoon. One good thing about fog is that it dims the light enough for blurring people and for panning.

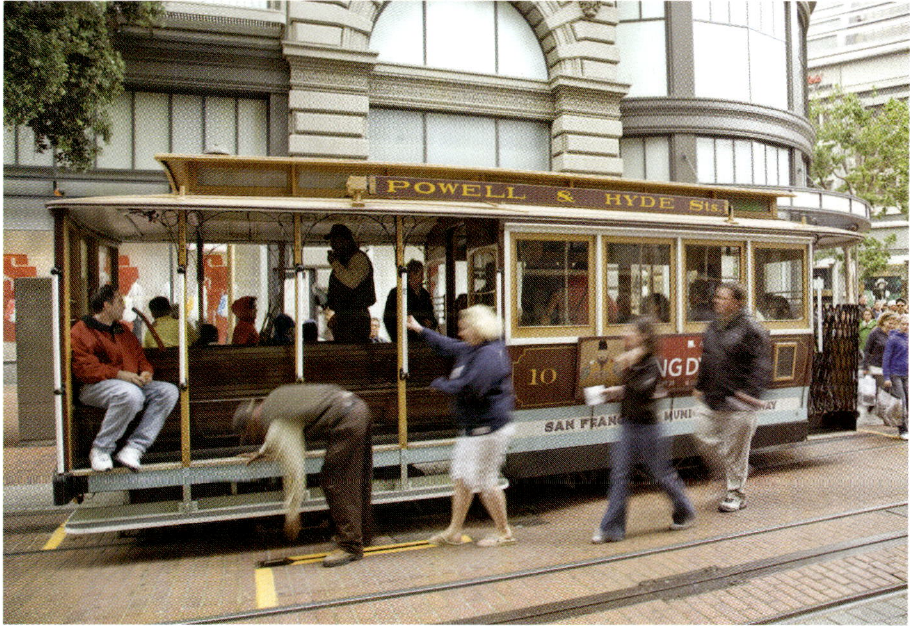

Focal length 24mm; ISO 100; aperture f/7.1; shutter speed 1/13; June 4:26 p.m.

The Shot

I took this picture to let people know what the inside of a cable car looks like. What's striking about it is that there's an awful lot of varnished wood that lines the cabin. This shot is a tricky one to get sharp, and you may have to try a couple of shots to get it right. First you have to find a cable car that's not crowded. The California-Van Ness line, which can be caught at the Embarcadero, is a good bet for a light crowd. Next, you have to place yourself at the entrance to the car and quickly take a shot so you don't block it for too long. The cable-car operator and the people on the train were perfectly polite when they saw I was taking a picture with a sizable camera (the Canon 5D). To darken the harsh sunlight that comes through all of the car's sides, I lowered my EV values by multiple stops. Lowering the EV values will underexpose your shot, thus making bright light darker. I chose not to use a flash because I wanted the natural color of the sunlight to be the only source of light in the photo. I find that flash in these situations affects the color in the picture, and I wanted to pick up the varnished wood as it looks when it's lit by sunlight.

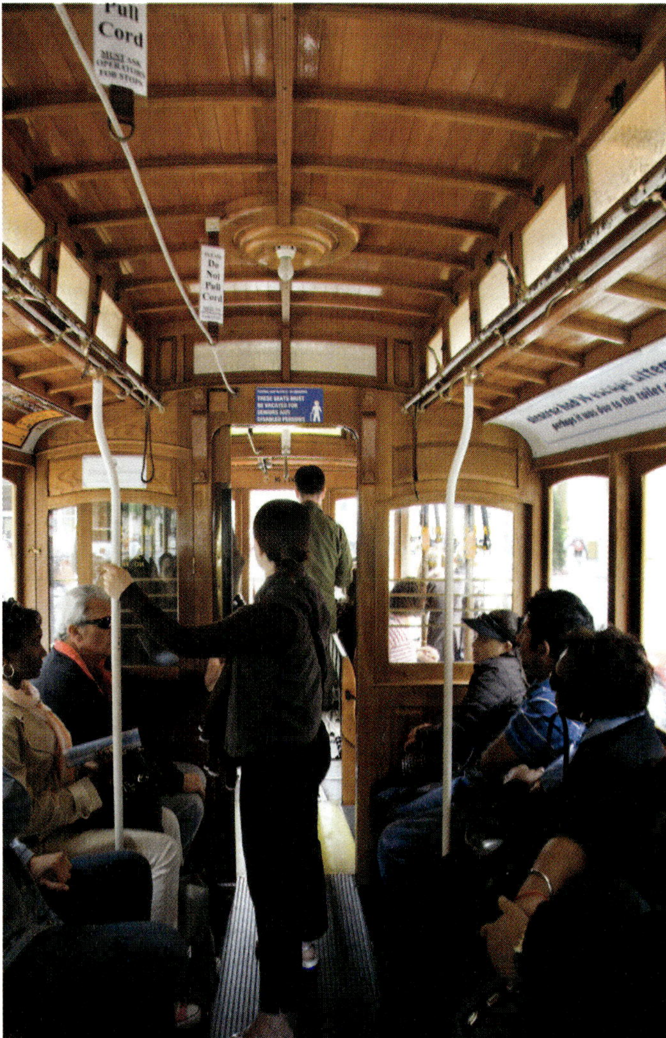

Focal length 24mm; ISO 400; aperture f/11; shutter speed 1/13; June 6:18 p.m.

Getting There

Three cable-car routes run up and down hills from downtown at Powell and Market (to Fisherman's Wharf and Ghirardelli Square) and the Embarcadero (to Van Ness). From Powell and Market, there are two lines: Powell-Mason and Powell-Hyde. The Powell-Mason ends up near Fisherman's Wharf at Taylor and Bay Streets via Mason Street, and the Powell-Hyde ends up near Ghirardelli Square at Hyde and Beach Streets via Hyde Street. At the Embarcadero, the California Street line runs to Van Ness, ending at California and Van Ness via California Street.

The best pictures are at the cable-car turnaround at Powell and Market near the Powell Street Muni and BART stations.

To get there using mass transit, the Powell Street station is one of the main stations in the city. You can take Muni Metro trains K, L, M, and N to Montgomery Street, Embarcadero, or AT&T Park, or outbound to other areas of the city. The buses on Market Street go all over the city.

If you're driving, from the South Bay, take 101 North to 280 North into San Francisco. Exit at 6th Street and take a right on Market Street. The Powell Street station is 1-1/2 blocks up on the left.

From the North Bay, take 101 South and exit at Lombard Street. Make a right on Van Ness Avenue and a left on Bush Street. Turn right on Jones Street and then left on O'Farrell. Turn right on Market Street. Go 1-1/2 blocks. The Powell Street station is on the left.

From the East Bay, take 80 West and exit at 5th Street. Take a right at Market. The Powell Street station is in the middle of the block on the left.

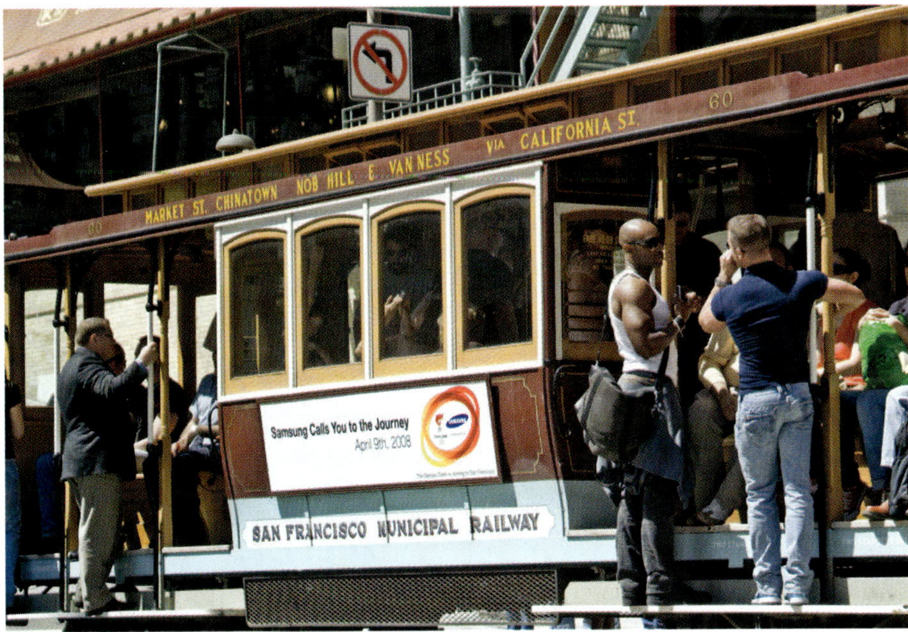

People holding onto the poles as the cable car moves.

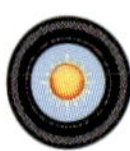 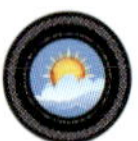 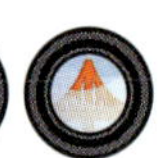

When to shoot: morning, afternoon, evening

BART Stations

A shot caught in a moment of time at a train station in Paris or the subway in San Francisco is unique in that the scene will never happen again. These types of shots are some of the easiest to get with respect to candid photography. To be sure, the surroundings can be the same, but the people coming and going won't be. These types of photo ops appear at any of the San Francisco BART stations: Embarcadero, Montgomery, Powell, Civic Center, 16th and Mission, 24th and Mission, Glen Park, and Balboa Park. By staying focused on one point in the station—the entrance/exit turnstile, for example, or the boarding of a train—you can build a picture of life in the world of mass transportation.

The Shot

Any BART station is filled with photo ops at any time of day or night. Because a BART train moves very fast as it comes into the station, it's easy to blur while keeping the rest of the frame (the station platform and the waiting passengers) relatively sharp. Usually a shot like this needs to be taken with a tripod to get the sharp background and blurred movement of the train. You can shoot without the tripod when you set your ISO speed to about 1000. By setting your ISO speed high, you can shoot with a bit longer shutter speed to catch the moving train blurred at the same time as getting a clear background. The ambient and reflective light in the BART station also helps you to get a sharp picture because of its uniform distribution well into the frame.

I've long been an aficionado of taking pictures in and around subway stations. The lighting inside the station is usually quite good, enabling me to get sharp hand-held shots when I set my ISO speed to a relatively high value. I set my camera to Tv (shutter priorty mode) with a shutter speed of 1/13 seconds. I know from experience that if I hold still I can get a sharp shot at that shutter speed when my camera is set to an ISO speed of 1000. After setting my camera, I stood waiting for the train to come. As soon as I saw it, I started taking a series of shots, pivoting as the train moved by until it finally stopped. As for the composition, there are two more notable points. The first is that if you look at the left edge of the frame, you can see that the train lines up to take up the bottom two-thirds of the frame and the station the remaining third, which follows the Rule of Thirds. The second is that the waiting passenger is situated in front of a solid-colored background (the door) to frame him in the best possible light. (He's literally framed by the door.) When I saw this composition, I immediately got out my camera and shot a series of several pictures, one of which turned out just the way I wanted it (a moving train with a passenger looking at it).

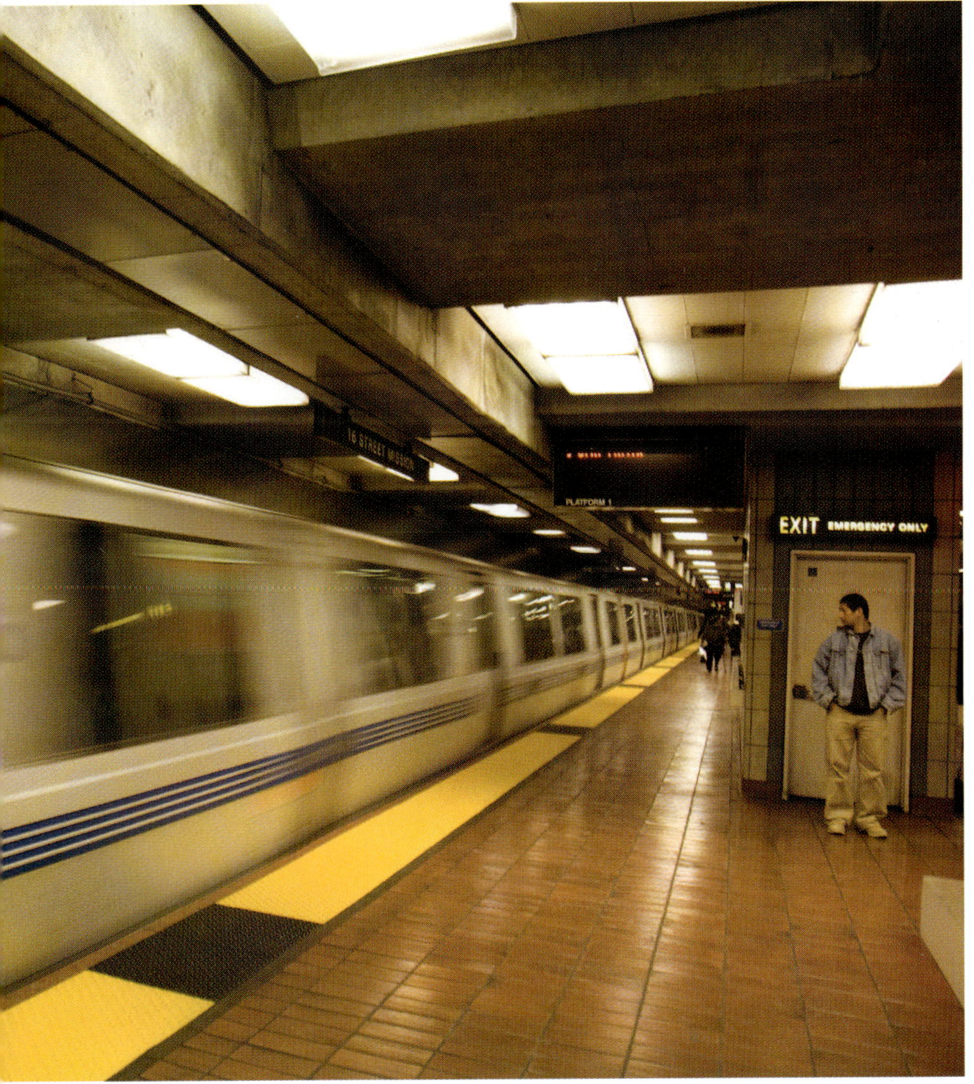

Focal length 24mm; ISO 1000; aperture f/7.1; shutter speed 1/13 seconds; June 2:18 p.m.

The Shot

This kind of shot is one where you are part of what's going on. It gives the illusion that the person on the far right of the frame is offering you a flier. Also prominent in the picture is the girl dancing. I asked the group if I could take their picture, and just afterward the girl raised her hands and swiveled her hips. Because my shutter speed was 1/13 seconds, the camera caught the girl's movement as motion blur—not a bad effect for not using a tripod. The two masked men in the front of the line of protesters have blurred hands, showing the movement of their hands passing out fliers. Their bodies, however, remain relatively sharp, showing that blur from camera shake was minimal. If they had been blurred, the shot would have lost its effect because it would have been hard to distinguish the blur from the subjects' motion versus the blur from camera shake.

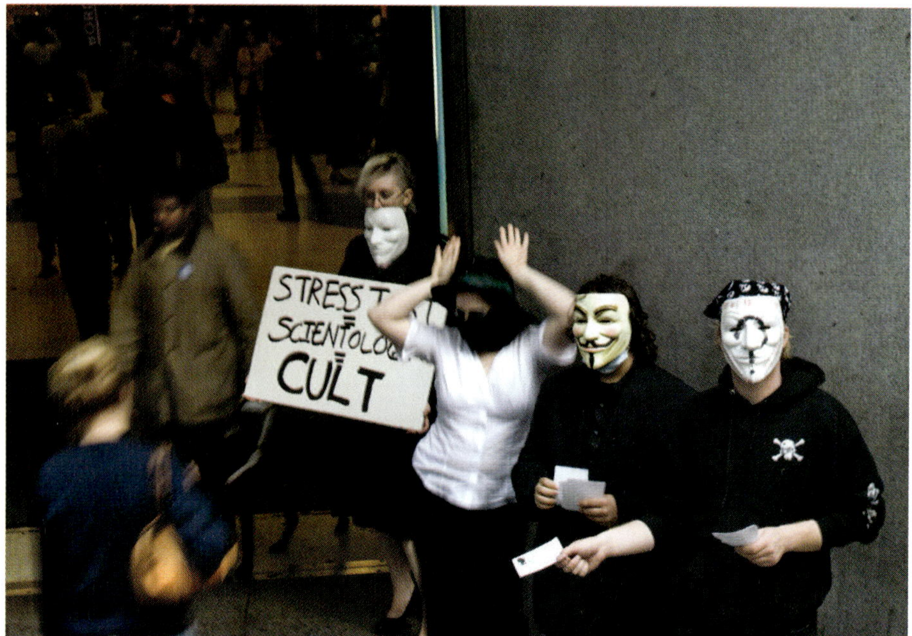

Focal length 45mm; ISO 100; aperture f/7.1; shutter speed 1/13; June 5:30 p.m.

Getting There

To get there using mass transit, the San Francisco BART stations are Embarcadero, Montgomery, Powell, Civic Center, 16th and Mission, 24th and Mission, Glen Park, and Balboa Park.

If you're driving, to get to the Powell Street station, follow the directions for getting to the cable-car turnaround in the "Cable Cars" photo op.

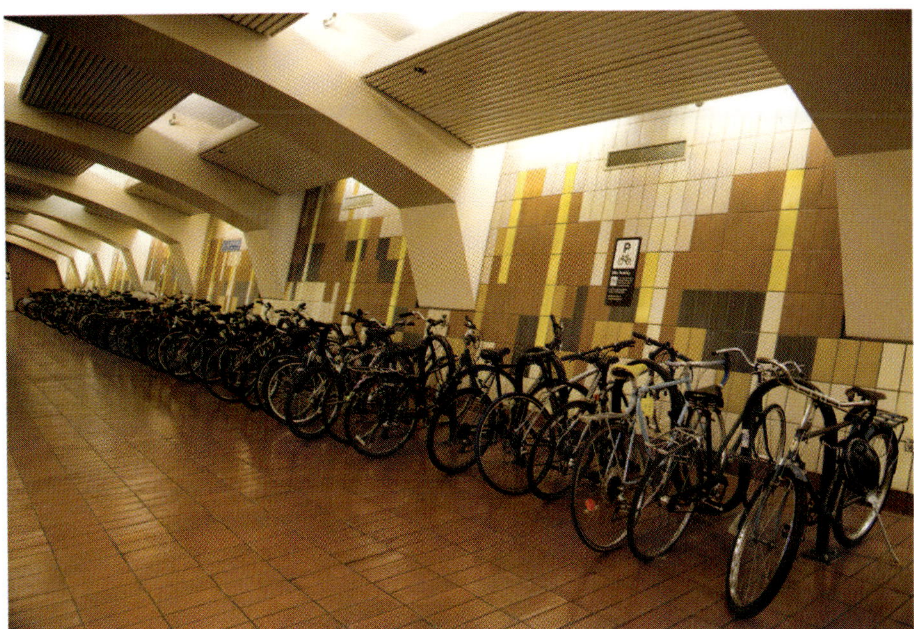

Bicycle parking at the 16th and Mission BART station.

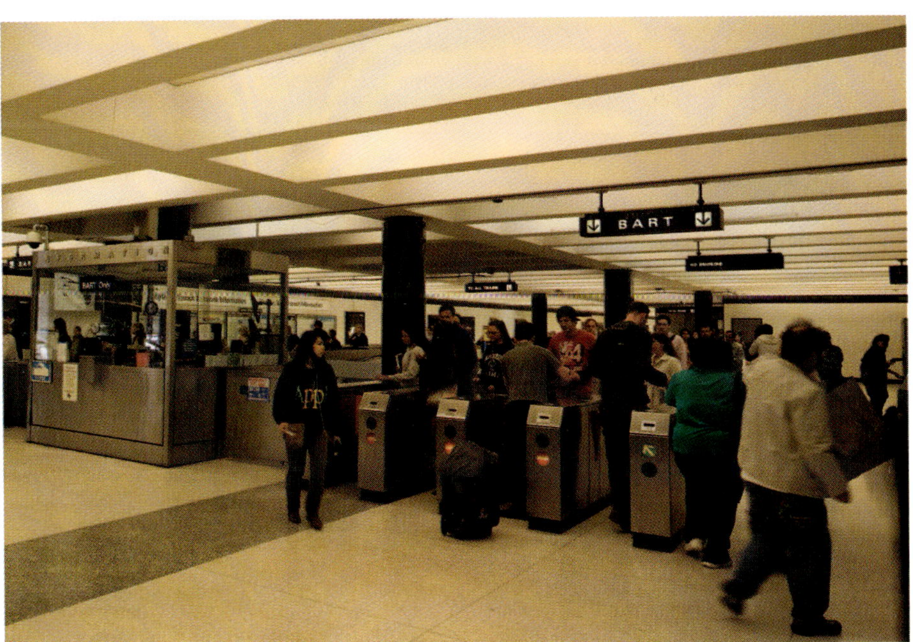

People going through the turnstile at the Powell Street station.

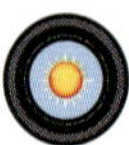 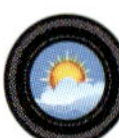 When to shoot: morning, afternoon, evening

F-Market Streetcars

In 1935, the Presidents' Conference Committee (PCC) of United States electric railway leaders decided that streetcars needed to be modernized from a boxy-type design to a more streamlined design. The result was the building of 4,500 streetcars that ran in 33 cities, including San Francisco. Today, the now-old streetcars have been put into service in what's known as the F-line, or the F-Market line. The line consists of streetcars that were refurbished and that had operated in San Francisco, Philadelphia, Newark, and other cities.

Shooting and then printing these vintage beauties is like obtaining a piece of the past—you'll want to spot and shoot all 17 of the models that run on the F-line. I've shot a few of them, each making up a part of one dynamic photo set.

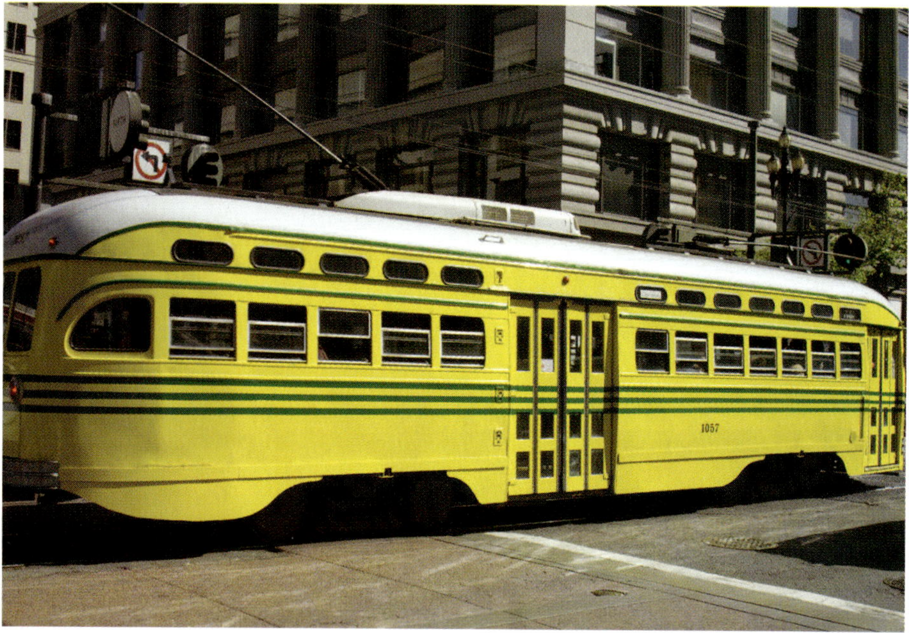

Streetcar in the sun.

The Shot

I found a nice background for a shot of the electric car traveling northeast on Market near Powell Street by standing on Market Street just southwest of the crosswalk between 4th and 5th Streets. I framed the downtown high rises in the background instead of a white sky. The fog added an interesting soft haze to the buildings in the background. The eye is drawn to the electric car, then down the street and up to the wedding-cake dome of the Humboldt Bank Building, which is in the top left of the frame. The background also matches the era in which the electric car was built because many of the buildings up and down the street were built during a time when these types of electric cars were put into service.

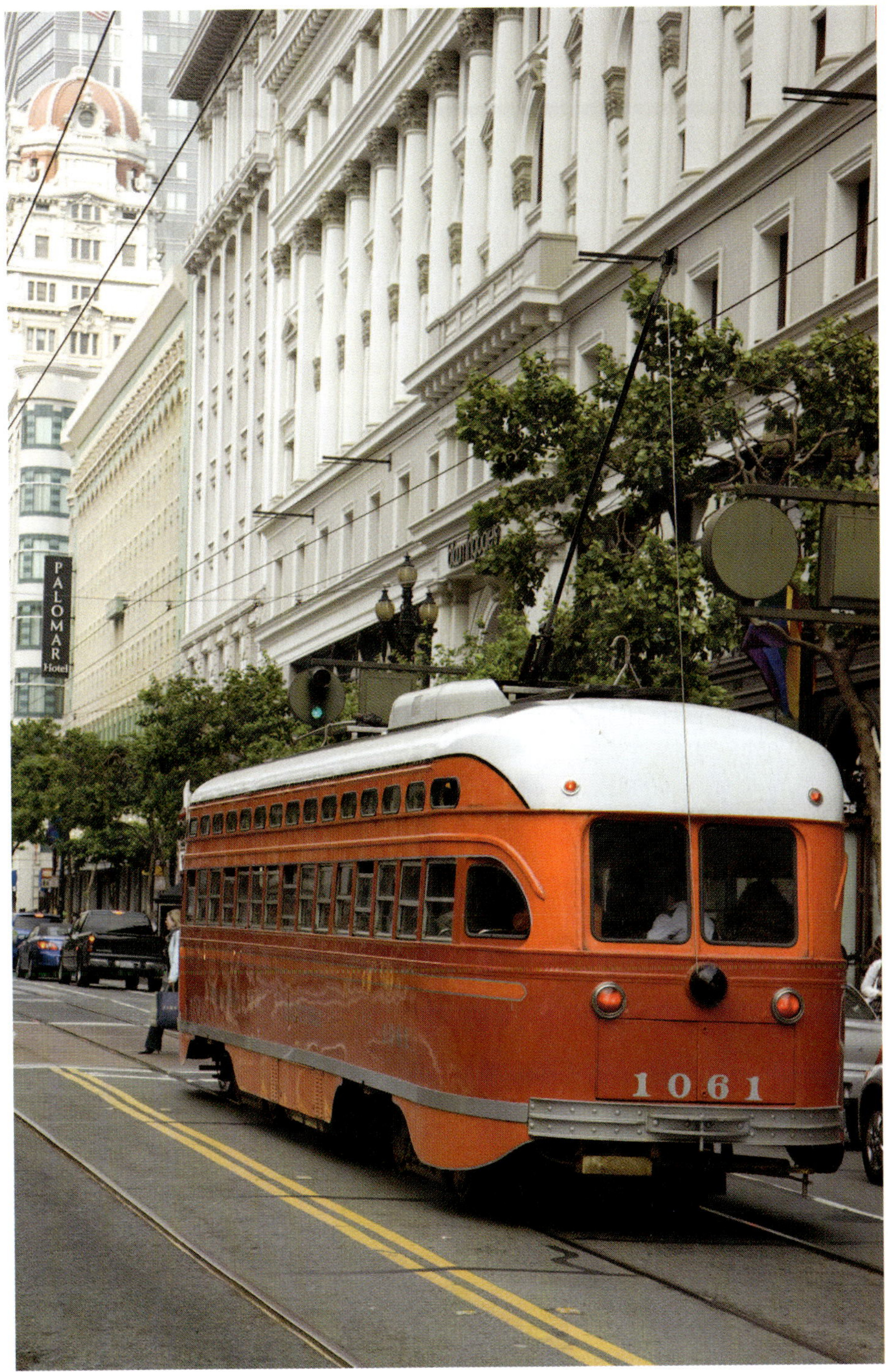

Focal length 82mm; ISO 200; aperture f/7.1; shutter speed 1/80; June 5:30 p.m.

The Shot

This is the first of a series of shots of the F-Market streetcars. There's an F-Market streetcar stop at the bus stop island just northwest of Main Street near the Embarcadero Hyatt Regency. Across the street from the island (on the same side where the Hyatt Regency is), you'll get a good vantage point for a shot of the F-Market when it stops to pick up and let off passengers. This shot was taken about 15 minutes after sunset and required a tripod to come out sharp and to pick up the light coming from inside the streetcar. To take the shot, I set up the tripod just northwest of the Hyatt. (Market Street runs southeast to northwest.) I waited for the steetcar to stop, then took a few shots of it. If I tried to shoot this without a tripod, you would get blur from camera shake because the 1/10 second shutter speed is too long for the shutter to be open to take a sharp shot. If you look closely, you can also see the passengers inside the streetcar.

It's fun to catch the streetcars as they are, wherever they are, with or without a tripod, at any time, day or night. I've seen pictures of them for sale around town, photographed every which way. I used a higher ISO speed because it was a foggy day, and I wanted to lessen the chances of getting a blurred shot. I used a smaller aperture to make sure that the entire car was in focus.

Most prominent on the back of the streetcar is the number of the train. This number can be looked up on the Internet to identify the place from where the car came.

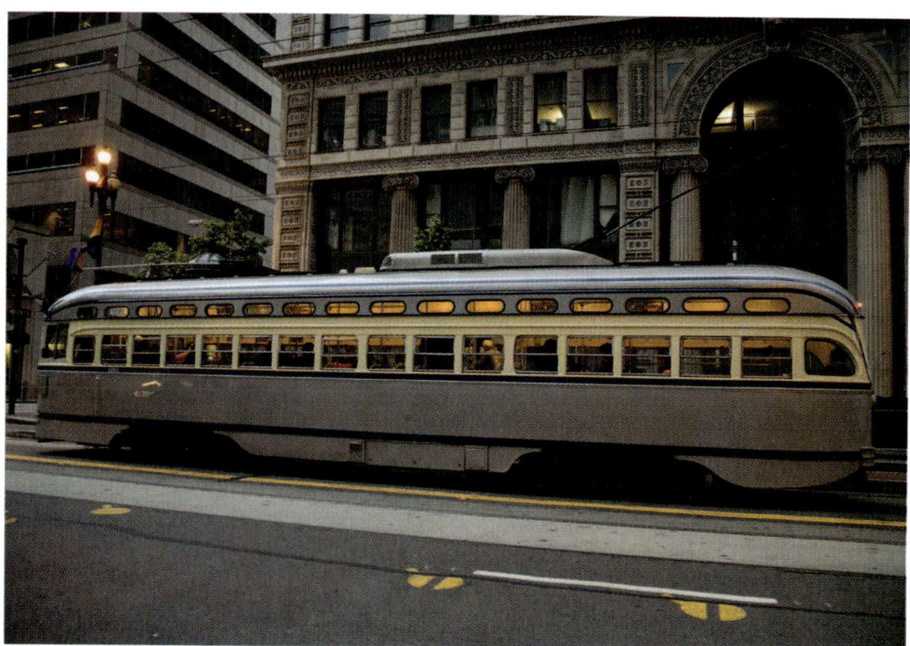

Focal length 24mm; ISO 200; aperture f/4; shutter speed 1/10; June 8:00 p.m.

Getting There

You'll see the electric cars on the F-Market line up and down Market Street and the Embarcadero, in front of the Ferry Building, in the Castro, and at Fisherman's Wharf. If you want to catch them all, wait around One Market Street near the Embarcadero BART station. Every F-line car passes there.

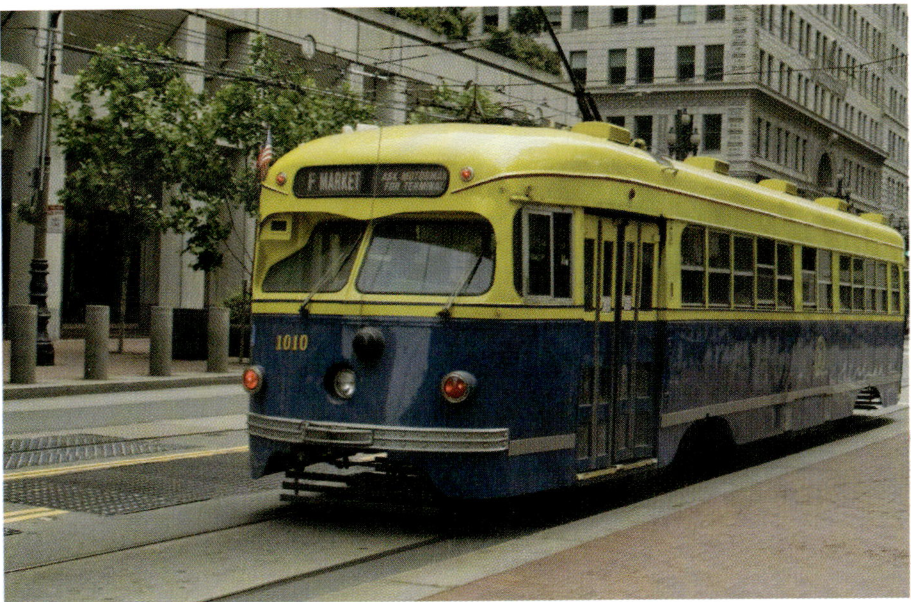

Streetcar front view.

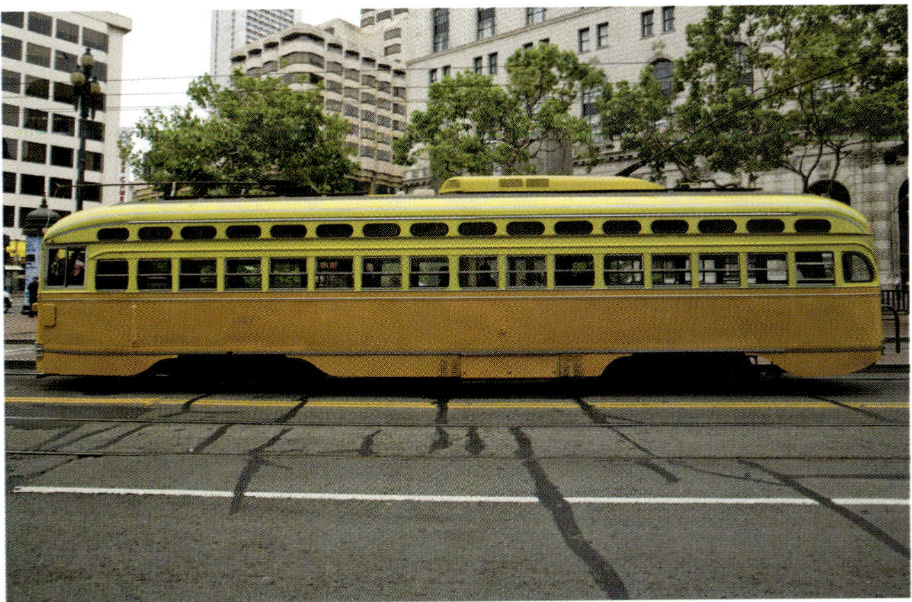

Side view of streetcar.

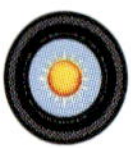 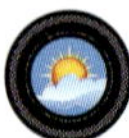

When to shoot: morning, afternoon, evening

Union Street

Union Street is one of the most popular business districts in the city. Retail stores, bars, and cafes line the street, housed in the first floors of Victorians. In the second and third floors are offices for lawyers, dentists, and doctors. For decades the street has catered to a younger population of business-people and the upwardly mobile, mostly heterosexual crowd. Some bars, such as Perry's, have been on the street for decades.

When walking west on the street after you cross Van Ness, you'll arrive at the Octagon House, a kind of entry point to the neighborhood. The Octagon House, which has eight sides, was built in 1961. Some people believe that the octagonal shape of the house improves the health of those who live in it. The house is open to the public as a museum from 12:00 to 3:00 p.m. on the second Sunday and the second and fourth Tuesdays of each month.

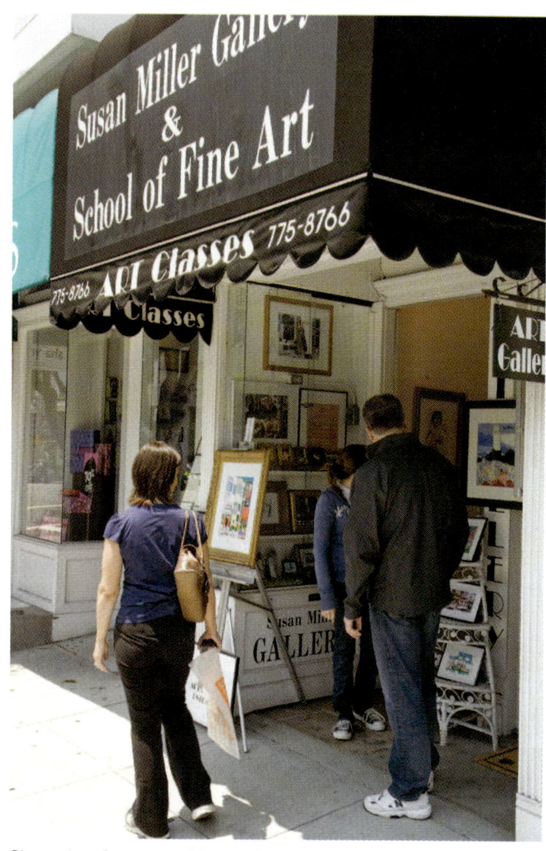

Shopping for something unique on Union Street.

The Shot

By including the wooden fence that leads up to the Octagon House on Octavia Street, you enhance the perspective and depth within the frame, more so than just photographing the house by itself. To get this shot, I walked from the house to the beginning of the fence near Union Street. Then I stooped down and rotated my camera to get a vertical shot so I could include as much of the fence as possible and so that the background included part of the light-blue sky. Each part of the picture—foreground, middle ground, and background—seems to be slightly varying shades of blue (the house and fence are the same shade of blue, but they appear different because of the variation of light that shines upon them), creating an interesting soft and subtle color match.

The fence leads to a payoff for the viewer because the eye moves deep into the frame, along the fence to the house. The payoff—or visual reward, if you will—is the house itself as it comes into view at the end of the fence. The small aperture I used (f/13) keeps everything in the picture in focus.

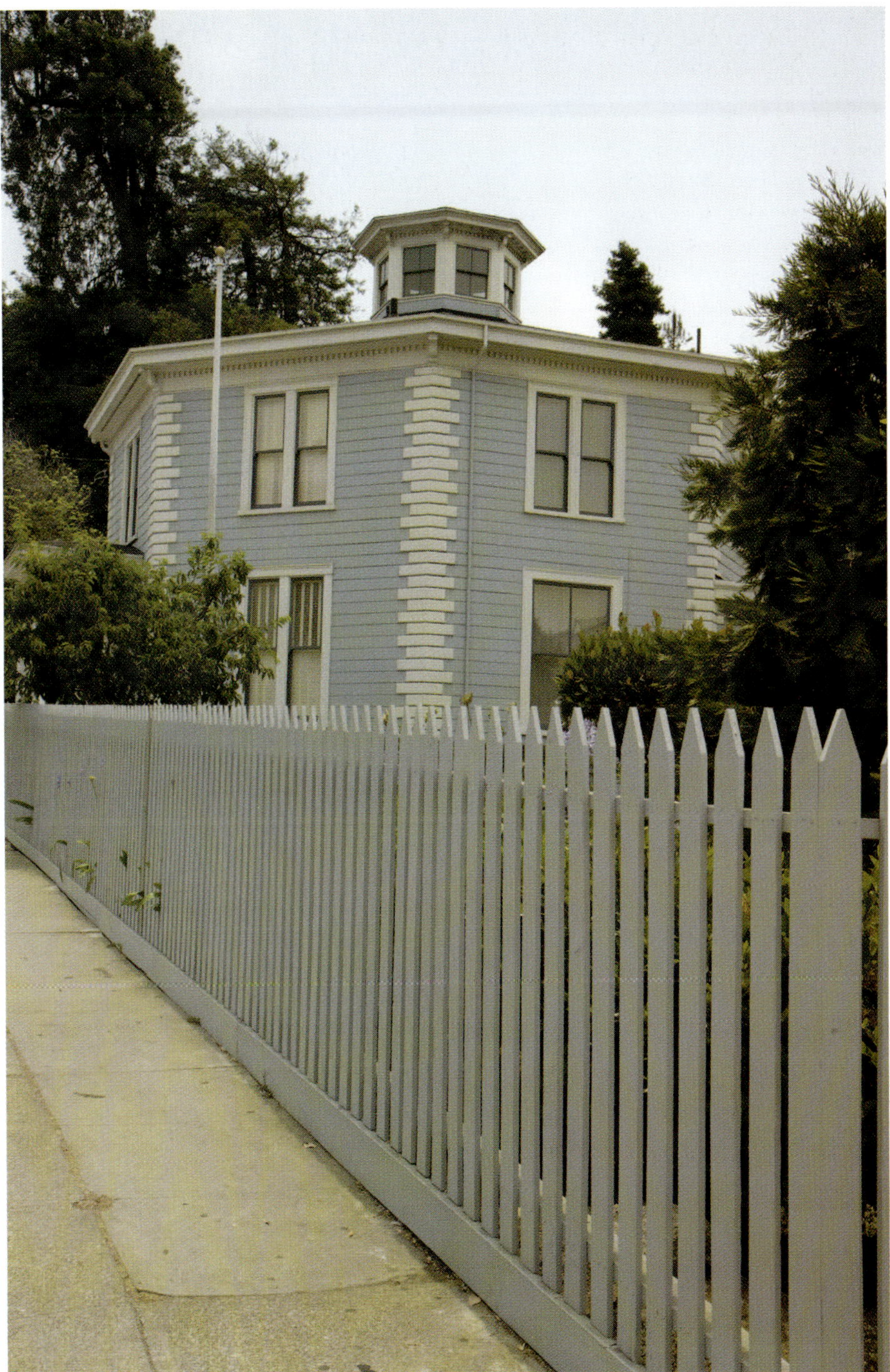

Focal length 40mm; ISO 200; aperture f/13; shutter speed 1/200; July 3:05 p.m.

The Shot

Next to San Francisco, San Franciscans like Paris best. Great French croissants can be had inside quaint Victorian buildings in just about every neighborhood. Union Street is no exception. There's a great French bakery inside an old Victorian with outdoor seating that photographs well straight on. To get this photograph of the bakery—La Boulange—I had to walk across the street to exactly the point where the bakery fits snugly into the frame. I was just far enough away to avoid converging lines. This bakery is a great place to photograph for a cafe scene, not only because of the building's brilliant shade of blue, but also because the windows are open during the day, eliminating any reflection from glass that would occur if the windows were closed. The symmetry of the woodwork is also worth noting in the top third of the frame, and the way the symmetry is broken up in the bottom two-thirds of the frame keeps the viewer looking inside and outside the doors and windows.

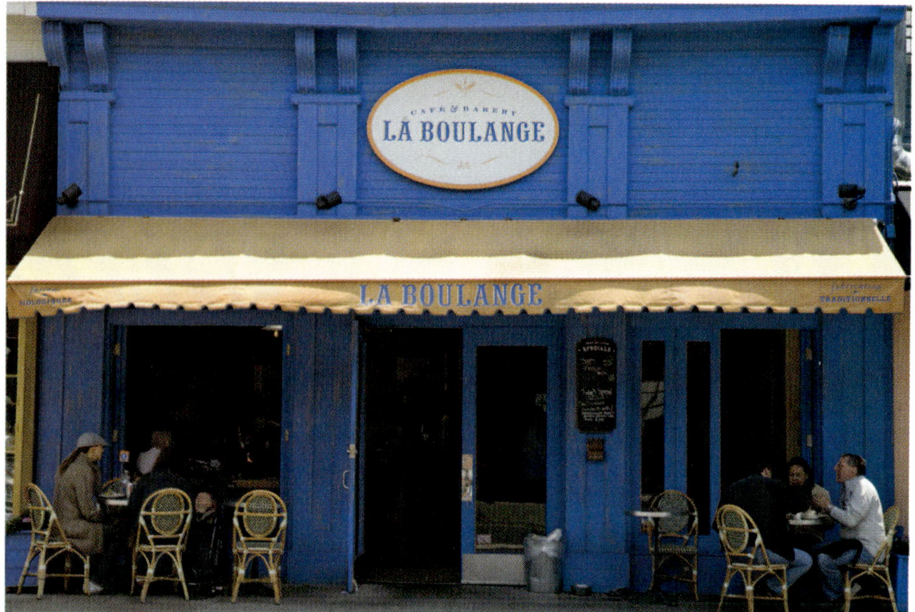

Focal length 70mm; ISO 200; aperture f/11; shutter speed 1/80; June 2:33 p.m.

Getting There

The Octagon House is at 2645 Gough Street at Union. The Union Street shopping district begins there and extends from the Octagon House westward to Divisadero.

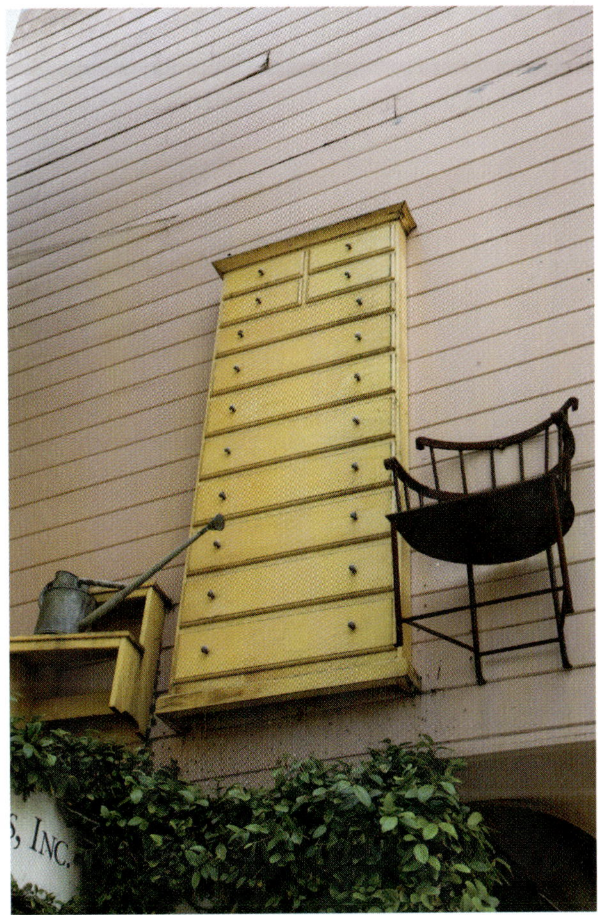

Furniture hung on the outside of a Victorian.

To get there using mass transit, from downtown, catch the J, K, L, M, or N to Van Ness Avenue, then transfer to the 47 Van Ness bus. Get off at Union Street. Or take the 41 Union bus from Main and Market Streets. Get off at Union and Octavia for the Octagon House. The Union Street business district runs west to Divisadero. La Boulange is at 1909 Union Street.

If you're driving, from the North Bay, take 101 South to the Marina exit. Take a right at Lyon Street and a left on Union. The Union Street shopping district will begin at Union and Divisadero and run to the Octagon House at Octavia.

From the East Bay, take 80 West to the 9th Street exit. Turn right on 9th, left on Hayes Street, right on Franklin Street, and left on Union to Octavia (for the Octagon House).

From the South Bay, take 101 North and exit at 9th Street, then follow the East Bay directions from 9th.

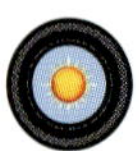 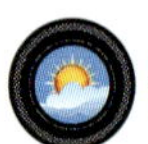 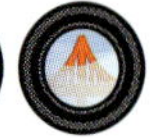

When to shoot: morning, afternoon, evening

Union Square

Union Square is a plaza in downtown San Francisco that is lined by Geary, Powell, Post, and Stockton Streets. The stores—Macy's, Bloomingdales, and Saks, to name a few—that face the square are part of the Union Square shopping district, which extends a few blocks from the square in every direction. San Francisco's theater district is also a part of the area known as Union Square.

John Geary, San Francisco's first American mayor, dedicated the square in 1850. In the mid-1800s, the square was a rallying point for the Union Army, which fought against the Confederate Army in the Civil War.

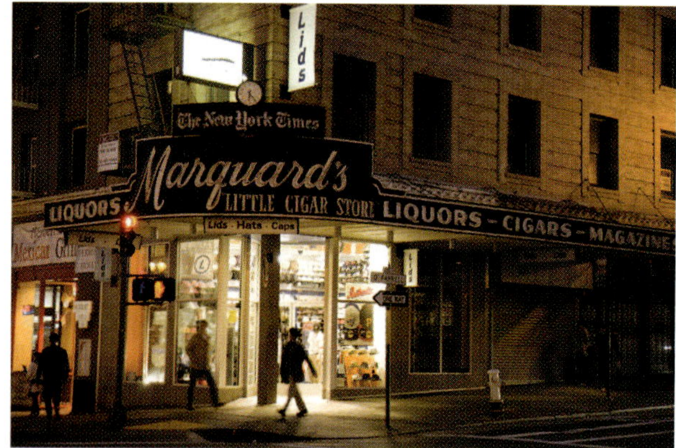

Marquard's on Union Square, a San Francisco landmark for decades.

The towering figurine known as "Victory" looks out upon the square from a 97-foot-tall Romanesque column. It represents a victory in one of the battles of the Spanish American War, which took place in the late 19th century.

The first underground parking garage was built under the square in 1940. A renovation of the square and garage was completed in 2000 to make room for outdoor cafes and open areas for concerts and other events.

The Shot

I chose to use a wide-angle lens (a Sigma 17-28mm lens) so that I could include a good bit of the paved area in the frame. This area contains interesting thick white lines that lead to the Victory statue. To get this shot I walked west from Maiden Lane (an alley east of Union Square that runs into Stockton Street) across Stockton Street until I reached the outdoor cafe that sits on the east side of the square. I took the picture on the north side of the cafe to get a western view of the square. Another advantage of using the wide-angle lens is that the buildings that line Geary Street to the south, along with the Saks store that lines Post Street to the north, can be included in the frame, adding a lot of depth to the image.

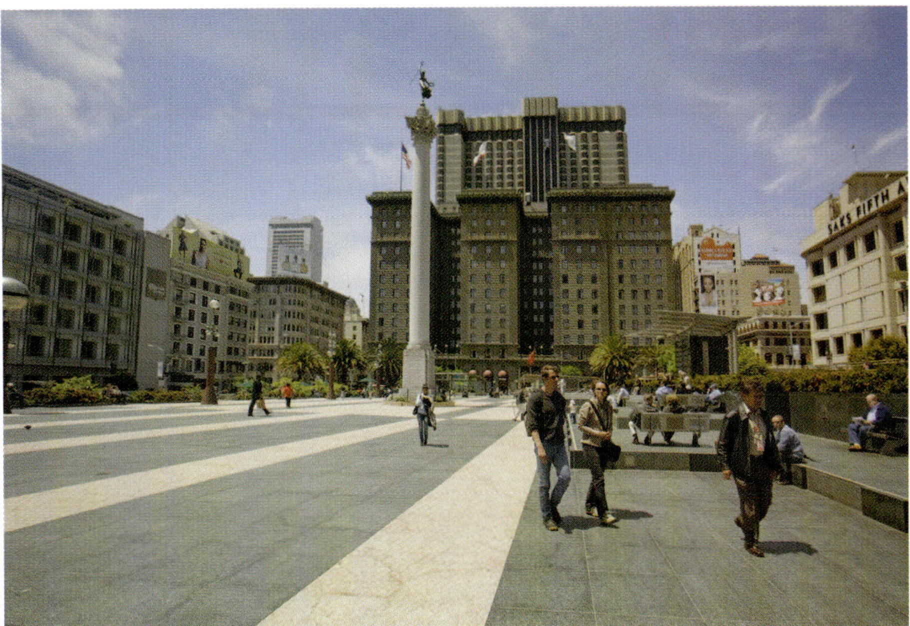

Focal length 17mm; ISO 200; aperture f/7.1; shutter speed 1/1000; May 2:15 p.m.

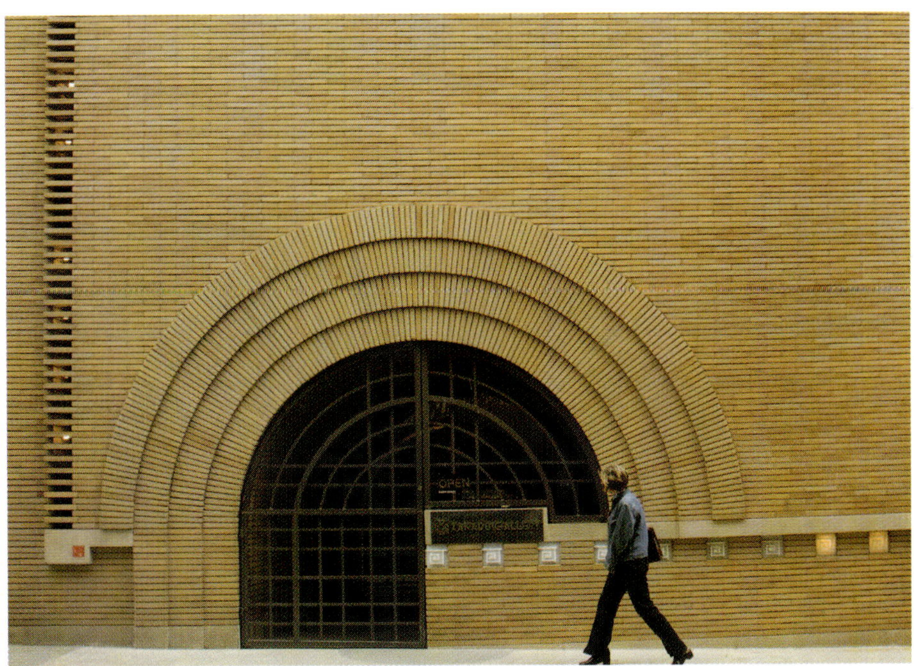

A woman on a foggy summer day walks by the gallery in a Maiden Lane building designed by Frank Lloyd Wright.

The Shot

This image was shot from a small alley—Maiden Lane—off Stockton Street. Maiden Lane is a street of galleries and shops across the street (east) from Union Square. The end of Maiden Lane looks out over Union Square and is blocked off to traffic with a guardrail. I took the picture standing just behind the guardrail, where the view of Union Square meets the front of the St. Francis Hotel. If you don't know the Union Square area, you wouldn't be able to tell whether the picture shows the front or back of the St. Francis Hotel. I take advantage of that fact by creating a kind of drama in the shot that's reminiscent of something you'd see in the famous Alfred Hitchcock movie, *Rear Window*. You just kind of wonder who is behind all those windows.

Technically, this image is a fine example of lines not converging in a shot of a building. This occurred because I was a good distance away from the building and I didn't have to tilt my camera upward to get a shot of the entire building.

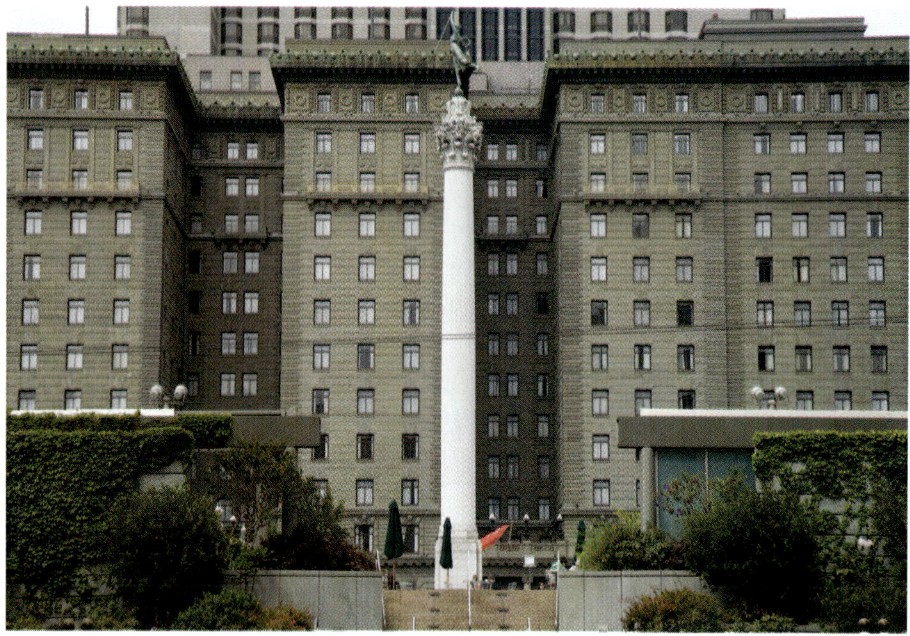

Focal length 80mm; ISO 200; aperture f/7.1; shutter speed 1/500; June 1:47 p.m.

Getting There

To get there using mass transit, from downtown, catch the 38 Geary on Market Street. Get off at Stockton or take the J, K, L, M, or N metro train to Powell Street and walk three blocks west to Union Square.

If you're driving, from the South Bay, take 101 North to the signs for I-80 East (signs for Oakland/I-80/Bay Bridge/Seventh St/US-101-N), then take the 4th Street exit. Make a slight left on Bryant and a left on 3rd. Continue until 3rd changes to Kearny and make a left on Sutter and then a left on Stockton to Post or Geary.

From the North Bay, take 101 South and exit at Lombard Street. Make a right on Van Ness Avenue and a left on Broadway. Turn right on Stockton to Post or Geary.

From the East Bay, take 80 West and exit at Fremont Street. Fremont turns to Front; continue on Front and make a left on Pine, a left on Montgomery, a right on Sutter, and a left on Stockton to Post or Geary.

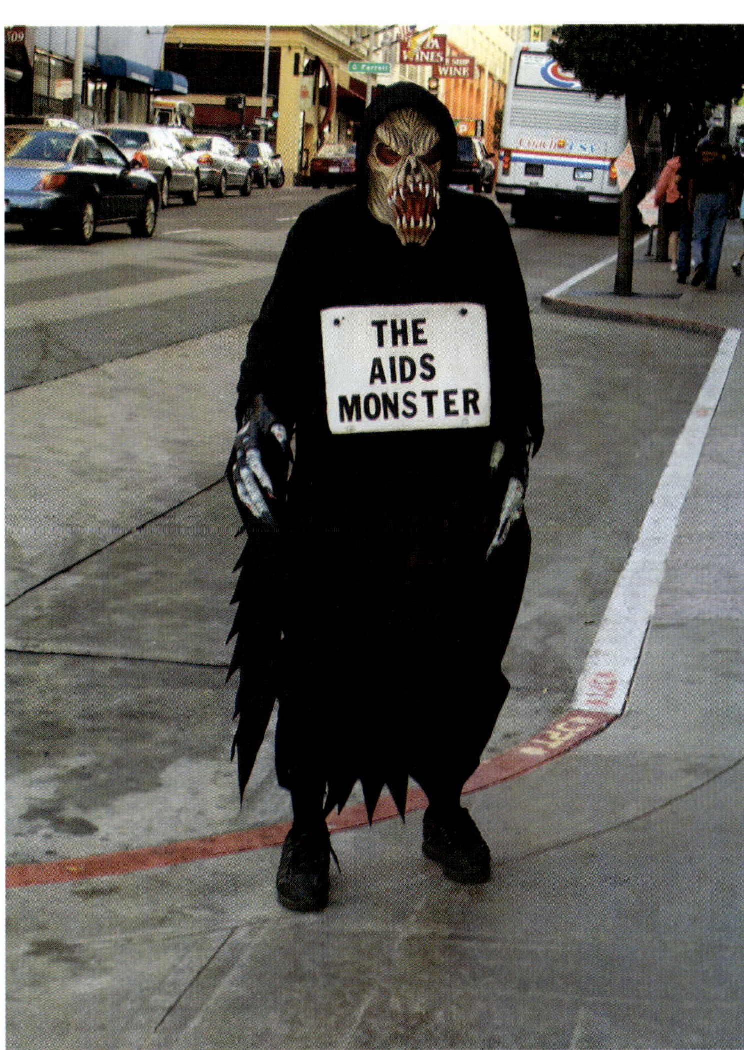

AIDS Monster spurs AIDS awareness near Union Square.

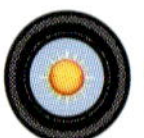 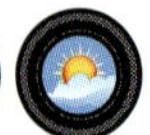 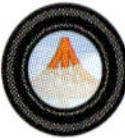

When to shoot: morning, afternoon, evening

Dolores Park

What a difference a decade makes. Just a decade ago, Dolores Park, a Mission District green area, was a host to drug deals and gang gatherings. Now the park is the number-one destination for the young and hip. Hundreds gather on the weekend to hang out in the sun and catch rays, and even more gather there for special events, such as movie nights and concerts. Every year the park hosts the lesbian motorcycle group Dykes on Bikes, and they begin a ride around the town, launching the Pink Saturday celebration. (See the Gay Pride parade photo op for more information about Pink Saturday.) On a normal weekend day, you'll see the park packed with people wearing the latest in fashion accessories and accompanied by canines that range from poodles to pit bulls.

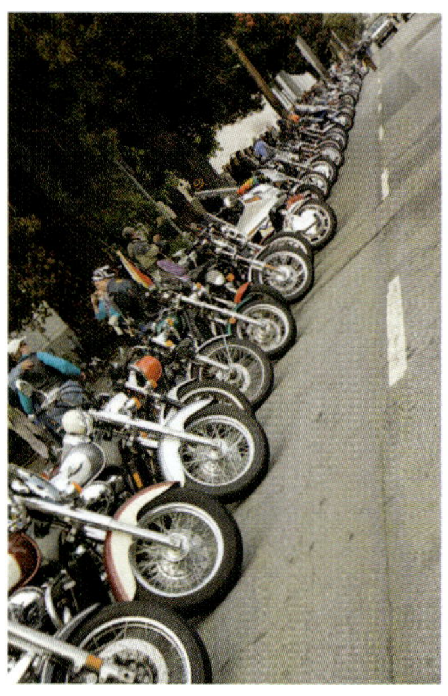

I tilted the camera to fit all motorcycles parked on Guerrero Street.

GETTING A RELEASE

When you take photographs of people who appear clearly in your picture and who are immediately recognizable, you might want to consider having them sign a release form. For example, it's very clear that I needed the woman whom I took a picture of in Dolores Park to sign a release form because she's easily identifiable and is the main subject in a published photograph. Under other circumstances, however, signing a release may or may not be something you have to do in order to publish the photograph or display it in an art show. For more detailed information about what to do regarding this matter, it's best to contact a publishing attorney.

You can get release forms from the Internet by typing the keywords "Adult Model Release" into Google. In short, a release form basically uses language that gives you the right to copyright and publish an image of the person who signs it. It also states that the person who signs the agreement has given up the right to approve the final version of the image that's to be published or displayed publicly. Finally, the form states that you (the photographer) are released from any claims that could make you responsible for the end product of the published photograph.

I have found that many people in San Francisco are familiar with release forms (especially those who wear attention-getting costumes), so having them sign one is usually not a problem. You should, however, always be aware of any person you don't know and handle all street photography sessions with care. Some neighborhoods in San Francisco are not all that safe when it comes to carrying on conversations with people on the street. If you're in a neighborhood where all there seems to be are liquor stores, you probably should take your candid photography elsewhere.

The Shot

A finger of fog divides this frame into two. Within the frame a balancing effect occurs between the three people who are in the foreground and Sutro Tower in the background. It's not hard to get the fog in this kind of position on the horizon, as it occurs frequently. The placement of people in the image follows the Rule of Thirds in that they are placed approximately one-third away from the right side of the frame. I also couldn't have asked the women to get in a better sitting configuration. I caught them as two were sitting facing the camera and one was sitting with her back to the camera, bringing the viewer a look over the latter's shoulder, as if he could hear what the women were saying. Last is the terrain. The women sit at the bottom of a small hill, which adds a bit of depth to the picture, and the fog begins a flow in the left side of the frame from behind another hill in the background. In order to bring out the green in the grass, deepen the light blue of the sky, and add detail to the gray and white fog, I lowered my camera's EV compensation by one stop to –.33 EV.

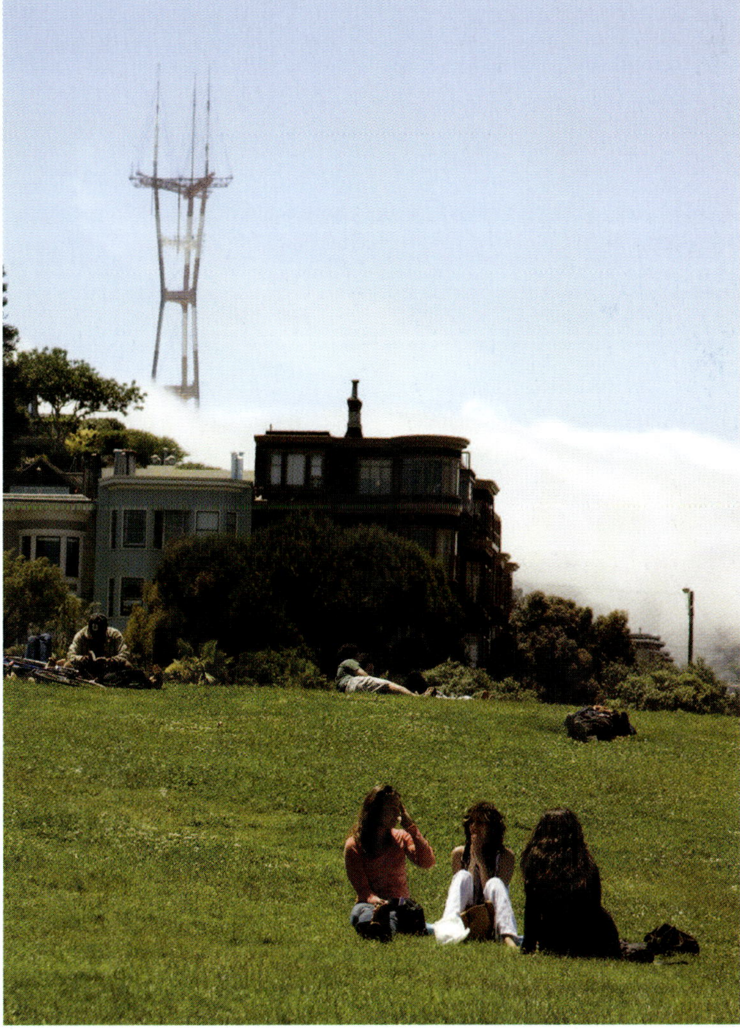

Focal Length 105mm; ISO 400; aperture f/7.1; shutter speed 1/1600; May 11:00 a.m.

The Shot

When I saw the woman in this image, her look struck me as…well, in a word, handsome. Then I saw the flag and put two and two together, meaning that I could place the woman in front of the flag for a great photo op. I asked the woman if I could take her picture and then asked her to sign a release (see the "Getting a Release" sidebar) to get her picture published. I then took a set of pictures varying the focal lengths and using a large aperture. Finally, I picked the best picture, and voila—here it is.

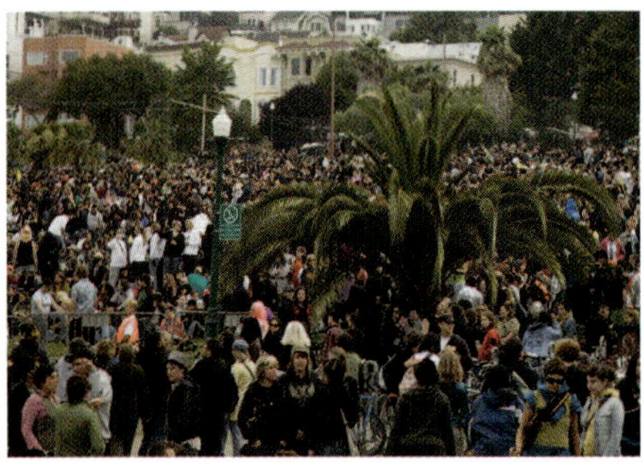

A sunny day attracts crowds to the park.

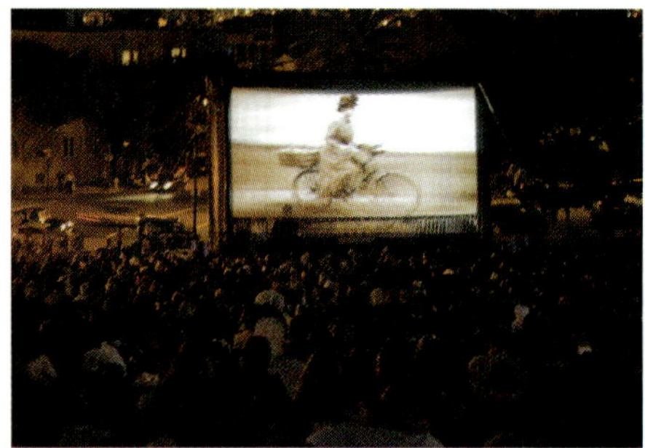

Watching *The Wizard of Oz* in Dolores Park.

Getting There

Dolores Park is in the Mission District of San Francisco between Church and Dolores and 18th and 20th Streets.

To get there using mass transit, from downtown, take the J Church to 18th and Church.

If you're driving, from the South Bay, take 101 North to the Cesar Chavez exit. Turn left on Cesar Chavez, right on Mission, and left on 18th to Church.

From the East Bay, take 80 West to 101 North until it ends at Market Street. Make a right on Market, a right on Valencia, and a right on 18th to Church.

From the North Bay, take 101 South. Make a slight left to exit on Lombard Street. Make a right on Van Ness, a right on Otis to Mission, and a right on 18th to Church.

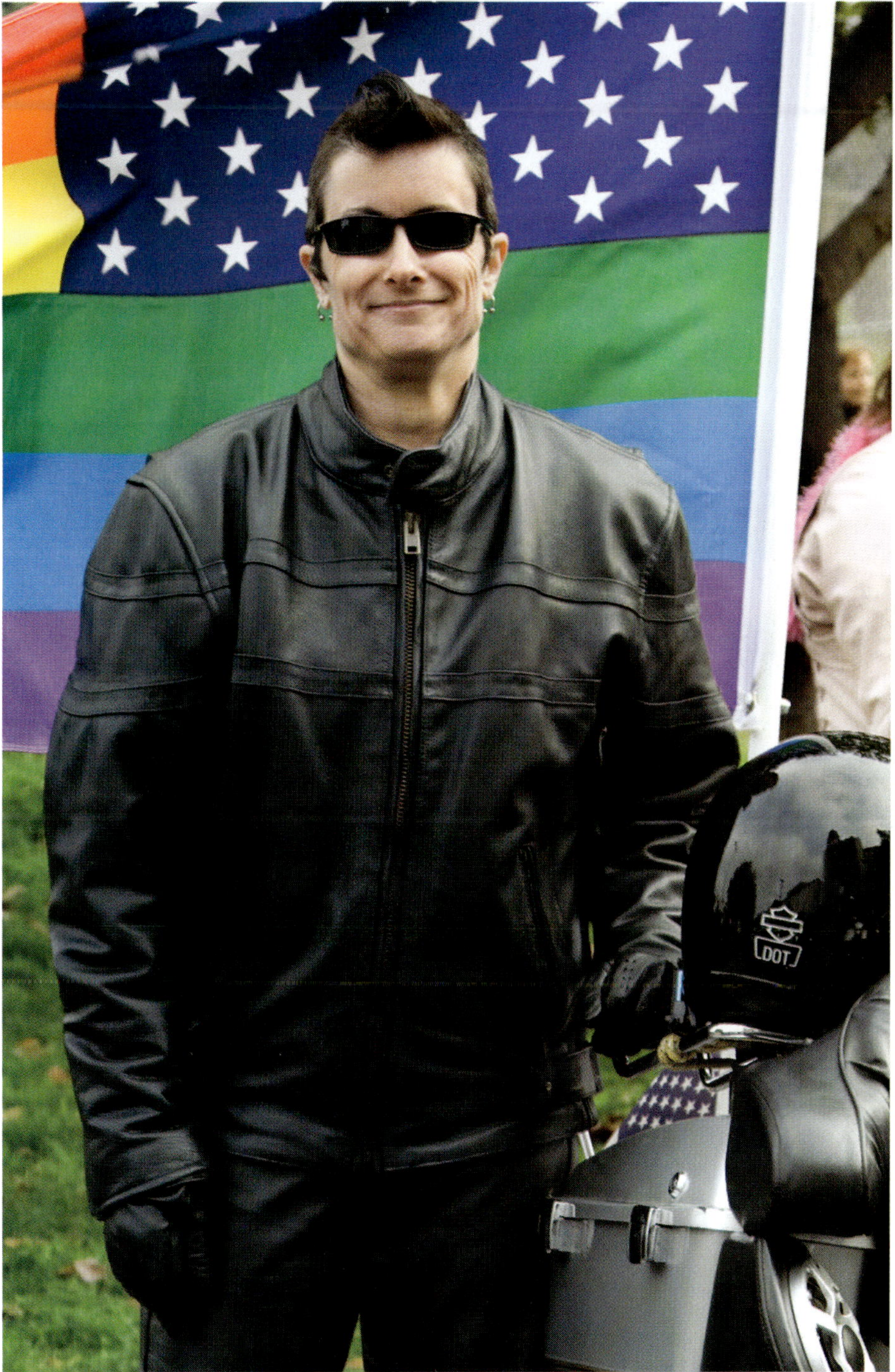

Focal length 58mm; ISO 400; aperture f/5.6; shutter speed 1/200; June 6:04 p.m.

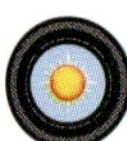 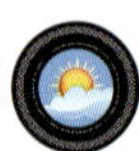

When to shoot: afternoon, night

Fisherman's Wharf

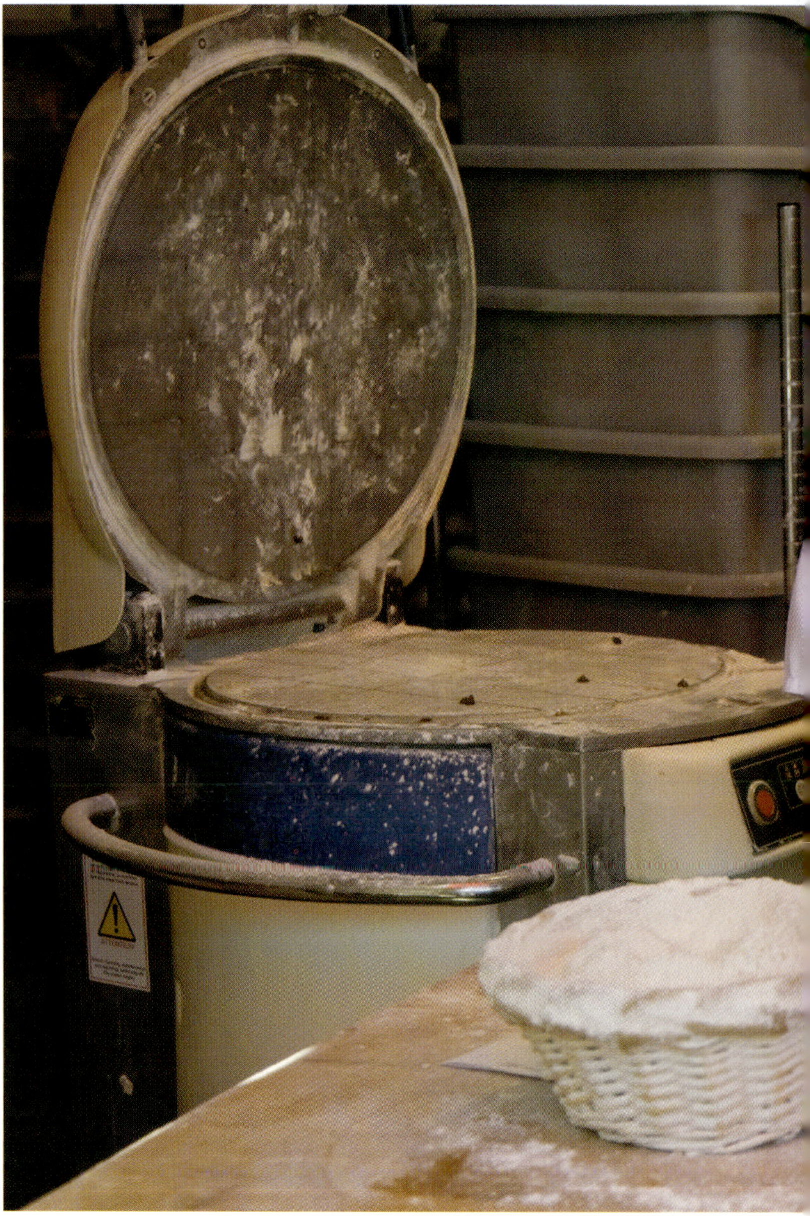

I don't know of any person who doesn't know of Fisherman's Wharf in San Francisco. Yet there are many who don't know about the fishing boats that once dominated the scene there. During the turn of the last century, *feluccas* (sailboats with a raking mast) brought in salmon, rockfish, herring, and crab. As technology progressed, motors replaced sails on fishing boats. By mid-century, boats with small motors, called *Monterey fishing boats*, became ubiquitous, replacing the feluccas. Among the hustle and bustle of tourists eating clam chowder in bowls of carved sourdough and the big hulls of boats and ferries that roam San Francisco Bay are nostalgic peeks at the wharf of yesterday. To be sure, there are some photo ops of today's goings-on at the Wharf, but the real excitement is bringing back the dynamic past.

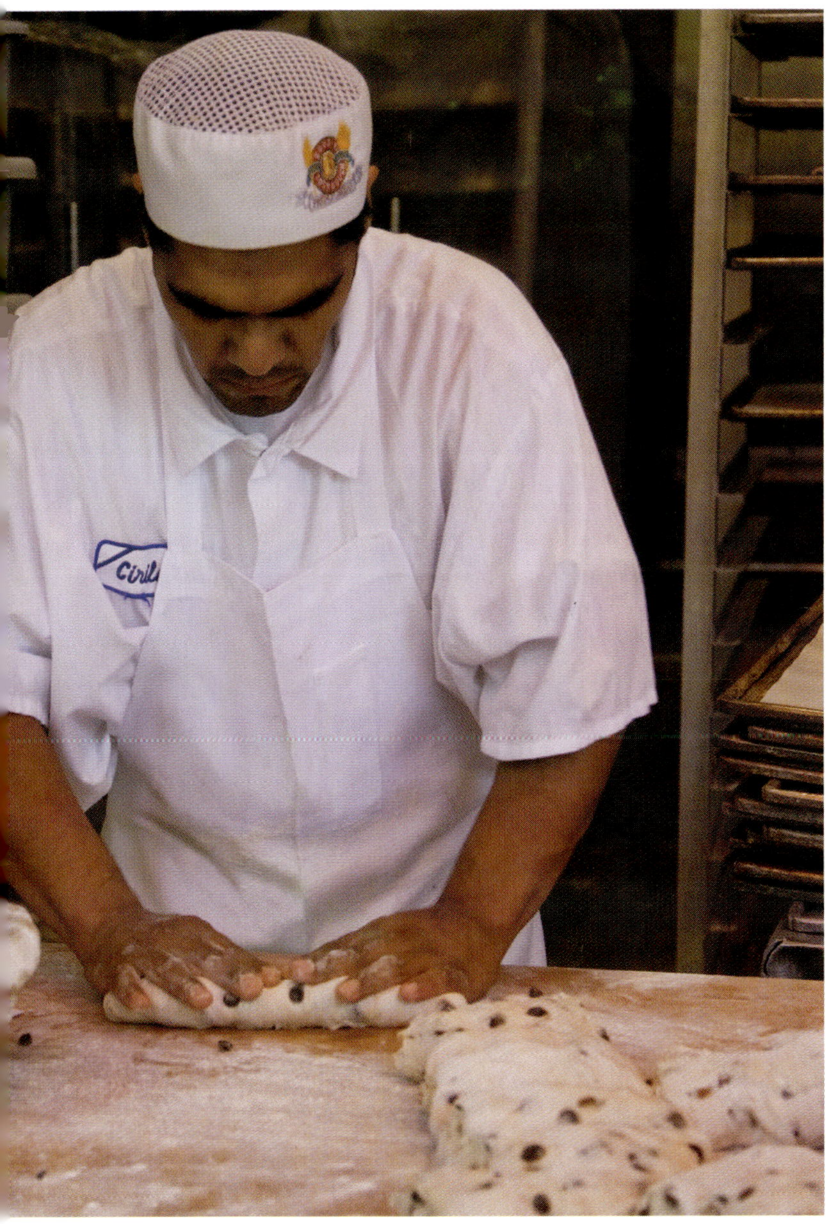

Baker makes bread at the Wharf.

The Shot

They're cute and colorful, wooden relics that have tested time. They're the Monterey fishing boats, a dying breed of marine craft that is at the top of my list of Fisherman's Wharf photo ops. They have names, too: Golden Gate, Nick, Pico, Baby Sal. The Monterey fishing boats are moored on the fishing fleet docks that are located on Jefferson between Taylor and Jones Street. In this picture I caught a man fixing his boat, which is fortunate because there are only 25 or so left. In the 1920s there were some 500 of these fishing boats. Many have sunk. I shot this picture with a wide aperture so I could frame the man clearly with some slight blur of the fishing boats in the background. This shot is one step above just taking a picture of the line of boats that you see in the background in that someone is doing something, so there's a narrative involved with it. In an article in the *San Francisco Chronicle,* Sal Alioto, one of the boat owners, said of the view of the boats from the restaurants above the wharf, "You got history right under your eyes here. Without the fishing boats, this would be just one more marina."

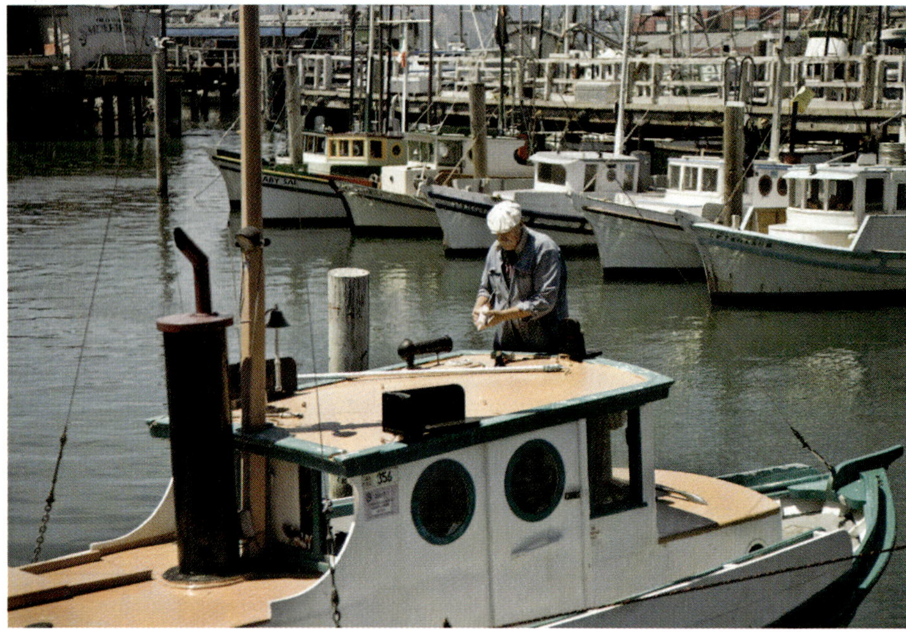

Focal length 75mm; ISO 200; aperture f/4; shutter speed 1/2000; August 10:55 a.m.

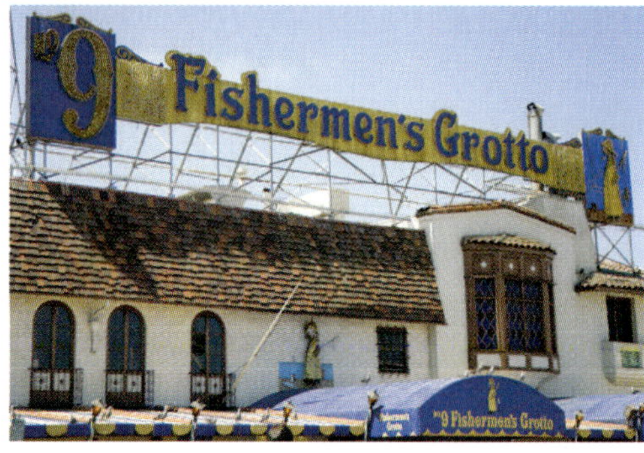

Fishermen's Grotto.

The Shot

The steam drew me to this photo op. Crabs are a quintessential Fisherman's Wharf treat, and when you can capture them in a cloud of steam, all the better to lure your viewer to the shot. In this shot, taken with a wide aperture in Av mode to maximize the shutter speed, I achieved blur in the foreground, which is the effect I wanted. I set my autofocus point to the back stack of crabs. This action resulted in a move gradually from the strainer in the blurred foreground to a clear background of a stack of crabs. The shot works because of the use of the Rule of Thirds in framing. The strainer, the first row of crabs, and the second row of crabs each occupy about one third of the frame, moving diagonally from the lower-left corner of the frame to the upper-right corner. Your eyes move up naturally along a diagonal line from the blurred strainer to the clear stack of crabs in the back. What really helps out the shot, though, is the crab that's right side up at the bottom right of the frame. If it weren't there, you wouldn't know what the crab's protective shell looks like.

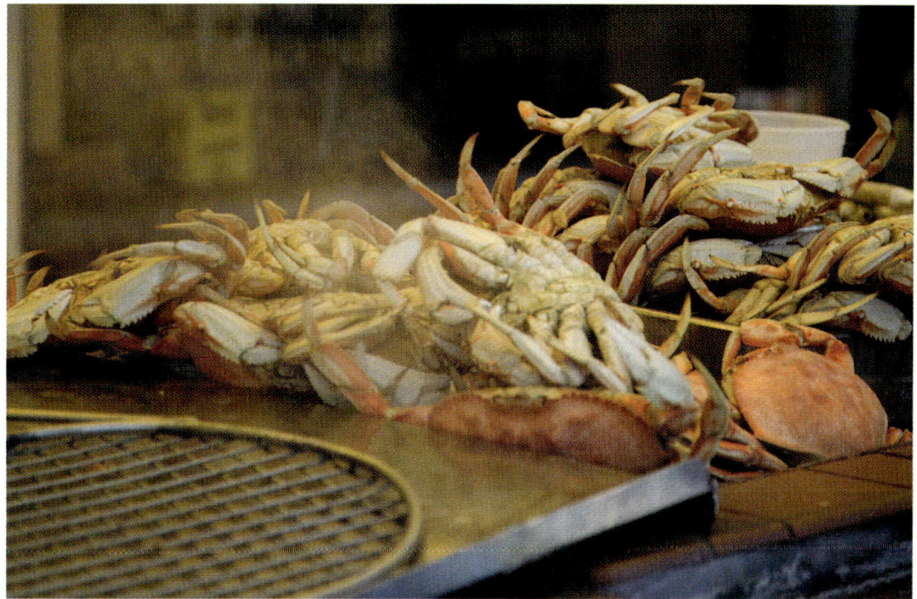

Focal length 97mm; ISO 200; aperture f/4; shutter speed 1/200; August 1:30 p.m.

Getting There

The heart of Fisherman's Wharf is around the historic F line streetcar stop at Jefferson and Jones Street.

To get there using mass transit, from downtown, catch the F line, which stops at the Ferry Building and lets you off at Jefferson and Jones Street.

If you're driving from the North Bay, take 101 South. Make a slight left onto Lombard, a left at Van Ness, a right at North Point, a left at Mason, and a left at Jefferson.

From the East Bay, take 80 West and exit at Fremont Street. Keep right at the fork and turn left on Folsom Street and left on Embarcadero, which turns into Jefferson.

From the South Bay, take 101 North to 280 North. Exit at King Street, which turns into the Embarcadero, which turns into Jefferson.

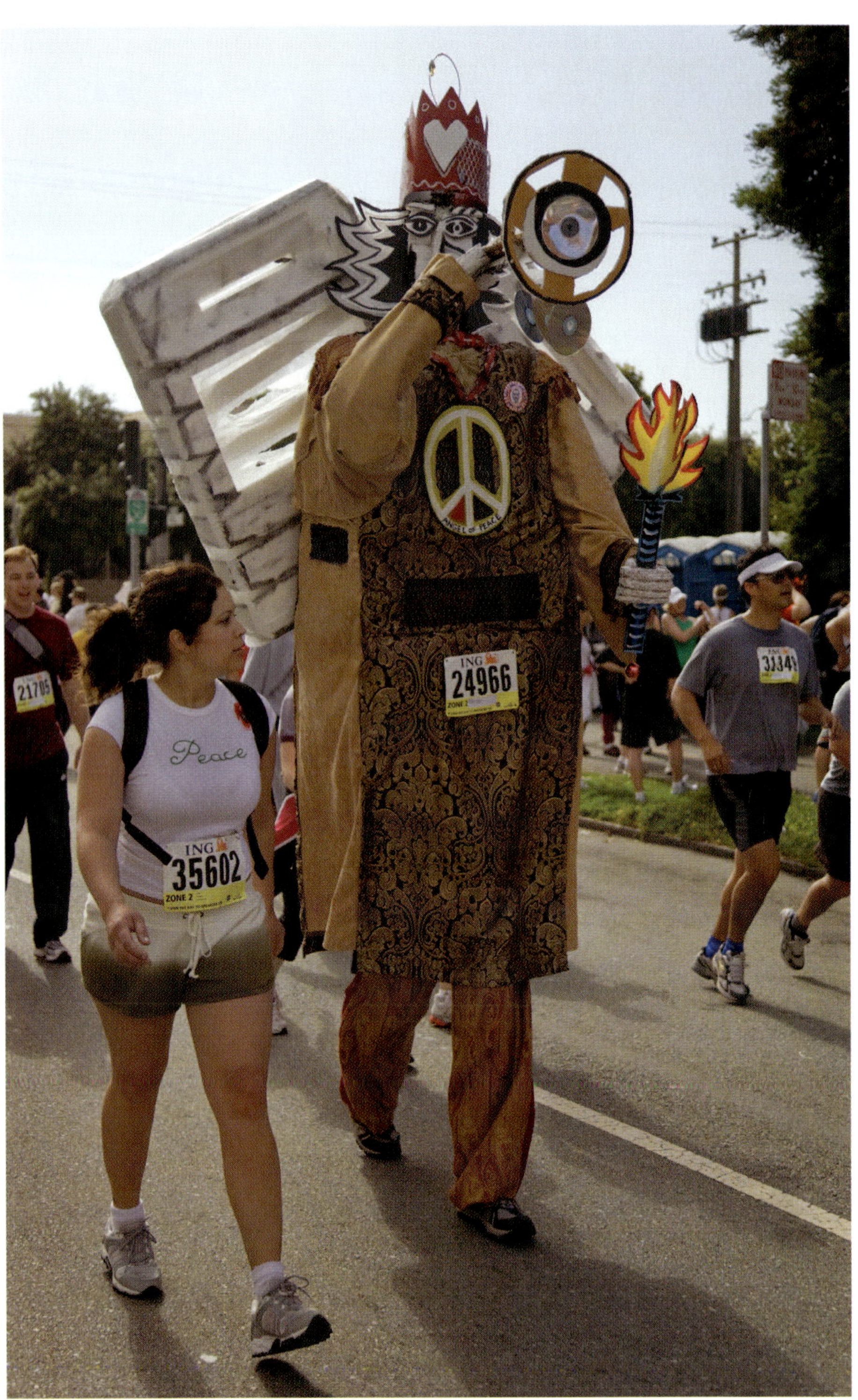

Elaborate costumes rule at the Bay to Breakers footrace.

CHAPTER 3

Events

There's a story about two people engaged in improprieties on top of a hydraulic piano in North Beach's Condor Club after it closed one night. A switch was pushed during the act, and the piano rose until the two were pinned together. One survived and one didn't, leaving us with one of the more bizarre memories of the city.

Since the rowdy prospectors on the hunt for gold made it to San Francisco, it has always been a place where the offbeat can happen at any moment. Go to any event, and you'll probably be able to take a picture of something you've never seen before. Many San Francisco events tend to be adult-oriented and boisterous, with some things not left to the imagination. Take the Bay to Breakers footrace, for instance: No matter how hard the city tries to stop people from running naked, it still happens. *C'est la vie.* You will see half-naked beefy guys and drag queens at the Gay Parade, and, well, who knows what will happen at the Love Parade.

To be sure, there are family-friendly events too, such as the Chinese New Year Parade and the Cherry Blossom Festival. Most people come to San Francisco not only with an open heart, but also with an open mind. Whatever your tastes, San Francisco is sure to have an event for you, and each and every one is sure to have photo ops beyond your wildest dreams.

Shooting Like a Pro

San Francisco events aren't big, they're massive, taking up miles of the city and involving tens of thousands of people. Getting a space to watch, much less photograph, can be a challenge. A word to the wise—get to where you're going along the path of the event at least an hour early. Time is on the photographer's side during most events, as they last several hours and usually move slowly.

When you're finding a place to photograph a parade, for example, be aware of all that surrounds you—that will be your background in the shot. Events that take place outside in the summer often take place under overcast skies caused by the fog. To eliminate the white areas of a foggy sky that often fill the frame of your photo, shoot without including the sky. During many events large, colorful floats pass by. When they do, take a series of shots of each, first photographing the entire float and the people around it, then zooming in and isolating people either individually or in groups. You can get some really good shots if you hone in on any action that takes place, as shown by the drummers in the Cherry Blossom Festival parade. If you see a pattern of people, say, leaning all in one direction in a dance, zoom in on the people's torsos and arms. Also, shoot what appeals to your eye. It's a good bet that what you like, others will like too.

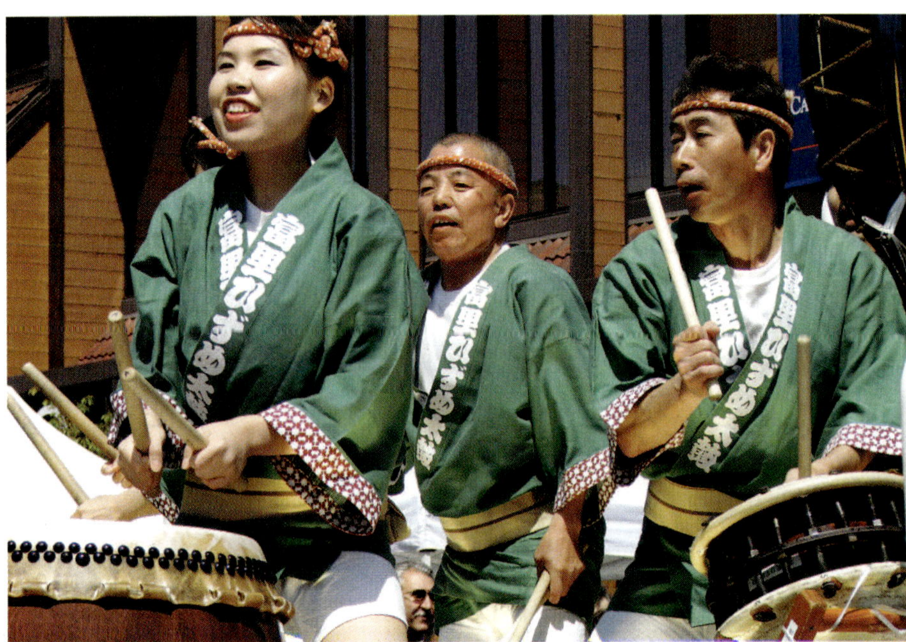

Hone in on the action during events.

The Gear

A fast lens (f/2.8 to f/4) is a good choice to photograph events to stop the motion of the people moving around. When you shoot at low f/stops (wide apertures), more light is let into your camera so that the shutter will open and close faster. You'll give up some depth of field, but you'll gain shutter speed. The image of the group of Bay to Breakers runners shows them caught with a relatively fast lens (f/4) so that they are stopped in their tracks without blur. The f/stop of the all-purpose lens I use stays constant no matter what the focal length is. A lens with a telephoto up to 200 or 300mm works well.

Be careful, though, because the higher the focal length you shoot at, the more the image is magnified, so shake from the camera is also magnified, making for a blurred image. There's a rule in photography about increasing shutter speeds when you increase your focal length. If you're shooting at a specified focal length, the shutter speed needs to be the inverse of that to keep from getting blur. For example, if you're shooting at 35mm, the longest shutter speed you should use is 1/35 second. If your shutter speed is 1/50 second, your image may appear sharp on a 35mm lens, but it will show camera shake on a 200mm lens due to the higher degree of magnification. To eliminate the blur, shoot at shutter speeds faster than 1/200 second.

Finally, a word about lenses: The best (and most expensive) zoom lenses have a constant maximum aperture throughout the range of focal lengths. If your camera can shoot with wide apertures in Av mode at all focal lengths with a telephoto lens, your shots will be sharper because the camera will calculate the fastest shutter speeds possible for each focal length you choose. A telephoto will also help when you want to zoom in on antics, such as the image I captured of people on stilts, or when you want to communicate something peaceful, such as the feeling you get from a Japanese dancer. A telephoto also lets you crop out distracting background and foreground elements.

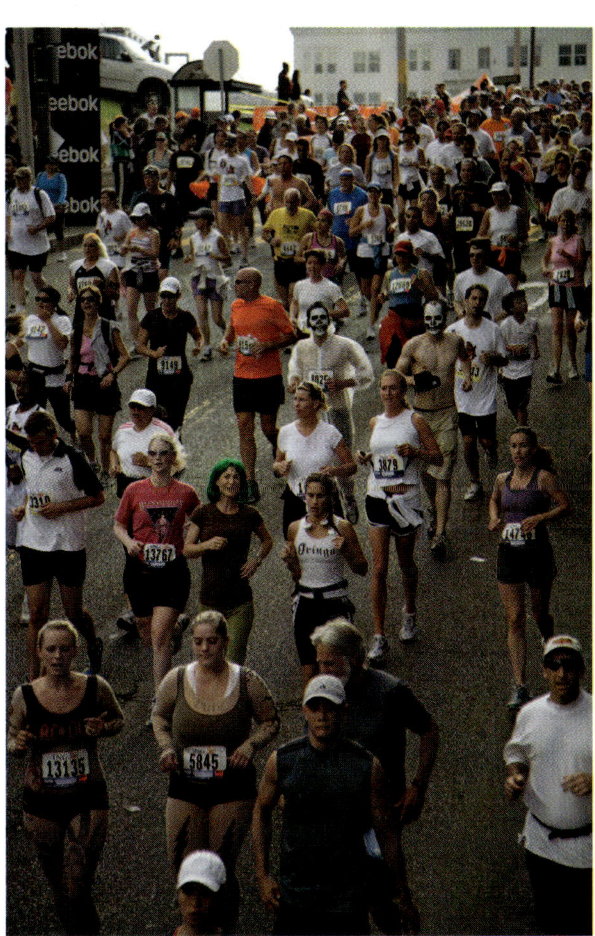

Bay to Breakers runners.

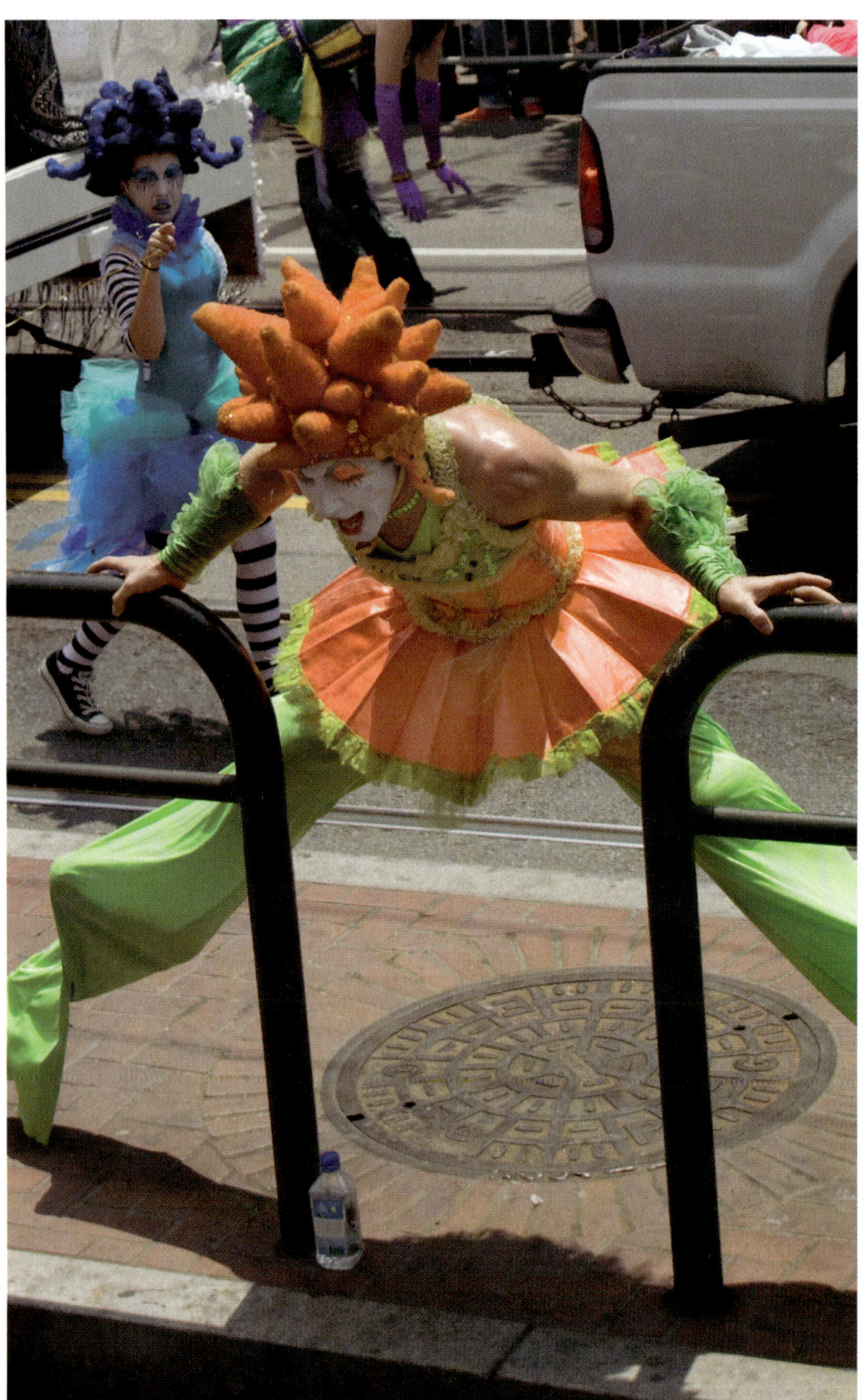

Antics on stilts at the Gay Parade.

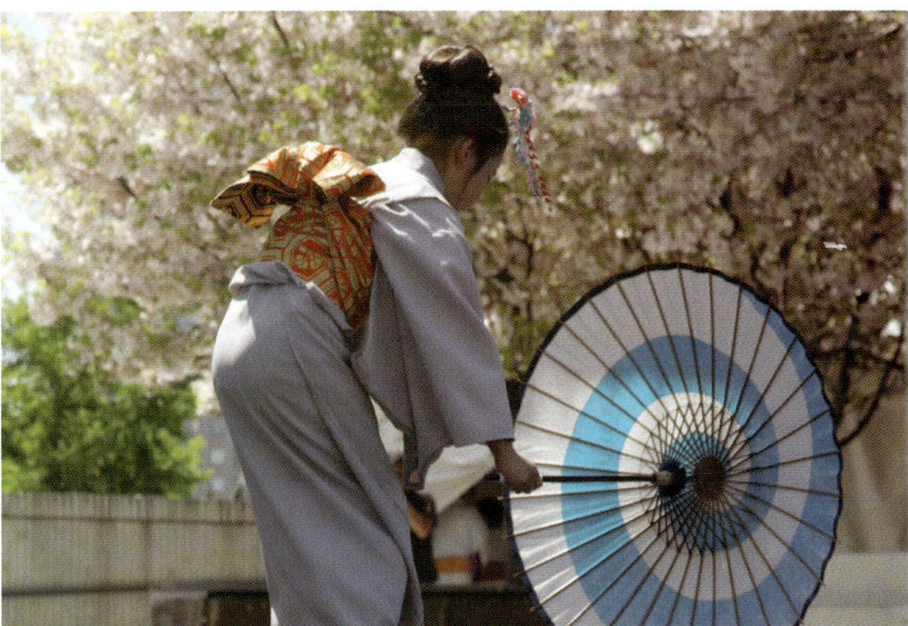

The peacefulness of a Japanese dancer.

The Plan

Find the place and time of the event and get there early to find a spot to photograph. Get as close to the event as possible. Try to find spots high up to capture all of the action up and down the path of the event. If it's foggy, set your camera's ISO to 400 (800 if you're shooting in the shade). When the fog lifts, set it at 200. Remember, if you set your ISO too high, you'll get noise.

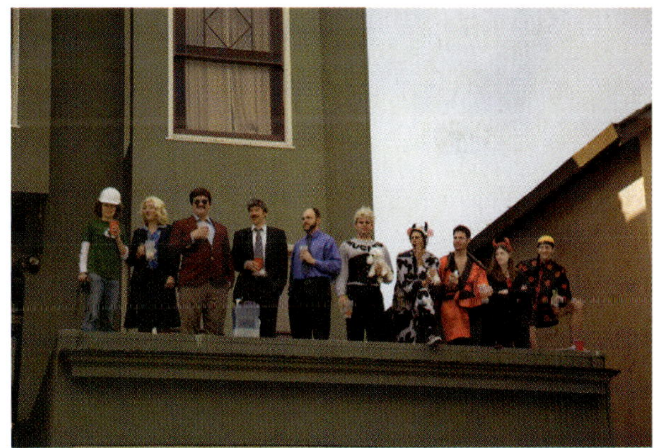

Spectators at Bay to Breakers.

Another good idea is to keep your camera in Av mode and shoot with its widest aperture setting. That way you'll almost ensure that all of your shots will be clear. Be warned, though, that when you're using a wide aperture, you have limited depth of field, so correct focus becomes critical. Make sure you set your auto-focus point on the object you want sharp in the frame.

When you're photographing, include the spectators as part of your repertoire of shots. Be on the lookout for colorful characters in the crowd. They can be interesting too, especially if they are wearing costumes or are lined up evenly within the frame, as in this image of spectators at the Bay to Breakers.

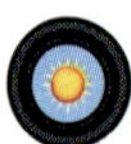 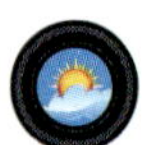

When to shoot: morning and early afternoon

Bay to Breakers Footrace

After the tragic 1906 earthquake and fire, San Franciscans craved a break from the rebuilding effort. In 1912, they decided to have a race from San Francisco Bay to the Pacific Ocean. It became known as the Bay to Breakers and has taken place every year since. Today, the footrace begins at 8:00 a.m. on the third Sunday in May.

While the race attracts some of the best runners from around the world, it's also a celebration for which participants and spectators dress up as anything or anybody, or wear nothing at all. (The city discourages this, but it happens anyway.) A flood of humankind (nearly 65,000 people) pours through the city streets all day long as more than 100,000 spectators look on.

This event is one you'll want to get up bright and early for—it generates enthusiasm for San Francisco like no other event the city has. I've found it best to shoot from near Alamo Square because you can see the runners go both up and down the Hayes Street hill. The participants start as a trickle of serious runners and end with a blast of serious partiers.

For more information about the race, including entering it, go to www.ingbaytobreakers.com.

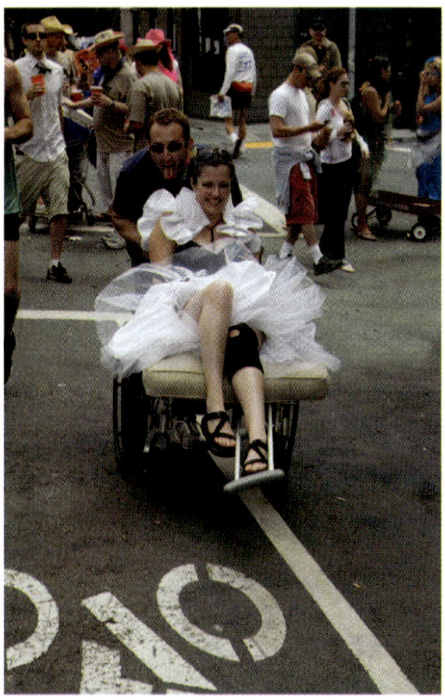

People have gags at the run.

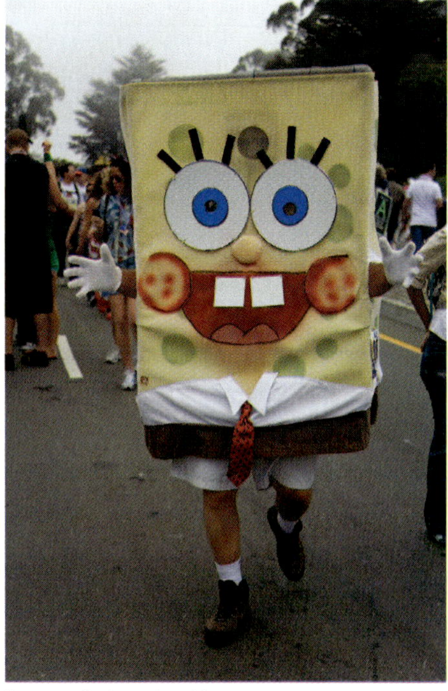

Sponge Bob makes his entrance.

The Shot

It's early morning with a thick fog overhead. The runners have begun to show off their gags. I want a sharp photograph, so what should I do? This is the scenario I have encountered almost every year I have photographed this event. To prepare for the shot, I adjust my ISO speed to a moderately fast one of 400. I choose this value to balance a sharp shot against one that has noise (as ISO speed increases, image quality decreases). Next, I set my camera to its widest aperture (f/4) in Av mode. Last, I quickly move my auto-focus point to the middle fish that I'm photographing, and I shoot. I chose this image as one of the best photo ops of the event because of its narrative—fish swimming upstream, or in this case, runners dressed up like fish, running against the tide. This is something that salmon do to die in real life, but in this case these runners are having a heck of a time. The photo is framed so that the "painted ladies" Victorians are in the background. Last, is the deep gray sky, which is typical of San Francisco during this time of year.

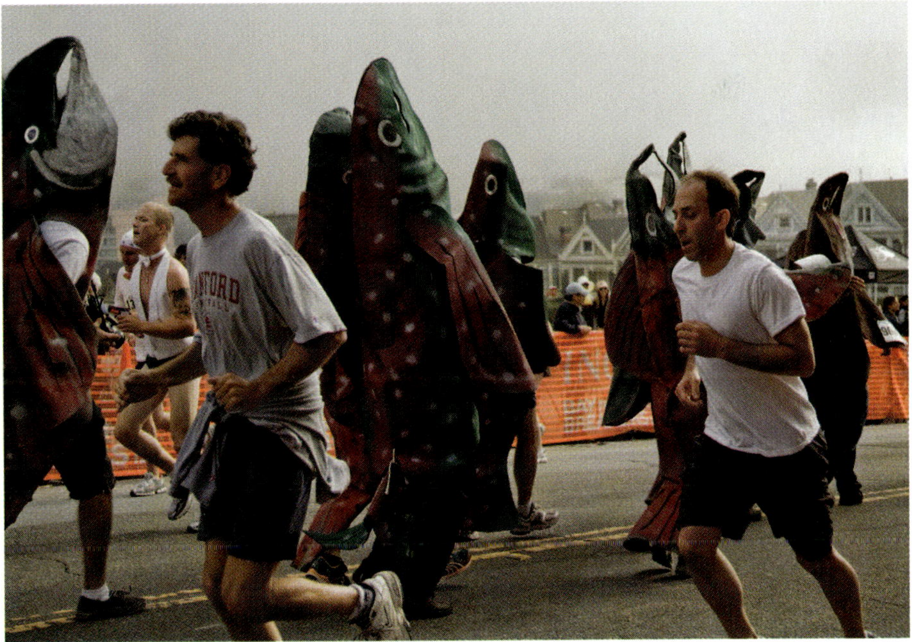

Focal length 47mm; ISO 400; aperture f/4; shutter speed 1/2500; May 8:26 a.m.

The Shot

In this shot, there's a Water Wiggle that people were crossing as they passed through the Panhandle, a green area before you reach Golden Gate Park. The peace sign, which is very often a symbol of San Francisco's counterculture, matches the color of the water droplets and is also the primary focus of the image. I couldn't have gotten a better opportunity for the middle ground than a curtain of splashing water. It helped to create the effect of the person in front of the curtain being sharp while the people behind it are blurred. Water scatters light, amplifying the contrast between the foreground and the background because of the light layer between the two. The additional light from the splashing water also caused the camera to use a faster shutter speed in Av mode (the f/stop was f/4) than it would have without it, stopping the action in the image in its tracks.

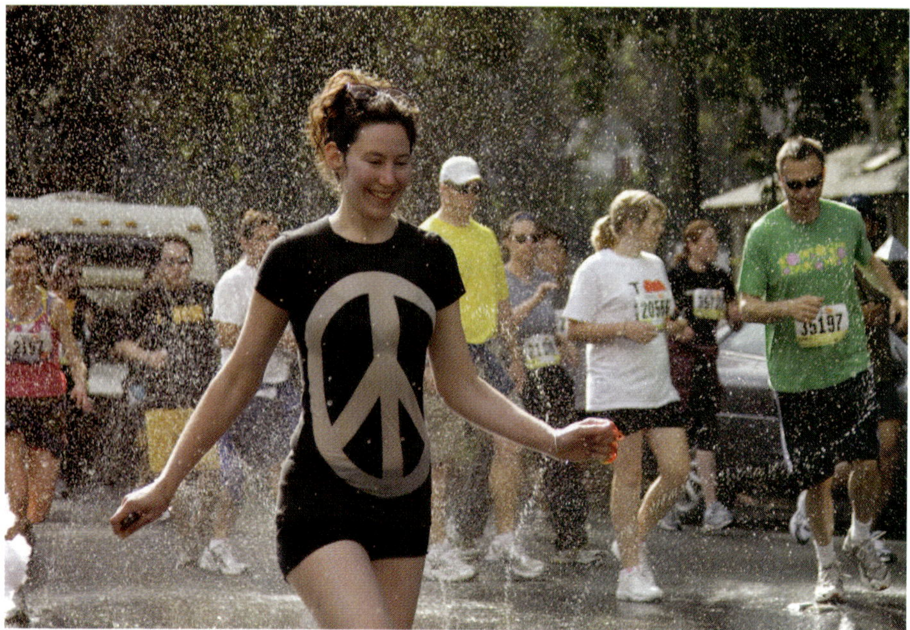

Focal length 73mm; ISO 400; aperture f/4; shutter speed 1/1600; May 10:02 a.m.

Getting There

The race starts at Howard Street and the Embarcadero and ends at the Great Highway. You can photograph anywhere along the route. The route follows a path westward along Howard Street to 9th Street, where the runners turn right. After crossing Market Street, 9th changes to Hayes Street, where runners climb a steep hill. After the hill, it's downhill to Fell Street. Fell Street runs through a green area called the Panhandle, which comes right before Golden Gate Park. When runners enter the park, Fell becomes John F. Kennedy Drive, which ends up at the Great Highway at Ocean Beach. One of the best places to photograph the race is near Alamo Square at the top of the Hayes Street hill. You can also follow the runners along the route anywhere from downtown to Ocean Beach.

To get there using mass transit, Muni provides buses to the starting area before the race and from the beach after the race on the N Judah and the 5 Fulton lines. They also run trains from West Portal station to the Embarcadero and from Judah and 19th Avenue to Church and Duboce, and then on to the Embarcadero.

If you're driving to the starting area at Howard and Embarcadero you can use parking lots that are open downtown. From the South Bay, take 101 North to 280 North. Exit at King Street, which turns into the Embarcadero. Take Embarcadero to Howard.

From the East Bay, take 80 West and exit at Fremont Street. Turn left at Folsom and left at the Embarcadero. Howard Street is one block northwest of Folsom.

From the North Bay, take 101 South to Lombard. Make a slight left on Lombard, a left at Van Ness, a right at Bay, and a right at the Embarcadero to Howard.

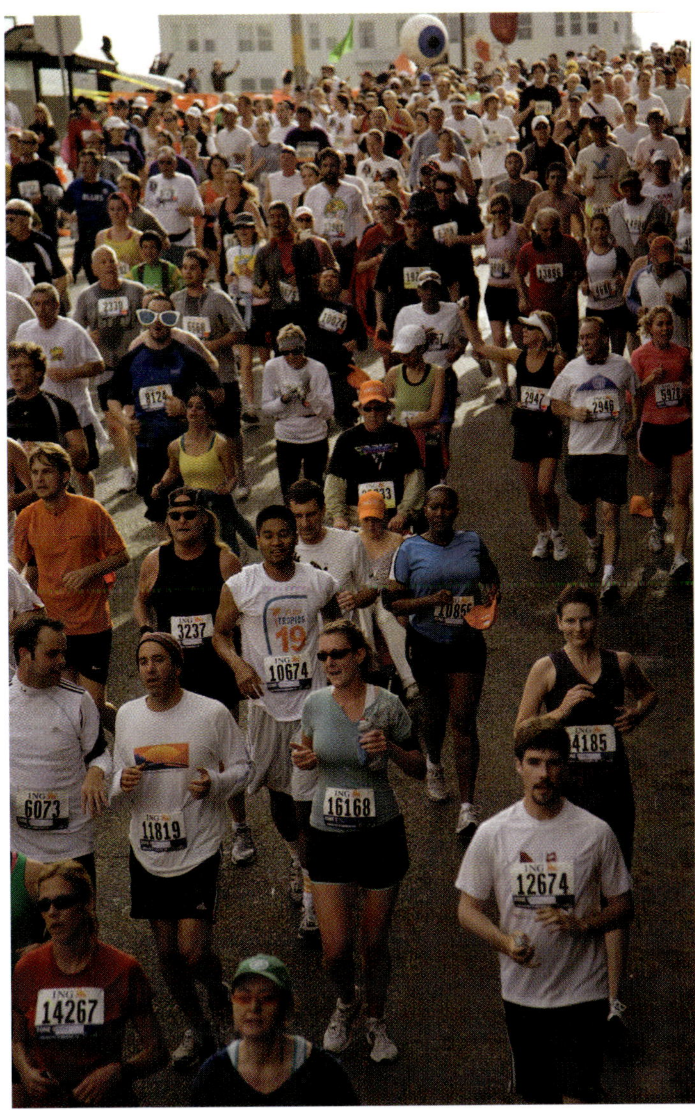

Runners come down the Hayes Street hill.

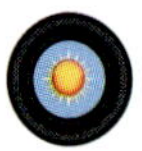 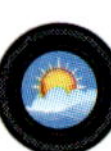 When to shoot: morning

Gay Pride Parade

In June of 1969, a group of gay people protested police harassment at their gathering place, the Stonewall Bar on Christopher Street in New York City. The protest turned into riots that lasted several days. A year later, a small group of gay people living in San Francisco wanted to commemorate what was to become known as "Stonewall," so they organized a small rally in Golden Gate Park. In 1972, the commemoration of Stonewall had been organized so that nearly 3,000 people marched down Polk Street, a gay area of the city. By 1977, the parade grew so that hundreds of thousands of people showed up to march for gay rights. The later years of the 1970s brought violence to the city when the mayor and the first openly gay supervisor were shot at City Hall. Crowds thinned at the parade due to fear that violence would erupt. However, since the 1970s, the parade has endured and grown to a celebration of a half a million people that takes place during the entire weekend of the last week of June. Coinciding with the parade are events such as Pink Saturday, a celebration the Saturday night before the parade, and the San Francisco International Lesbian and Gay Film Festival.

The parade begins at 10:30 a.m. most years. It begins at the Embarcadero and ends around noon at the Civic Center. There's a big celebration until 6:00 p.m. at Civic Center Plaza. Check www.sfpride.org for the latest information on the coming year's parade.

The Shot

The first thing you'll notice is the crowds on the sides of Market Street. They line up almost a dozen deep to get a glimpse of the passing parade. Word to the wise: Get there early if you want any photographs. There is another option for photographing, though, other than the side of the street. If you walk up and down Market Street, look for places to watch the parade, such as on top of newspaper stands and telephone booths. That's the option I chose and how I got the particular vantage point you see here. I took the picture from atop a telephone booth on the northwest side of Market Street, just northeast of where Taylor Street and Golden Gate Avenue meet Market Street.

Notice that in the picture it's sunny. During June, the fog usually lifts before the parade starts, so expect bright sun, which will affect how you set your camera. To deepen my depth of field a bit so I can get the line of people in the street in sharp focus, I increase my f/stop (decrease my aperture opening) to about 6.3. For more information about depth of field, see the sidebar entitled "Zooming and Depth of Field" coming up shortly.

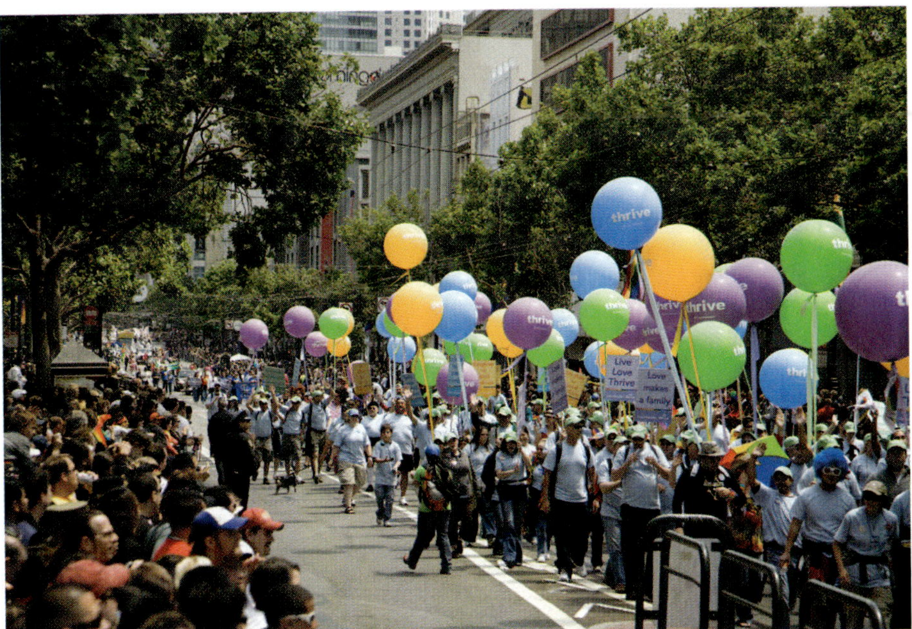

Focal length 105mm; ISO 200; aperture f/6.3; shutter speed 1/500; June 11:19 a.m.

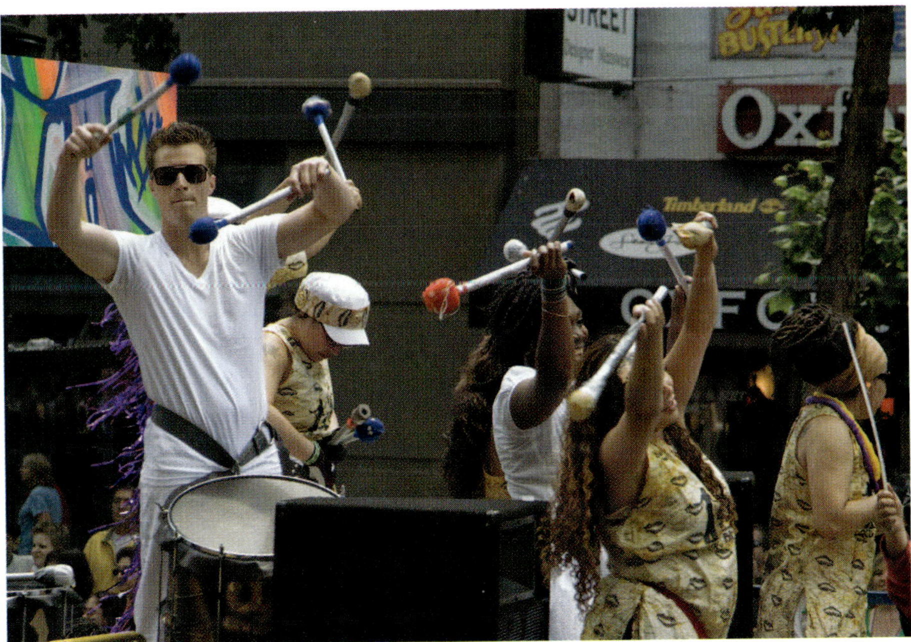

Dancing with the mallets.

The Shot

The subjects—the singer in the middle and dancers on the sides—are well-balanced with respect to each other. The way they are facing—the singer and pair of girls dancing for the crowd on one side of the street and the guy for the crowd on the other side—makes the parade come to life as if you're watching it live. The shot is sharp thanks to an aperture that's relatively narrow. The focal length is considered "normal" for a full-sized sensor camera, such as the Canon 5D used for this photo—normal meaning that the lens' focal length is neither wide angle nor telephoto. (See the upcoming "Zooming and Depth of Field" sidebar.) When I got home, I picked the best shots from the dozen or so I took. If you look closely, I caught each performer with arms extended as part of their performance, which shows their involvement in what they are doing. It all goes to show you that taking just one or two shots might not be enough to get the action you want.

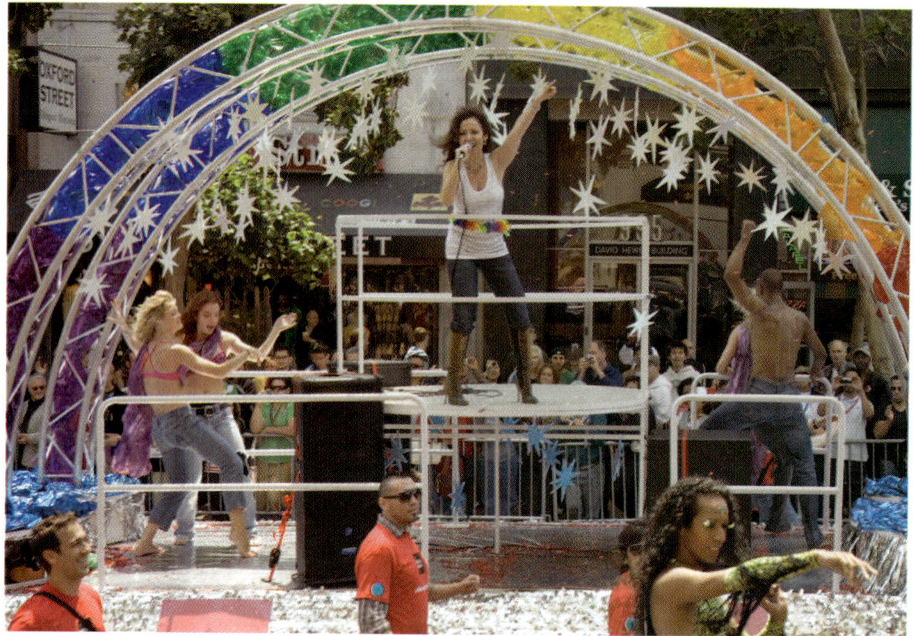

Focal length 50mm; ISO 200; aperture f/6.3; shutter speed 1/200; June 11:28 a.m.

Getting There

The San Francisco LGBT (Lesbian, Gay, Bisexual, and Transgender) Pride Parade, as it's formally called, begins in the same general area as the Bay to Breakers footrace. It also follows the same path along Market Street up until 9th Street.

To get there using mass transit, the beginning of the parade route is near the Embarcadero station. The end of the parade route is near the Civic Center station. You can get to either one or from one to another by taking the J, K, L, M, or N Muni Metro subway car.

If you're driving to the starting area at Market and Embarcadero, to get close to the staging area and the beginning of the parade, drive to Howard Street and take a left to look for parking lots in the area.

From the South Bay, take 101 North to 280 North. Exit at King Street, which turns into the Embarcadero. Take Embarcadero to Howard.

From the East Bay, take 80 West and exit at Fremont Street. Make a left at Folsom and a left at the Embarcadero. Howard Street is one block northwest of Folsom.

From the North Bay, take 101 South to Lombard. Make a slight left on Lombard, a left at Van Ness, a right at Bay, and a right at the Embarcadero to Howard.

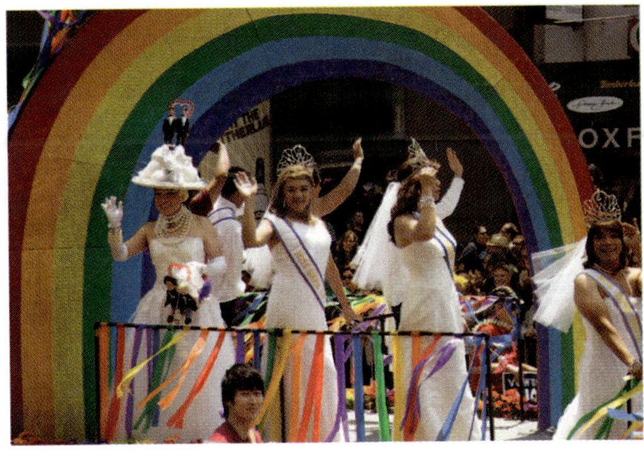

Rainbow float.

ZOOMING AND DEPTH OF FIELD

You might already know that when you use a wide aperture, your depth of field is going to decrease. There are other factors that affect depth of field other than aperture, namely the focal length at which you shoot your picture and the distance between the lens and subject/object (where your set your autofocus point). The longer the focal length of your lens when you shoot, the shorter the depth of field. Shooting at 200mm will give you less depth of field than shooting at 50mm. Last, the farther away your subject is, the greater your depth of field. Shooting with your subject 50 feet away will give you more depth of field in front of and behind your subject than shooting 5 feet away from your subject. The picture of the flags shows you a large depth of field. The picture of the drums shows you a small depth of field.

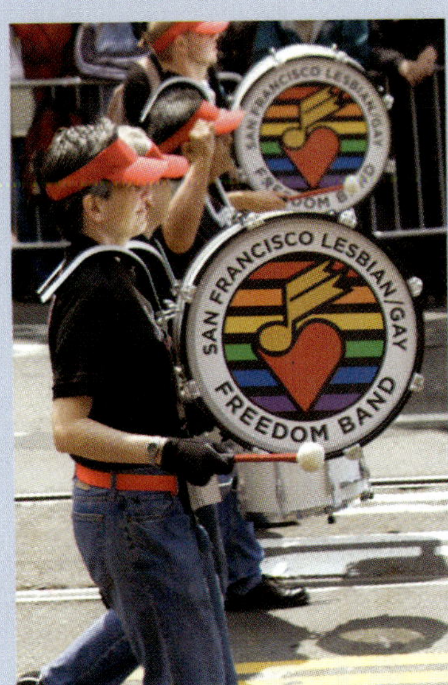

A small depth of field shows only one drum that's sharp.

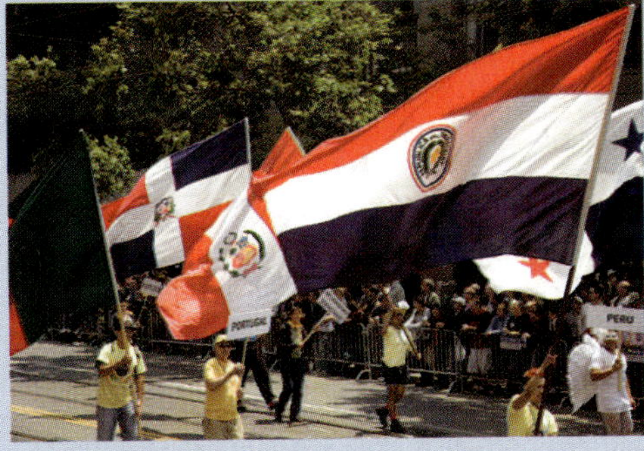

Use a large depth of field to view all flags clearly.

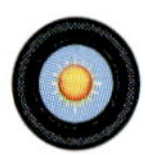 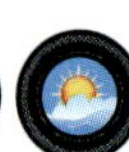 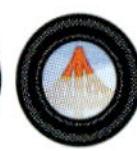

When to shoot: afternoon

Cherry Blossom Festival

The cherry blossom, a longstanding icon in Japan, has been around for a long, long time. It's as important as spring. The *hanami*, or viewing of the flowers, brings family and friends together. San Franciscans of Japanese heritage gather with the rest of the community for *hanami* and a larger celebration—the Northern California Cherry Blossom Festival. The event takes place over two weekends in April. To be sure, there are flower viewings, but there are also tea ceremonies, concerts, Japanese dance recitals, martial arts demonstrations, and a big parade. Streets are closed for the festival in the area of Japan Center in the city's Japantown, around Post and Buchanan Streets. Japantown is one of three such neighborhoods in the United States. It was founded during the year of the great earthquake (1906). Japan Center was built in 1968. Peace Plaza, a sizable square, has a giant five-tiered pagoda that rises in the south part of the plaza near Geary Street. For information about the current year's Cherry Blossom Festival go to www.nccbf.org

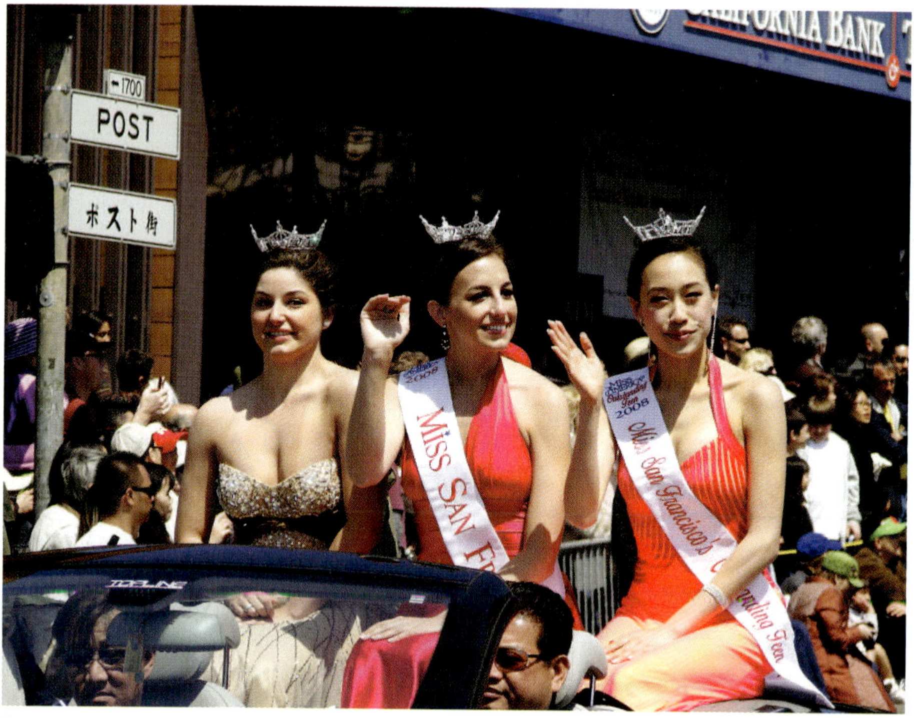

Beauty queens ride in parade.

The Shot

First, the Cherry Blossom Parade on the second weekend of the festival has numerous floats, dancers, musicians, and several beauty queens. It's important to point out that this parade is much easier to access than the Gay Pride Parade. You'll get the most action on Post Street at the end of Buchanan Street, across the street from Soko Hardware. This is on the northern edge of Peace Plaza, the plaza where the Peace Pagoda is located. In this shot, I emphasize a float that warranted some focus because of the great off-white background of the drum behind the subjects. Also significant in the frame is the subject placement. The man and woman are about one-third from the left side of the frame, following the Rule of Thirds. They also wear kimonos, one red and one blue, which contrast each other and match the neutral color black of the drum. Texture, shape, and form play roles in making this photograph compelling. The blue metallic decorative confetti in the background and the rope on the drum have very different surfaces—the confetti is smooth, and the rope is rough. The circular shape of the drum's face and the diagonal lines of rope on its body offer added dimension to the frame. The face sits on a two-dimensional frame, and the body extends inward into the frame.

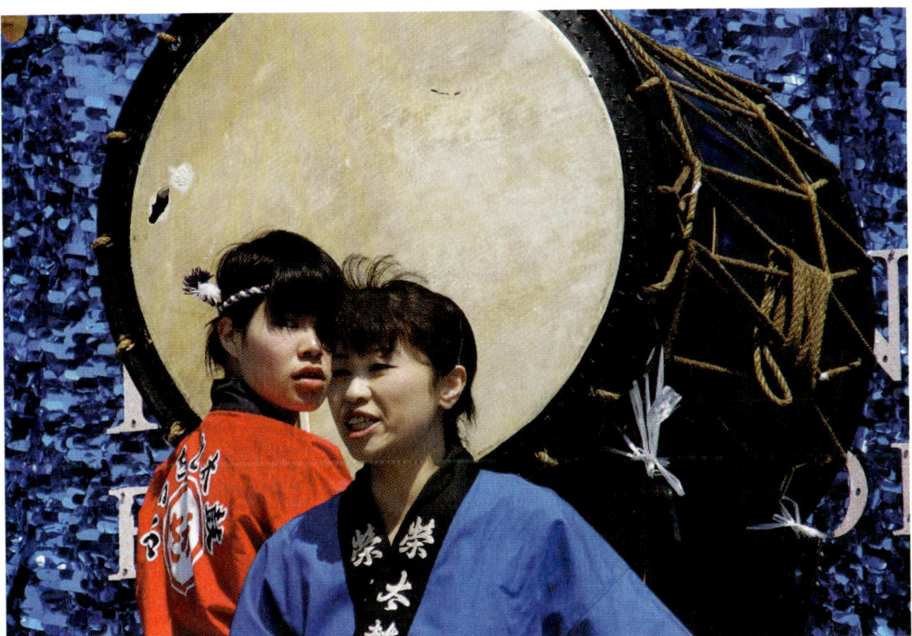

Focal length 200mm; ISO 100; aperture f/4; shutter speed 1/1000; April 1:03 p.m.

The Shot

This photo shows an unusual act of a man twirling a box on an umbrella in the foreground with a crowd in the background. There's lots of narrative in this shot of umbrella and umbrella twirler. First is the obvious: He's attracting quite a crowd. That's because he is balancing a sizable wooden cube on an umbrella made of paper, hence the expression of concentration and the upward tilt to his head. Second is the framing: The man, the umbrella, and the box create a curve that sweeps upward throughout the frame. Last is the color of the three objects: All offer good contrast to the color of the people and the sky in the background.

Whatever one may think, the symbolism here is more than meets the eye. First, these umbrellas are more appropriately described as paper parasols. The use of them in Japanese art is widespread. The mere fact that one is used in this photograph makes it a kind of Japanese-inspired work of art. Second, these parasols are fragile, with thin wooden sticks holding them together. The fact that this man is balancing an object with sharp corners on the top of it explains why he looks so involved in his twirling. Add these elements together, and you've got one interesting photograph.

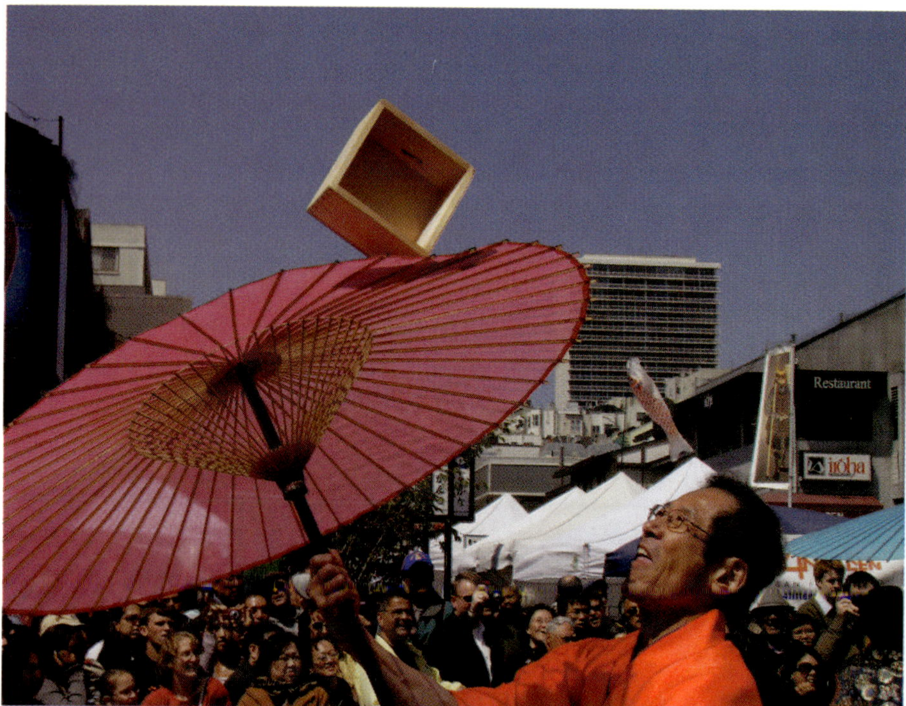

Focal length 180mm; ISO 100; aperture f/4; shutter speed 1/1000; April 1:12 p.m.

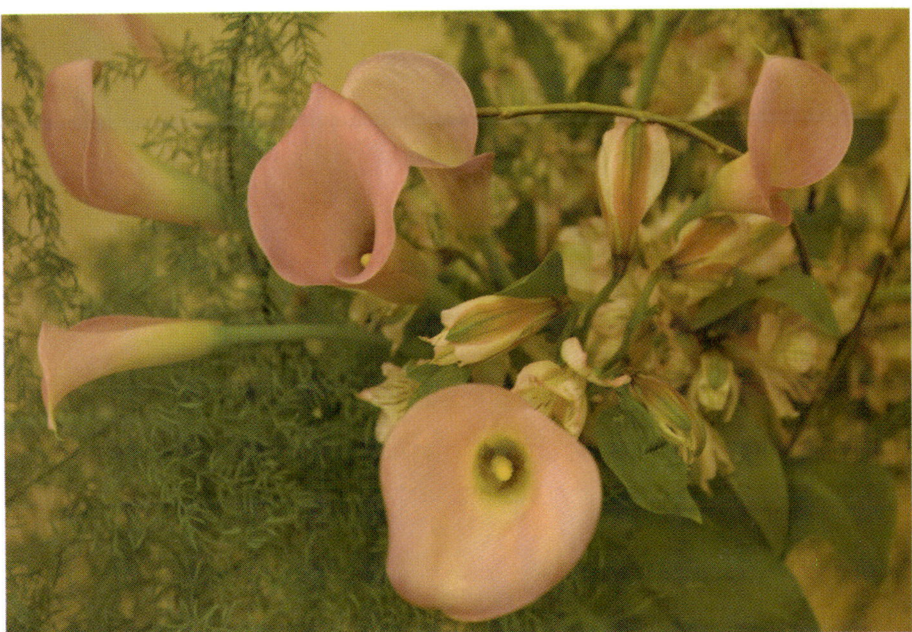

Flowers from the indoor flower show look like a painting.

Getting There

On the first weekend, the events take place at Japan Center, which is between Post and Geary Streets and Laguna and Webster. Buchanan ends as a pedestrian alley at Sutter Street, one block north of Post Street, and continues as an alley all the way though Peace Plaza to Geary Street. On the second weekend, the parade begins at the Civic Center at 1:00 p.m. It winds north up Polk, then west on Post Street.

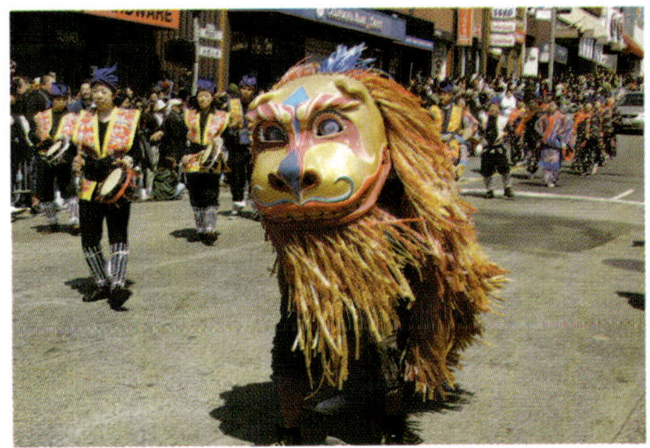

Masked character at parade.

To get there using mass transit, take the 2 Clement bus from Market and Drum Streets downtown to Sutter and Buchanan, then walk one block south down the Buchanan pedestrian walkway to Peace Plaza.

If you're driving to Peace Plaza from the South Bay, take 101 North via the ramp to SF. Continue on Octavia and make a left at Fell, a right at Fillmore, and a right at Post.

From the East Bay, take 80 West. Exit at Central Fry/101 North toward GG Bridge. Continue on Octavia and make a left on Fell, a right on Fillmore, and a right on Post.

From the North Bay, take 101 South to Lombard. Make a slight left on Lombard, a right on Fillmore, and a left on Post.

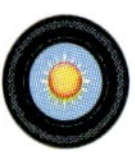 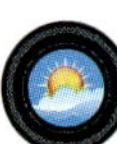 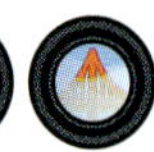

When to shoot: afternoon

Critical Mass

Critical Mass is a bike ride that started in San Francisco in 1992. The bike ride is an effort to raise awareness of bicyclists' rights to the road and to remind people of the advantages bicycles have in reducing emissions, urban sprawl, and congestion. There are now Critical Mass bike rides all over the world. In many United States' cities, police and citizens have not tolerated the overflow of bicycles on the roadways, which has caused bicyclists to get in trouble with the law. However, the city of San Francisco has always tolerated the event so that police and motorists do not harass bicyclists. The event offers photographers great opportunities for panning shots. (See the upcoming sidebar entitled "A Perfect Time to Pan.") In most cities, including San Francisco, the event takes place on the last Friday of each month. The bicyclists meet at a specified time and place, but no one knows the route until they get to the starting point.

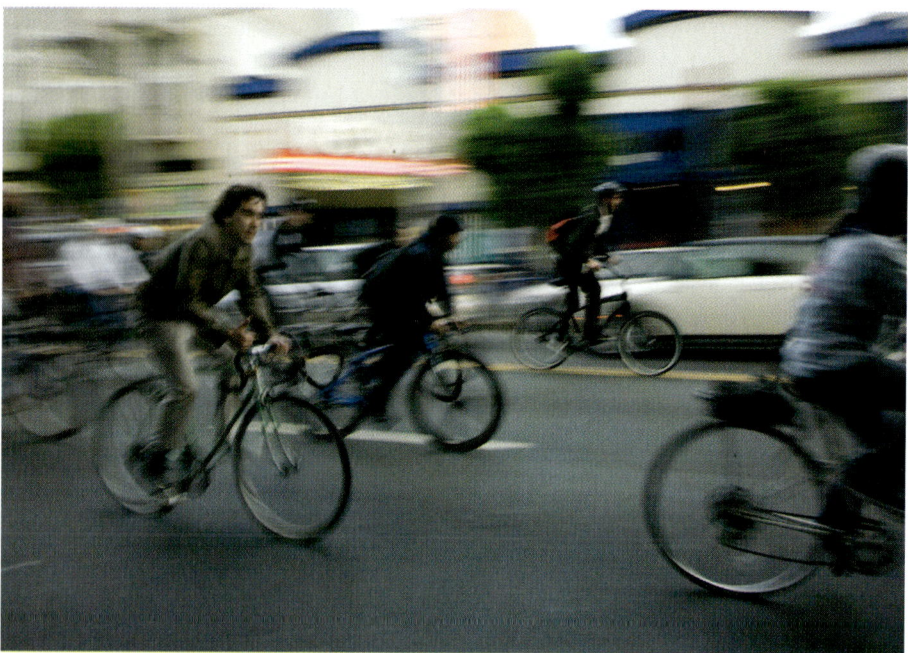

Panned shot with face of bicyclist coming into focus.

The Shot

This shot was taken as the bicyclists passed the Roxie Theater on 16th Street, a few miles southwest of the starting point of the ride. Because rides are spontaneous, no one knows the route until the day of the ride. I caught these bicyclists on a Friday evening in late June. Since the street was shaded because it was late in the day, I used a high ISO. This is one of a series of panned shots I took. The bicyclist in the foreground, two bicyclists in the middle ground, and cars and buildings in the background help to enhance the depth in the photo. The sharpness of the orange and blue horizontal-striped shirt of the bicyclist in the middle ground draws the eye into the scene. I panned by following the bicyclist in the foreground. She is sharp because I was able to keep the auto-focus point on the same place in the middle of her body throughout the time the shutter was open. Also, helping to maintain the sharpness of the figure is the fact she was moving on a horizontal trajectory. The background is very blurred because of the movement of the camera. It causes the viewer to see the bicyclists as if they are moving in the frame. I was able to achieve some clarity in the background because I used a narrow aperture.

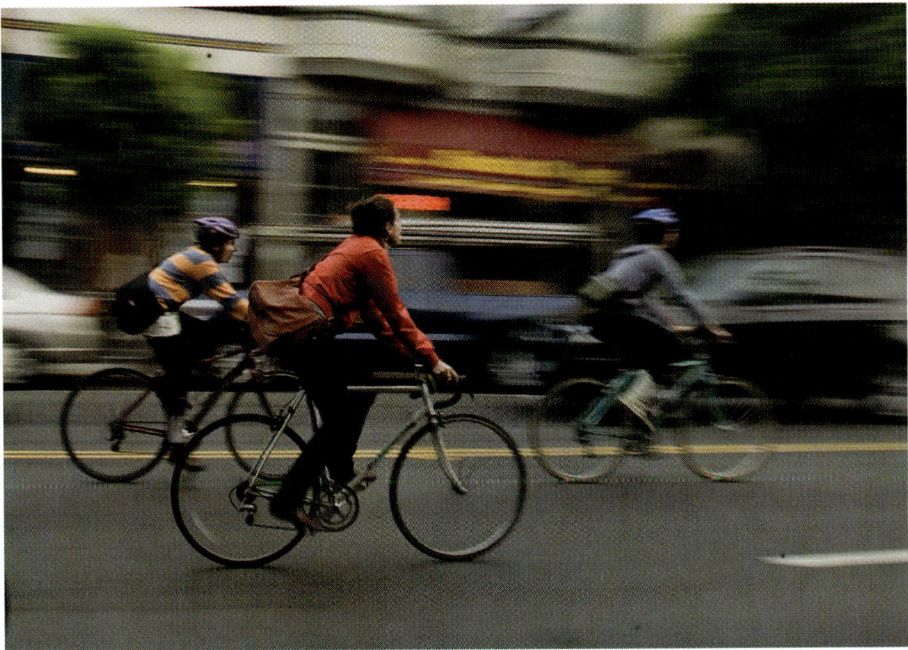

Focal length 24mm; ISO 1000; aperture f/22; shutter speed 1/25; June 6:38 p.m.

A PERFECT TIME TO PAN

Many things can happen when you leave your shutter open. People move or traffic flows, leaving trails if you leave your shutter open long enough. In this image of the Golden Gate Bridge toll plaza, I left the shutter open for four seconds, long enough to blur headlights and taillights over the course of the entire frame in some spots.

There's another way to use blur to show movement. You can blur the background in a shot while keeping your subject sharp to create the illusion of movement by panning your camera while you follow the moving subject when the shutter is open. The first thing you have to remember when using this technique is that you're creating the illusion of the subject, which is still in the frame, as moving by blurring the background. If you use a tripod, the subject is more likely to appear sharper because you won't get any additional blur around it from camera shake. The first image of the three bicyclers riding as part of Critical Mass shows the sharp subject and blurred background resulting from the panning described above. If your subject is severely blurred with the background after you pan, you probably want to try panning over and over again until you get the subject relatively sharp.

To blur the background, first get on the side of the road so that you can pan from left to right as the bicyclists move down the road. Then, set your camera on a tripod with the lens pointing at the passing subjects. Manually set the shutter speed on your camera to 1/20 to 1/30 in Tv mode, the mode that lets you set the shutter speed while your camera sets the f/stop. When you see the bicyclists on the left getting closer, pick one of them to set your focus point on. Press your shutter all the way down and follow the bicyclist, keeping the focus point on him as you move your camera from left to right. All this happens quickly, so you'll have to move your camera quickly and then repeat over and over again as more bicyclists pass by.

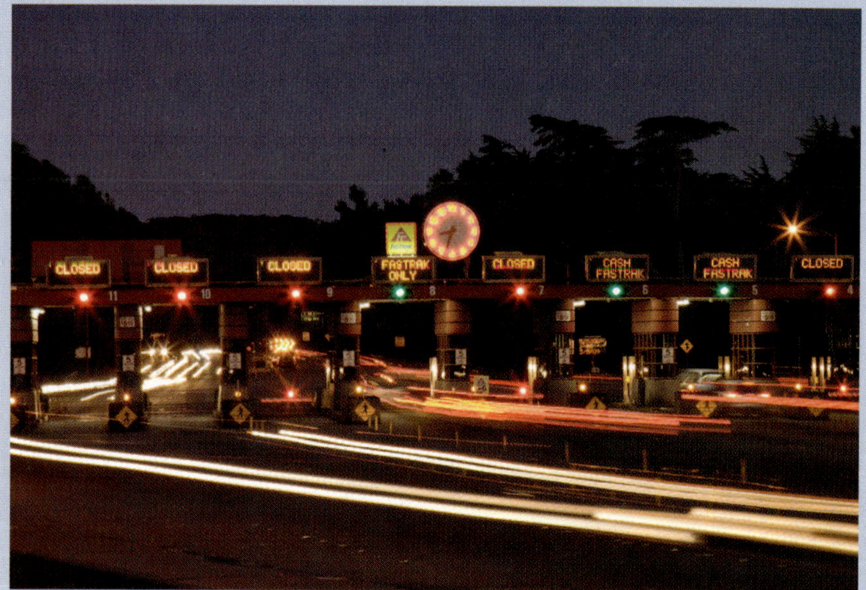

Vehicle trails at Golden Gate Bridge toll plaza.

The Shot

This is a shot that gives you a look at the bikes and riders. I shot at a narrower aperture so I could get all of the bikes in the shot as sharp as possible. I used the Rule of Thirds to frame the shot. The road and bicycles take up the lower two-thirds of the frame, and the buildings take up the upper third. I tried to get the movie theater in the background to give the shot some added character. Finally, I shot facing down the road so that you can see the bicyclists coming up it.

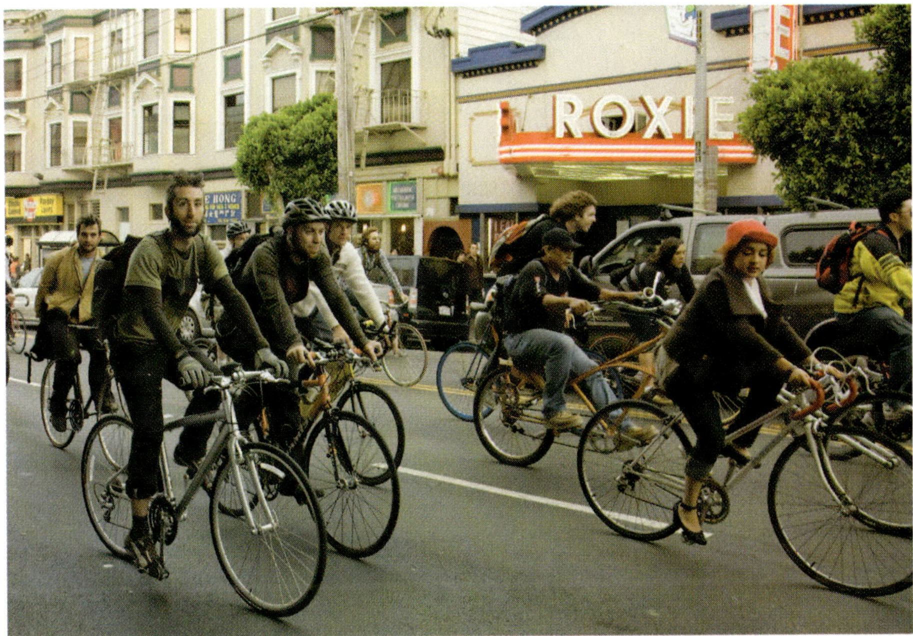

Focal length 36mm; ISO 800; aperture f/7.1; shutter speed 1/400; June 6:16 p.m.

Getting There

The bike riders meet at 5:30 p.m. at Justin Herman Plaza, between Embarcadero BART and the Ferry Building. The route they take is different every time they meet.

To get there using mass transit, Justin Herman Plaza is across the street from the Ferry Building. The plaza runs into the Embarcadero BART and Muni station. The Embarcadero station is the last downtown stop and is accessible to trains that come and go to various points in the city, including the K, L, M, N, and J trains that travel underground. The F train (vintage streetcars) stops directly in front of the Ferry Building. Buses on the ground go all over the city.

If you're driving, Justin Herman Plaza is just west of the Embarcadero. From the South Bay, take 101 North to 280 North. Exit at King Street, which turns into the Embarcadero.

From the East Bay, take 80 West and exit at Fremont Street. Turn left at Folsom and left at the Embarcadero.

From the North Bay, take 101 South to Lombard. Make a slight left on Lombard, a left at Van Ness, a right at Bay, and a right at the Embarcadero. Make a U-turn at Howard Street because you'll overshoot the Ferry Building by a couple of blocks.

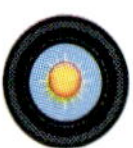 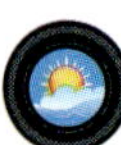 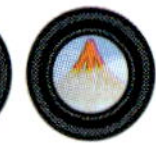

When to shoot: morning, afternoon

Farmers Market

Visit the San Francisco Farmers Market on a Saturday, and you'll find more than a dozen artists selling their wares in front of the Ferry Building and all kinds of food vendors in the back. It's also packed inside the Ferry Building, where everything from fresh-baked bread to exotic mushrooms is sold. On Tuesday, the market's a bit smaller. Officially, the market is called the Ferry Plaza Farmers Market. It's run by the Center for Urban Education about Sustainable Agriculture. The market opened in 1992 as a special one-time event—an event that was so successful that it was opened on a regular basis year-round. At the market is bustling activity among dramatic views of downtown high rises. On Saturday, some of the artists work on their pieces while they are running their booths. Also, don't miss the photographers who display their shots of San Francisco. You can never learn enough about shooting in the city, and you'll probably find shots where you learn a new technique or two. For more information go to www.ferrybuildingmarketplace.com.

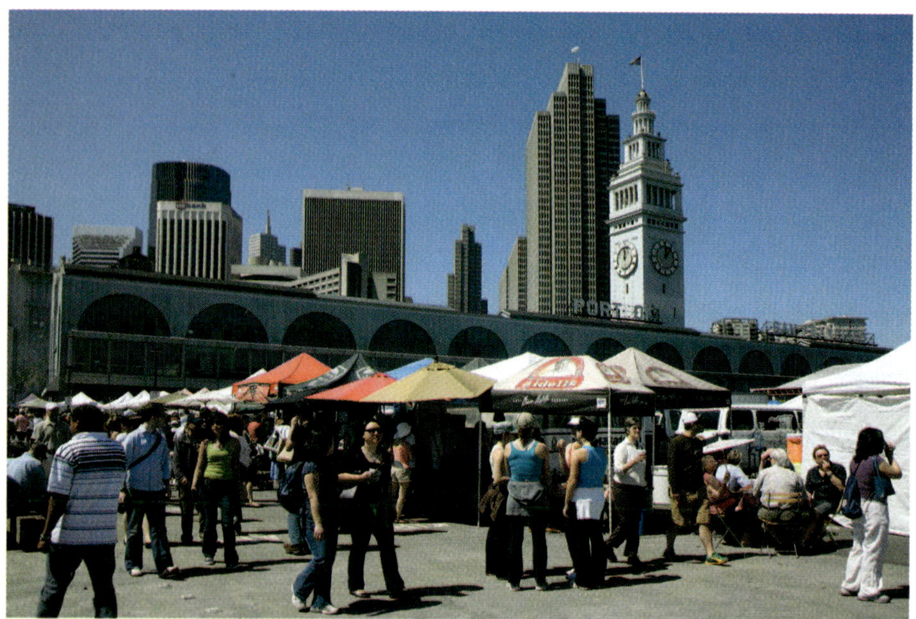

Farmers Market behind the Ferry Building, looking northwest.

The Shot

One of the great things about coming to the Farmers Market at the Ferry Building is that there are great views everywhere you look. This is a shot that shows the setting of the Farmers Market with western views of downtown. Tents are put up to house the artists in this part of the market. Because I wanted the entire shot sharp, I used a small aperture (f/13). The composition doesn't follow the Rule of Thirds vertically, with one third of the buildings on one side of the frame and two thirds on the other side. Instead, there's a dividing line at mid-frame (Market Street) that balances the skyscrapers on the right with those on the left. When shots are symmetrical or almost symmetrical, like this one was, it works to set the dividing line in the middle of the frame. There is a distinction between the two sides, though. The high rises in the left side of the frame are much older than those on the right, which is an interesting aspect of how the city was built. Finally, if you look at the detail in the foreground, you'll find that they also sell clothes at the Farmers Market.

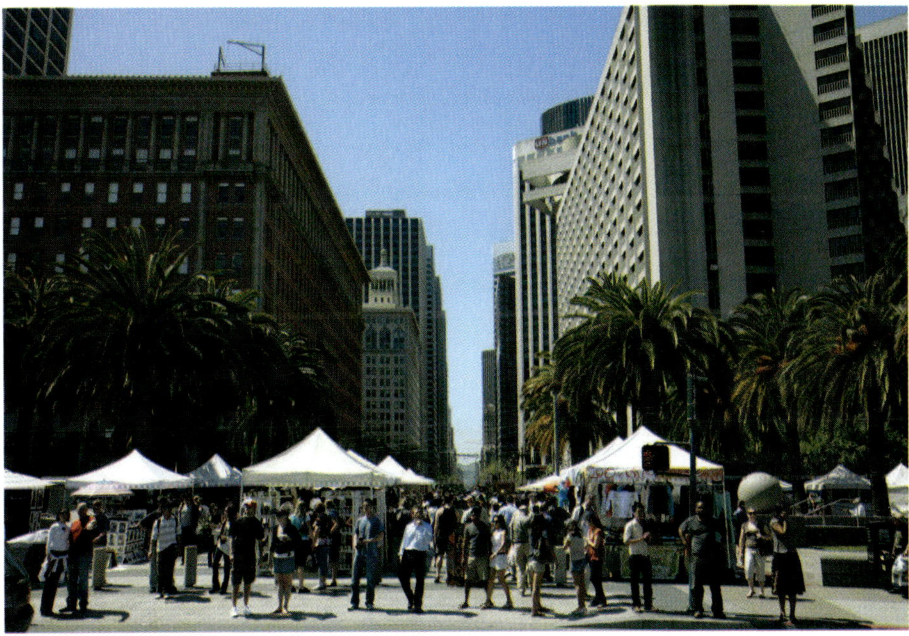

Focal length 32mm; ISO 400; aperture f/13; shutter speed 1/320; May 11:21 a.m.

The Shot

To get this shot, I had to take a few from different angles. I chose this one from the set because it clearly shows the work of the artist. What's even more interesting is that it shows in detail the tools with which he works. It's as if you're standing directly over him watching the work he is doing. Since there wasn't much use of the zoom (the shot was taken at 36mm), there's not much background blur, even though the aperture was open fairly wide. Part of the fun of this shot was watching the painter work and getting to talk to him after he signed the release.

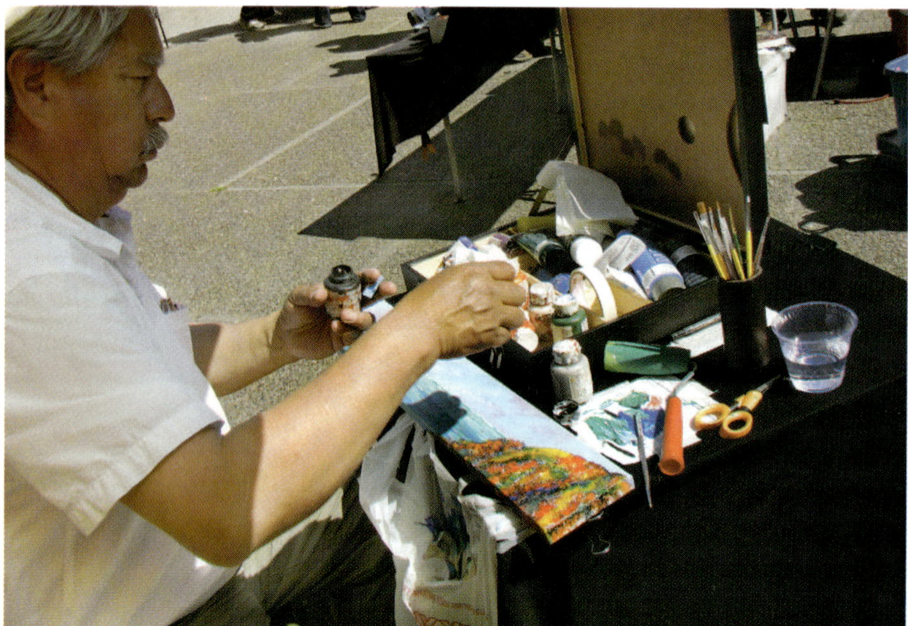

Focal length 36mm; ISO 100; aperture f/5.6; shutter speed 1/500; May 12:03 p.m.

SAN FRANCISCO EVENTS THROUGHOUT THE YEAR

Most weekends San Francisco has some sort of event, festival, or parade. On weekdays, too, there are things going on that warrant a camera. From protest marches to visiting dignitaries, the city is filled with spontaneous gatherings. However, there are events that happen on a regular basis. Some major events and their websites are:

- Chinese New Year Festival and Parade in January: www.chineseparade.com
- St. Patrick's Day Parade in March: www.sfstpatricksdayparade.com
- Carnaval San Francisco in May: www.carnavalsf.com
- Shakespeare in the Park in September: www.sfshakes.org
- LoveFest and Parade in October: www.sflovefest.org
- The Great Dickens Christmas Fair in December: www.dickensfair.com
- San Francisco Mime Troupe Show throughout the year: www.sfmt.org

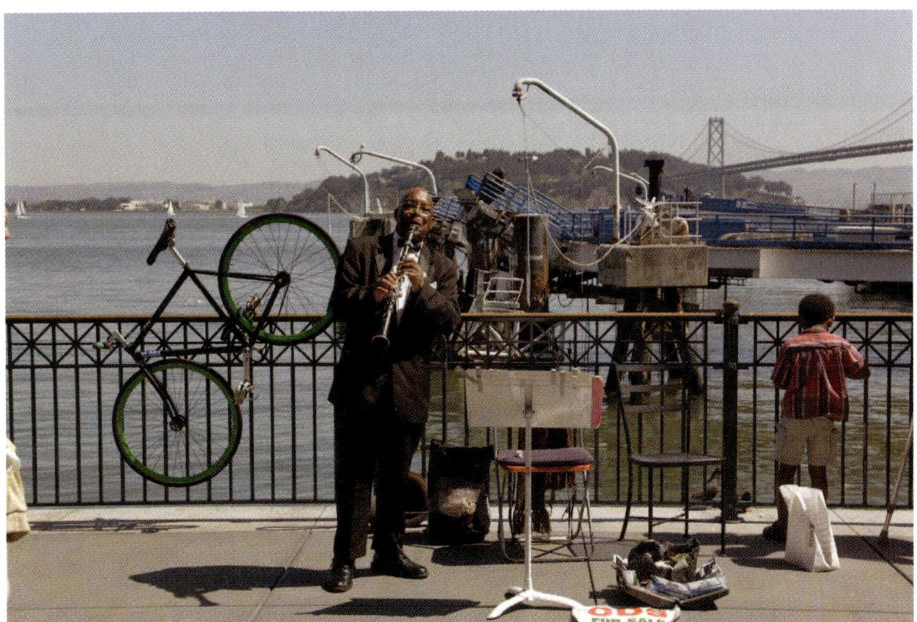

Musician playing behind the Ferry Building, looking east.

Getting There

The Farmers Market takes place across the street from the Ferry Building, in front of the Ferry Building, in the Ferry Building, and behind it.

To get there using mass transit, the Embarcadero BART and Muni station is just outside the area where the market takes place. The Embarcadero station is the last downtown stop and is accessible to trains that come from and go to various points in the city, including the K, L, M, N, and J trains that travel underground. The F train (vintage streetcars) stops directly in front of the Ferry Building. Buses on the ground go all over the city.

If you're driving from the South Bay, take 101 North to 280 North. Exit at King Street, which turns into the Embarcadero.

From the East Bay, take 80 West and exit at Fremont St. Make a left at Folsom and a left at the Embarcadero.

From the North Bay, take 101 South to Lombard. Make a slight left on Lombard, a left at Van Ness, a right at Bay, and a right at the Embarcadero. Make a U-turn at Howard Street because you'll overshoot the Ferry Building by a couple of blocks.

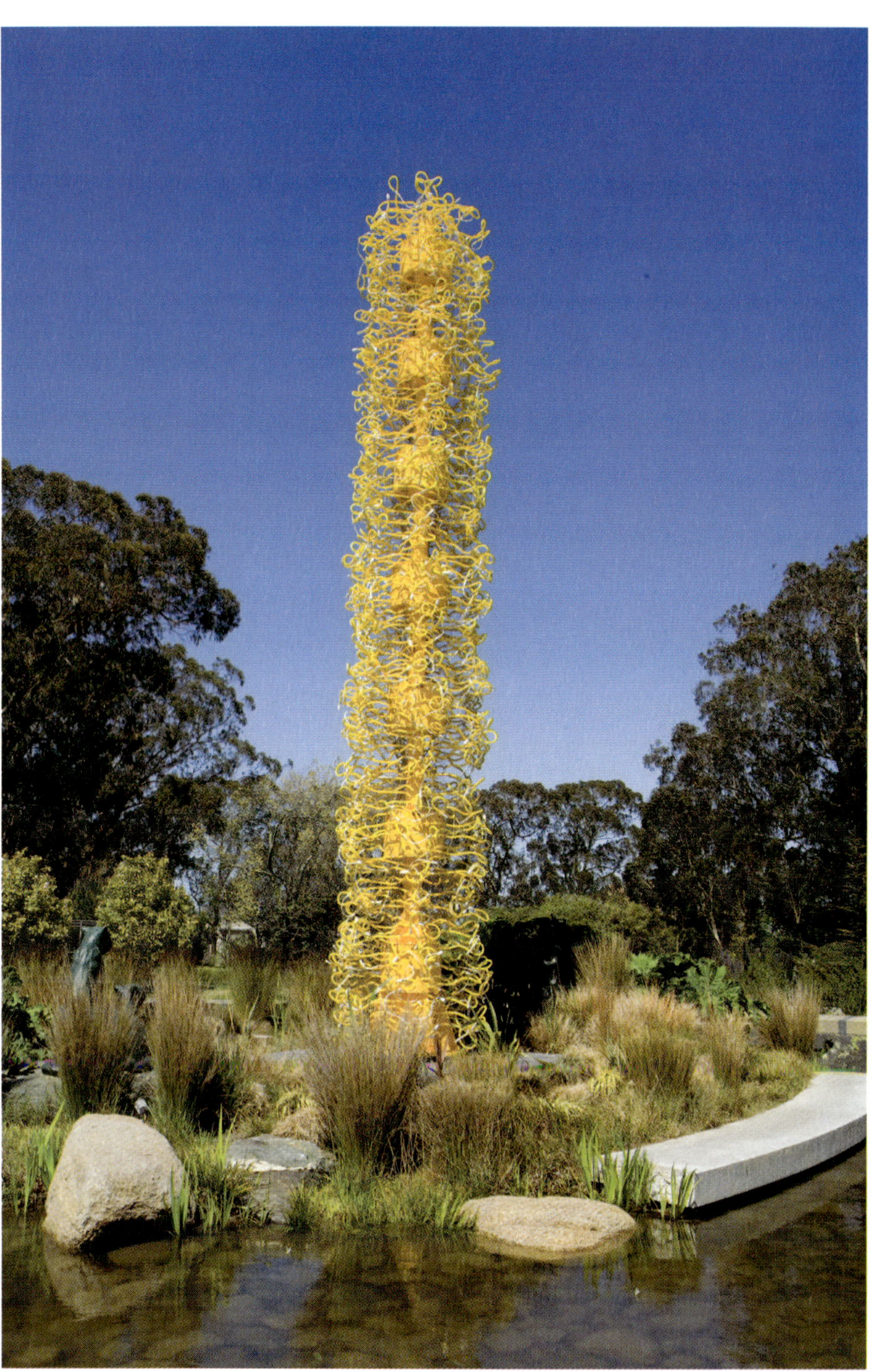

Thirty-foot "Saffron Tower" in the Pool of Enchantment on the east side of the de Young Museum in Golden Gate Park.

Chapter 4

Urban Oasis

No big city in the world has as rustic of an environment as that found in San Francisco. If you consider the wide range of choices you have for photographing the great outdoors, San Francisco seems to have it all: beaches, gardens, lakes, wetlands, and vast great escapes that have you thinking there's no city nearby for hundreds of miles. For the photographer, opportunities abound to experiment with many of your camera's settings to obtain vibrant, sharp images that fit your definition of the city's great outdoors.

Shooting Like a Pro

With miles of beaches, rocky shorelines, and coastal marshes, taking pictures of unobstructed landscapes is fairly easy in San Francisco. There are also nooks and crannies—city parks and gardens—in the city where people getting fresh air and relaxation can be made into inviting themes for your photos, such as this shot of Woh Hei Yuen Park tucked into Chinatown.

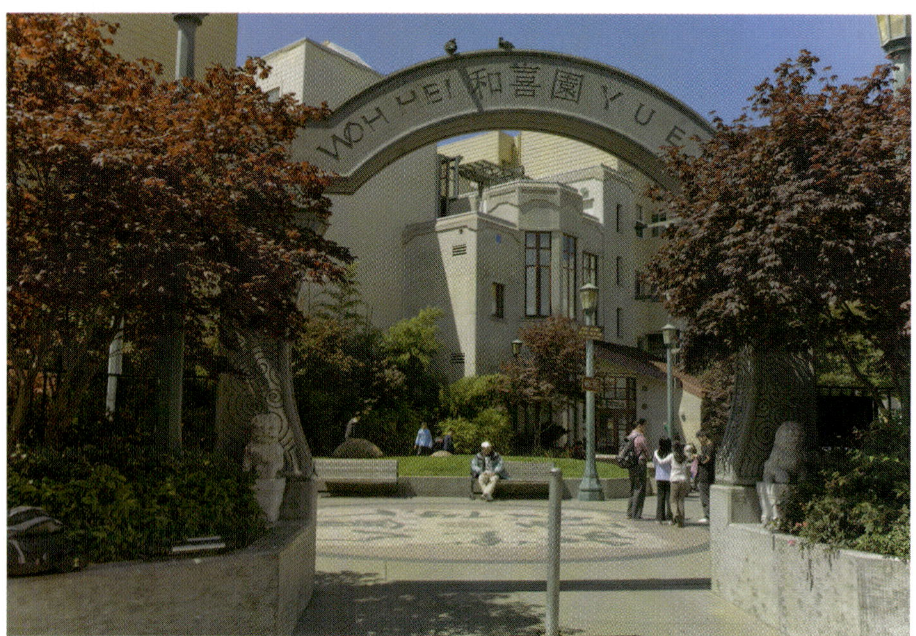

Woh Hei Yuen Park in Chinatown.

While beautiful landscapes are easy to come by, shooting them so that they are vibrant and interesting takes some technical knowledge and some creativity. You may know well-tested techniques of the great landscape photographers, the first being to shoot with a narrow aperture so that there is a deep depth of field (see the "Photographing San Francisco Landscapes" sidebar at the end of this chapter). But you can also restrict areas of sharp focus to a specific location in the frame. The viewer's attention is naturally drawn to a sharp, well-defined area of a landscape within an out-of-focus frame. Placing the subject (or area within the landscape) in sharp focus separates it visually from elements in the frame that could otherwise be a distraction. In the shot of seagulls at Lake Merced, only the birds that are flying are in sharp focus. The viewer may begin by looking at the dock in the foreground, but the eye is quickly drawn up through the frame, emulating the flight path of the departing birds.

Another thing you can do with landscapes is to add objects, such as trees or gates, to the edges of your image to frame it. This view looking south from Corona Heights is framed by the trees close to where I took the shot.

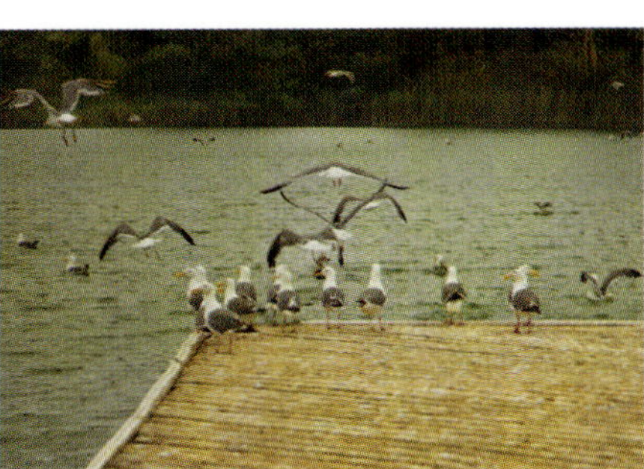

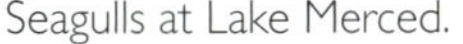

Seagulls at Lake Merced.

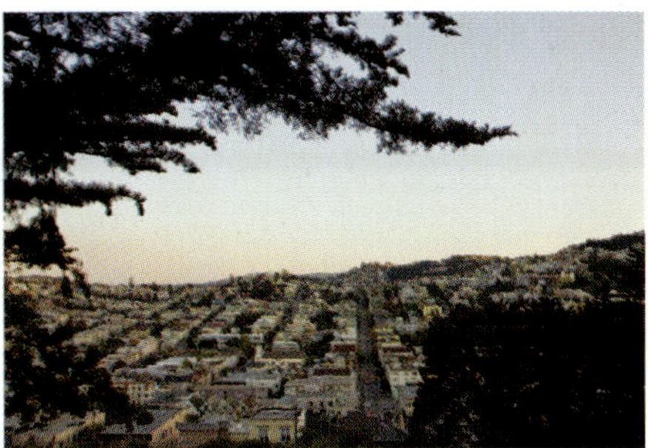

View looking south from Corona Heights.

The range of shots you can find in the urban outdoors of San Francisco can range from the small and detailed (such as a shot of California poppies) to the vast and far-reaching. One option you have in San Francisco is to find those areas that look untouched by humans. You can find these along trails and on the shoreline. The view from a cliff that sinks down hundreds of feet to the beach at Fort Funston shows a changing terrain as you move from the bottom to the top of the frame—fascinating changes of texture that the viewer can almost feel as he moves through them.

If by chance you don't have a tripod or you are not inclined to use one, you'll have to work with wide apertures on foggy days so that only part of your photo will be in focus. If you shoot with narrow apertures in these conditions, it requires slow shutter speeds, which will induce camera shake, ruining your photo.

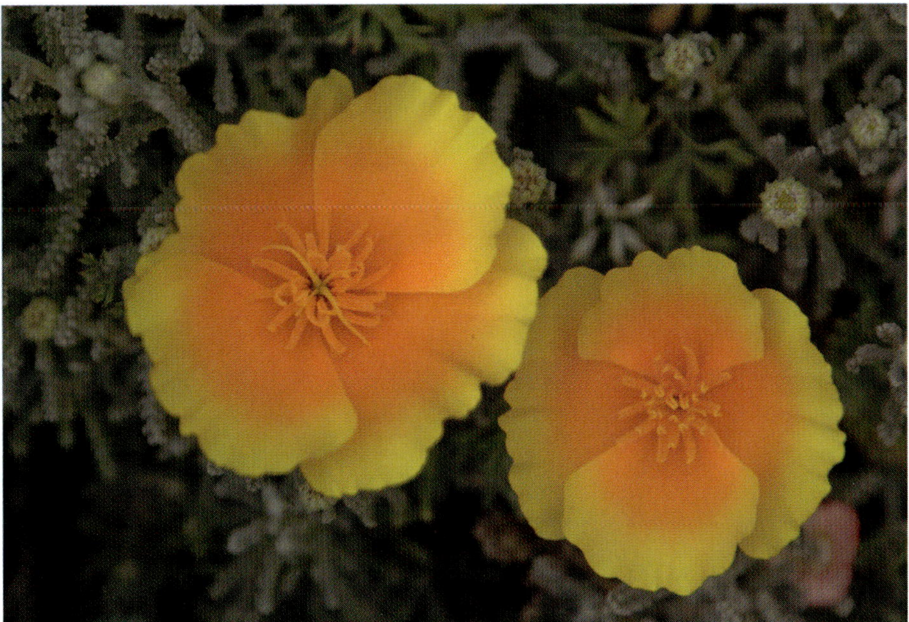

California poppies.

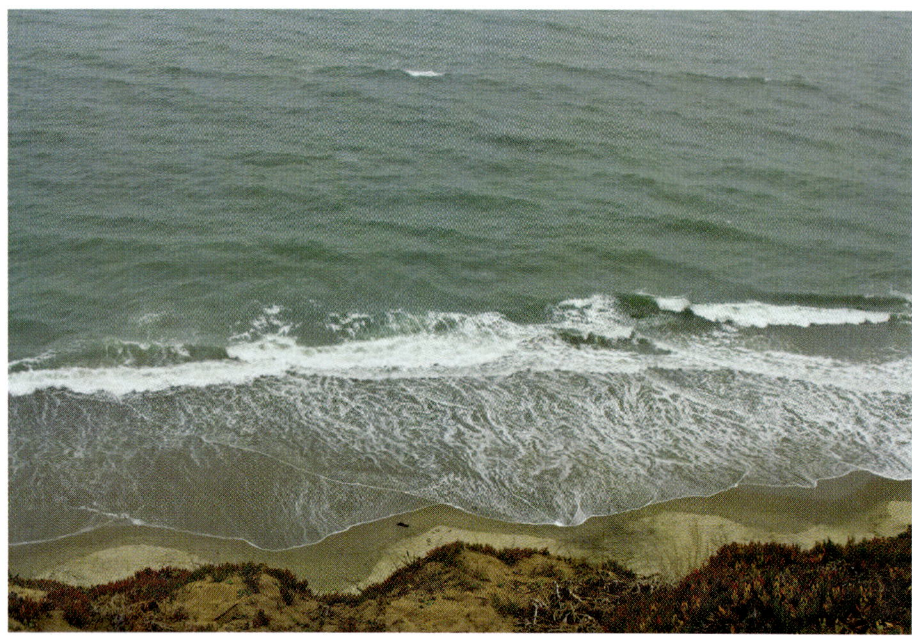

Beach at Fort Funston.

The Gear

A tripod is essential for shots like the one of Yerba Buena Gardens, so you can turn water to silky sheets in manmade waterfalls. Consider taking along a flashlight; many photo ops are best shot at dusk, and since some are quite far out, where there are no city lights, you might need extra light to guide you on the trails as night approaches. Macro modes (including the ones that come with a general-purpose telephoto lens on dSLR cameras and the ones that come with point-and-shoot cameras) are almost comparable to traditional macro lenses. You can use macro mode or a macro lens to catch the details like those shown in the picture of the California poppies. You can also use a telephoto lens to capture part of a landscape, focusing on interesting elements in the scene, or to capture wildlife, such as a squirrel in Golden Gate Park or the giraffe at the San Francisco Zoo. Last, a wide-angle lens, such as a 17-40 mm f/4 lens, is good to have to capture the coastal landscapes.

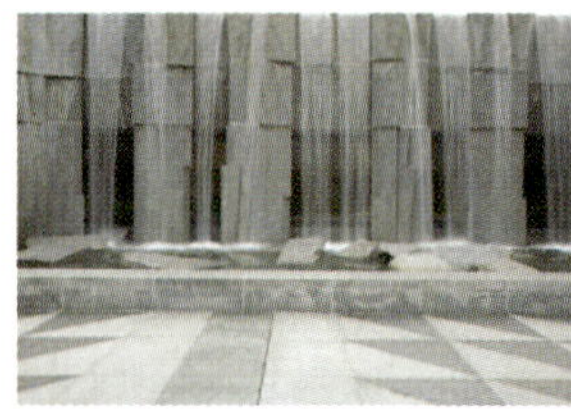

Waterfall of Yerba Buena Gardens.

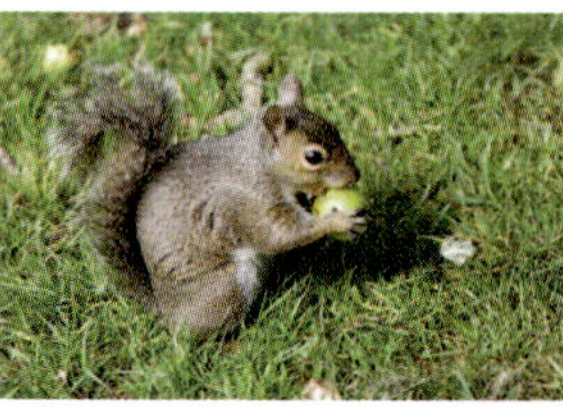

Squirrel in Golden Gate Park.

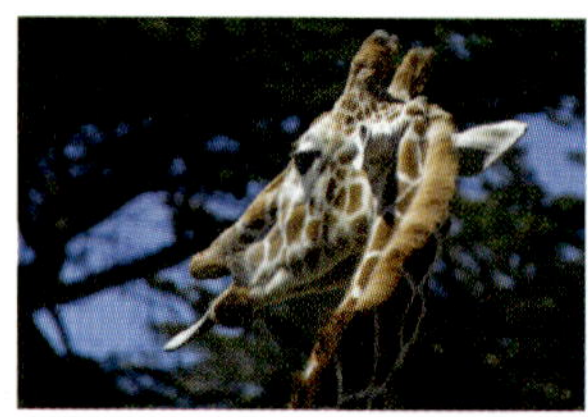

Giraffe at the San Francisco Zoo.

The Plan

Any outing to the best photo spots of the city outdoors requires at least a couple of hours. If you have limited time, a car is the best way to catch a good variety of shots from Ocean Beach to Baker Beach on one day, and Golden Gate Park on another. This trek is best on late fall or winter days when there is no fog or rain. There are some spring and summer days, though, that are clear and warm or the fog breaks up for a couple of hours in the afternoon.

Sunny areas of the city, such as those to the west of Fisherman's Wharf, are also filled with photo ops of beaches by the bay. If you're shooting landscapes during the day, use an ISO of around 200. The same ISO speed can be used at night if you're using a tripod. You'll get a cleaner image with less noise.

Finally, for each landscape, bracket your exposures by changing f/stops and/or shutter speeds (shutter speeds if they're taken at night). Bracketing can be used as a creative tool and also as a tool for choosing the sharpest image. Once you've settled on a composition, don't be afraid to experiment. Take a series of shots at varying apertures and shutter speeds. By changing the aperture, you determine how far the area of sharp focus will extend from the point on which you focused the lens. You also have to be on guard for lens diffraction (more bending of the light waves at narrow apertures), which can cause softness in pictures taken at narrow apertures (see the "Photographing San Francisco Landscapes" sidebar). If moving objects are in the frame, changing the shutter speed will determine whether they are frozen in motion or appear as a blur passing through the image. If you have shadows in the frame, be careful not to underexpose them, as dark areas in a photograph are susceptible to noise, or tiny multicolored dots in darker areas of the frame.

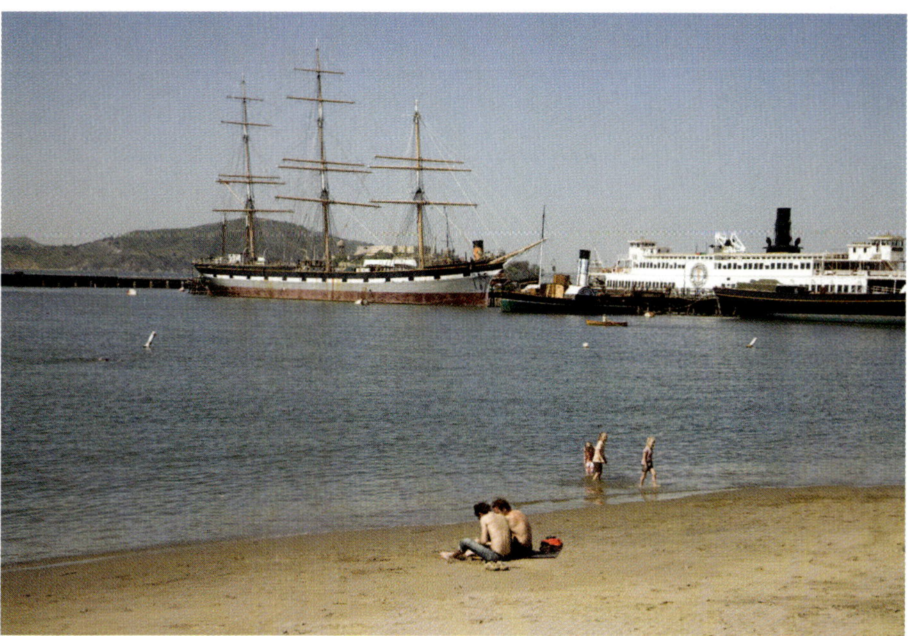

Beach near Fisherman's Wharf.

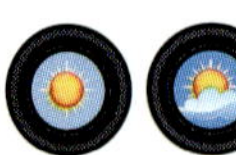
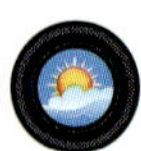

When to shoot: morning, afternoon

Botanical Garden at Strybing Arboretum

During the 1860s, San Francisco civic leaders imagined a great park and arboretum in the western part of the city. At the time, the area was made up of fog-enshrouded sand dunes. After gardeners planted some 60,000 trees to temper the west wind that blew over the area, planning of the arboretum began. John McLaren, superintendent of Golden Gate Park, led the effort. In the 1920s, Helene Strybing left sufficient funds in her will to establish the garden. In the 1930s, McLaren and a gardener, Eric Walther, planned out an area in Golden Gate Park that would include plants from all over the world. The garden opened in 1940.

In 2004, the Strybing Arboretum became the San Francisco Botanical Garden. Today, people use both names or a combination of the two to refer to a 55-acre area of Golden Gate Park. The garden is free to the public and open weekdays from 8:00 a.m. to 5:30 p.m. and weekends/holidays from 10:00 a.m. to 5:00 p.m.

The Arboretum is best photographed during winter because the sun sets while the Arboretum is still open, so you have the subtle light of dusk to work with. However, that doesn't mean you can't get good photographs in spring and summer. Fog occurs frequently during those times of year and usually lifts by late afternoon. When it starts to burn off, white willows sketch a deep blue sky.

The Shot

If you walk about a tenth of a mile along the path from the main gate (west-northwest), you'll find the Library Terrace Garden, a patio area with several wooden benches and a fountain. If you look above and below the fountain before you take a shot of it, you'll find that the intensity of the reflected light on the water varies considerably. When you're looking at the fountain, preparing to take a picture of it, you can assess the light reflecting from the fountain water by stooping down slowly to different levels to see the various reflections you get. There will be a point where you get a maximum reflection, and that will be the point from which you shoot. I picked up a silvery reflection from the water just about three inches above the horizontal plane upon which the water surface lies. At that point I wanted to take a picture. I then set my camera to a wide aperture in Av mode because I wanted the foreground of water and rock in the right side of the frame sharp and the background of curved rock formation within the wall softened. The overall effect of the photograph gives the viewer a sense of "wet," still water in front of peaceful rocks, a kind of contrast of feeling and texture.

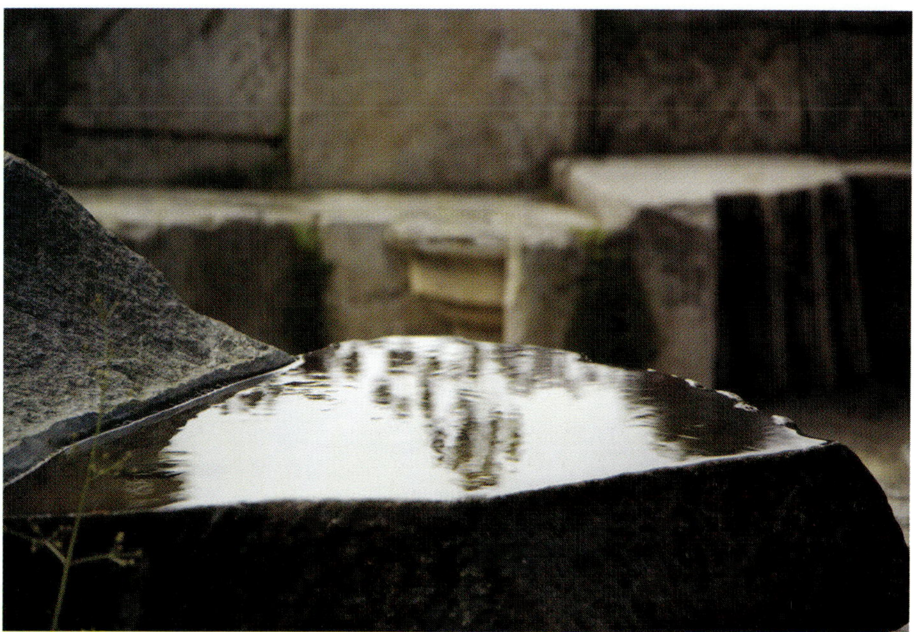

Focal length 105mm; ISO 200; aperture f/4; shutter speed 1/800; May 3:40 p.m.

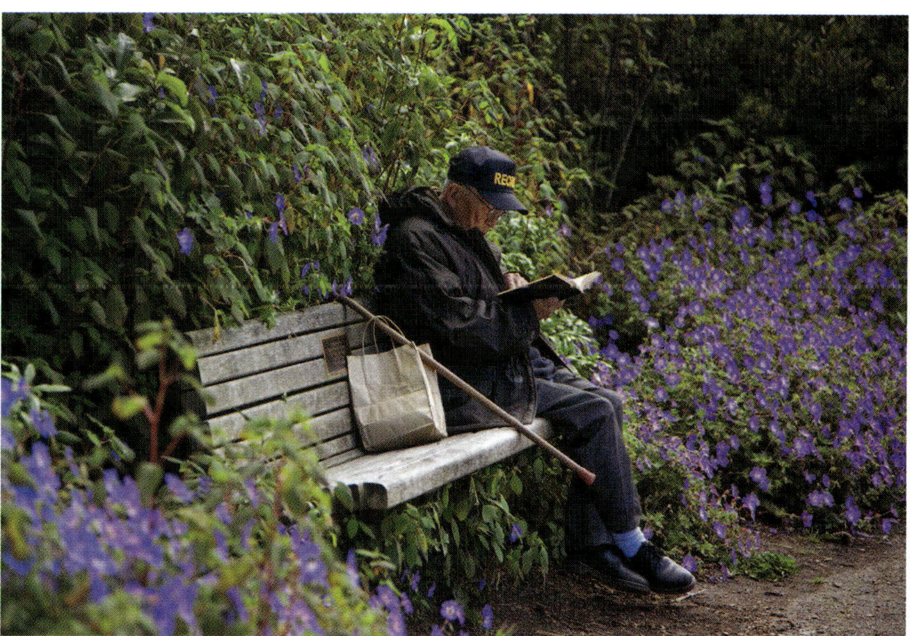

A man reads in the garden.

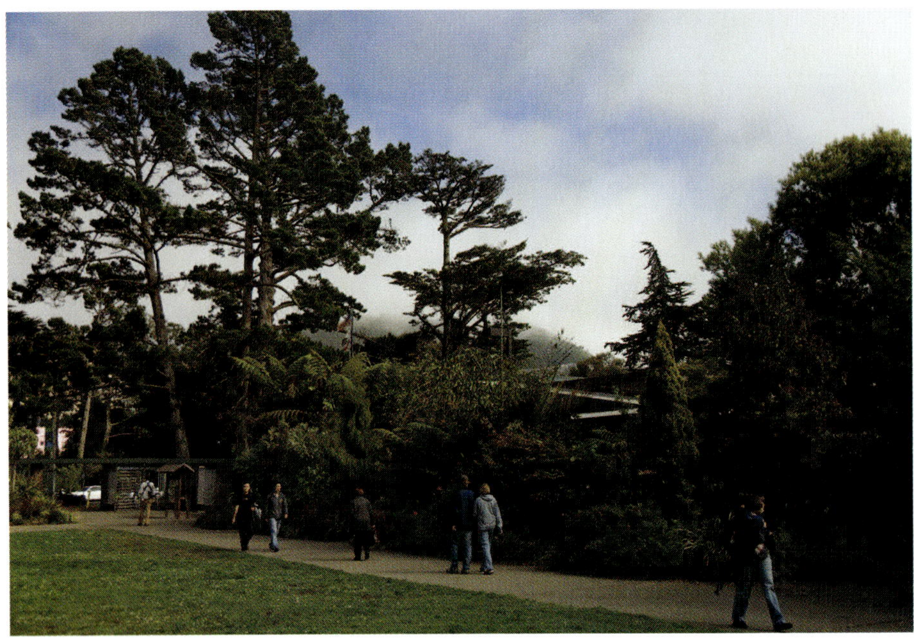

Walkway to the garden.

The Shot

The grounds of the botanical gardens are divided into regions of the world. When you walk along the main path from the entrance gate, you'll pass the entry gardens. Continue walking northwest, and you'll get to the Great Meadow, an area where people have picnics. Just before you get to it, there's a small path that winds southeast to southwest from the Great Meadow. This is the East Asia area—the area where you will find bamboo.

San Francisco's climate is a perfect match for growing bamboo. Plant most varieties, and they'll take over any space not occupied by other plants in a few weeks. The bamboo in the park grows in tight patches that contain dozens of almost-vertical stems that are smooth to the touch and that are marked with rings at almost regular intervals up and down the stem. These stems are very photogenic, especially when photographed from up close. The smooth golden surface of the bamboo reflects sunlight so that your frame turns a golden hue.

By using a wide aperture (f/4) in Av mode, I was able to soften some of the bamboo stems, while others remained sharp. In the far background, you can see good *bokeh*, or a pleasant out-of-focus area—a softening that is smooth and silky. For more information about good and bad bokeh, see the upcoming "Bokeh: Discovering Photography's New Term" sidebar. Finally, don't forget that close-ups of flowers, leaves, and stems of garden plants can be some of the best photos you take in a garden.

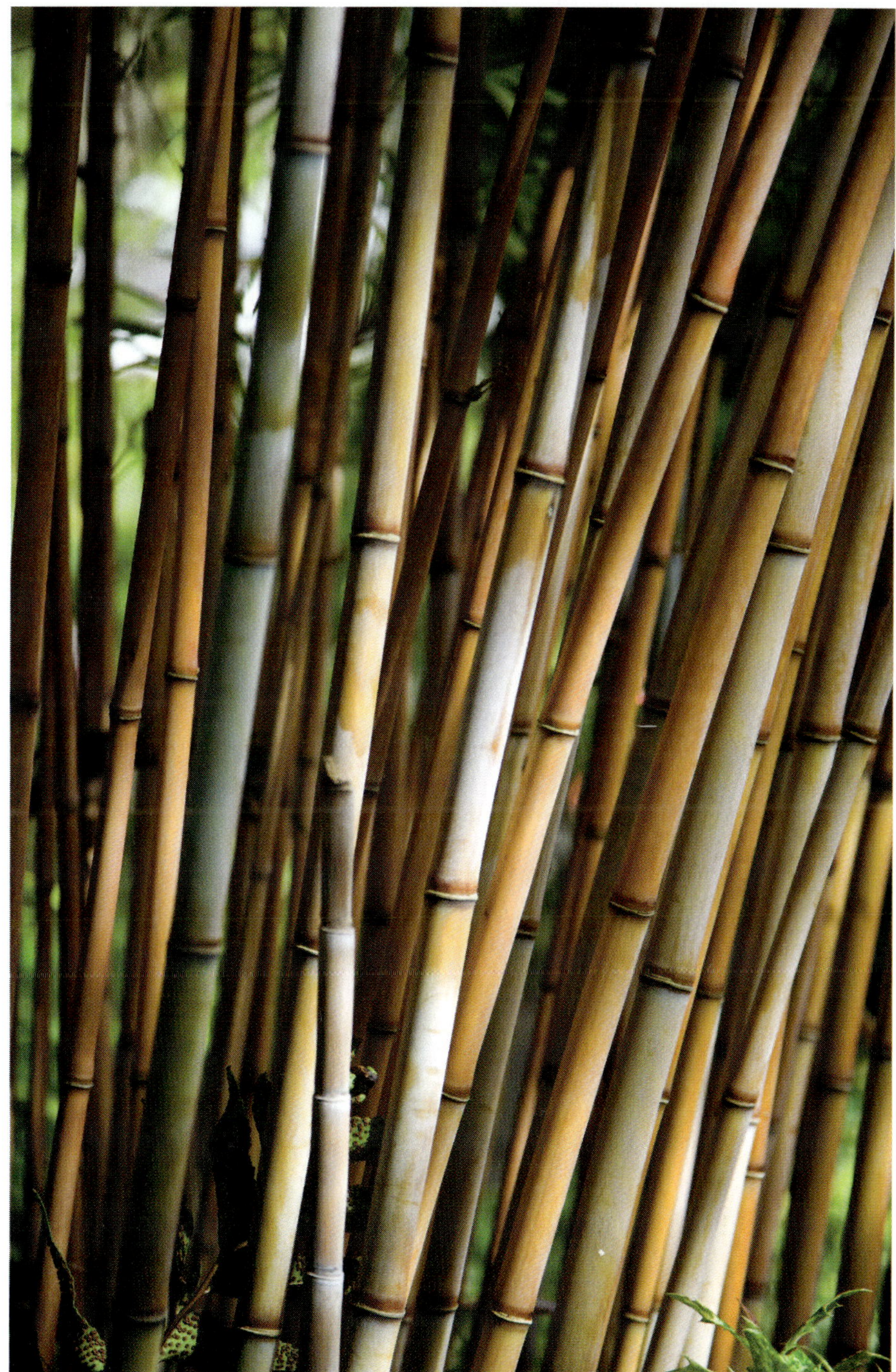

Focal length 105mm; ISO 200; aperture f/4; shutter speed 1/160; May 3:53 p.m.

BOKEH: STRANGE WORD, SIMPLE MEANING

Bokeh comes from the Japanese term meaning fuzzy. Since about 2000, it's been widely used to describe an aesthetically pleasing rendering of out-of-focus areas of an image.

Whether or not you get good bokeh depends on the contents of your background, the size of your aperture opening, and/or the construction of your camera's lens. Good bokeh is smooth and is contained in a photograph whose background has no sharp edges in its contents, nor any drastic changes of light. If you don't open your aperture wide enough in a close-up shot, you'll get bad bokeh because the background won't be soft enough. Bokeh also has to do with how well your lens is built. Within each lens there's an aperture diaphragm through which light enters. The construction and design of the aperture diaphragm determines the bokeh. More expensive lenses have a greater number of aperture blades, which produces smooth, round bokeh. Cheaper lenses use fewer blades, which yields hard-edged hexagons.

Small shapes, usually circles or hexagons that make up the out-of-focus background area, should meld smoothly into one another, so much so that you don't notice them. In order to do that, the circles of light that are seen when you blow up a photo and that make up the bokeh should brighten as you move to the center, as shown in this image of a succulent at the Conservatory of Flowers. Bad bokeh happens when you have bright outer rings in the shapes that make up the bokeh, as shown in the picture of a peacock at the zoo.

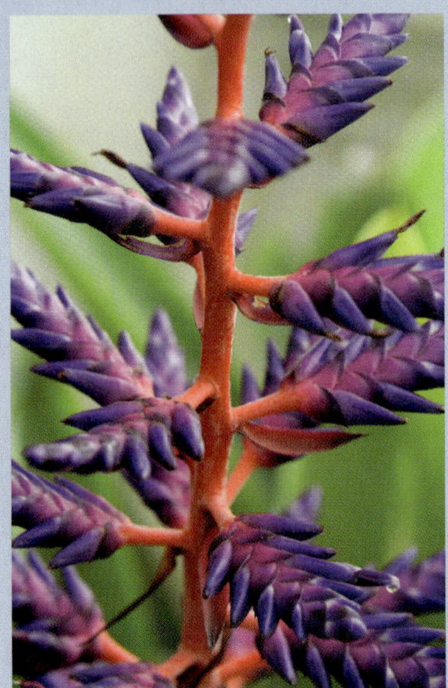

Good bokeh in photograph of a succulent plant at the San Francisco Conservatory of Flowers.

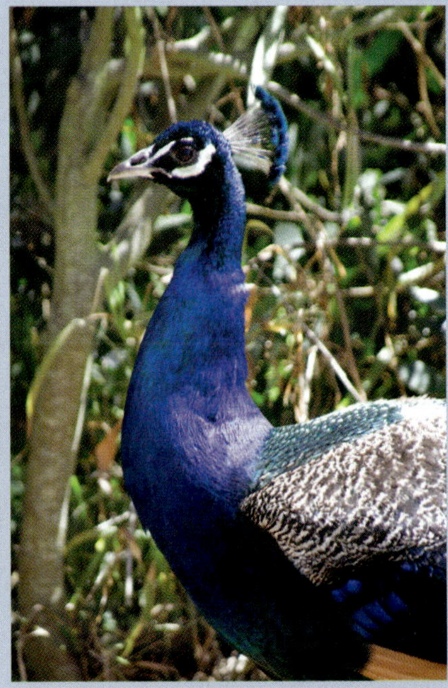

Bad bokeh in photograph of a peacock at the San Francisco Zoo.

Getting There

The main entrance to the San Francisco Botanical Garden is at the corner of 9th Avenue and Lincoln Way.

To get there using mass transit, take the N-Judah Muni line and get off at Irving and 9th Avenue. Walk one block north along 9th to Lincoln Way. The garden is just north of 9th and Lincoln on Martin Luther King Drive (a continuation of 9th Avenue into the park).

If you're driving, from the North Bay, take the Golden Gate Bridge to the Park Presidio/19th Avenue exit. Make a right on Kirkham, a right on 20th, and a right on Judah to 9th Avenue. Make a left on 9th to Lincoln Way.

From the East Bay, take 80 West to 101 South. Exit at Golden Gate Bridge/101-N (Exit 1B), then take the Octavia/Fell exit. Continue on Octavia and make a left on Fell. Fell will merge left onto Lincoln Way in Golden Gate Park. Continue on Lincoln Way to 9th Avenue.

From the South Bay, take 101 North to the 9th Street exit. Go straight on Harrison one block. Make a right on 9th Street, which turns to Hayes after crossing Market. Continue on Hayes, then make a left on Gough and a right on Fell, which merges into Lincoln Way on the left at the park. Take Lincoln Way to 9th Avenue. (Note: 9th Street is a street and 9th Avenue is an avenue. The streets run from downtown. The avenues run parallel to Golden Gate Park.)

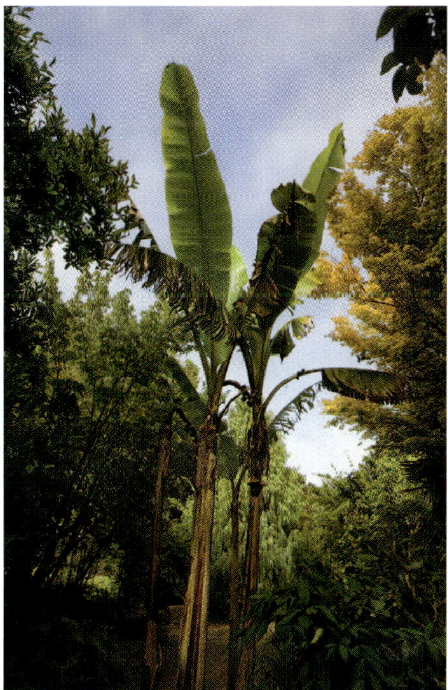

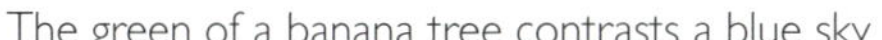

The green of a banana tree contrasts a blue sky

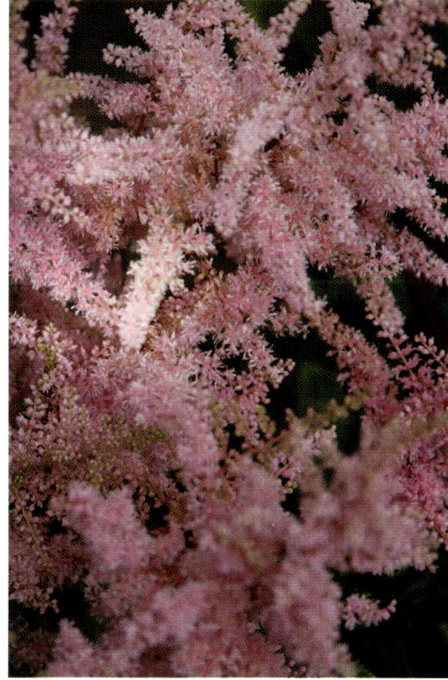

Great natural lighting can be found in the garden.

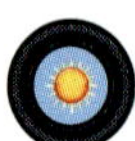 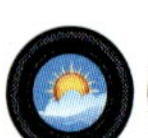 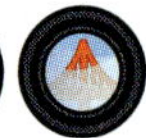

When to shoot: morning, afternoon

Conservatory of Flowers

James Lick, the wealthiest man in California in 1876, had planned to build a giant greenhouse at his Santa Clara, California, estate. The crates that contained wood and glass pieces to build the greenhouse had been purchased and were ready to be erected. Shortly before the building started, Lick died. About a year later, a businessman bought the crates and donated them to the Golden Gate Park commission. By 1879, the greenhouse had been put together and opened to the public.

The greenhouse is a complex piece of architecture consisting of different kinds of rooflines—gable, Tudor, and dome. The architectural elements of whitewashed wood and glass are interwoven so that the entire structure has hundreds of intersecting lines, each surrounded by glass and created by vertical and horizontal pieces of wood crossing each other. Almost any part of the building you photograph shows interesting patterns of line, shape, and form.

Inside the Conservatory are exhibits of tropical, aquatic, and potted plants. The greenhouse structure is surrounded by elaborate planted areas, one of which makes up a giant clock that sits on the lawn just to the east of the main building. While the grounds are open at any time to get into the Conservatory, it costs $5 to get into the greenhouse. The greenhouse is open from 9:00 a.m. to 4:30 p.m. Tuesday through Sunday.

The Shot

The most beautiful architectural detail of the Conservatory is located just above the entrance. I stepped back about 100 feet from the structure and zoomed in to prevent converging lines. I framed the shot to include the text that names the building; two gabled roofs, one on top of the other; and an abundant amount of colored glass. I could have framed just the dome, but it's all white, making it a washout for a photograph. Front and center in this photograph are the long, vertical pieces of glass just below the first gabled roof. This glass, along with the glass that makes up the gabled roof, gives one a feeling that, indeed, this is not an ordinary Victorian building; it is a greenhouse. I set my camera to a narrow aperture (large f/stop number) so that both the foreground and background would be sharp, leaving all of the architectural detail in focus.

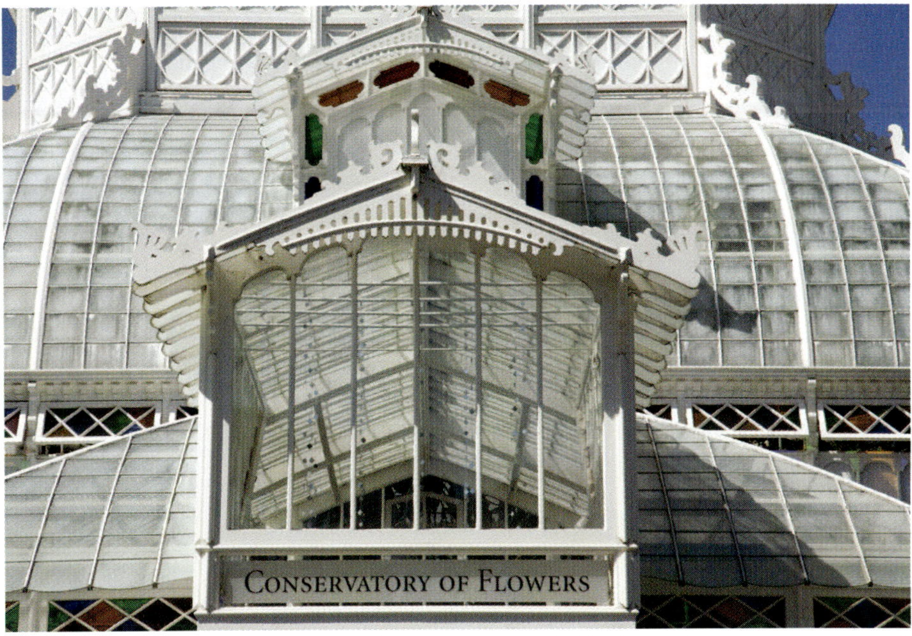

Focal length 105mm; ISO 400; aperture f/14; shutter speed 1/1250; May 1:40 p.m.

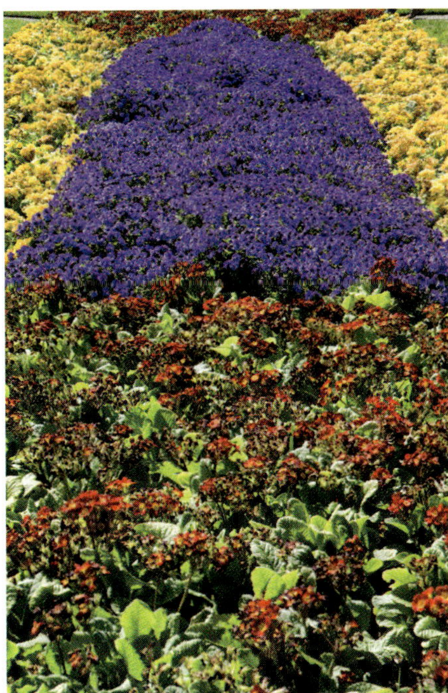

Bed of flowers in front of the Conservatory.

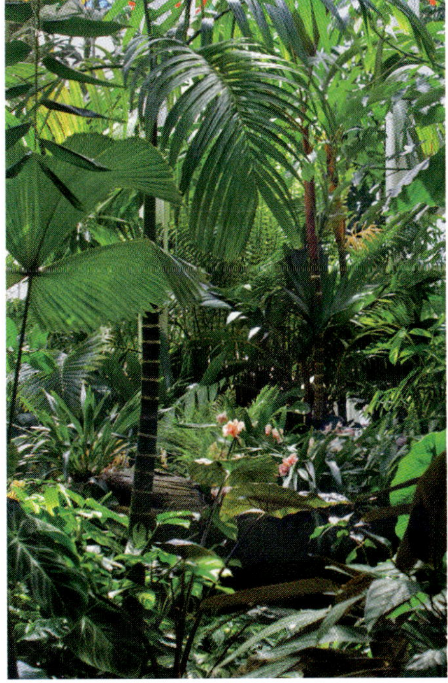

Tropical plants inside the Conservatory.

The Shot

Since I walked right up to the clock and shot at a relatively wide angle, it appears elongated in the shot. The space that the clock occupies is actually a square. I wanted to make the clock look more artful while showing the wide expanse of this area of the park. When you look at the shot, the width of the clock gets smaller as you move into the frame. This happened because I was so close to the clock that it enhanced the perspective. The effect also makes each number of the clock vary in size, with 7, 6, and 5 being the most prominent, emphasizing that these numbers symbolize more than just a measurement of time. Another interesting aspect of this shot is that the frame is divided into thirds at the horizon, marking three different areas of the park in the background. In the left third is the edge of the Conservatory with people sitting on the grass, in the middle third is the large palm tree, and in the right third is a forest of trees.

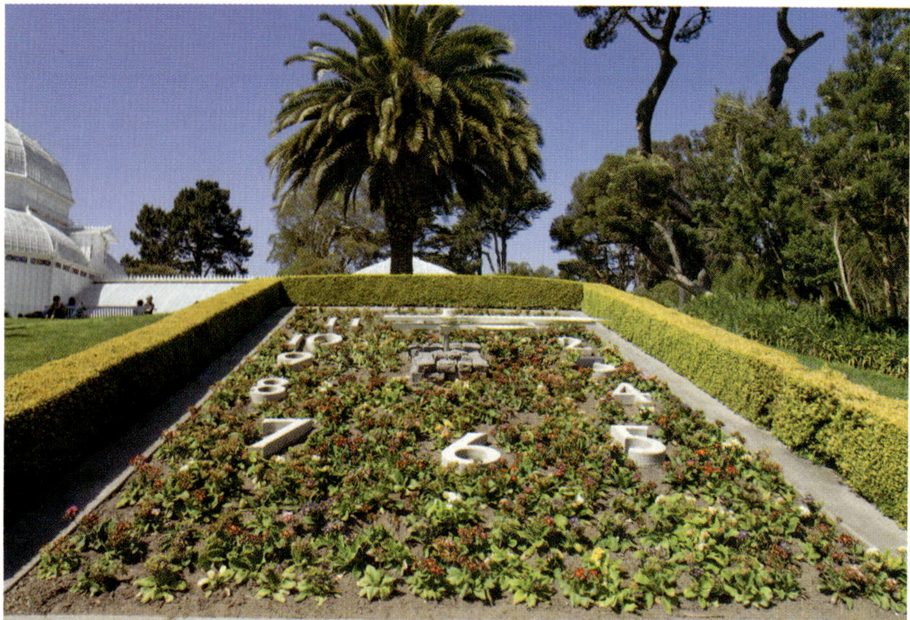

Focal length 24mm; ISO 400; aperture f/16; shutter speed 1/500; May 1:18 p.m.

Getting There

The main entrance to the Conservatory of Flowers is a short walk north of John F. Kennedy Drive. The facility is also close to Conservatory Drive West, which is closest to city streets, making a bus in close proximity to that street the best option for public transit.

To get there using mass transit, the easiest way is to take a bus from downtown and walk through Golden Gate Park to the main entrance of the building. From downtown, you can take the 5 Fulton bus from various points on Market Street in the Financial District.

Get off at Fulton Street and 4th Avenue. You'll be on the northwest side of the street. You'll see the park across the street on the south side of Fulton. You can enter the park via a path that begins half a block east of the bus stop on the south side of Fulton, between 3rd and 4th Avenues. Walk south along the path until you get to a three-way intersection on the path. Veer right (so you're walking southeast) until you get to Conservatory Drive West. Cross the street and continue southeast along the path until you reach the greenhouse.

If you're driving, from the North Bay, take the Golden Gate Bridge to the Park Presidio/19th Avenue exit. Make a right on Cabrillo, go one short block, and then turn left on 14th. Go one block, then turn left on Fulton, right on 8th Avenue, and left on JFK Drive. The Conservatory will be on the left.

From the East Bay, take 80 West to 101 South and exit at Golden Gate Bridge/101-N (Exit 1B). Then take the Octavia/Fell exit. Continue on Octavia and make a left on Fell. Fell will merge right onto JFK Dr. The Conservatory will be on the right.

From the South Bay, take 101 North to the 9th Street exit. Go straight on Harrison one block, then turn right on 9th, which turns into Hayes after crossing Market. Continue on Hayes, then make a left on Gough, a right on Fell, and veer right onto JFK Drive when you enter the park. The Conservatory will be on the right.

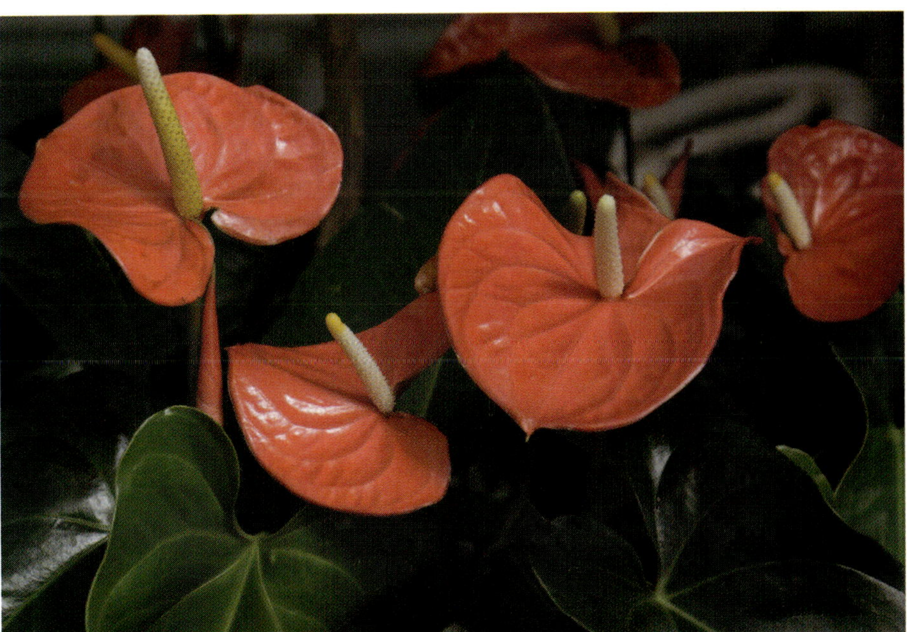

Anthurium grown inside the Conservatory

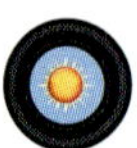 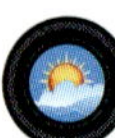 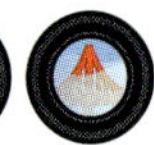

When to shoot: morning, afternoon

Yerba Buena Gardens

Art, diversity, and sustainability are the themes of Yerba Buena Gardens. The complex addresses these themes with a number of cultural, convention, and entertainment facilities that are spread out over two blocks in the SOMA (South of Market) neighborhood.

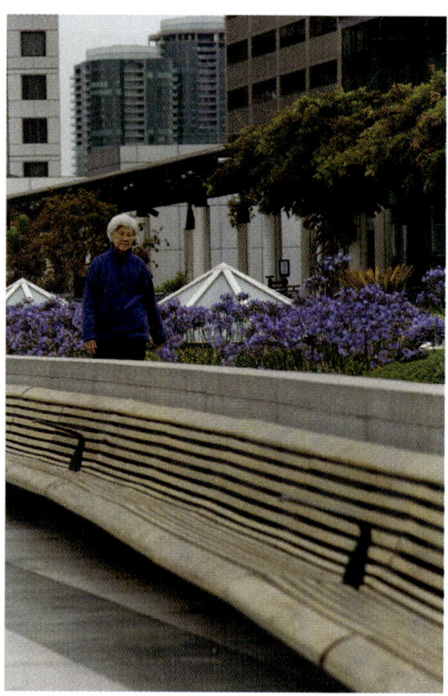

Woman walking in the garden.

Yerba Buena translates from Spanish to "good herb." When the area that includes the parcel of land upon which the complex sits was named in the early 1800s, there were wild mint plants growing in the hills nearby. In the 1950s, the San Francisco Board of Supervisors designated a several-block area of Yerba Buena as a redevelopment site. Nothing was done with the land until the 1970s, when Dianne Feinstein, who was mayor of San Francisco at the time, and the San Francisco Redevelopment Agency announced that the land was open to development to those who had a vision of it being a "magnificent" urban garden. It took two decades after that announcement for the cultural facilities and the garden to finally open. It opened to the public in 1993.

There are many outside structures to photograph in the garden, from the façade of MOMA (the Museum of Modern Art) to the Martin Luther King Memorial. The gardens of this complex are few and far between, and, in my opinion, are not the primary focus of the property; however, there are great water features, including two large waterfall fountains.

The Shot

This is part of a large, elongated fountain (water feature) in the garden near the gallery and theater buildings. In the photo you can see part the San Francisco Museum of Modern Art (SFMOMA), which is on 3rd Street just to the northeast of the end of the fountain. The colors, shapes, and forms of this image are notable. I set up my tripod to include the fountain's sharp curve as the largest element that enhances perspective and adds depth to the image. The silvery water and the vertical lines of the waterfall complement the lines and shapes in the background. The circular shape of SFMOMA's large, round skylight contains silver geometric patterns that match not only the rectangles of glass of the building in front of it, but also the gray concrete that edges out the frame. Also, the red brick adds a bit of contrast to the image. Finally, the fountain's curve ends with a payoff: the woman wearing a heavy coat and walking behind the fountain. All the elements add up to a postmodern feel, meaning that eclectic, complex shapes have replaced simple, formal ones.

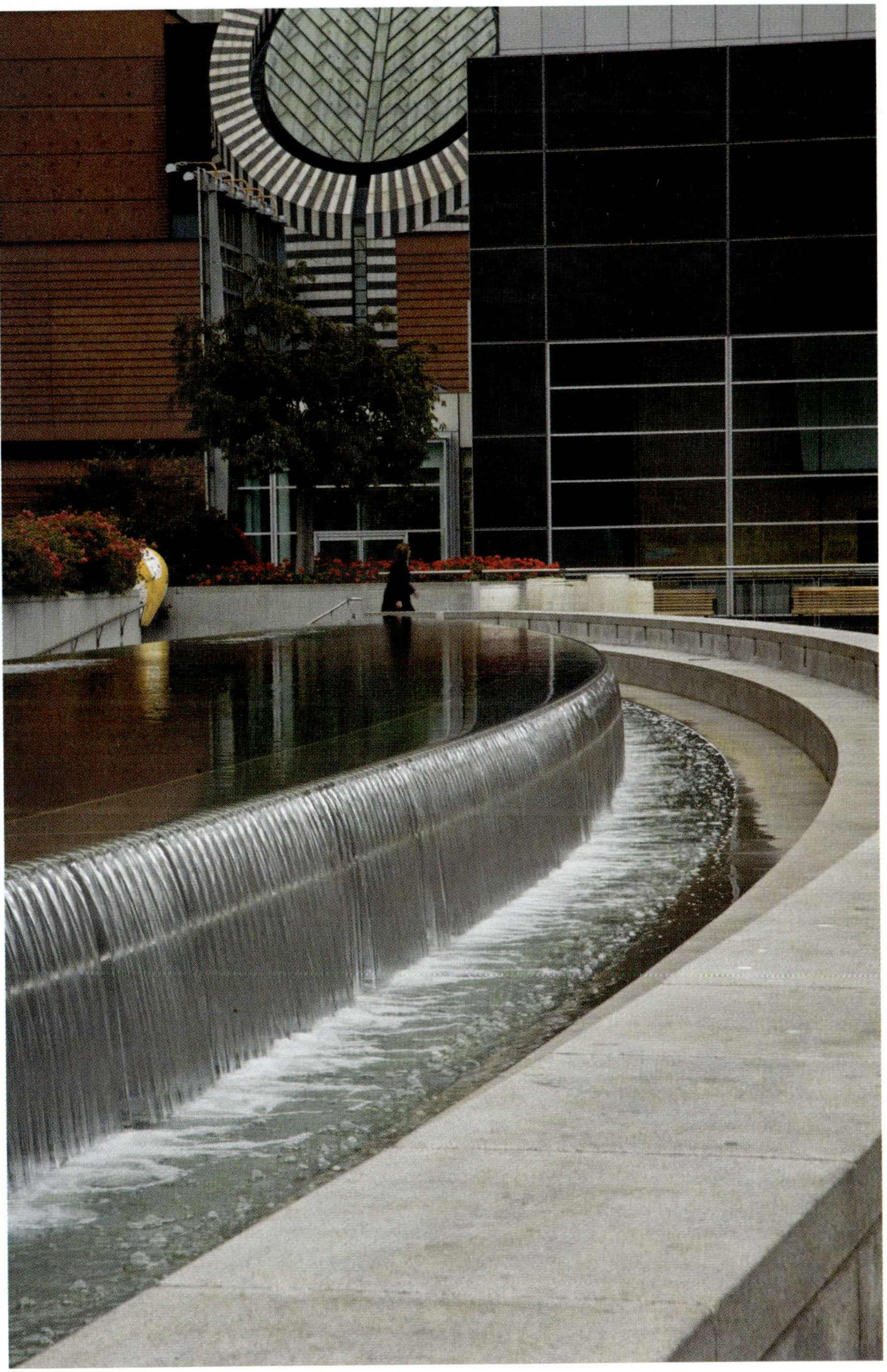

Focal length 105mm; ISO 200; aperture f/22; shutter speed 1/30; August 10:24 a.m.

The Shot

The Martin Luther King Memorial at Yerba Buena is a powerful monument. To capture its symbolism, I included the picture of Martin Luther King Jr. in the frame. In fact, it's the centerpiece of the frame. It was necessary to use a tripod on the path that leads under the waterfall for this shot for two reasons: First, to get the photograph of King sharp because this part of the memorial is in a dark place, and second, to get the waterfall to look silky. To achieve this, I had to lower the exposure compensation as low as it would go (–2 EV) so I could use a longer shutter speed. I was also successful in getting a smoky effect where the water falls around the rocks. If I let the shutter open any longer, all I would have achieved would've been a waterfall of blown highlights.

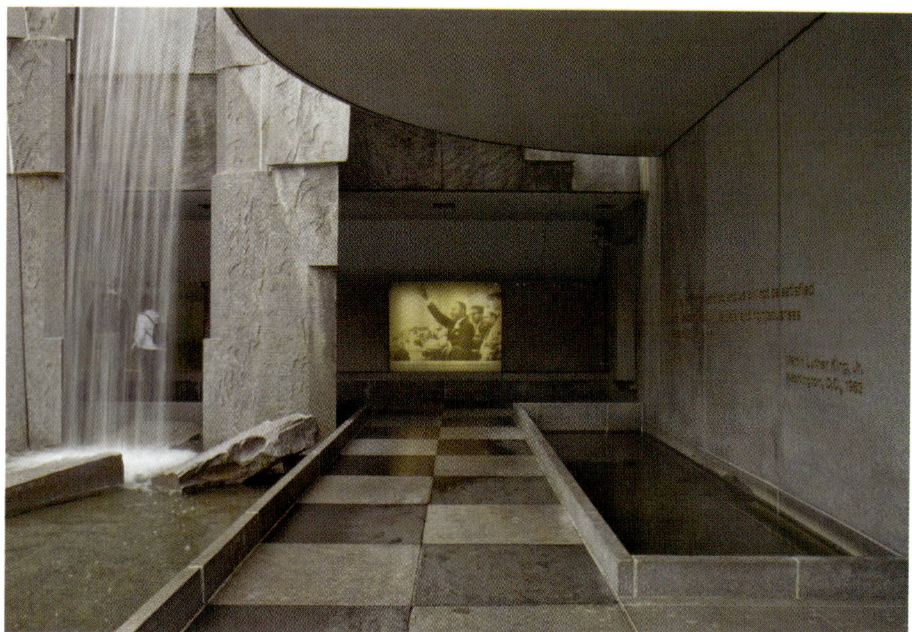

Focal length 28mm; ISO 200; aperture f/22; shutter speed 1/6; August 11:30 a.m.

Getting There

Yerba Buena Gardens covers two square blocks in the South of Market (SOMA) neighborhood. The parts of the gardens that have a giant waterfall and a huge fountain are great to photograph and occupy one city block located between Mission and Howard Streets and 3rd and 4th Streets.

To get there using mass transit, Yerba Buena Gardens is located near the Montgomery Street and Powell Street BART/Muni stations. To get there from the Montgomery Street station, walk southwest on Market Street to 3rd Street. Make a left on 3rd Street and walk half a block (southeast) past Mission (one-and-a-half blocks southeast of Market Street).

You'll see the Museum of Modern Art (SFMOMA) on your left. There's a large crosswalk on 3rd that goes from SFMOMA to Yerba Buena Gardens. On the right, just past the crosswalk, is a large walkway that takes you into Yerba Buena Gardens. The walkway takes you from between the Center for the Arts Gallery and the Center for the Arts Theater to the Martin Luther King Memorial, which will be on your left after you pass between the two buildings.

If you're driving, from the North Bay, take 101 South. Make a slight left to exit on Lombard Street. Make a right on Van Ness and a left on Golden Gate Avenue. Follow Golden Gate across Market Street, where it changes to 6th Street. Make a left on Folsom and a left on 3rd. The gardens will be on the left between Howard and Mission Streets.

From the East Bay, take 80 West to 101 South. Exit at Fremont Street and make a left at Howard, and then a right on 3rd Street. The gardens will be on the left between Howard and Mission Streets.

From the South Bay, take 101 North to the 4th Street exit. Stay straight coming off the freeway to Bryant Street, and make a left on 3rd.

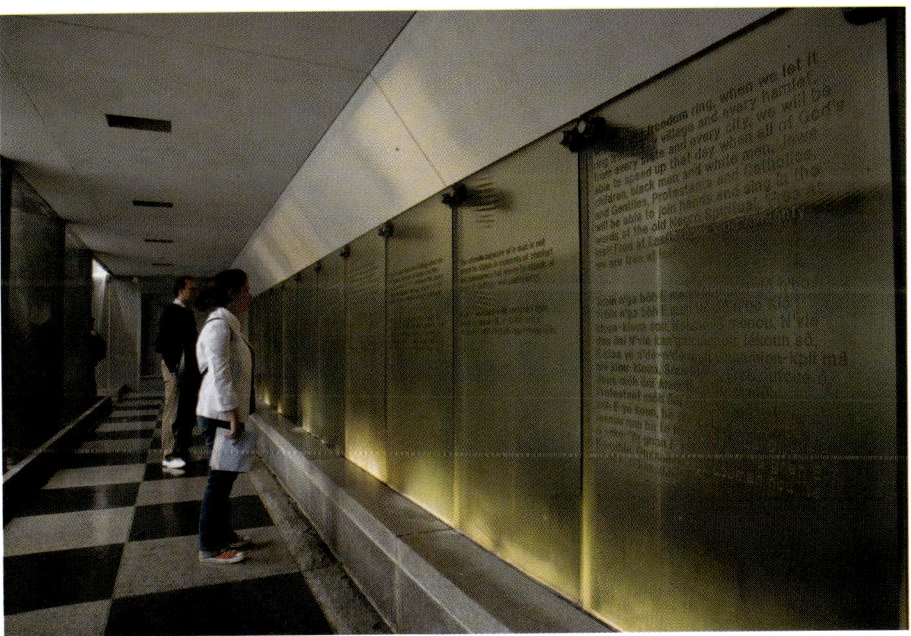

Reading about Martin Luther King Jr.

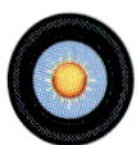 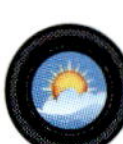 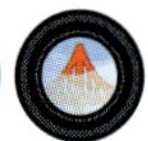

When to shoot: morning, afternoon

Japanese Tea Garden

The Japanese Tea Garden is a peaceful place of ponds and pagodas. The gardens were planted for the World's Fair of 1894. Baron Makoto Hagiwara wanted the garden to be a permanent part of Golden Gate Park. He made a deal to build and plant the garden with John McLaren, then superintendent of Golden Gate Park. Hagiwara used his own money to build the garden. His family lived there until 1942. During WWII, they were forced to move to the Japanese internment camps, at which time the garden went into disrepair. Some time after the war, the Hagiwara family returned to the garden. Today, the garden has many pathways that look upon secluded plant and water areas, perfect for taking photographs. White sky is a problem in summer when the fog is sometimes present nearly all day.

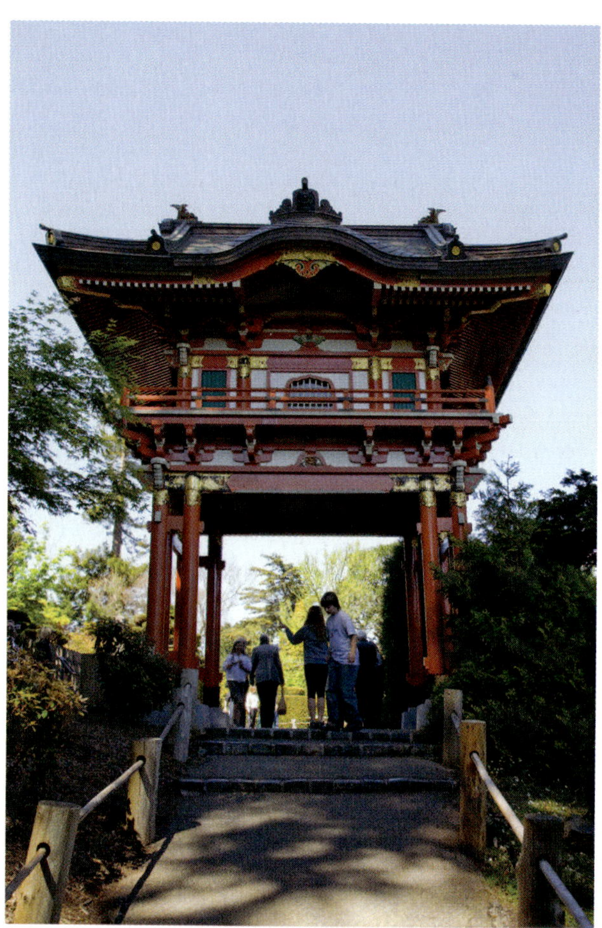

Temple Gate.

The Shot

Peace lanterns represent a significant part of Japanese culture, and this one was found in a near-perfect setting—good light, clear water, and great plants around it. Since this lantern had a dark shadow cast on it, I used it as a quasi-background object and placed it one-third from the left side of the frame so that your eye goes from the lighted foreground and middle ground to the shadow on the lantern. I placed my focus point on the ferns in the middle ground so that they would be sharp and the lantern slightly soft, smoothing out the hard stone of it. Bordering the bottom of the frame is a line of red bougainvillea. That, along with the nearly-red tree branch that hangs over the lantern, adds splashes of color to the frame. Without these two items, the photograph wouldn't have nearly as much depth. It's also interesting to note that the lantern has four parts: the base stone (*jirin* in Japanese), the light compartment, the roof (*kasa*), and the jewel (*kurin*) at the top.

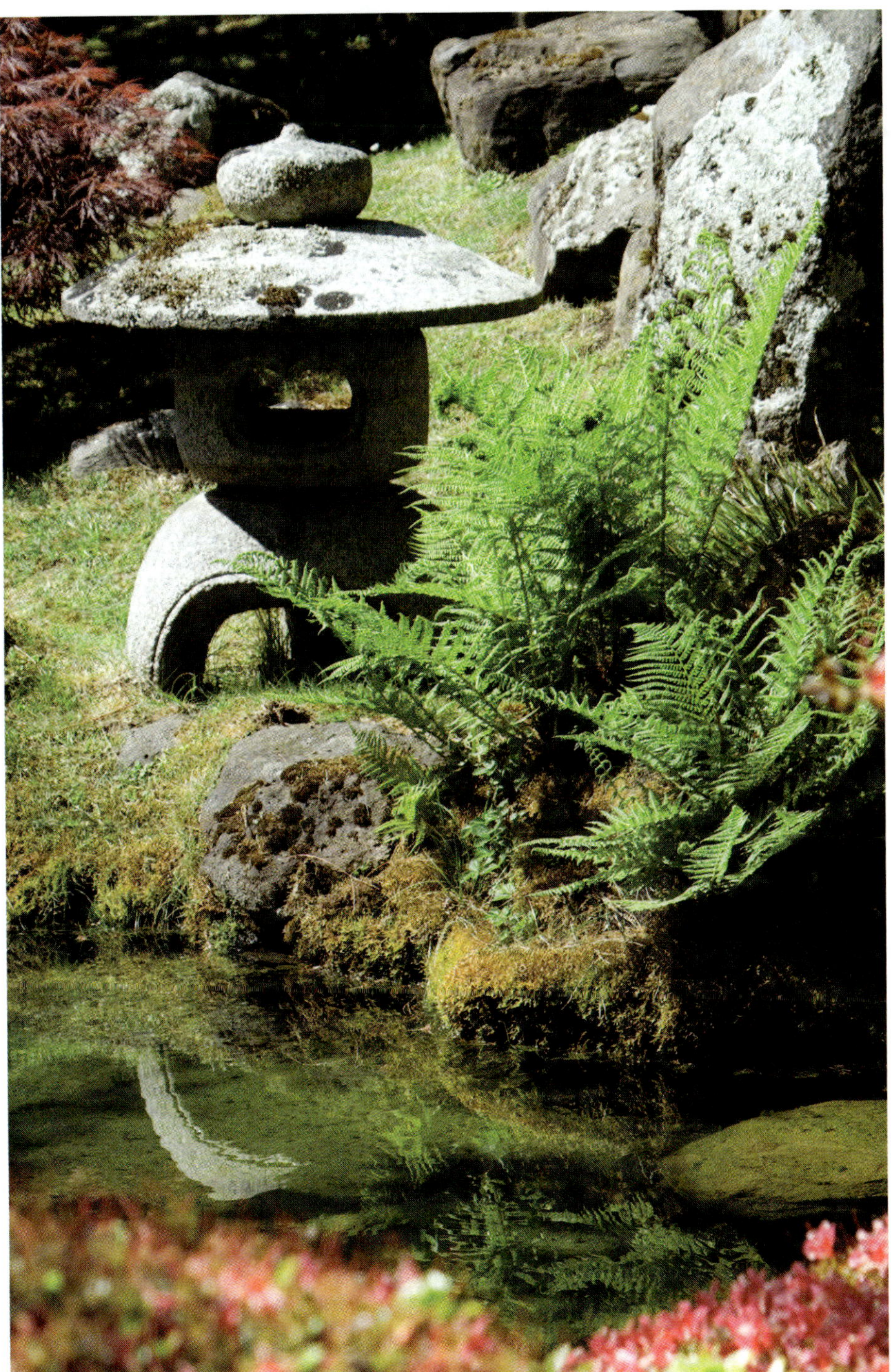

Focal length 84mm; ISO 200; aperture f/8; shutter speed 1/250; April 2:00 p.m.

The Shot

This pagoda is a five-story Buddhist shrine. You can get to it via the Long Bridge or through the Temple Gate, both of which can be accessed by a number of curvy trails that gradually make their way northwest from the main gate. There's a plaque at the pagoda that says it's derived from ancient Indian funeral mounds (*stupas*) that first the Chinese

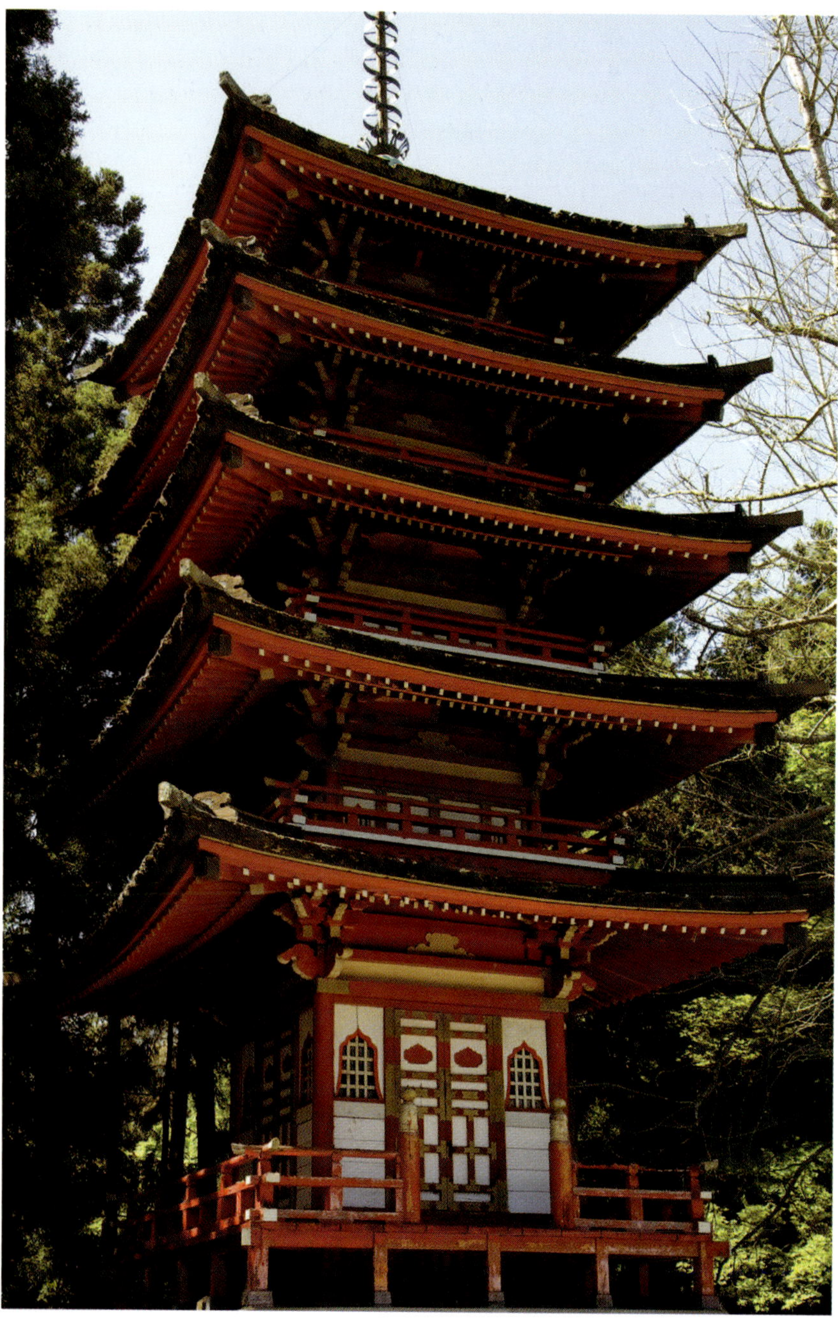

Focal length 35mm; ISO 200; aperture f/9; shutter speed 1/160; April 10:24 a.m.

adopted, and then the Japanese. This pagoda is an original from the Panama-Pacific International Exposition of 1915. You can't go inside the pagoda, but you can get good photographs of it from a variety of points around it. The biggest challenge in getting a good picture of it is to avoid a white sky. As with so many other pictures that you take in Golden Gate Park, you have to time it right to get a sky clear from fog. If you're visiting the park in the spring or summer, avoid it in the morning because that's when the fog is the worst. In the summer it usually clears by 2:00 p.m., but sometimes it's later. You'll get the best photographs of the pagoda on a clear late-fall or winter day. For the best picture of a full view of the pagoda, go to the west side of it in the afternoon in spring and summer so you're looking east to a blue sky. I shot this in Av mode with my aperture set to f/9. I set a narrow aperture so the eaves would be sharp from top to bottom. Finally, I lowered my exposure compensation two stops to –.67 to deepen the red color of the structure.

Getting There

The Japanese Tea Garden is at 7 Hagiwara Tea Garden Drive.

To get there using mass transit, from downtown, take the K or T toward Balboa Park. Get off at the Forest Hill Station. Walk across Laguna Honda Boulevard to transfer to the 44 O'Shaughnessy. Get off at Concourse Drive/Academy of Sciences. Walk northwest from California Academy of Sciences toward The de Young Museum. The Japanese Tea Garden is just to the east of the de Young Museum. A more direct way to get there (with a bit of a longer walk) is to take the 5 Fulton and get off at 8th and Fulton. After you cross Fulton Street on 8th Avenue, you'll see a path at the southwestern corner of Fulton and 8th. That path leads directly to the Japanese Tea Garden.

If you're driving, from the North Bay, take the Golden Gate Bridge to the Park Presidio/19th Avenue exit. Make a right on Cabrillo, go one short block, then make a left on 14th. Go one block, then turn left on Fulton, right on 8th Avenue, left on JFK Drive, and then left on Hagiwara Tea Garden Drive.

From the East Bay, take 80 West to 101 South. Exit at Golden Gate Bridge/101-N (Exit 1B), then take the Octavia/Fell exit. Continue on Octavia and make a left on Fell. Fell will merge right onto JFK Drive. Make a left on Hagiwara Tea Garden Drive.

From the South Bay, take 101 North to the 9th Street exit. Go straight on Harrison one block and make a right on 9th, which turns into Hayes after crossing Market. Continue on Hayes, then turn left on Gough, right on Fell, and veer right onto JFK Drive when you enter the park. Make a left on Hagiwara Tea Garden Drive.

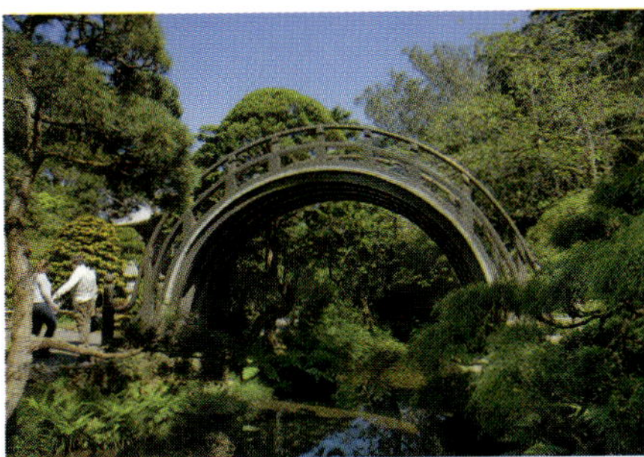

Drum bridge in garden.

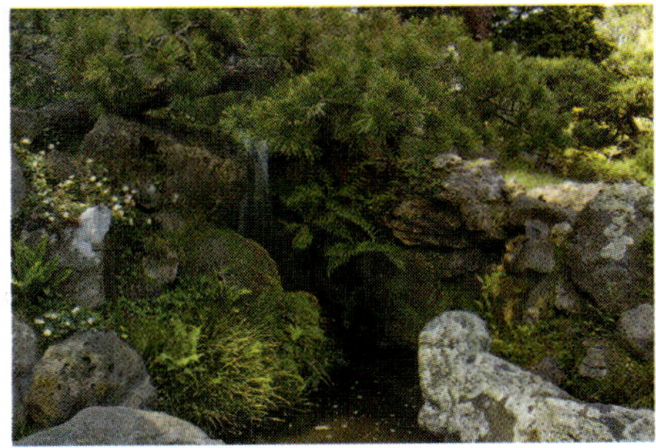

Small waterfall in garden.

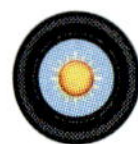 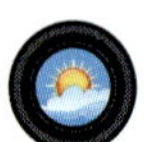 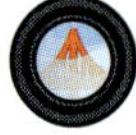

When to shoot: morning, afternoon

China Beach

Once called Phelan Beach, China Beach is a small cove in the shoreline just southwest of the Golden Gate Bridge. The neighborhood near the beach is surrounded by expensive early twentieth-century homes of all colors, shapes, and sizes. Before you go down some stairs to get to the beach, you'll see a stone plaque that tells of the cove area being used as a campsite by Chinese fishermen during the Gold Rush. Right at the bottom of the stairs is a large structure, an old lifeguard station that serves as a sundeck. The second floor of the structure offers interesting views of the beach below. Once you get down to the beach, you'll find a quaint sandy area with few tourists. As you get closer to the water, the sand changes to beautiful, small, multicolored rocks. The beach can be fogged in during spring and summer, so taking photos there can be a challenge. During the afternoon the fog can creep in and out, leaving only a small window of time to photograph the scenic views of the seashore. During winter and fall, there are great views of the Golden Gate Bridge from the beach.

The Shot

In this shot I took advantage of the lens curvature and wide angle to shoot a compelling landscape filled with color and texture. In order to get this shot, I stooped down right smack in the center of the beach. I angled the camera slightly downward so I could include (in order) the rocks, the whitecaps, the ocean water, and the sky. I lowered my exposure compensation by two stops to deepen all of the colors in the frame, from the reds of some of the rocks to the deep blue of the ocean water as it approaches the horizon. The combination of an aperture that wasn't too wide and the wide angle of the lens increased the depth of field. In doing so, all of the rocks are sharp, as are the bird and the whitecaps. The crispness of the foreground and middle ground leave you feeling as if you are touching the textures of the rounded, smooth rocks and the foamy wake near them. Then there is the bird. You get a sense of what it might see as it looks out over the great Pacific Ocean.

The Shot

I shot this picture standing near to where the beach becomes impassable due to the rocks. I included the brown sand in the shot because of the contrast it provides with the ocean water. This picture is framed so that the curve in the coastline takes the viewer's eye out to sea (and into the fog). Also, the whitecaps and fog almost make a semicircle within the frame. You might think that this composition—the shoreline with the fog at sea—doesn't happen very often, but indeed it does. Fog often hangs off the shoreline of many nooks along the coast. It has to do with the topography of the coastline and the fact that low clouds and fog can't get over the hills as fast as the fog over the ocean. I used a relatively narrow aperture so the entire image stays sharp throughout.

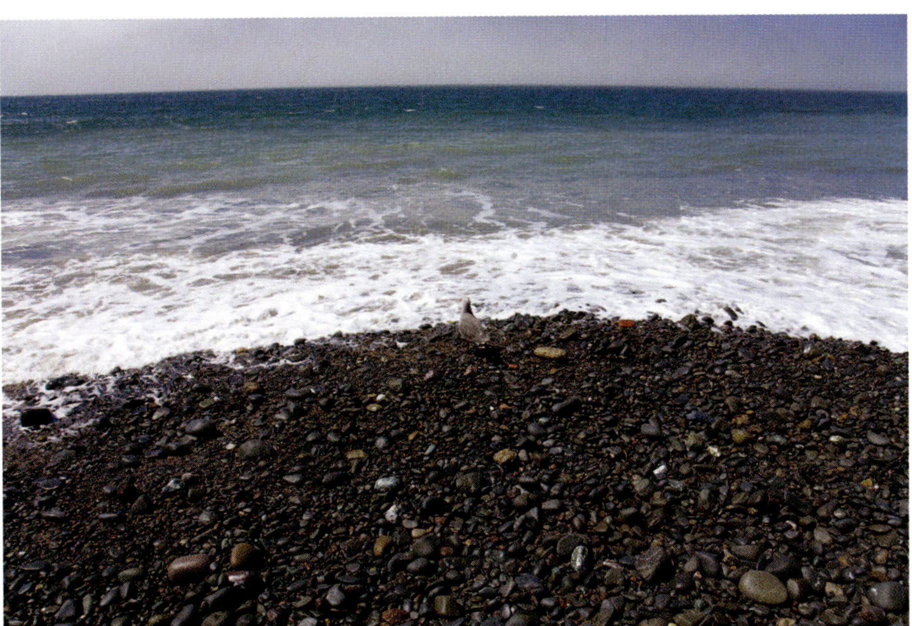

Focal length 24mm; ISO 200; aperture f/9; shutter speed 1/400; August 3:35 p.m.

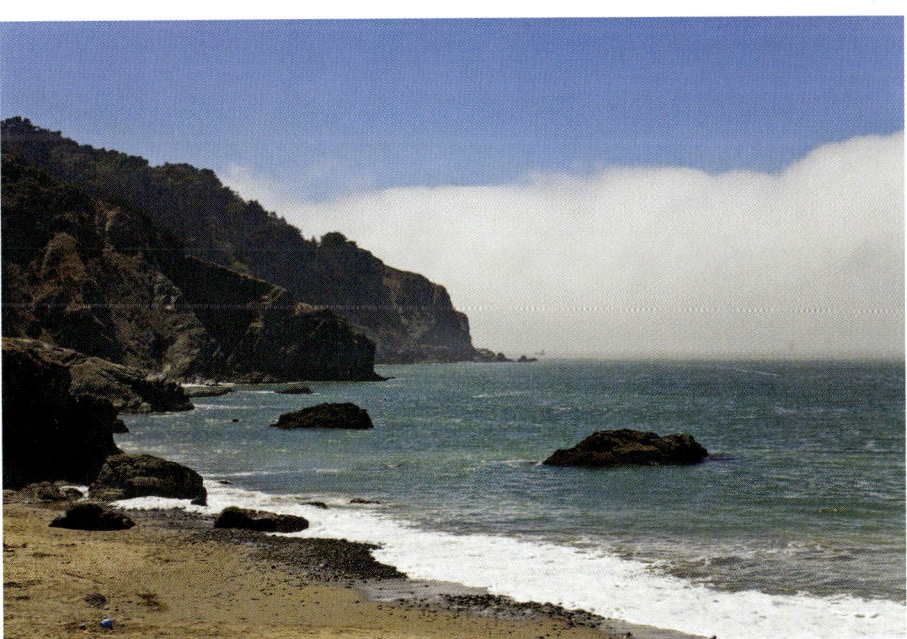

Focal length 50mm; ISO 200; aperture f/9; shutter speed 1/500; August 3:48 p.m.

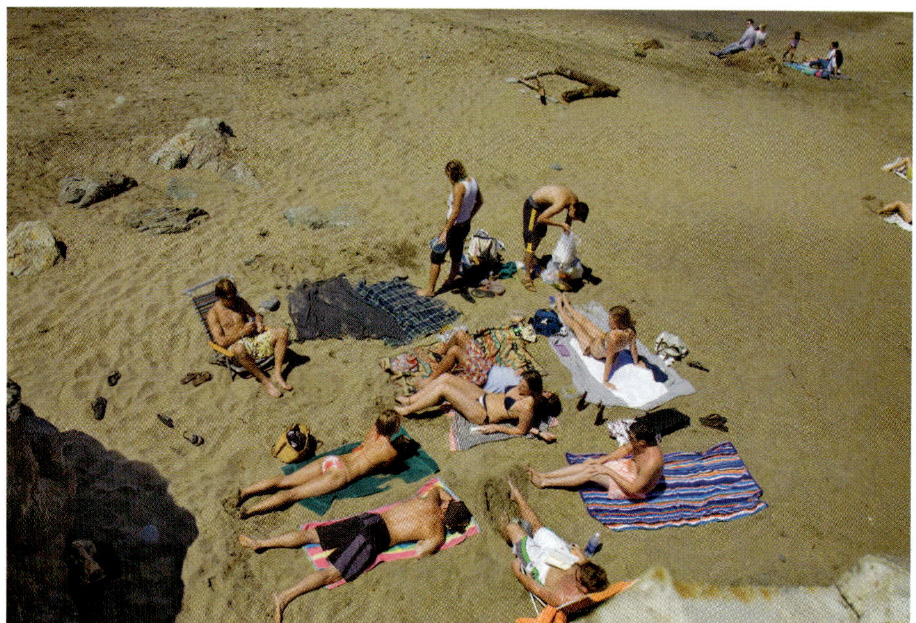

Sunbathers on the beach.

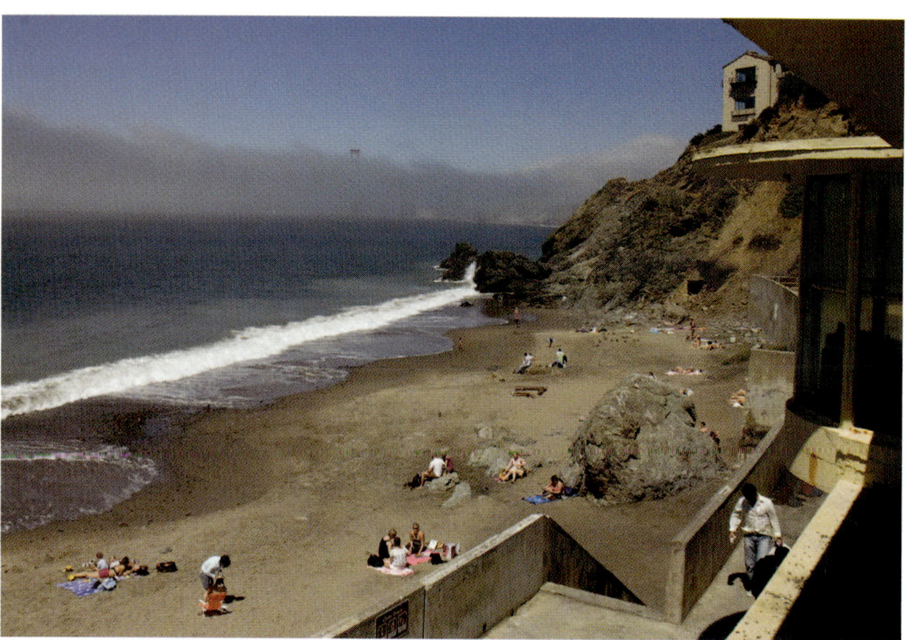

View looking southwest.

Getting There

China Beach is at 490 Sea Cliff Avenue at the end of El Camino del Mar.

To get there using mass transit, take the 1 California bus from the northeast corner of Sacramento and Davis Street. Get off at California and 30th. Walk west on 30th and turn left on El Camino del Mar. El Camino del Mar will split in two. Where it does, don't turn right. Continue straight on to the beach.

If you're driving, from the North Bay, take the Golden Gate Bridge toward the 25th Avenue exit. Merge onto Merchant Road and make a right on Lincoln, a right on 25th Avenue, and a left on Sea Cliff Avenue.

From the East Bay, take 80 West and exit at Central Fwy/101-N toward Golden Gate Bridge. Make a slight left on Van Ness, a left on Geary, a right on 27th, and a left on Sea Cliff Avenue.

From the South Bay, take 280 North to San Francisco. It will turn into CA-1 N/19th Avenue. Veer left just after you get into Golden Gate Park. 19th Avenue will change to 25th Avenue after you get out of the park. Make a left on Sea Cliff Avenue.

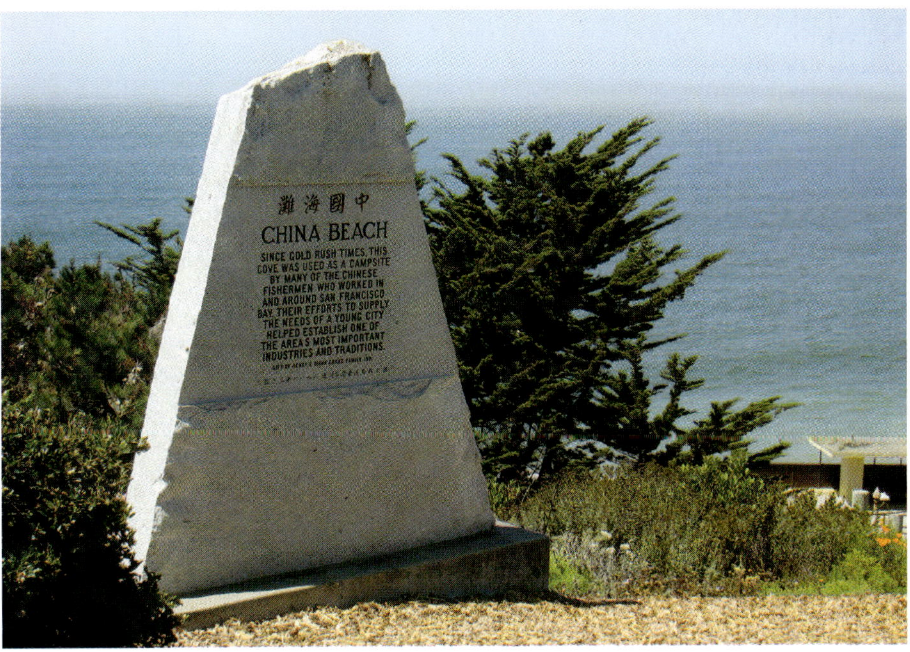

China Beach monument.

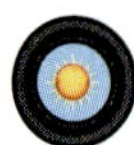 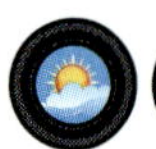 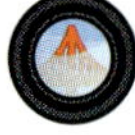 When to shoot: morning, afternoon

Lands End

Of all the places in San Francisco, Lands End is the most remote. With stunning views of rocky, windswept cliffs and the Pacific Ocean at every glance, you'll have a lot of choices when composing a landscape photo of the area. It all begins on a trail—the Coastal Trail (or Lands End Trail), which extends about 2 miles from near 32nd Avenue in the Sea Cliff neighborhood of the Richmond District through Sutro Heights Park to the Cliff House. This trail used to be a railroad track of the Cliff House Railroad, which brought people from downtown to Sutro Baths and the Cliff House. The photos in this section come from the only accessible beach, Mile Rock Beach (locals call it Lands End Beach), along the trail, which is a little over a half-mile hike from the back of the parking lot that's just north of Point Lobos and 48th Avenue on El Camino del Mar. The hike isn't for the faint of heart; there's a steep staircase that comes up from the beach after you've hiked down it. You'll see and can photograph isolated beaches along the trail, but it is highly recommended that you do not veer off the path. People have fallen from the rocks and cliffs and drowned in the very cold water, which is filled with rip currents.

The Shot

The one good thing about the often fogged-in beach of Lands End is that you can take shots with longer shutter speeds to get a silky look to the water because of the lower light conditions from the sun being blocked by the fog. If you're there on a foggy day and you lower your exposure compensation a few stops, you can leave your shutter open at least a third of a second in late afternoon or early morning. I hit the beach shortly after the sunset on a foggy July evening. It's quite a hike with camera equipment and tripod in tow. I walked on the rocks to very near the water, and I set up my tripod so that it faced northeast toward a cliff. I framed the cliff so it appears two-thirds into the frame from the right end. It acts as a dividing point between the middle ground and background (the background being the Marin Headlands that occupies the upper-left third of the frame). By leaving the shutter open for 8 seconds, the waves crashing on the beach turned into a soft, billowing layer that looks as if smoke is rising from the rocks. Before I knew it, it was time to wrap it up as the dark was encroaching the beach, leaving my assistant (Fred Rimando) and I in near-darkness a good distance from civilization.

The Shot

This photo is from the eastern end of the Coastal Trail (Lands End trail). You can enter this part of the trail from 32nd Avenue and El Camino del Mar in the Richmond District. This secluded beach is a few hundred feet past the lookout tower, which is at the entrance to this part of the trail. When you're walking west along the trail, be on the lookout for this beach by glancing down the cliffs as you walk. Before you set off, check the times when low tide occurs in the newspaper, as this shot will be absent a beach if it's taken at high tide. To get this shot, you have to have a zoom lens of at least 100mm (35mm equivalent).

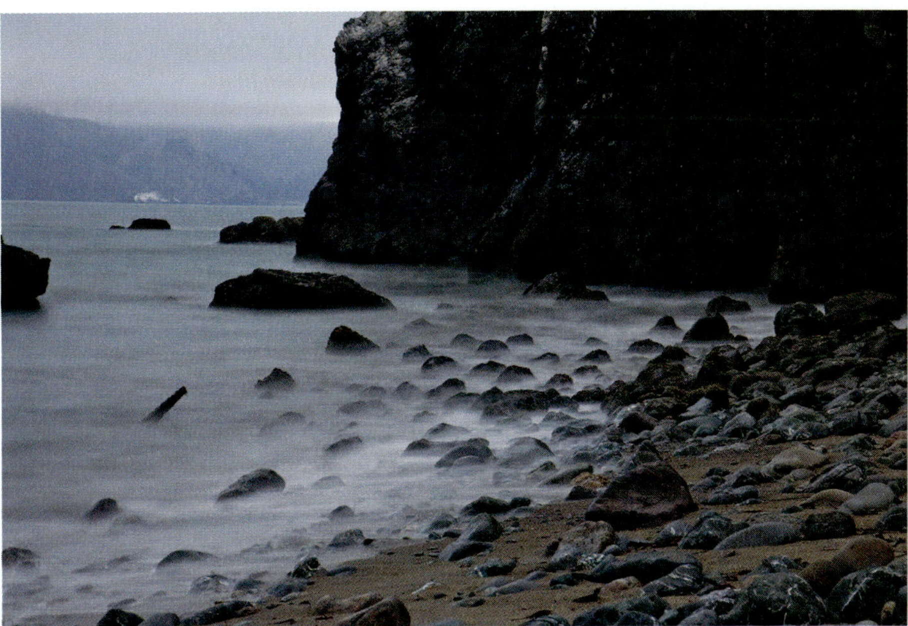

Focal length 73mm; ISO 200; aperture f/9; shutter speed 8 seconds; July 8:25 p.m.

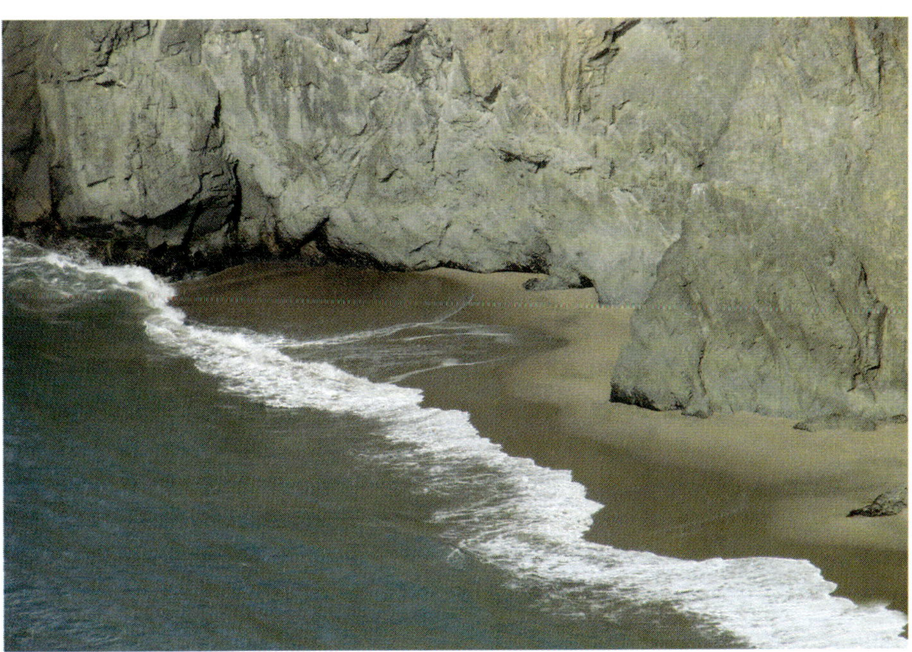

Focal length 200mm; ISO 200; aperture f/5.6; shutter speed 1/500; June 2:16 p.m.

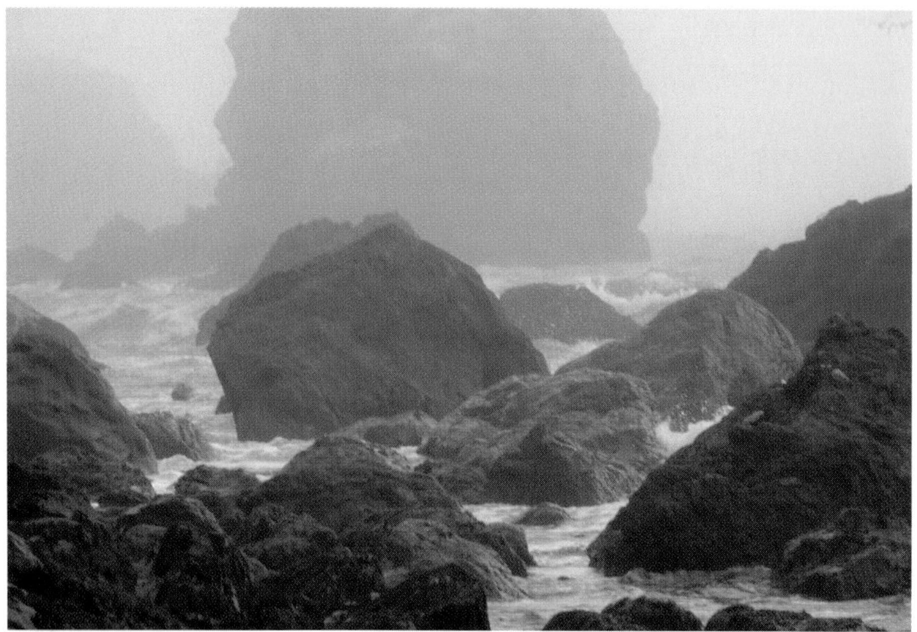

Huge boulders in the fog at Lands End.

Getting There

Lands End extends along the Coastal Trail from Sutro Baths to the Richmond District. The trailhead can be accessed from a parking lot on El Camino Real just north of 48th and Point Lobos Avenue.

To get there using mass transit, take the 38 Geary bus from Davis and Pine Street downtown to 48th and Point Lobos in the Richmond District. Walk north on 48th to the parking lot on El Camino del Mar. The trailhead is in the back of the parking lot. Take a right to walk north to Lands End Beach.

If you're driving, from the North Bay, take the Golden Gate Bridge toward the 25th Avenue exit. Merge onto Merchant Road and make a right on Lincoln, a right on 25th Avenue, and a right on Geary, which turns into Point Lobos Avenue.

From the East Bay, take 80 West to exit at Central Fwy/101-N toward the Golden Gate Bridge. Make a slight left on Van Ness and a left on Geary, which turns into Point Lobos Avenue.

From the South Bay, take 280 North to San Francisco. It will turn into CA-1 N/19th Avenue. Veer left just after you get into Golden Gate Park. 19th Avenue will change to 25th Avenue after you get out of the park. Make a left on Geary, which turns into Point Lobos Avenue.

Miles Rock Lighthouse in the fog off Lands End Beach.

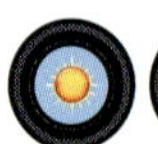
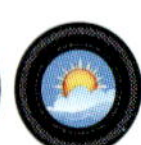

When to shoot: morning, afternoon, evening

Twin Peaks

At nearly 1,000 feet high, Twin Peaks are two hills that run north to south in the middle of the city. They serve as fog blockers for many city neighborhoods. After traveling on windy Twin Peaks Boulevard, you get to a lookout spot where tourists snap pictures left and right. Joining them is no problem, as there's plenty of room up there for everybody. But one thing is for sure about the Twin Peaks photo op: It's absolutely undoable when there is fog. That's because the fog that comes in from the ocean fiercely blows up and around both peaks, obscuring the view in an emulsion of white. Whether the fog is coming in or going out, there's sure to be a howling wind at the top of the peaks; so if you do go up there, dress warmly. Now for the good news: If you hit this place after the fog has lifted, you'll get a stunning blue sky wrapped around a downtown view that's the best in the city.

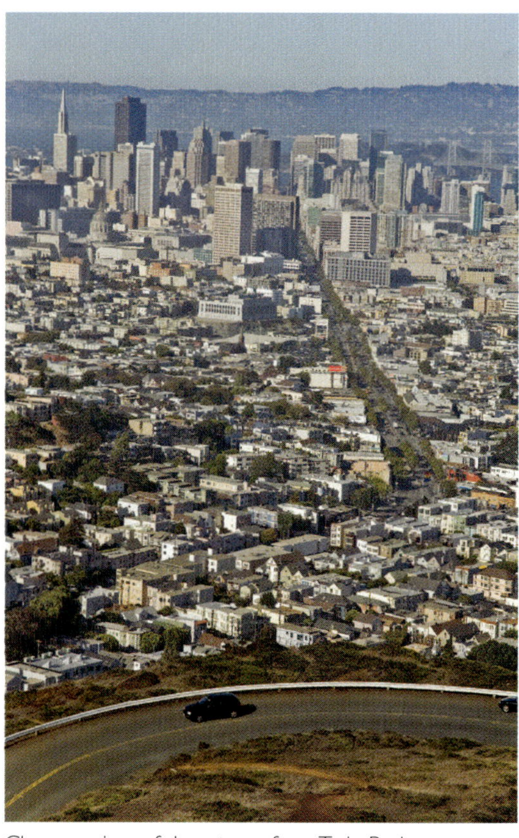

Close-up view of downtown from Twin Peaks.

The Shot

For many photographers, busloads of tourists are an annoyance. They seem to get in the way of pictures at the most inopportune times. But they can be interesting subjects unto themselves, particularly when they're riveted by their surroundings. If you like to people-watch with your camera, this is as good a place as any to find people gazing at the drama below them, not to mention their activities, from taking pictures (of course!) to looking though the colorful telescopes that have been placed all along the lookout area. In this picture, taken from a top of a wall that is just behind the main barrier wall of the lookout area, the first thing that caught my eye was the color balance between the pink of one subject's sweater and the blue of the telescope, perfect complementing colors centered a third in from the left side of the frame and a third of the way down from the top of the frame. The next interesting point of this photo is a technical one. The area of sharp focus is the tourists. But I used a relatively narrow aperture to minimize bokeh in the background. Including details in the faraway buildings adds to the dimension of the shot.

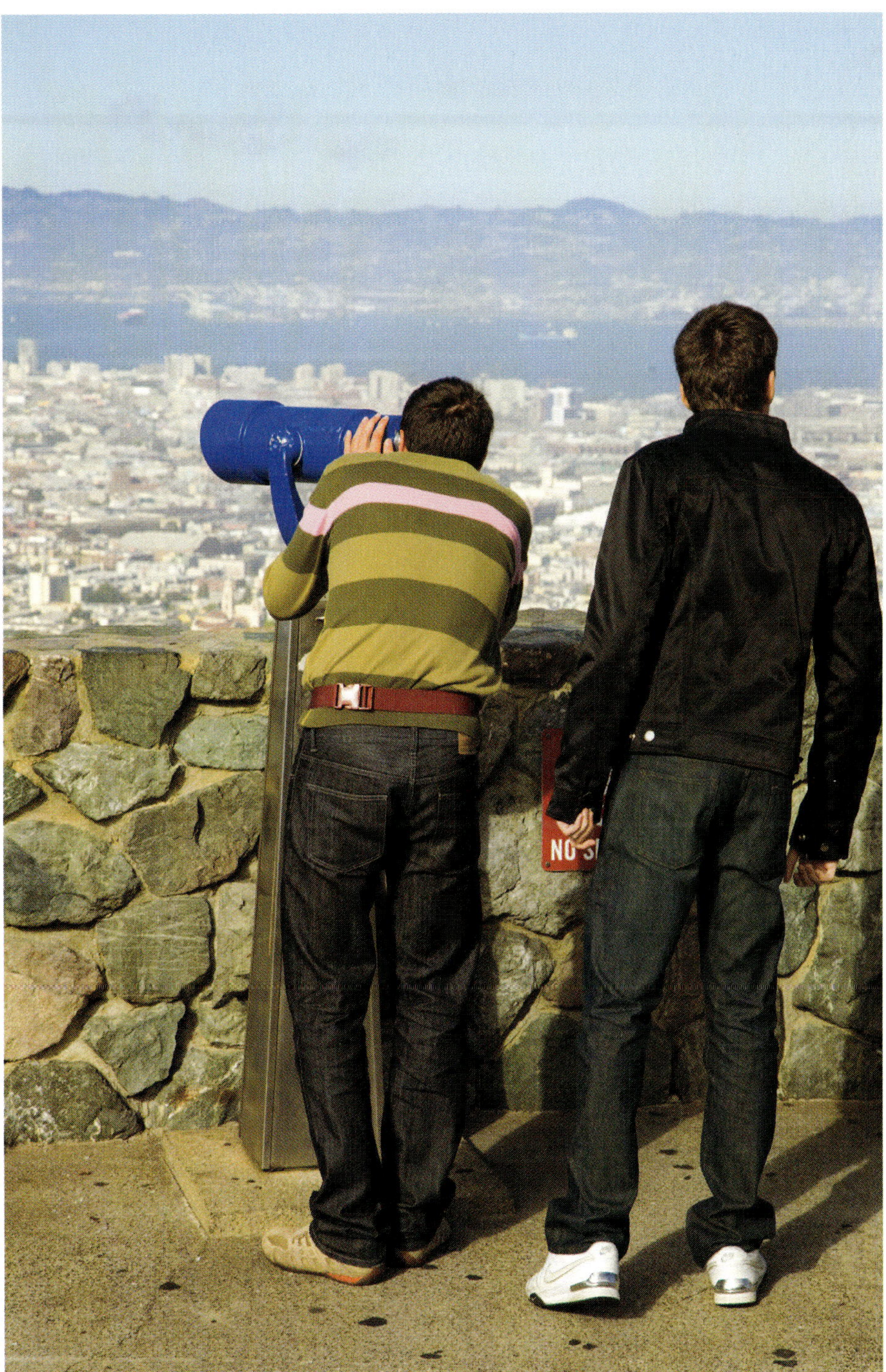

Focal length 92mm; ISO 200; aperture f/11; shutter speed 1/200; August 5:00 p.m.

The Shot

One of the advantages of having wide-angle capability on my zoom lens is being able to catch the wide expanse of a landscape, and there's no better place to find as thrilling a view as the top of Twin Peaks in San Francisco. Right below the overlook at the top of Twin Peaks, you can see Twin Peaks Boulevard snake around the mountain. I framed this photo so that it's divided up into thirds: The bottom third, the foreground, is of the Twin Peaks hill; the middle third, the middle ground, is of the city; and the top third, the background, is of the bay and sky together. If you look at the picture as a whole, the thirds meld together with varying colors and textures. On the right side of the frame you can see part of the East Bay in the background. Once the fog left on that day, the sky was so clear that you could see Mt. Diablo in the far-right corner of the frame. Mt. Diablo is about 30 miles from where the shot was taken.

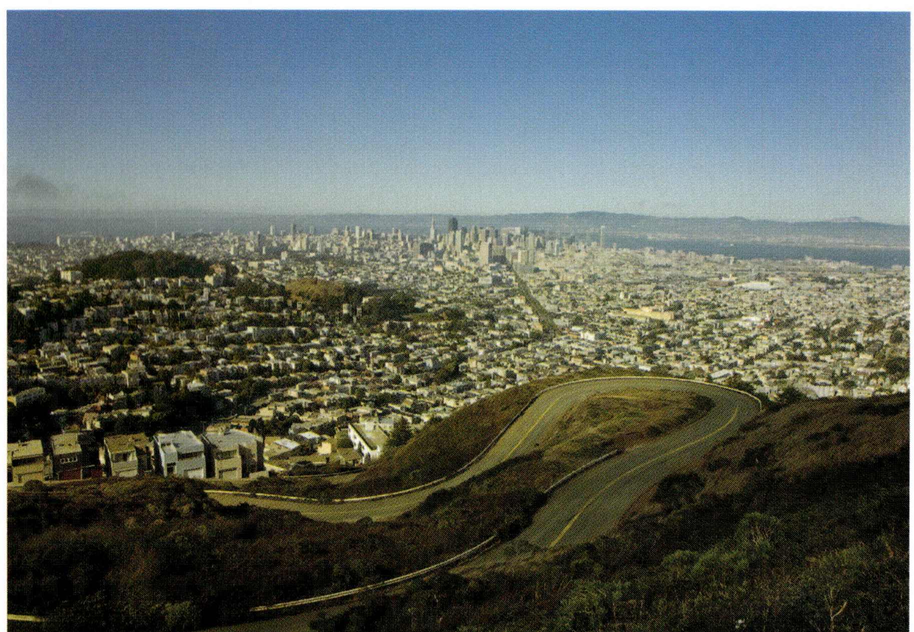

Focal length 24mm; ISO 200; aperture f/11; shutter speed 1/400; August 4:49 p.m.

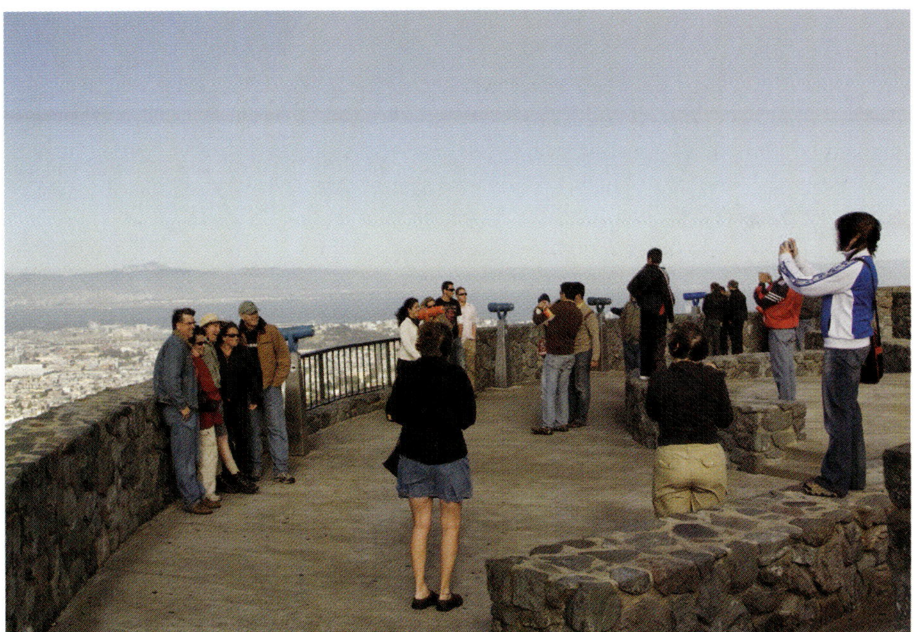

Tourists at Twin Peaks lookout.

Getting There

The Twin Peaks observation area is at Twin Peaks Boulevard and Christmas Tree Point Road.

To get there using mass transit,from downtown take the K, L, or M Muni Metro train to Castro Street. Transfer to the 37 Corbett bus, which stops on the west corner of Market and Castro Streets. Get off at Corbett and Clayton. Walk west on Clayton to Pemberton Place. Make a left, then a sharp left on Twin Peaks Boulevard to Christmas Tree Point Road.

If you are driving, from the North Bay, take the Golden Gate Bridge to the Park Presidio/19th Avenue exit. Make a right on Cabrillo, go one short block, then turn left on 14th Avenue, left on Fulton, right on Stanyan, left on 17th Street, right on Clayton, and right on Twin Peaks Boulevard to Christmas Tree Point Road.

From the East Bay, take 80 West to 101 North, then follow the directions for the South Bay route.

From the South Bay, take 101 North to 280 South. Exit on Monterey Boulevard and make a left on Bosworth Street, which changes to Oshaughnessy Boulevard. Make a right on Portola Drive and left on Twin Peaks Boulevard to Christmas Tree Point Road.

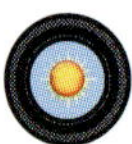 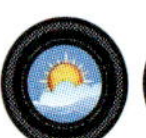 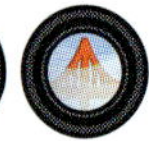

When to shoot: morning, afternoon

Sutro Baths

If I could wish back one thing about San Francisco that existed in the past and is no longer there, I'd wish to bring back the Sutro Baths. In 1894, after Adolf Sutro rebuilt the Cliff House, which had burned down, he decided to develop the beachfront land he owned next to it. Sutro built a multilevel complex, which he referred to as the "Palace of the People." When the baths opened in 1896, up to 25,000 patrons had a choice of six heated saltwater pools and a cold freshwater pool, into which they could enter via flying rings, trampolines, slides, or swings. The pools sat under a glass roof that contained 100,000 panes. When you photograph the ruins, you'll see what were once the saltwater and freshwater pools.

The Shot

When you walk around the ruins of Sutro Baths, you'll find a couple of staircases that provided access to the different levels of the building. This staircase is embedded in the westernmost wall of the pool at the north end of the Sutro Bath right near the ocean. The small staircase, which is exposed to the wave action much of the time, contains a variety of ocean plant life of different shades of green that make for an interesting shot. To catch the details on and around the staircase, I used a narrow aperture in Av mode. The bottom of the staircase is deep in the center of the frame with the water at the bottom, which adds depth and a variety of textures to the site.

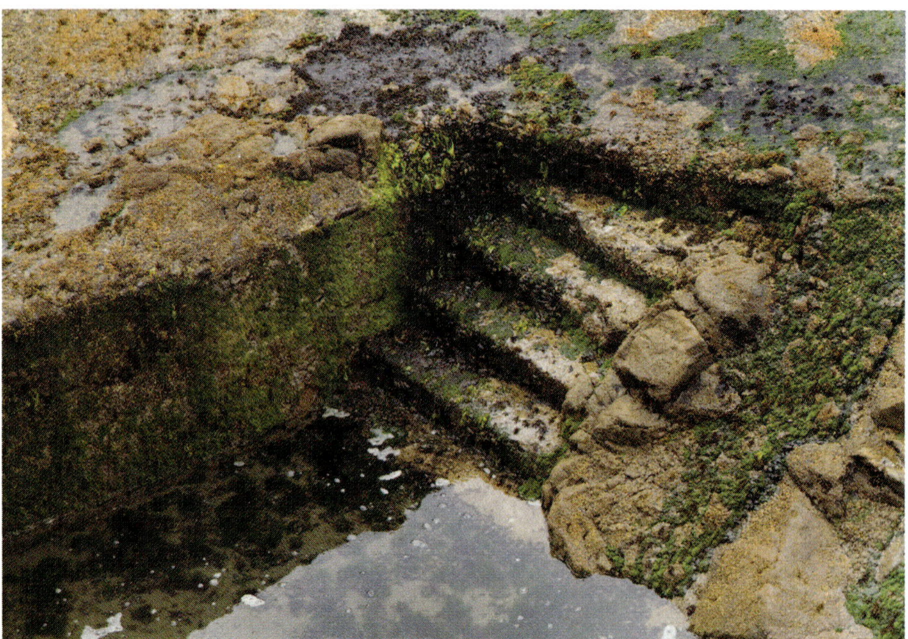

Focal length 105mm; ISO 200; aperture f/9; shutter speed 1/125; August 3:05 p.m.

The Shot

You can get a great view of the Sutro Baths from behind the north end of the Cliff House building. The north end of the building is a newer addition (2004) to a 1909 main structure on the south end. Enter the north end of the building from Point Lobos Avenue and take the staircase to the bottom level. There you'll find overlooks of the Sutro Baths on the north end and Ocean Beach on the south end. This picture was taken in late afternoon, just after the fog had broken to reveal a blue sky. I had to wait a good two hours for the fog to break, and when it did, I quickly took this and other shots. Just as quickly as the fog broke, it reappeared, which left me with only a small window of time to get a good shot. The sky's color provides a stark contrast to that of the land below. In the middle ground on the right side of the frame, you can see the remains of one of the pools of Sutro Baths.

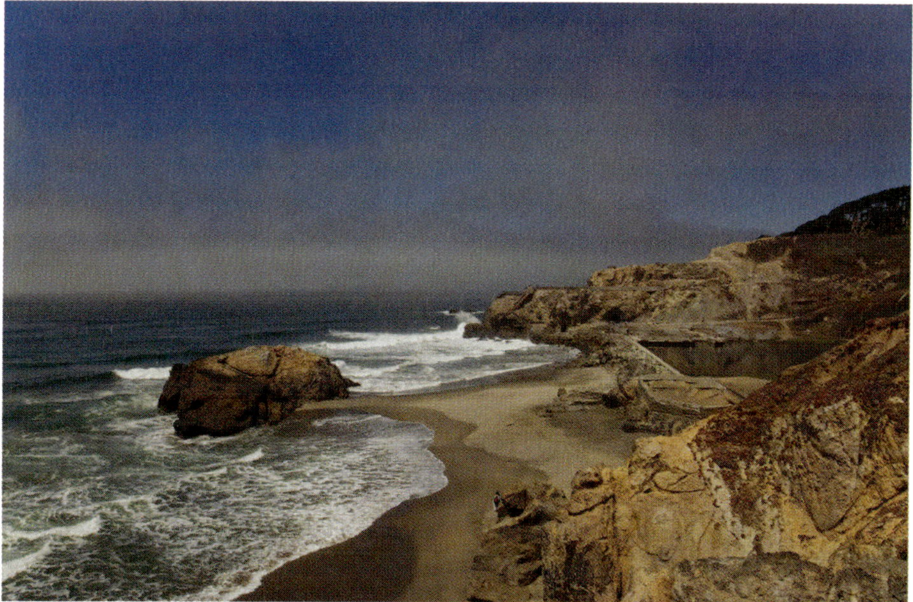

Focal length 24mm; ISO 200; aperture f/9; shutter speed 1/500; August 4:20 p.m.

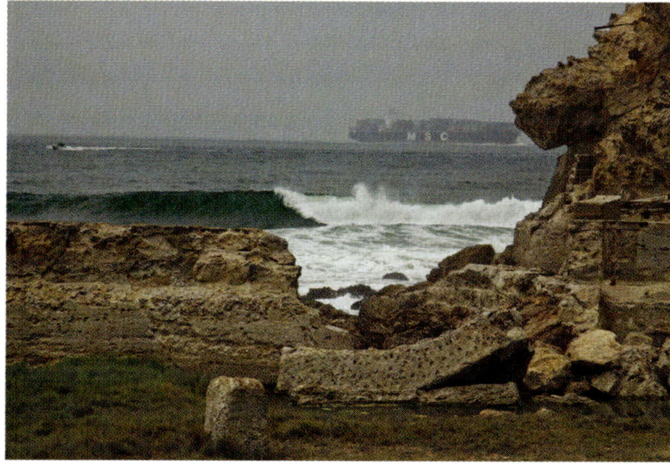

A ship passes by the ruins.

Getting There

Sutro Baths is located next to (just north of) the Cliff House, which is at 1090 Point Lobos Avenue.

To get there using mass transit, take the 38 Geary bus from Davis and Pine Street downtown to 48th and Point Lobos in the Richmond District. Walk west on Point Lobos to just before the road curves south. You'll see the baths on your right.

If you're driving, from the North Bay, take the Golden Gate Bridge toward the 25th

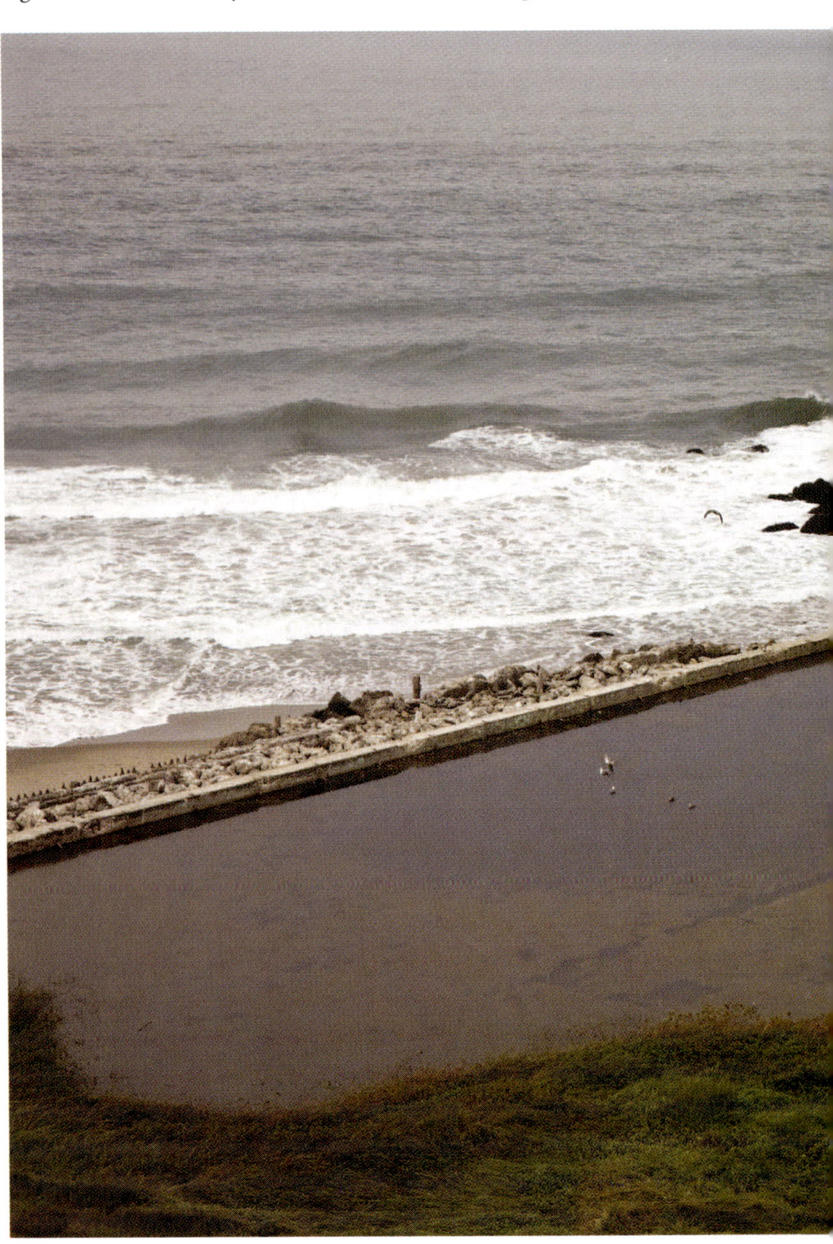

Avenue exit and merge onto Merchant Road. Make a right on Lincoln, a right on 25th Avenue, and a right on Geary, which turns into Point Lobos Avenue.

From the East Bay, take 80 West to exit at Central Fwy/101-N toward the Golden Gate Bridge. Make a slight left on Van Ness and a left on Geary, which turns into Point Lobos Avenue.

From the South Bay, take 280 North to San Francisco. It will turn into CA-1 N/19th Avenue. Veer left just after you get into Golden Gate Park. 19th Avenue will change to 25th Avenue after you get out of the park. Make a left on Geary, which turns into Point Lobos Avenue.

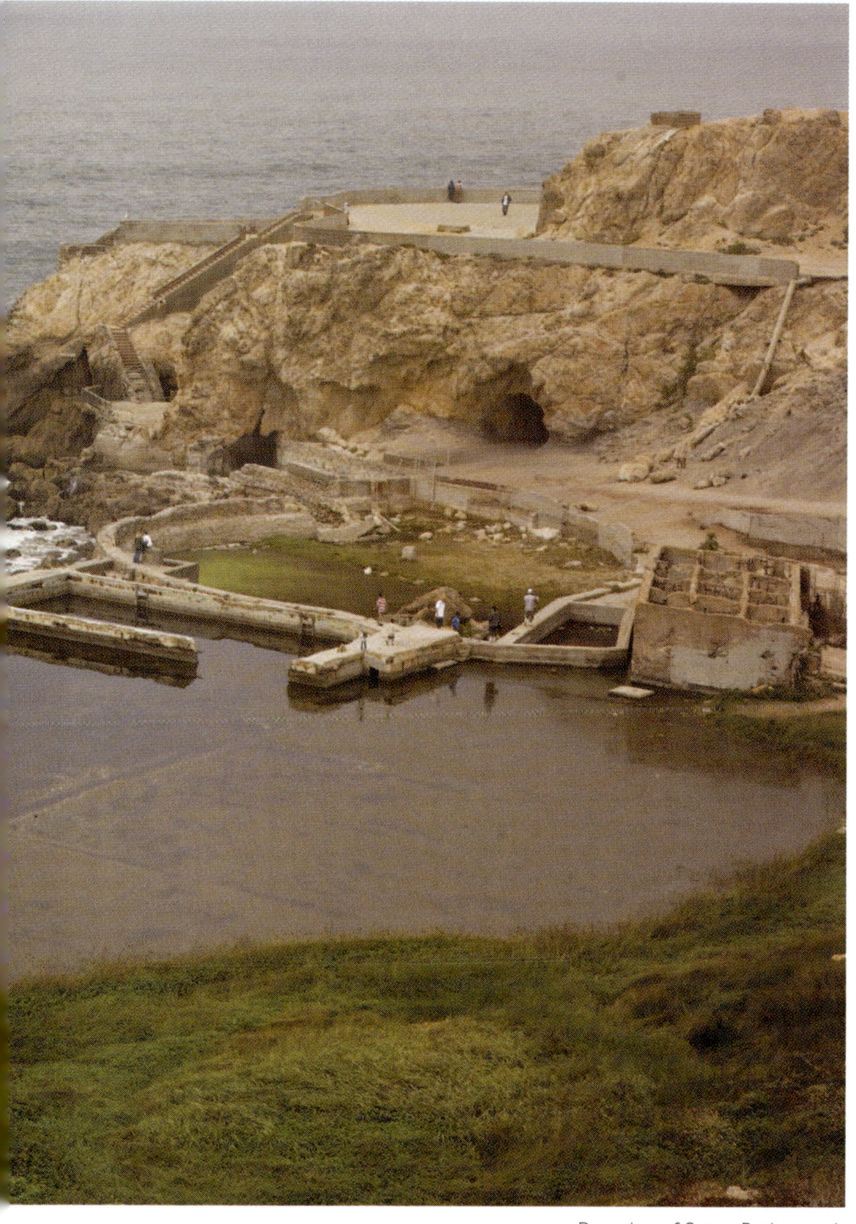

Remains of Sutro Baths pool.

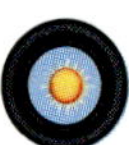 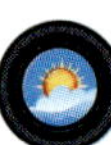

When to shoot: morning, afternoon

Candlestick Park

On a gorgeous October day in 1989, the third game of the World Series was about to begin at Candlestick Park. At 5:04 p.m., the ground started to shake. Then the field rose and fell in a giant wave. It looked as if the Candlestick Park stadium was going to split apart. For 15 seconds, 65,000 fans wondered what was going on. The Loma Prieta earthquake had hit the Bay Area with a vengeance. The moment the earthquake hit Candlestick Park is perhaps one of the most significant historical events to take place in San Francisco in the twentieth century.

The stadium, now referred to as Monster Park, opened in 1960 with Richard Nixon delivering the first pitch. In 1966, the Beatles performed at the park. Today, the park is home to the San Francisco 49ers football team. One of the reasons why the San Francisco Giants baseball team moved from this location to AT&T Park (see the AT&T Park photo op) is because of strong winds that can swirl into the stadium from all directions. The 49ers also plan to move in part because of the wind problem. They will be moving to a stadium that will be built in Santa Clara, California.

Locals refer to the area around the stadium as Candlestick Park, but officially it's known as Candlestick Point. Across the street from the stadium is the Candlestick Point State Recreation Area. Jamestown Avenue, which is bordered by the parking lots on the south side of the stadium and San Francisco Bay, and the recreation area, which lies at the southernmost point of Candlestick, are filled with spots to take great photographs.

The Shot

There's parking along Jamestown Avenue. Just before you get to the curve in the road before Candlestick Point State Park, there's a pier extending into the water on the right side of the road (south). You can park along the road while taking a picture of the pier. I framed this shot so the pier shoots out just above the left corner of the frame. The diagonal line that the pier makes within the frame ends at a point right below where the tallest building on the skyline is. When your eye goes to the end of the pier, it's rewarded with a modern building. In this image I used a wide aperture to limit the depth of field so that the sharpest part of the image was placed at the end of the pier and its surroundings just to the right of the center of the frame. Since the middle ground is tack sharp and the background somewhat soft, the photo almost looks as if it's three-dimensional. The diagonal lines in the pier also add dimension to the frame.

The Shot

The best view of the façade of the Candlestick Park stadium is from the back, off of Hunters Point Expressway. There are fewer trees blocking the structure in the back than in the front of the stadium. To get there by car, you drive southeast on Jamestown Avenue. The road turns north at a curve and then turns into Hunters Point Expressway. The entire area on the left side of the road as you turn the corner is the parking lot of the stadium.

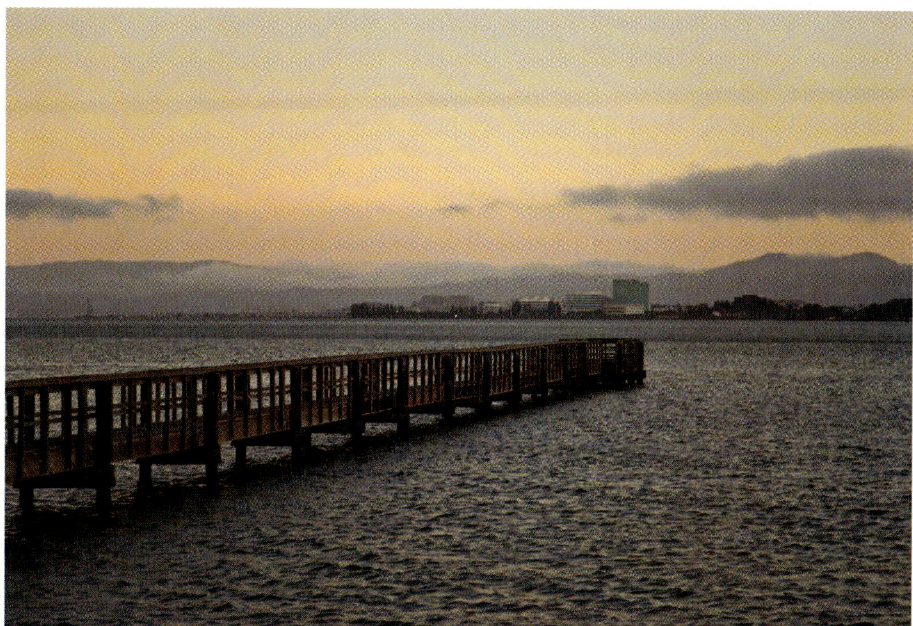

Focal length 97mm; ISO 200; aperture f/4; shutter speed 1/125; August 7:22 p.m.

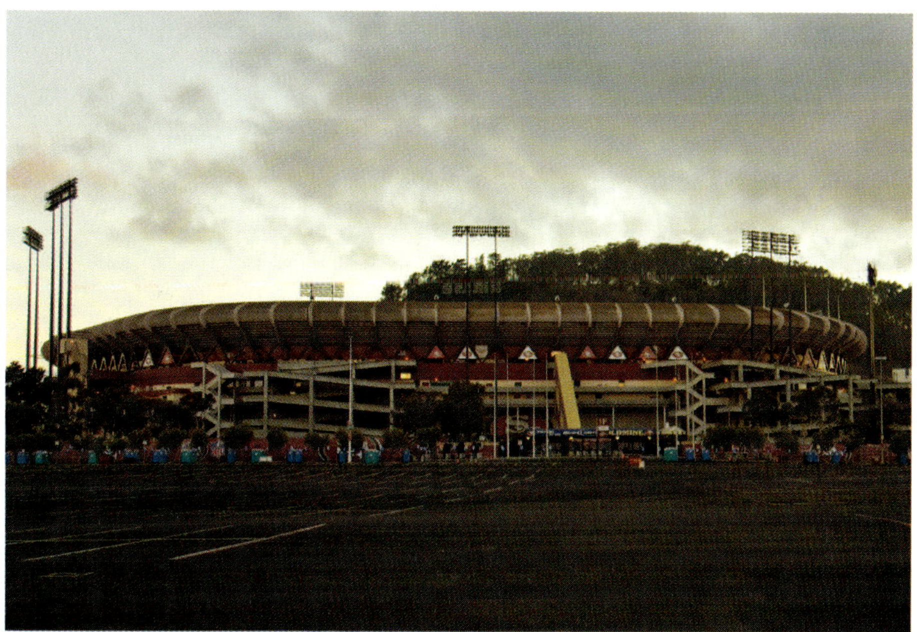

Focal length 35mm; ISO 200; aperture f/4; shutter speed 1/80; August 7:35 p.m.

It is surrounded by a large fence. There's a break in the fence at some gates on the left (west) side of the road about 1,000 feet after you pass the corner where the road changes its name. There's also a pull-off on that side of the road where you can park when you take the picture. As far as stadium architecture is concerned, this structure is a classic of mid-century modern design simply because the parking lot surrounds the building. When the stadium was built in the late '50s, the auto was king, and single-level parking lots were the name of the game. Back then, open parking lots were considered showplaces for automobiles with screaming colors and sleek designs. I caught the stadium as the fog was coming and as the sun was setting on the right side of it. There's lots of repeating patterns on the structure, from the triangles with "SF" inside them to the diagonal lines that make up the ramps. The frame is roughly divided into three parts: the surface of the parking lot at the bottom, the stadium in the middle, and the sky and fog at the top. Since the sun was setting, I got some light peachy tones in the left side of the frame.

Getting There

The back of Candlestick Park and the Candlestick Point State Recreation Area are on Hunters Point Expressway. There are bay views and parking on Jamestown Avenue (which turns into Hunters Point Expressway after the road curves from east to north). The recreation area is located just after the road changes names after the curve.

To get there using mass transit, from the south corner of 4th and Market downtown, take the 9X and get off at Bay Shore Boulevard and Leland Avenue. Walk northwest on Bay Shore Boulevard to the northwest corner of Blanken and Tunnel Avenue, where you'll take the 56 bus. Get off at 50 Thomas Mellon Drive. Walk south on Thomas Mellon Drive and make a left on Harney Way and a right on Jamestown Avenue to the pier, stadium, and park.

If you're driving, from the North Bay, take 101 South to Lombard Street. Turn right at Van Ness. Merge onto 101 South and take exit 429 A toward Monster Park/Tunnel Avenue. Keep right at the fork and merge onto Alanna Road. Take a slight left on Harney Way and a right on Jamestown, which turns into Hunters Point Expressway.

From the East Bay, take 80 West and continue on 101 South. Take exit 429 A toward Monster Park/Tunnel Avenue. Keep right at the fork and merge onto Alanna Road. Take a slight left on Harney Way and a right on Jamestown, which turns into Hunters Point Expressway.

From the South Bay, take 101 North. Exit at 429 A toward Monster Park and merge onto Harney Way. Make a right on Jamestown Avenue, which turns into Hunters Point Expressway.

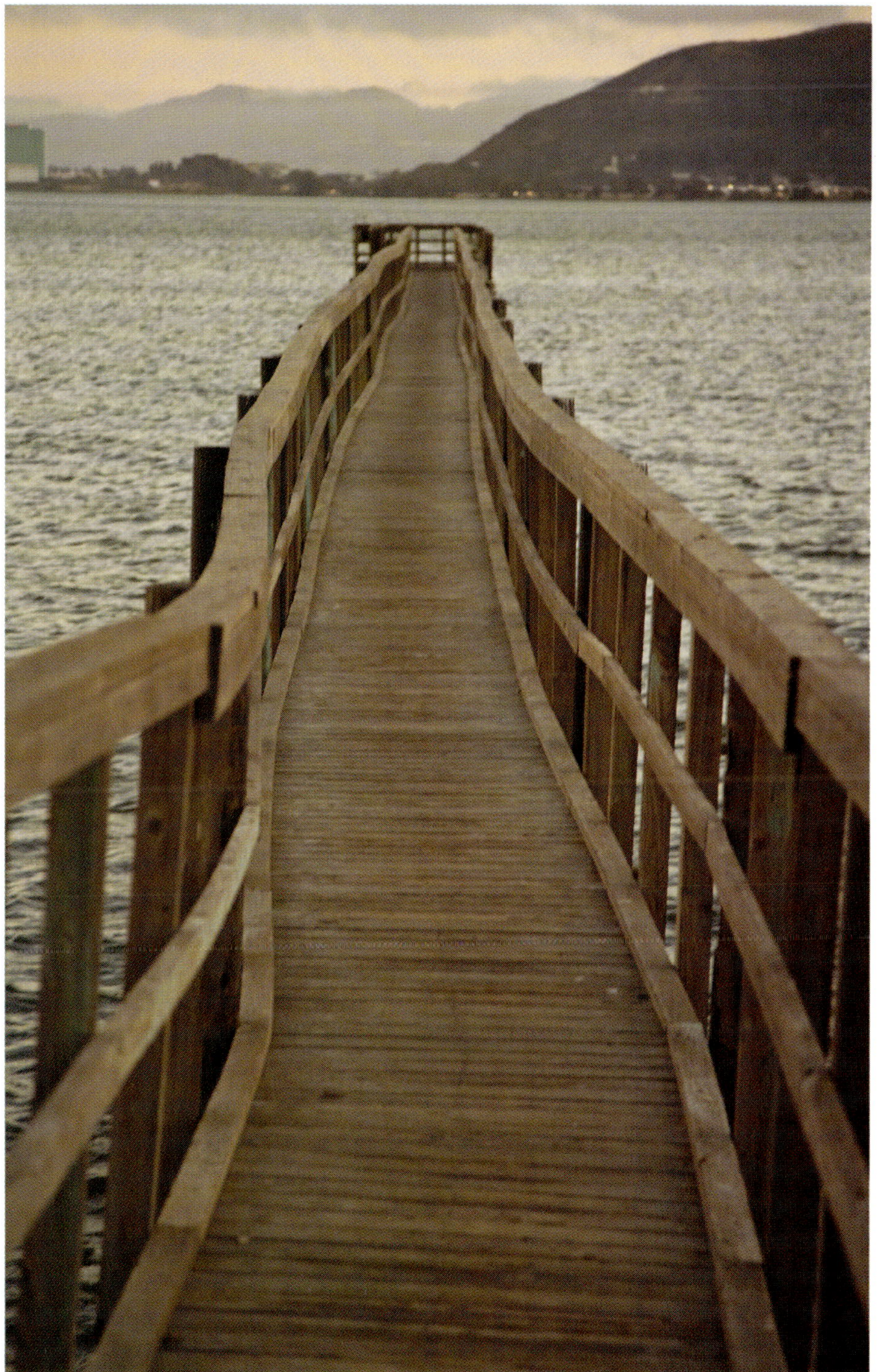

View of another pier shot at a wide aperture to restrict sharpness to a small area in the center of the frame.

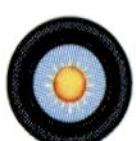 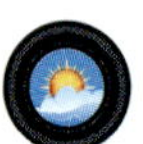 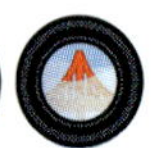

When to shoot: morning, afternoon

Ocean Beach

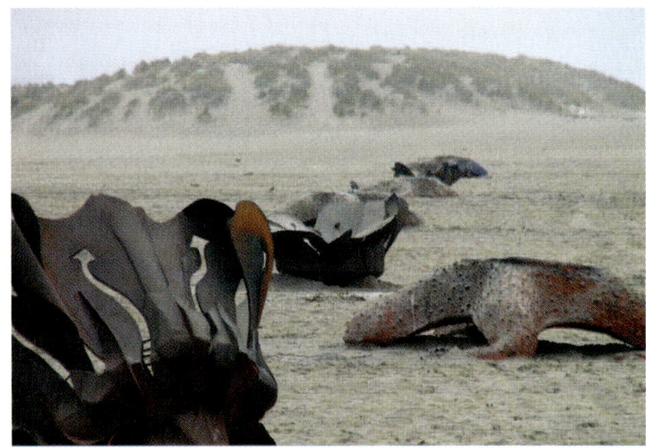

Fire pit sculptures on the beach.

With treacherous currents; dull, gray sand; and foggy skies, why would anyone want to go to Ocean Beach in San Francisco? In spite of the fact that the beach isn't a lay-down-your-blanket-and-get-some-sun kind of place, there's a lot going on there. The beach, which stretches from north to south for more than three miles, is a place where people fish, surf, jog, walk dogs, light bonfires (there are pits for this), fly kites, and, yes, drown. The last thing you want to do here is go for a swim. The undercurrents from the upwelled waters can suck you up as if there were a suction cup pumping underneath you. The beach's wide expanse of sand, sea, and sky make it a great place for photography, though, fog or shine. For some great landscapes, you can get some fantastic shots from above, up at the Cliff House at the beach's northern end. For candid shots, there's everything from surfers riding waves to fishermen casting their lines. Extra special is the windmill that can be photographed from the Great Highway across the street from the beach. The windmill has been there since 1902. It was originally built to irrigate the sand dunes so that plants could grow in what was to be Golden Gate Park. Soon electric pumps delivered the water to the park, and the windmill became obsolete.

The Shot

The best view of Ocean Beach comes from the south end of the observation deck at the Cliff House. (See the Sutro Baths photo op for directions to the Cliff House.) When you first look at this image, you might think that the rocky area you see in the foreground is closer than it is. It's quite a ways down to the ocean from the vantage point of the Cliff House observation area. In this shot I used a relatively narrow aperture so as not to soften both the rocky outcropping at the left side of the frame and the ocean that seems to stretch endlessly to the horizon.

The Shot

This picture of the windmill can be taken by walking from the east side of the Great Highway at Ocean Beach between the Beach Chalet and Fulton Street. The windmill is surrounded by lots of shrubbery, but if you use the Rule of Thirds you can fit the greenery into the picture so it complements the windmill. If you photograph the windmill straight on, it will look flat and two-dimensional. To give the picture more depth and to see the curvature of the blades, move a little to the south of the windmill to get it from a slight angle.

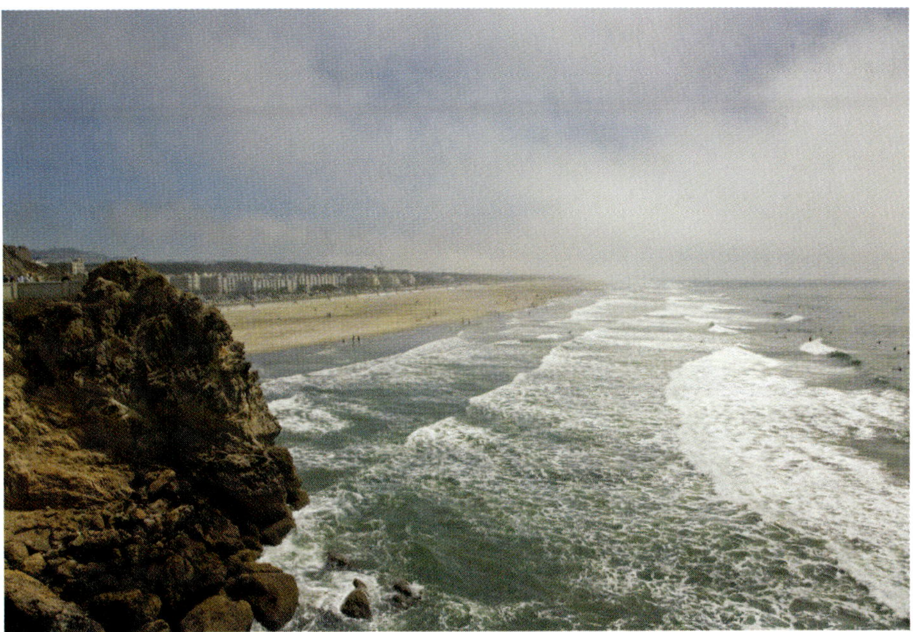

Focal length 24mm; ISO 100; aperture f/9; shutter speed 1/500; August 2:55 p.m.

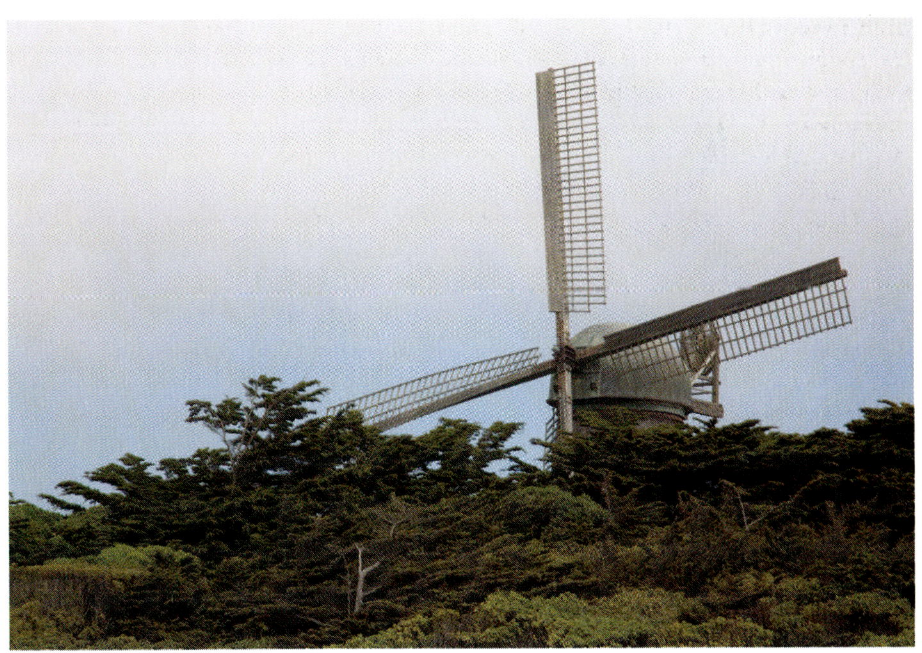

Focal length 105mm; ISO 200; aperture f/9; shutter speed 1/400; June 1:17 p.m.

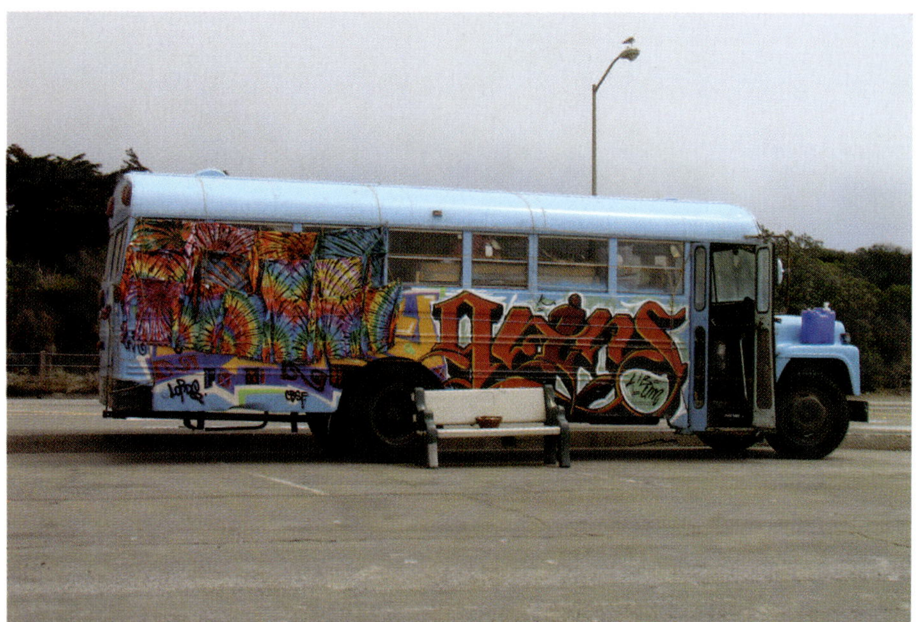

Tie-dyed T-shirts sold from a bus in the beach parking lot.

Getting There

The most popular part of Ocean Beach, the Beach Chalet (see the Beach Chalet photo op in Chapter 5), and the southern end of Golden Gate Park are within walking distance of one another.

To get there using mass transit, take the 5 Fulton from Powell and Market (north end) and get off at La Playa and Fulton Street. Walk west on Fulton to the beach.

If you're driving, from the North Bay, take 101 South toward the 19th Avenue exit. Merge onto CA-1, which turns into Park Presidio Boulevard. Make a right on Fulton to the Great Highway.

From the East Bay, take 80 West to exit 1B to merge onto 101 North. Take exit 434B toward Fell Street/Octavia Boulevard. Merge onto Octavia and make a left at Fell Street, a right at Shrader Street, and a left at Fulton Street to the Great Highway.

From the South Bay, take 280 North to San Francisco. It will turn into CA-1 N/19th Avenue. Veer left just after you get into Golden Gate Park. Take a left on Fulton, which is the street bordering the north end of the park. Make a left on the Great Highway.

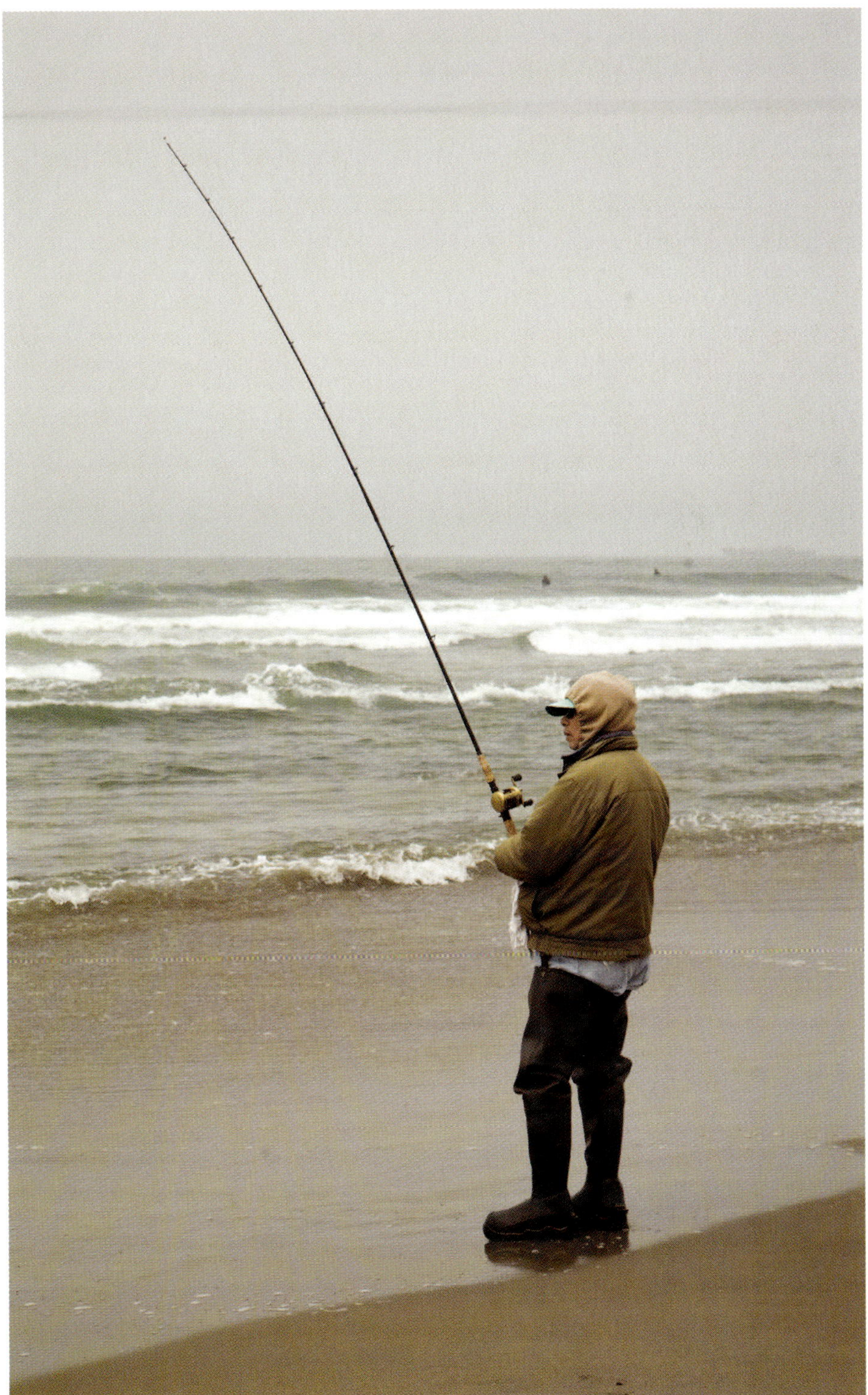

Fisherman on the beach.

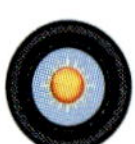 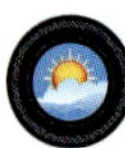 When to shoot: morning, afternoon

Stern Grove

In the 1870s, George M. Greene homesteaded the property that is now Stern Grove and planted eucalyptus trees. In 1931, Rosalie Meyer Stern bought the property from Greene for a memorial for her husband, Sigmund Stern. She deeded the grove to the city of San Francisco under the conditions that it be used as a place for the performing arts. In the '30s, the city purchased more land around the grove, and the federally funded Works Progress Administration helped to fix up the park. Today, the 63-acre park hosts a Midsummer Music Festival from June through August every year. Aside from eucalyptus trees, the grove has a cluster of redwood trees around a pond, which offers a brilliant reflection of the forest.

The Shot

To get to the redwood grove, enter the Stern Grove main entrance and go downhill (west) on the footpath until you run into the redwood grove and pond. I set up my tripod (see the upcoming "Photographing San Francisco Landscapes" sidebar) on the east side of the pond, aiming it away from the clubhouse, near the pond and toward the redwood grove. My goal was to bring out the rusty red color of the redwood tree trunks. I lowered the exposure compensation on my camera three stops so I could maximize my shutter speed. I was able to use a long shutter speed because the tree canopy covered the sky over the grove, letting in only a little light. That, combined with lowering my exposure compensation, gave me a one-second exposure. The very narrow aperture I used kept each tree trunk tack sharp.

The Shot

This is a wooden bridge right next to the pond. I set up my tripod in front of the side of the bridge to catch it lengthwise. In this I have a clearly delineated foreground, middle ground, and background, all of which contribute to a craggy setting. The primary subject in the image is the bridge, which I put tightly into the frame. The narrow aperture contributed to a sharp focus throughout the frame, and a (relatively) long exposure combined with a negative exposure compensation and the natural light that filtered though the trees enriched the color in the frame

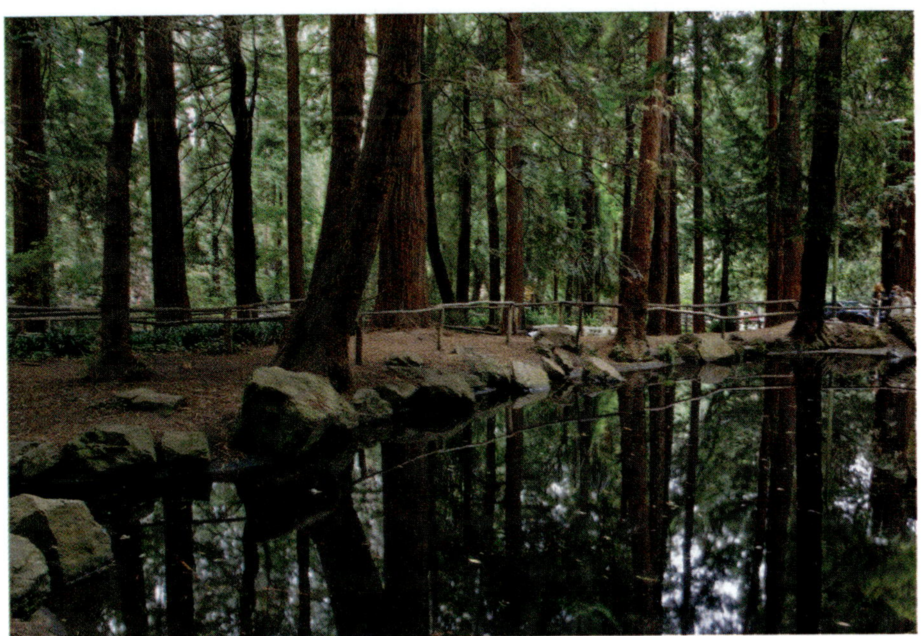

Focal length 28mm; ISO 200; aperture f/20; shutter speed 1 second; August 1:22 p.m.

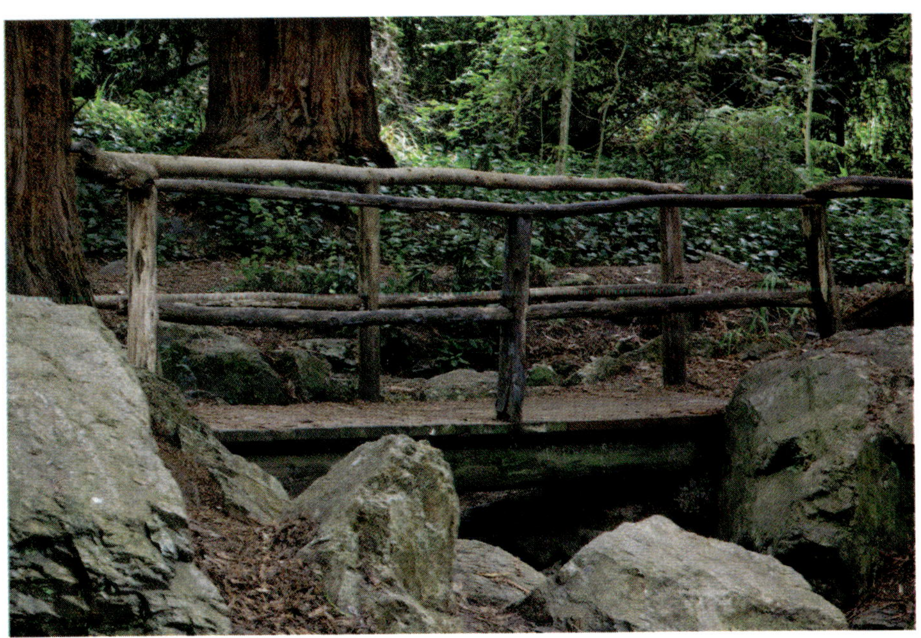

Focal length 82mm; ISO 200; aperture f/20; shutter speed 0.8 seconds; August 1:45 p.m.

PHOTOGRAPHING SAN FRANCISCO LANDSCAPES

You might already know all the tips for photographing landscapes: Use narrow apertures with the autofocus point set in the middle of the frame, use a tripod, scope out the spot a few times to find the best time of day to photograph it, and so on. Since San Francisco has special weather elements to consider, you'll want to add a few more tips to your knowledge base of landscape photography.

Getting a good photograph when there's a constant gray, overcast sky day after day, especially in late spring, summer, and early fall, is not impossible—in fact, it's highly likely. If you want to photograph during those times, the first thing to remember is to try to avoid photographing the sky. If you take a look at the Stern Grove shots, you'll see that there is no sky in the frame in either image.

But framing the image without the sky is only the first step. The next thing you'll want to do is set your camera on a tripod, especially if you find yourself in the middle of a redwood forest. It's just too dark under the giant trees' canopy to get a sharp photograph without one.

Finally, you'll want to set your camera to a narrow aperture in Av mode and then play with a few shutter speeds to see which ones give you the exposure you want. If you want longer shutter speeds, you can lower your exposure compensation a few stops, as I did in the two Stern Grove images.

You don't always have to photograph landscapes at narrow apertures. For special effects, you can try using wide apertures, which will cause a narrow depth of field. Experiment with placing the area of sharp focus at different locations throughout the frame. This can be a really cool effect in landscapes, as you saw in the second shot of the pier at Candlestick.

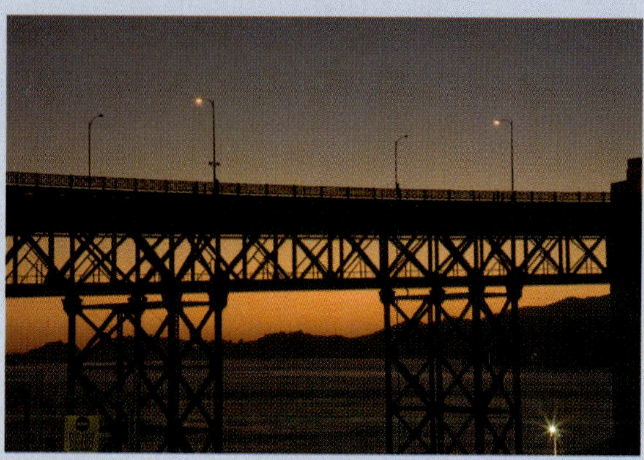

Golden Gate Bridge entrance, San Francisco side.

Finally if you use narrow apertures, there's a chance for your image to become soft due to lens diffraction, or light bending in different directions when it goes through a narrow opening. Take a few shots of the landscape at apertures smaller than f/9 so that you can pick out the one that comes out the sharpest and with the largest depth of field.

Don't forget the blessings of perfect weather. On sunny days or partly cloudy days, get out there and photograph just after dusk when the sky turns midnight blue, as shown in this shot of the Golden Gate Bridge entrance. Under these conditions, all the landscape photography tips you probably know work best.

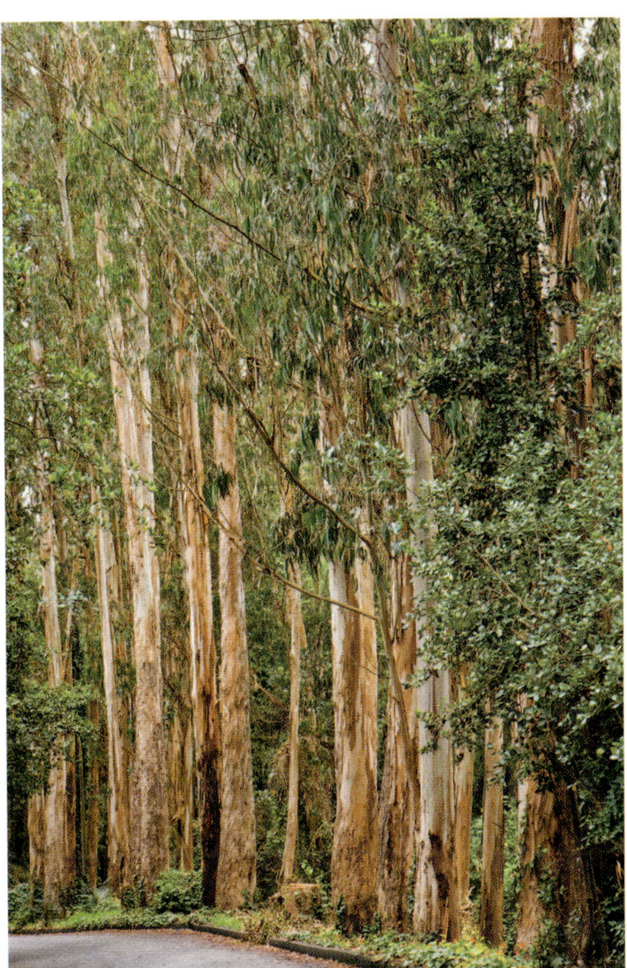
Eucalyptus trees in Stern Grove.

Getting There

The main entrance to Stern Grove is at the corner of 19th Avenue and Sloat Boulevard.

To get there using mass transit, from downtown, you can take the K Ingleside Muni line to West Portal Avenue and Sloat Boulevard. Walk one block west on Sloat Boulevard to Stern Grove. Note that West Portal Avenue turns into Sloat Boulevard one block east of Stern Grove.

If you're driving, from the North Bay, take 101 South and exit at 19th Avenue. Take 19th Avenue to Sloat.

From the East Bay, take 80 West and continue on 101 South to 280 South. Exit at Geneva Avenue and make a left on Geneva, a right on San Jose Avenue, a right on Sagamore Street, a slight right on Brotherhood Way, and a right onto the ramp for Junipero Serra. Veer left onto 19th Avenue to Sloat.

From the South Bay, take 280 North and make a slight left at 19th Avenue (the freeway turns into 19th Avenue on the left side) to Sloat.

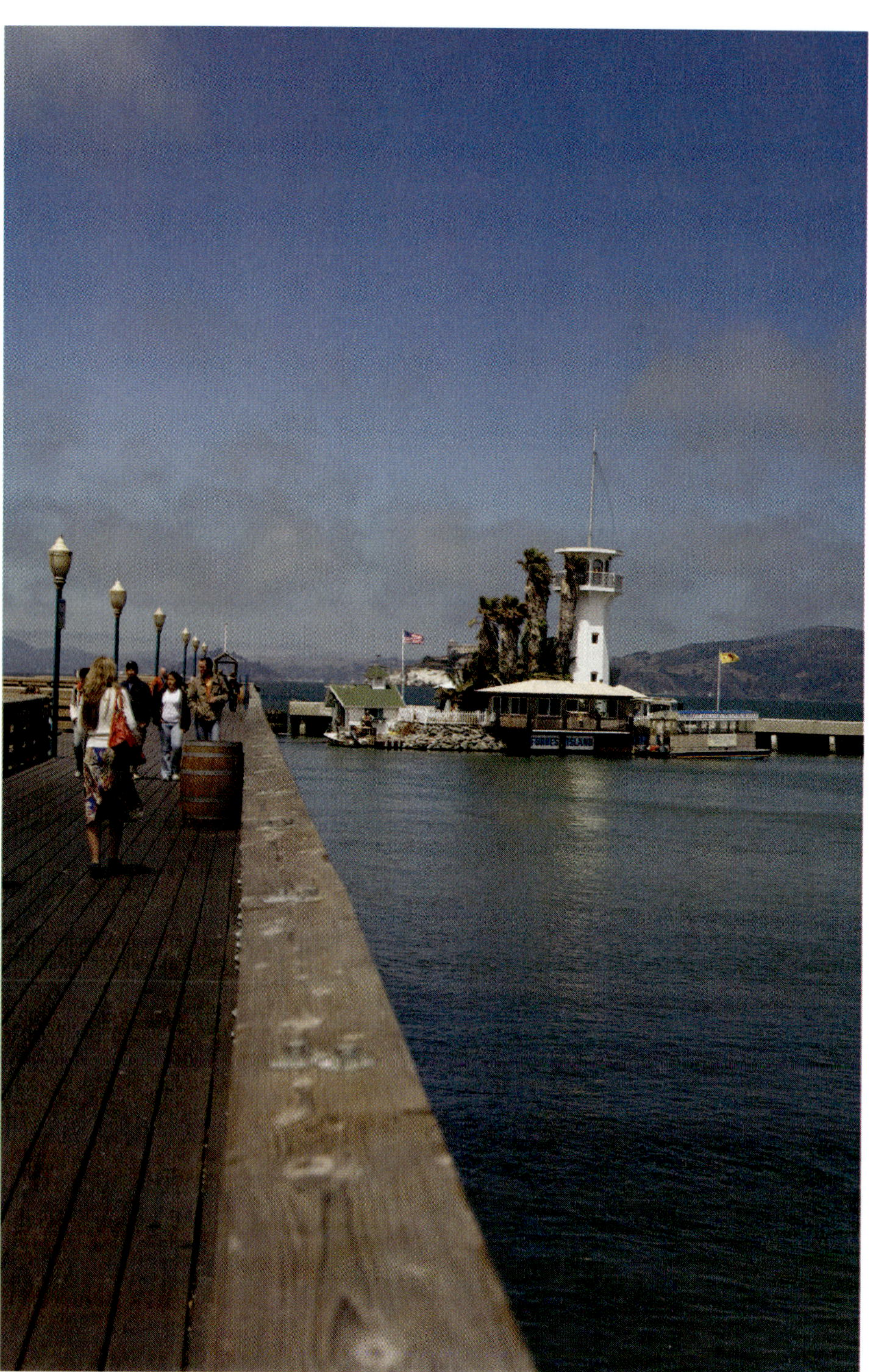

Lighthouse at Pier 41.

CHAPTER 5

Secret Places

A secret place in San Francisco can involve a set of stairs hidden under vegetative overgrowth or a narrow pier off of the bay. These types of photo ops will create serendipitous moments for your viewers. There's an alley that muralists have transformed into a place where people become aware of social justice, there are spectacular views from a neighborhood at the top of a hill in the south end of the city, and there's a beach house filled with artwork from the 1930s' Work Projects Administration. That's not all, either. Even if you're in the city only a few days, you're likely to find your own secret—a person, place, or thing so unique you'd be hard-pressed to find it anywhere else in the world.

Shooting Like a Pro

The first thing to remember when considering secret places in San Francisco is to have your camera with you as much as possible. You never know when you'll stumble on that perfect photo op. San Francisco has many staircases that are used by pedestrians—staircases that climb steep hills and that wind through neighborhood after neighborhood. When you have your camera and are climbing one of these staircases (the Filbert Steps are described in the Levi's Plaza and Filbert Steps photo op), you're likely to find a photo opportunity similar to this shot of flower pots overlooking the Bay Bridge.

Shooting like a pro in secret places means being willing to assume all kinds of positions to get the right angle in your shot. In the shot of the flower pots, I had to lie down on the ground to frame the planted pots with the Bay Bridge in the background and that wonderful design on the apartment building in the middle ground.

If you find just the ground interesting like it is in this garden shot, frame it alone. You don't have to include the sky and trees—in fact, including them would take away from the beauty of the shot.

Last on the pro list for secret places is shooting murals or other artistic works. Try to do more than just shoot the murals or part of them. Include some other elements from the surrounding environment in your picture to give it a personal touch. Also, shoot murals and sculptures at unique angles, including from above and below, and play with the light and shadows shining on or around them. Finally, if you're going to put a picture of someone else's artwork on your website or blog, it's always good to give credit where credit is due. List the artists or arts organization that did the work.

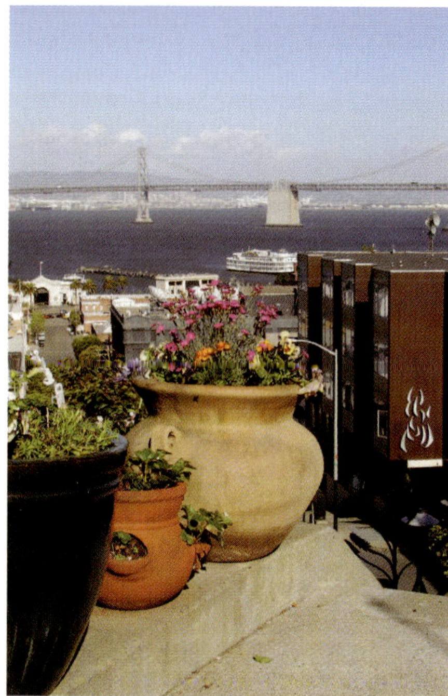

Sometimes you have to lie down to get a good photo.

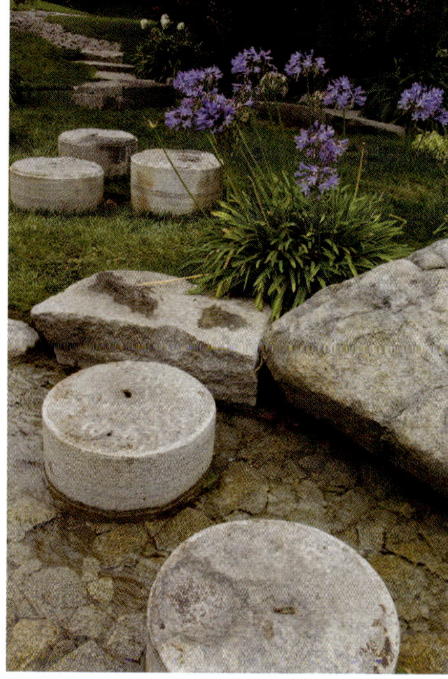

Include only the ground in your frame.

The Gear

Some of the lesser-known places in San Francisco that provide great photo ops are indoors. The Musée Mécanique and Beach Chalet offer excellent indoor shots, but they are busy places, not the kinds of places where you can set up a tripod. In this case you'll have to make your ISO speed a bit greater. There is one place—Grace Cathedral—that does let you shoot with a tripod inside. This image shows the church's labyrinth. While Grace Cathedral is no secret, the labyrinth might be to some. A general-purpose 28-105mm lens is a good one to photograph most of the secret places listed in this chapter. A wide-angle lens—say, 18 to 28mm—is also good, especially for shooting the San Francisco National Cemetery.

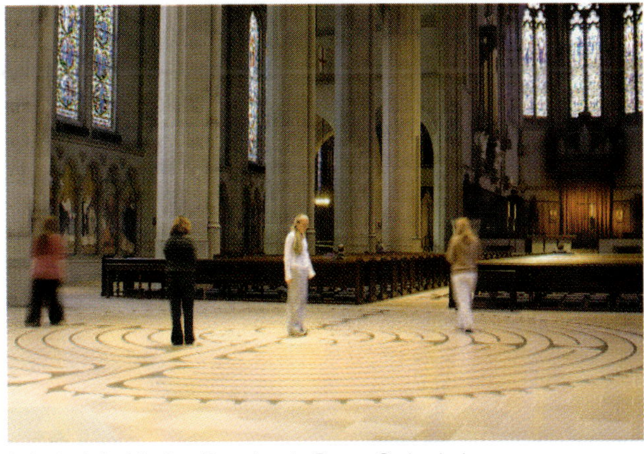

Labyrinth inside San Francisco's Grace Cathedral.

The Plan

Public transportation is the best way to get to many of the secret places in this chapter. For example, the Beach Chalet is very near the Cliff House, Sutro Baths, and Ocean Beach. If you're planning an outing, it's a good idea to visit all the attractions at one time. The same goes for the Fisherman's Wharf area. There are many "secret" piers, alleys, waterways, and parking lots where the views change upon each glance, and lots of people on the streets, including performance artists, make for some great photography. This shot shows how one pier, Pier 39, with its throngs of people and sea lions, looks from another pier, Pier 41.

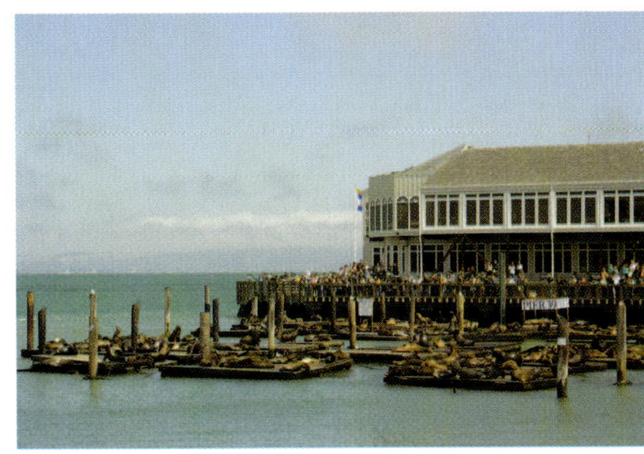

Sea lions off of Pier 39.

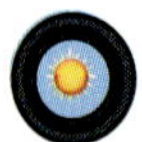 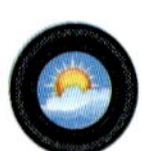

When to shoot: morning, afternoon

Balmy Alley

The Mission District is a mural haven, and Balmy Street (it's really an alley) is the haven's focal point. It's one of three alleys in the area lined by 24th and 25th Streets and Folsom and Harrison Streets. The alley has more than 30 murals that change from time to time, with themes such as human rights and Latin American culture that bring tolerance and justice front and center. These murals have been likened to those of the WPA (Work Projects Administration). WPA murals can be found in the Coit Tower and Beach Chalet photo ops. Unlike the WPA murals, the Balmy Alley murals (and the hundreds of other murals throughout the city) are very diverse both in the media used and in the subject matter.

The mural project on Balmy Street began in the '70s, when various muralist groups, such as the Mujeres Muralistas (women muralists), constructed works to celebrate women's lives. In 1985, Balmy Alley went into full swing with mural displays. During that year, 22 artists painted murals up and down the street to educate people about topics such as the United States' intervention in Central America. Precita Eyes (precitaeyes.org), which sponsors and implements mural projects, offers maps of locations of Mission District murals ($3) and Saturday tours on which you can see more than 60 murals in a 10-block walk.

The Shot

Precita Eyes muralists painted the mural at the bottom of the picture. It's situated on the east side of the street about 100 feet south of the northeastern corner of 24th and Balmy Streets. To take the picture, I stepped back from the mural to the west side of the street and framed the entire building vertically so viewers can get a sense of the mural as it appears on the façade of the flat building. Note that the iron work on the railing and front gate adds an additional artistic element to the shot. I had to be careful when taking this shot because the sun was shining on the building—a time when my camera tends to overexpose when I shoot in aperture priority mode. I lowered my exposure compensation to –.5 to get a better exposure. I checked the exposure after I took the shot by looking at the histogram. (For more about histograms, see the "Just What Are Those Diagrams Called Histograms?" sidebar.) The histogram was weighted in the center, as shown in the middle graph of the histogram diagram. This let me know that I had a good exposure.

NOTE

Because I captured this image in raw mode I could have achieved an identical result while shooting at a normal exposure by using raw conversion software to lower the overall exposure once the image was uploaded to the computer. A major benefit of shooting in raw mode is the degree of high-quality post-capture processing available. But shooting in raw mode isn't an excuse to get careless when setting your exposure in the field. If your camera fails to record any information at all in the highlights, no amount of post-capture exposure reduction can recover the missing information.

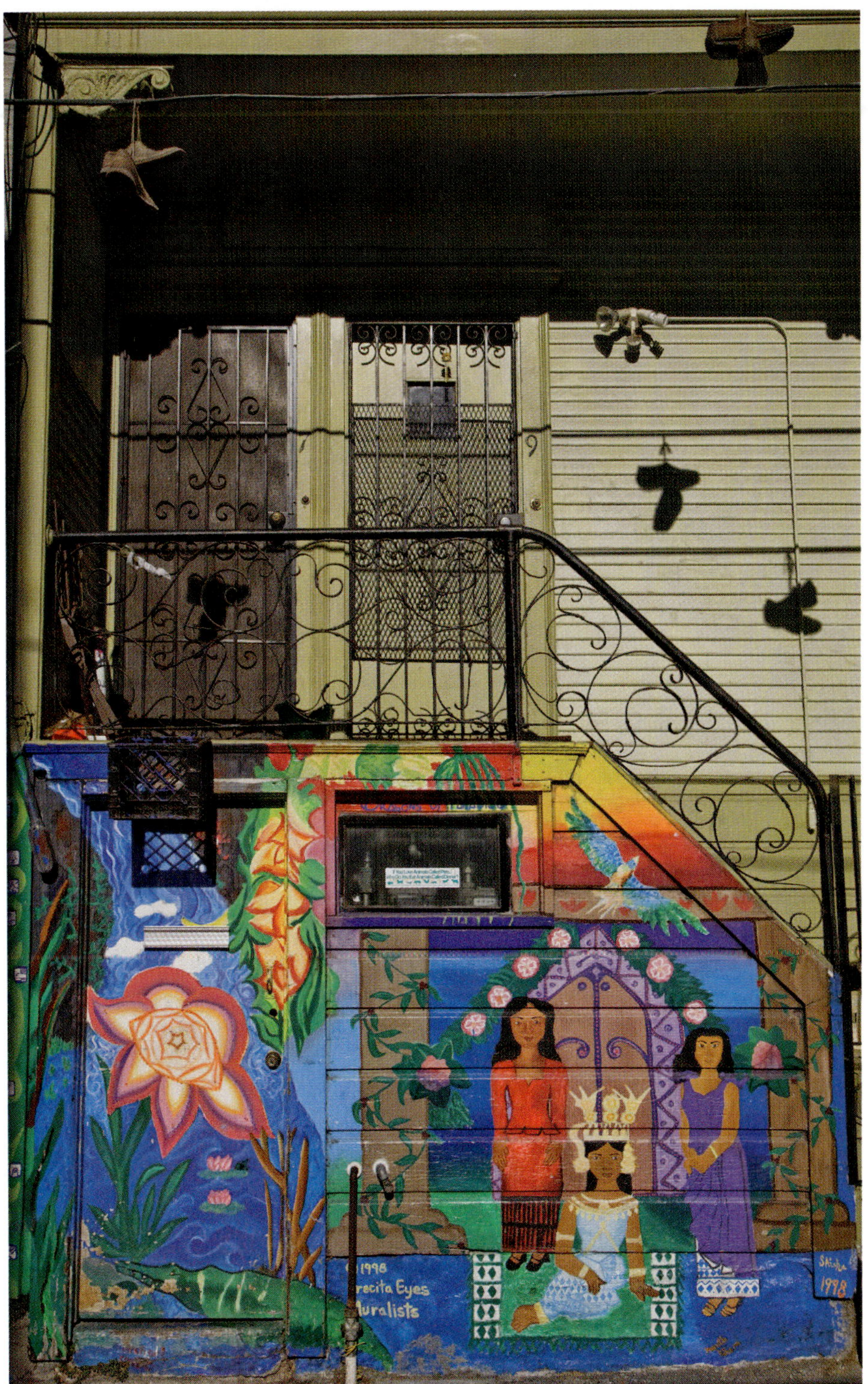

Focal length 32mm; ISO 200; aperture f/8; shutter speed 1/1000; August 5:42 p.m.

If you look closely at the picture, there is some other stuff going on that's kind of fun. There's a pair of shadows cast on the building that look as if they are emanating from birds. If you look at the top of the frame, you'll see they are tennis shoes. What's nice about these shadows is that they fill the blank space of the building with shadow shapes, which kind of balance the picture so there's something going on in all quadrants of the shot (the bottom of the building and the left and right sides of the top of the building).

JUST WHAT ARE THOSE DIAGRAMS CALLED HISTOGRAMS?

High-end digital cameras can display a histogram of each recorded image. Why is this important? A histogram is a visual representation of the relative number of pixels at any given luminance, or brightness level. In the illustrations here, I've divided the histogram range into five sections, representing from left to right: blacks, shadows, midtones, lights, and highlights. The location of the tallest peak along a histogram indicates the highest concentration of pixels. A histogram that is bunched toward the right indicates an exposure of primarily bright luminance levels. A histogram bunched toward the left means the camera recorded the scene as a very dark one. A proper exposure of a scene with a "normal" contrast range will show pixel values across the full range of the histogram with most data residing in the middle luminance ranges and tapering off at the endpoints. It's worth noting that there is no such thing as a perfect histogram. A black cat in a coal mine and a polar bear in the snow photographed at their optimum exposures will yield completely different histogram shapes. Something you should always avoid, however, are peaks at extreme ends of the histogram range. These indicate an exposure in which shadow and/or highlight information has been clipped and cannot be recovered.

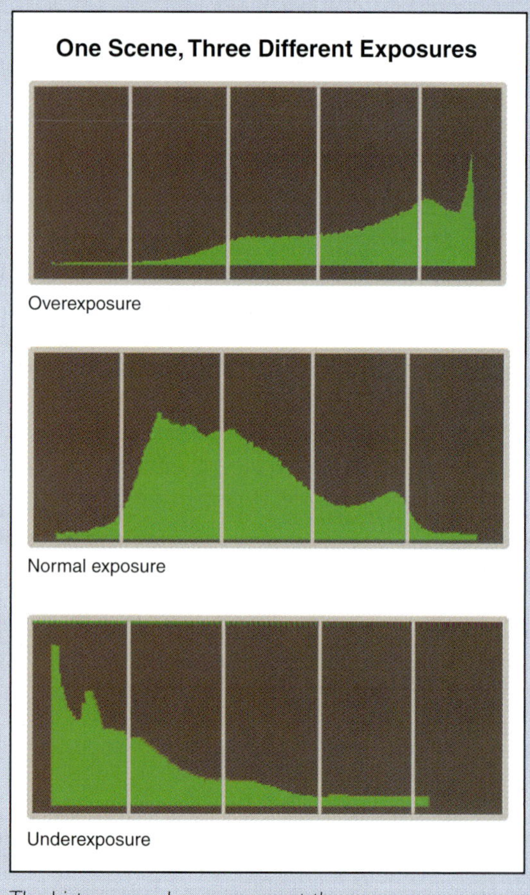

The histograms above represent the same scene captured at different exposure values.

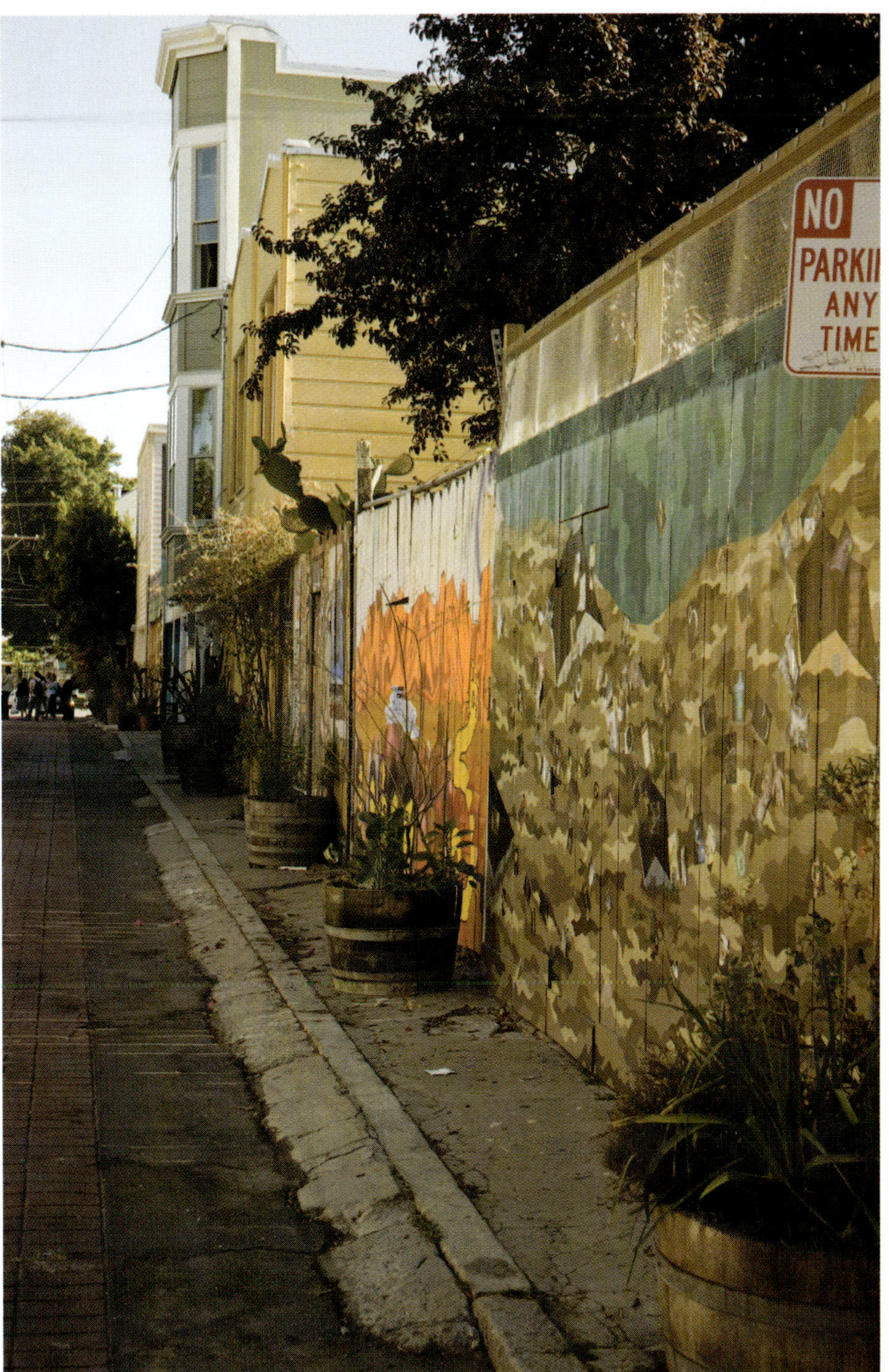

Balmy Street looking south.

The Shot

This mural and bougainvillea plant is on the east side of the alley, right in the middle of the block. If you step back a bit from the mural and the bush, they're easily photographed. One word that would describe this image is *patina.* As painted wood is exposed to the elements, it wears down so that you can see the grain of it appearing though the painted surface. The grain made from the wood leaching though the paint provides interesting designs, which overlay half of the woman. When painted surfaces are exposed to the outdoors for long periods of time, the color of the paint changes, sometimes to colors that you've never seen before. Since there's really no prominent subject or object in this shot, it's a great shot to experiment with your camera's light metering system. I got the most balanced light in this shot by setting my metering system so that the camera averages the light from the entire frame.

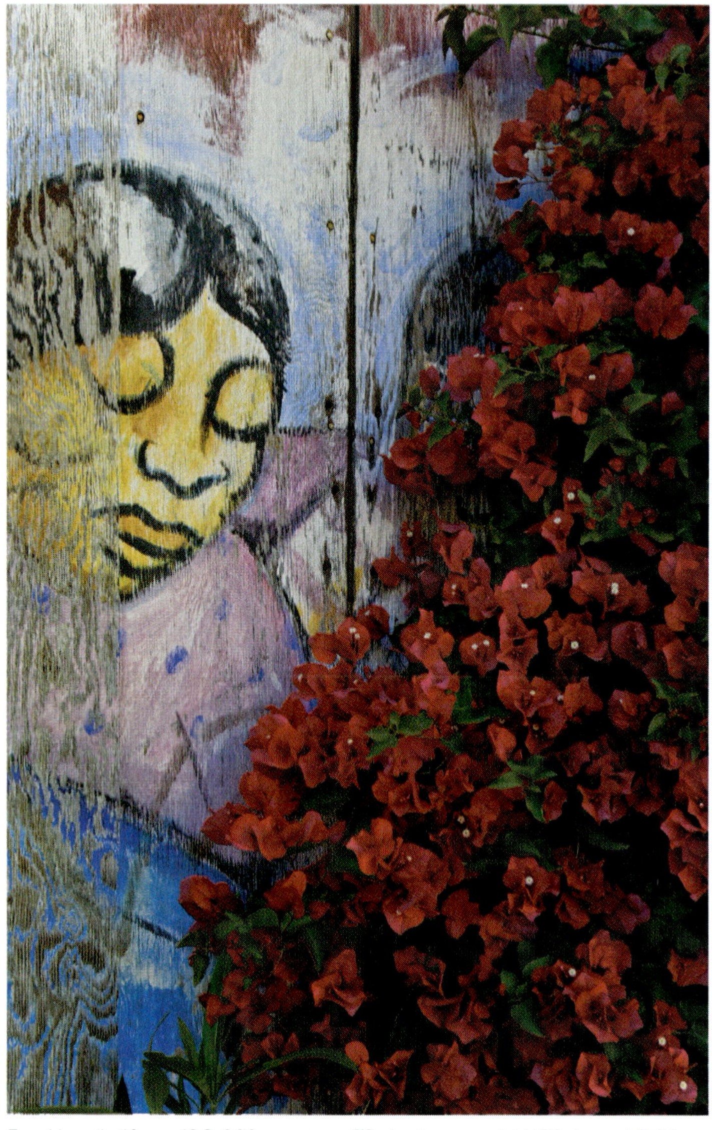

Focal length 40mm; ISO 200; aperture f/9; shutter speed 1/100; August 5:04 p.m.

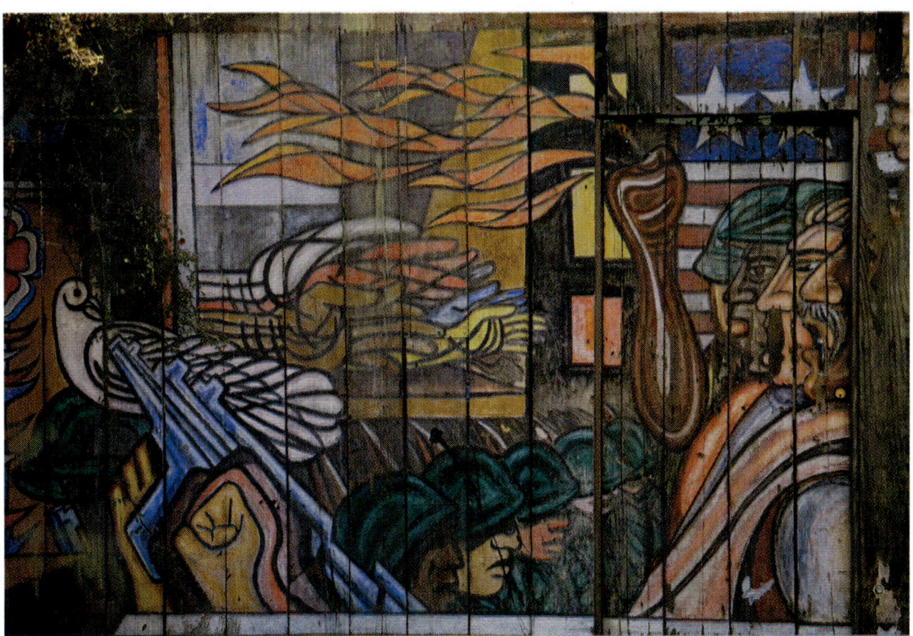

Some of the murals depict political themes.

Getting There

To get there using mass transit, from downtown, take BART to the 24th and Mission station. You can also take the 14 Mission bus anywhere along Mission Street downtown.

If you're driving, from the North Bay, take 101 South. Veer right onto Richardson Street, which turns into Lombard Street. Make a right on Van Ness, which turns into S. Van Ness after Market Street, then turn left on 25th Street.

From the East Bay, take 80 West to 101 South to Cesar Chavez Street. Make a right at Harrison Street and a left on 25th.

From the South Bay, take 101 North to the Cesar Chavez exit. Make a left on the Cesar Chavez ramp, a right on Harrison Street, and a left on 25th Street.

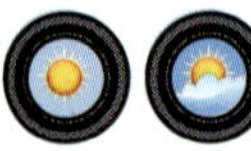
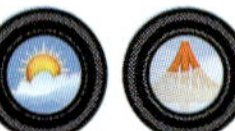

When to shoot: morning, afternoon

Beach Chalet

In 1996, the Spanish-style building designed by Willis Polk underwent a major restoration. The 1925 building originally was a changing room and restaurant for Ocean Beach bathers. It later went on to be a lascivious gambling hall. After WW II, it was taken over by the army and later rented to the Veterans of Foreign Wars. In 1979, the building was closed until some college students recognized its potential and worked out a plan to open a restaurant there. Today, there's a visitor center on the first floor and the restaurant and brewery on the second. Some of the most interesting things about the Beach Chalet are the 1930s' WPA (Work Projects Administration) frescoes that wrap around the inside of the building, all 1500 feet of them. Lucien Labaudt, an artist who opened a school of fashion and design on Powell Street, designed all of them. If you take a close look at the people he painted in them, you'll get the connection between Labaudt's fashion background and the characters he painted.

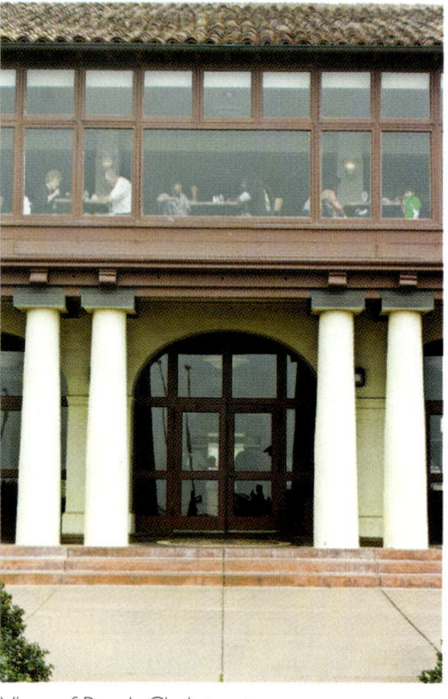

View of Beach Chalet entrance.

The Shot

The portico of the Beach Chalet is a typical Spanish-style—wood plank ceiling, tile floor, and rows of columns that support the roof. I shot this by standing at the southern end of the building looking north, so that the entire portico is in the frame. This shot's perspective enhances the depth of the frame. I shot with a relatively narrow aperture to keep everything in the frame in sharp focus, including the bushes at the end. The green of the bushes at the end of the portico is the payoff when the viewer looks through the hallway into the frame's center. It, too, adds even more depth to the picture. Also adding to viewer's interest in the picture is the repetition of both the columns on the left and the light fixtures on the right, which enhance the elongated perspective of the shot.

I know from my experiences with my camera that 1000 is the highest ISO speed I can use before I see major image degradation (noise and loss of detail). One example of image degradation is the tiny multicolored dots that appear in an area where the color is actually solid. Every camera is different. Some cameras do really well at higher ISO speeds, and some don't. Practicing with your camera will help you to get to know what ISO speeds you can use and still maintain acceptable image quality.

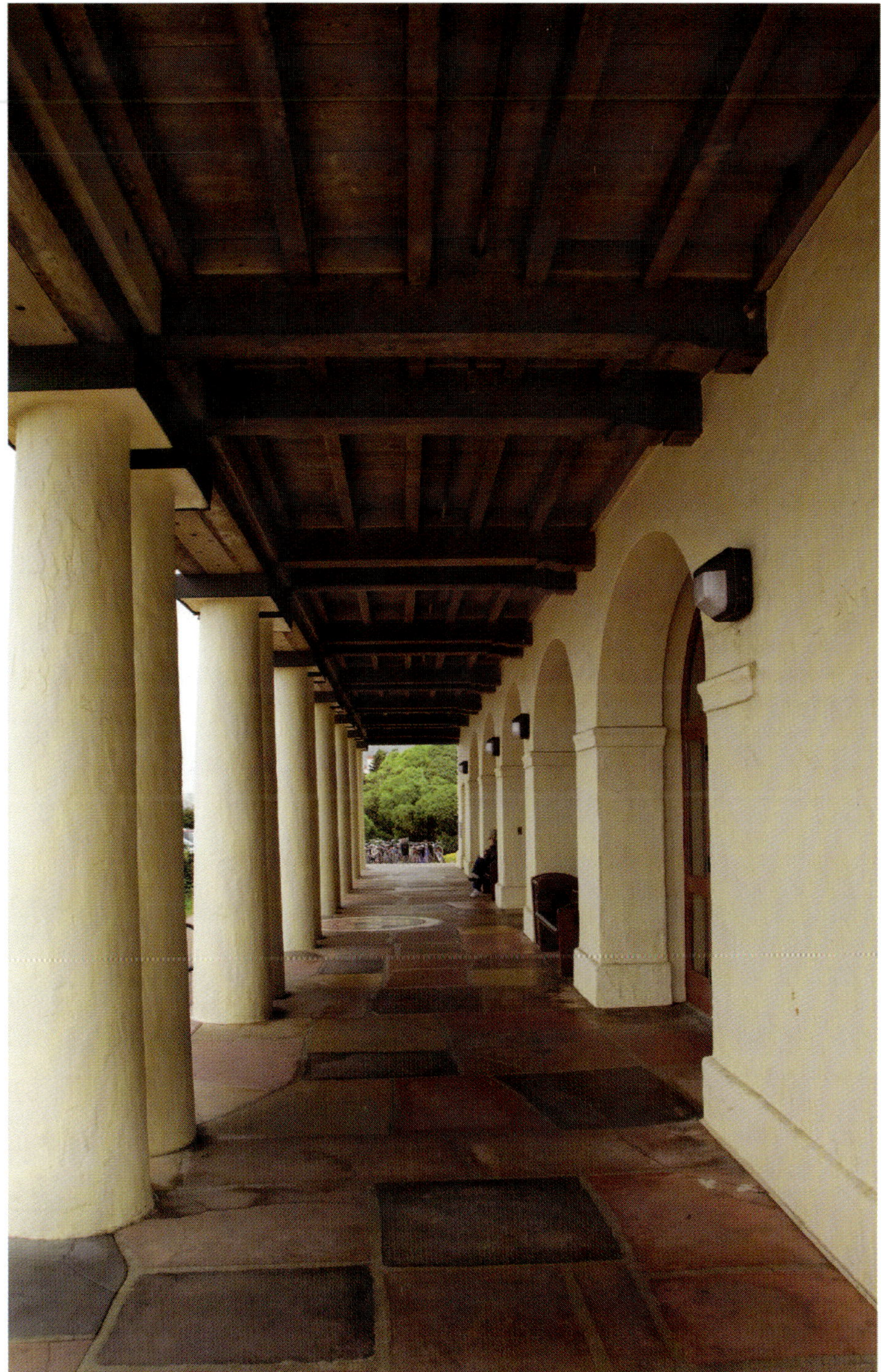

Focal length 24mm; ISO 200; aperture f/9; shutter speed 1/100; August 2:55 p.m.

The Shot

The first thing that comes to mind when looking at these frescoes is the women—they're full-figured, very much unlike the women depicted in the media today. The bathing suits are also filled with details that give you clues to when these pictures were constructed. Last in terms of the content of the picture is the Golden Gate Bridge and fog, which lets you know the scene takes place in San Francisco. Since I was indoors and didn't use a tripod (there's not enough room in the place to set one up), I set my ISO speed to a higher value in order to enable a shutter speed fast enough to minimize camera shake. I took a couple of shots while being as still as I could and holding my breath when I was shooting. Then I picked the shot that was the sharpest.

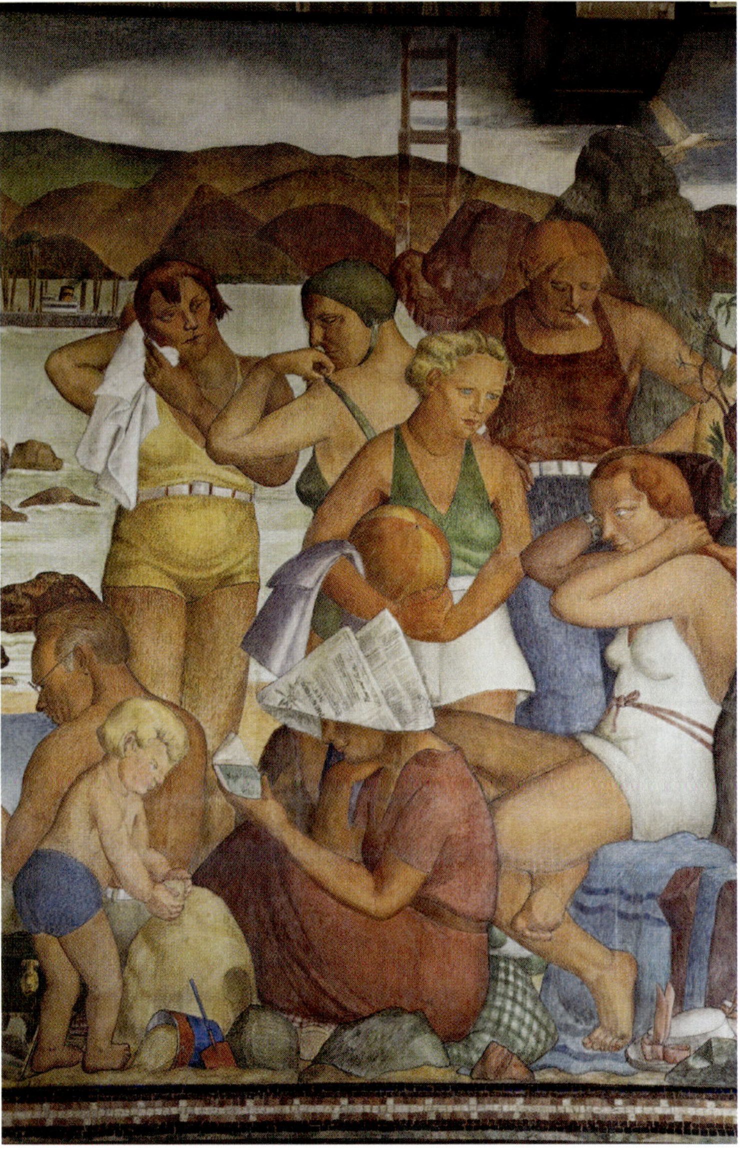

Focal length 45mm; ISO 1000; aperture f/9; shutter speed 1/30; August 2:04 p.m.

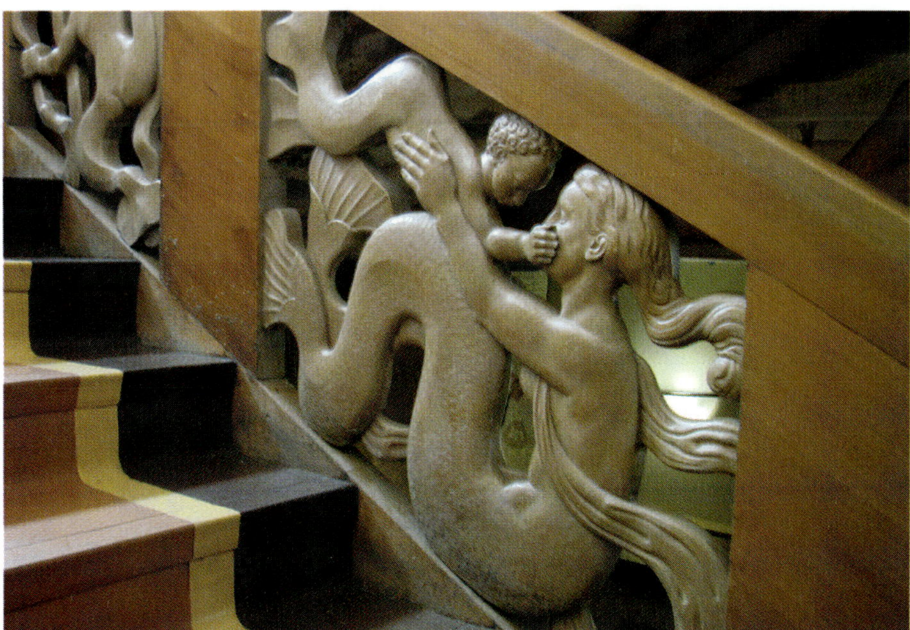

Sculptural work on stairway.

Getting There

The Beach Chalet is across the street from Ocean Beach in the western end of Golden Gate Park, on the Great Highway between Fulton Street and Lincoln Way.

To get there using mass transit, take the 5 Fulton from Powell and Market (north end) and get off at La Playa and Fulton Street. Walk west on Fulton to the Great Highway and take a left. The Beach Chalet will be on your left.

If you're driving, from the North Bay, take 101 South toward the 19th Avenue exit. Merge onto CA-1, which turns into Park Presidio Boulevard. Make a right on Fulton to the Great Highway.

From the East Bay, take 80 West to exit 1B to merge onto 101 North. Take exit 434B toward Fell Street/Octavia Boulevard and merge onto Octavia. Make a left at Fell Street, a right at Shrader Street, and a left at Fulton Street to the Great Highway.

From the South Bay, take 280 North to San Francisco, which will turn into CA-1 N/19th Ave. Veer left just after you get into Golden Gate Park. Make a left on Fulton, which is the street bordering the north end of the park. Make a left on the Great Highway.

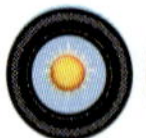 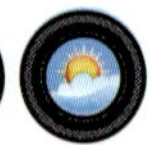 When to shoot: morning

Bernal Heights

With narrow, curvy streets that wind up and down steep hills that are challenging to navigate, the Bernal Heights neighborhood is tightly packed with ribbons of houses. At the top of it all is a gigantic park and tops of hills that are brown in the summer and green in the winter. The park is unique in that you can find city views in all directions, from north to south and east to west, without obstructions. The neighborhood is named after José Cornelio de Bernal, who owned the land (which was part of Rancho de las Salinas y Potrero Nuevo) when this part of California was Mexican territory. Irish immigrants then built small farms and houses after the land was subdivided into small parcels. Since the land is on solid bedrock, damage from the 1906 earthquake was minor. Today, the neighborhood thrives with small shops and restaurants that line Courtland Avenue. The neighborhood escape is the Bernal Heights Park, where you can observe all kinds of people jogging and walking their dogs. To learn more about the neighborhood and park, go to www.sfgate.com/neighborhoods/sf/bernalheights.

The Shot

In one of the compelling views from Bernal Heights, the Bay Bridge is included in the background. To get this view, walk up the hill on the east side of the park. When you get to the top, you'll see the Bay Bridge well off in the distance. Frame the shot so the bridge is in the background by zooming in to a focal length of about 105mm. By using the Rule of Thirds, I restricted the sky to the upper third of the composition. The framing shows a rise and fall of a series of hills, which adds much depth to this photo. I used a narrow aperture so that everything in the frame is sharp. Noteworthy in this photo are the red-brick buildings of San Francisco General Hospital in the right third of the frame. They offer stark contrast to the surrounding buildings and background sky.

The Shot

As soon as you get to the top of the hill by walking west across the barren, rocky surface, you'll see gorgeous downtown views off to your right (north). In order to give the shot a dramatic feel, I caught as much of the view as I could get into the lens. I used a wide-angle lens, framing the shot so that the center of downtown lays one-third from the left edge of the frame. Along the bottom of the frame I included a sliver of the top of the hill, letting the viewer feel as if he's standing on the precipice looking out at the view.

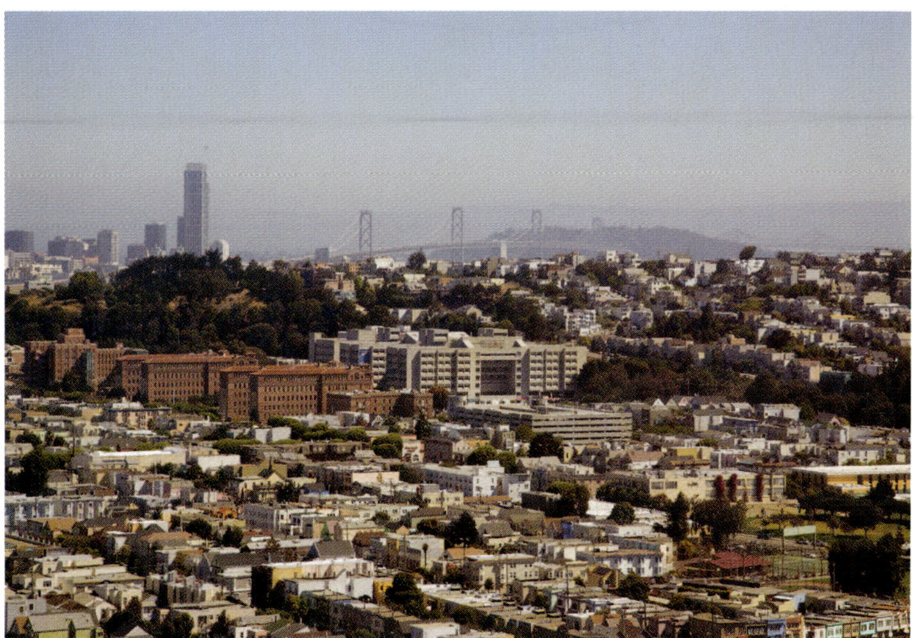

Focal length 105mm; ISO 200; aperture f/13; shutter speed 1/200; August 9:30 a.m.

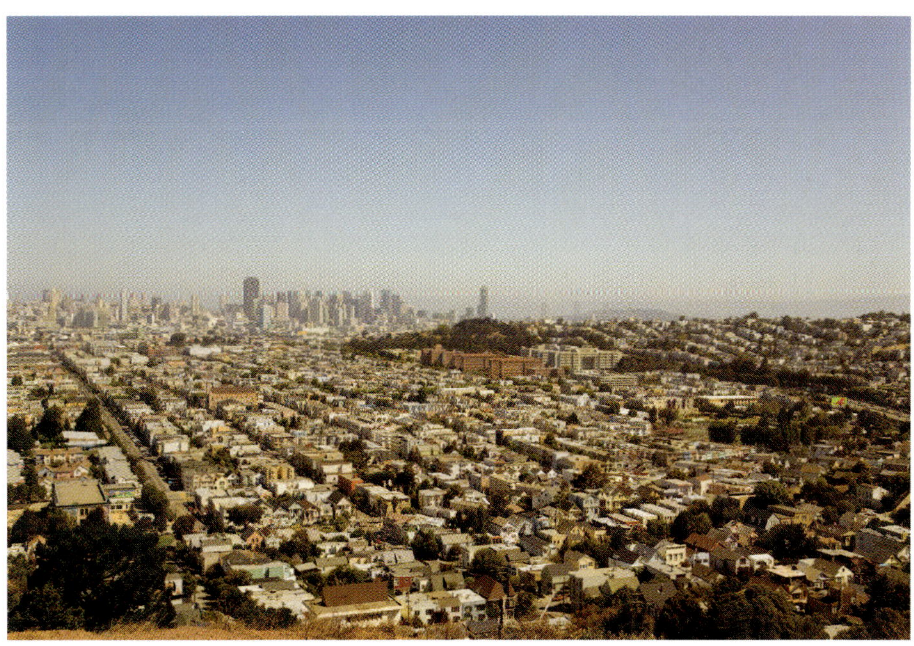

Focal length 40mm; ISO 200; aperture f/7.1; shutter speed 1/800; August 9:44 a.m.

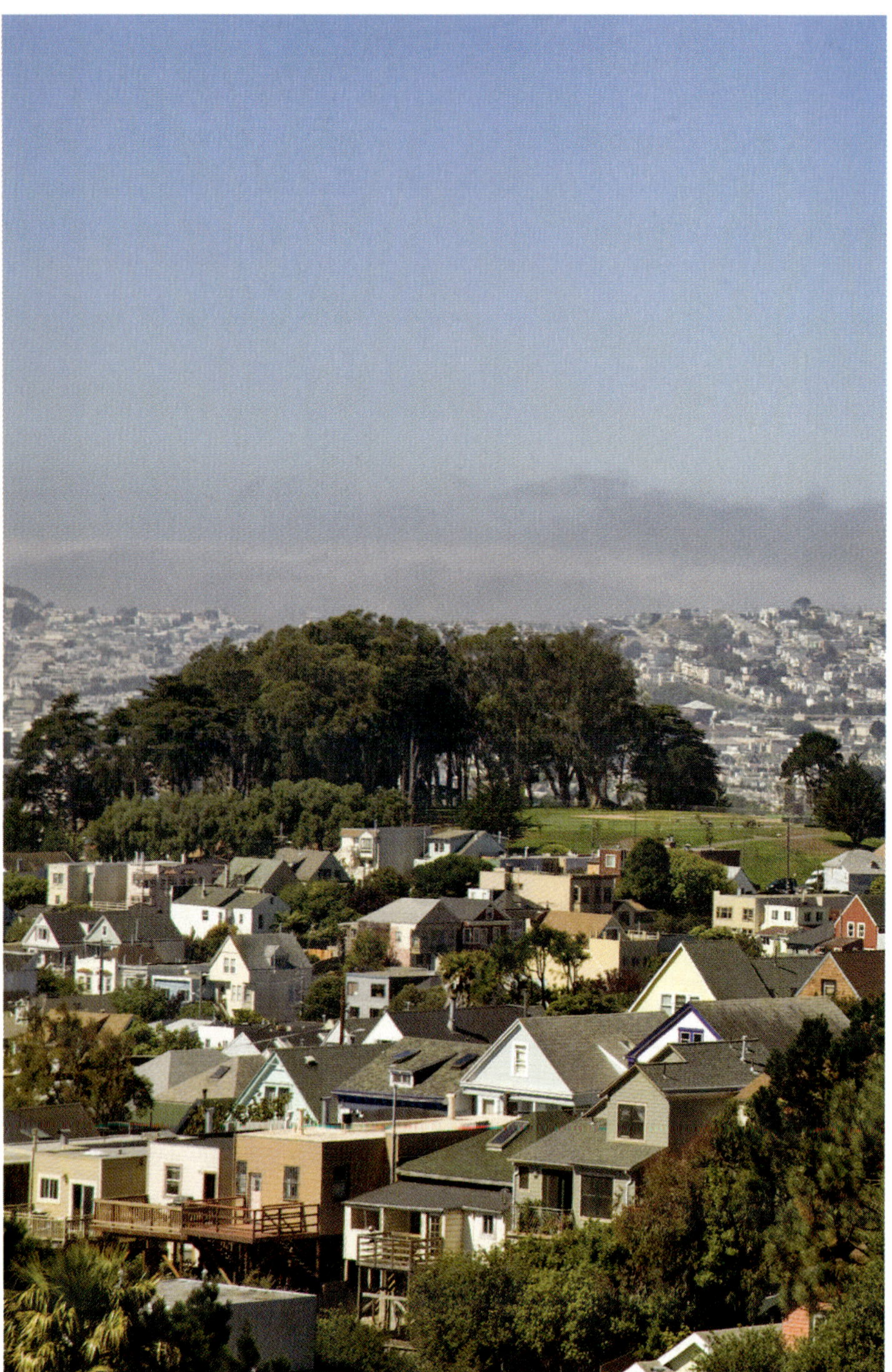

View of Bernal Heights neighborhood.

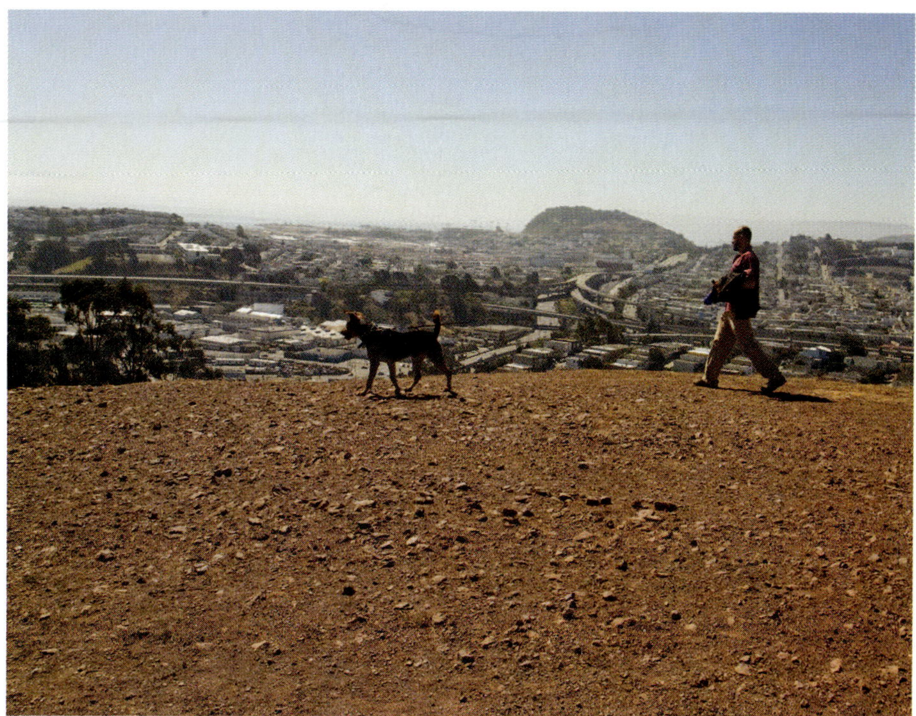

Man walking dog with view in background.

Getting There

Bernal Heights Boulevard circles the park. The best place to photograph is just up the hill on the east side of the park, where Bernal Heights Boulevard changes to Carver Street.

To get there using mass transit, from downtown (Embarcadero, Montgomery, or Powell stations), take BART to 24th and Mission Street. Take the 67 bus from the southwest corner of Mission to Ripley and Folsom Street. Walk southeast on Folsom Street, which changes to Bernal Heights Boulevard. You'll be at the far eastern end of the park when Bernal Heights Boulevard changes to Carver Street.

If you're driving, from the North Bay, take 101 South to Richardson, which turns into Lombard. Make a right on Van Ness, which changes to South Van Ness after Market Street. Make a left on Cesar Chavez and a right on Folsom, which turns into Bernal Heights Boulevard.

From the East Bay, take 80 West to 101 South. Exit at Cesar Chavez and turn left at Folsom, which turns into Bernal Heights Boulevard.

From the South Bay, take 101 North to Alemany Boulevard. Exit toward Bayshore Boulevard. Stay to the right and then take a left on Bayshore. Make a left on Cortland Avenue, a right on Nevada Street, and a slight right on Bernal Heights Boulevard, which changes to Bradford Street. Turn left at Bernal Heights Boulevard.

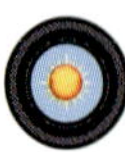 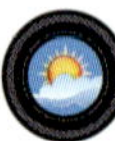

When to shoot: morning, afternoon

Levi's Plaza and Filbert Steps

Levi's Plaza Park is one of what some would consider a dying breed of modernist creations. In some cities, such as Denver, urban parks dotted with water features, cobblestones, trees, grass, and granite have been demolished. Levi's Plaza, the urban park in San Francisco, however, still thrives. Designed by Lawrence Halprin, the park was constructed in 1978—a tranquil place where the flatlands off the bay meet the steep inclines of Telegraph Hill. If you were to walk the area from one of the parking lots in the vicinity of Pier 23 on San Francisco Bay, you'd cross the busy Embarcadero (at Greenwich) and run into a thicket of trees a few feet on your left, which is the eastern border of Levi's Plaza. You'd see Coit Tower on the top of the hill from the plaza. You'd then walk east through the plaza, first crossing Battery Street, then Sansome, to the Filbert Steps, which straddle a hill. This area, considered the east slope of Telegraph Hill, used to be a rock quarry site in the late 1800s. The rugged slope had been torn apart by explosions in an effort to remove rocks. Since the slope was rock, many of the homes that were built before the 1906 earthquake survived, and you can see them as you walk up the wooden stairs.

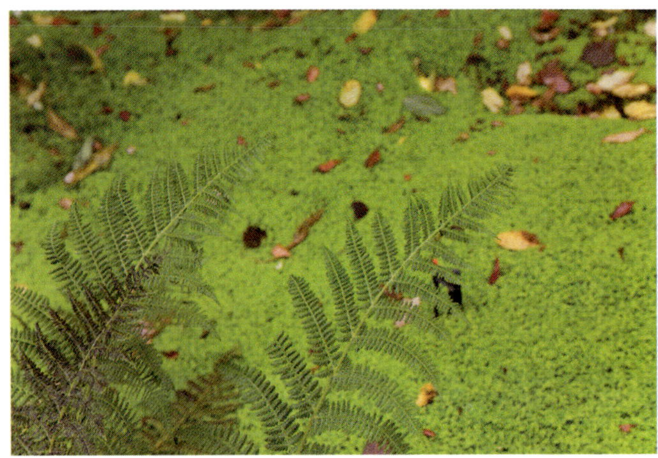

Ferns with light-green ground cover in the background.

The Shot

This shot concentrates on the construction of the staircase and the vegetation that grows around and under it. The staircase is made of redwood, which actually turns from red to gray when exposed to the elements. Most notable in the shot is what's in the foreground—a soft close-up of the stairs, which moves into sharp focus as you move up. Including objects (in this case, three wooden steps) in the foreground really adds depth to the photo. The light, too, is of interest. The railings are reflecting the subtle light that has come through the fog from up above (especially in the middle ground), which contrasts the shadowy view in between the stairs.

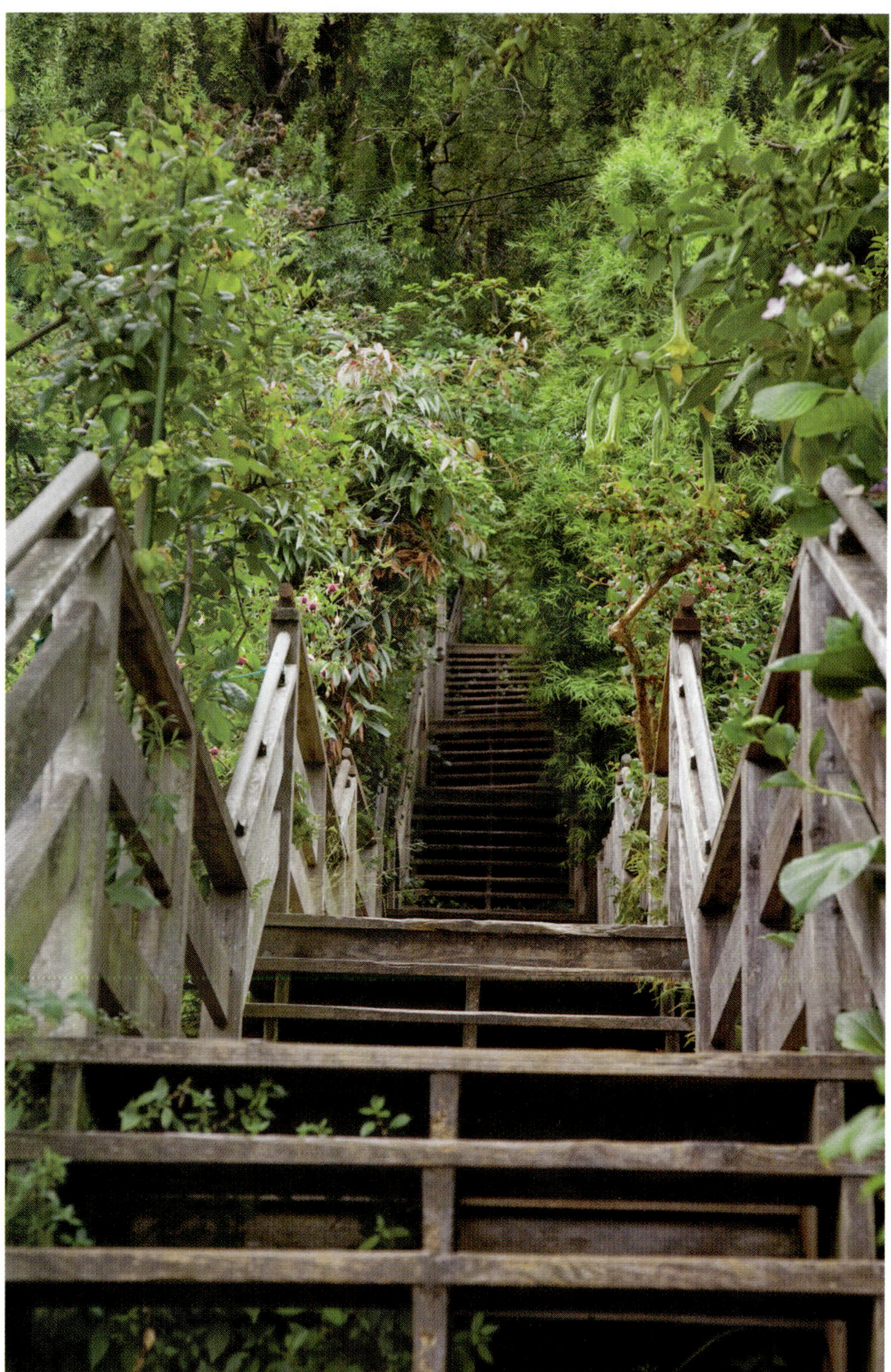

Focal length 45mm; ISO 200; aperture f/6.3; shutter speed 1/125; August 11:04 a.m.

The Shot

In this shot I first set my exposure compensation to the lowest value of underexposure (–2) because I wanted to be able to keep the shutter open long enough to make the water silky. The result was excellent; I was able to keep the shutter open a half second. I framed the shot, leaving space above and below the waterfalls, where each contrasts the other. Each part of the photograph has drastic differences in texture, from the concrete at the bottom, to the water in the middle, to the leaves at the top.

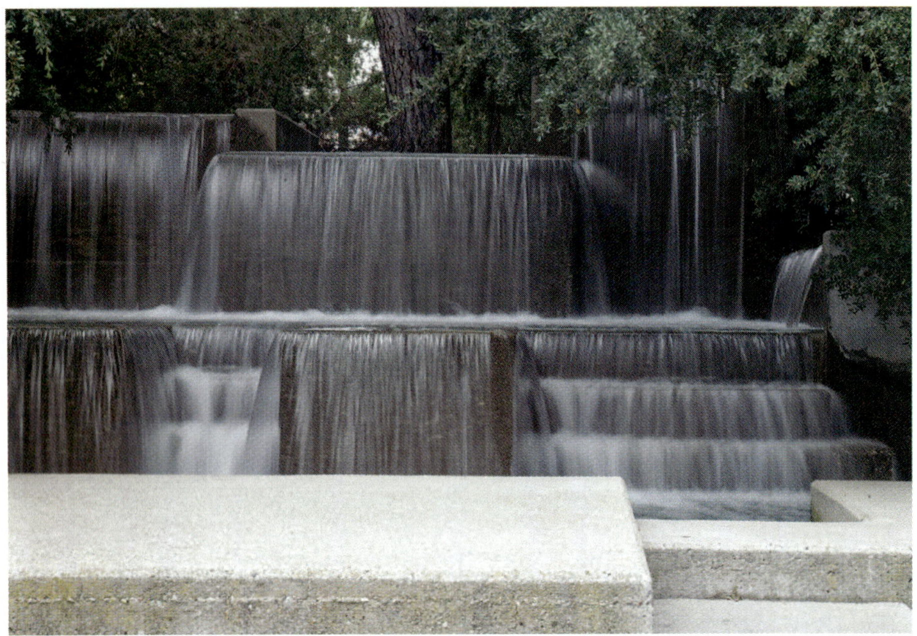

Focal length 60mm; ISO 200; aperture f/22; shutter speed 0.5 seconds; August 10:40 a.m.

Getting There

Levi's Plaza Park is at 1160 Battery Street near Greenwich Street and the Embarcadero, which is near Pier 23, where there is parking.

To get there using mass transit, from downtown, take the F streetcar from the Ferry Building and get off at Greenwich and the Embarcadero. Walk across the street, then go left a few steps to Levi's Plaza Park.

If you're driving, from the South Bay, take 101 North to 280 North. Exit at King Street, which turns into the Embarcadero, and take it to Greenwich.

From the East Bay, take 80 West and exit at Fremont Street. Turn left at Folsom and left at the Embarcadero to Greenwich.

From the North Bay, take 101 South to Lombard. Make a slight left on Lombard, a left at Van Ness, a right at Bay, and a right at the Embarcadero to Greenwich.

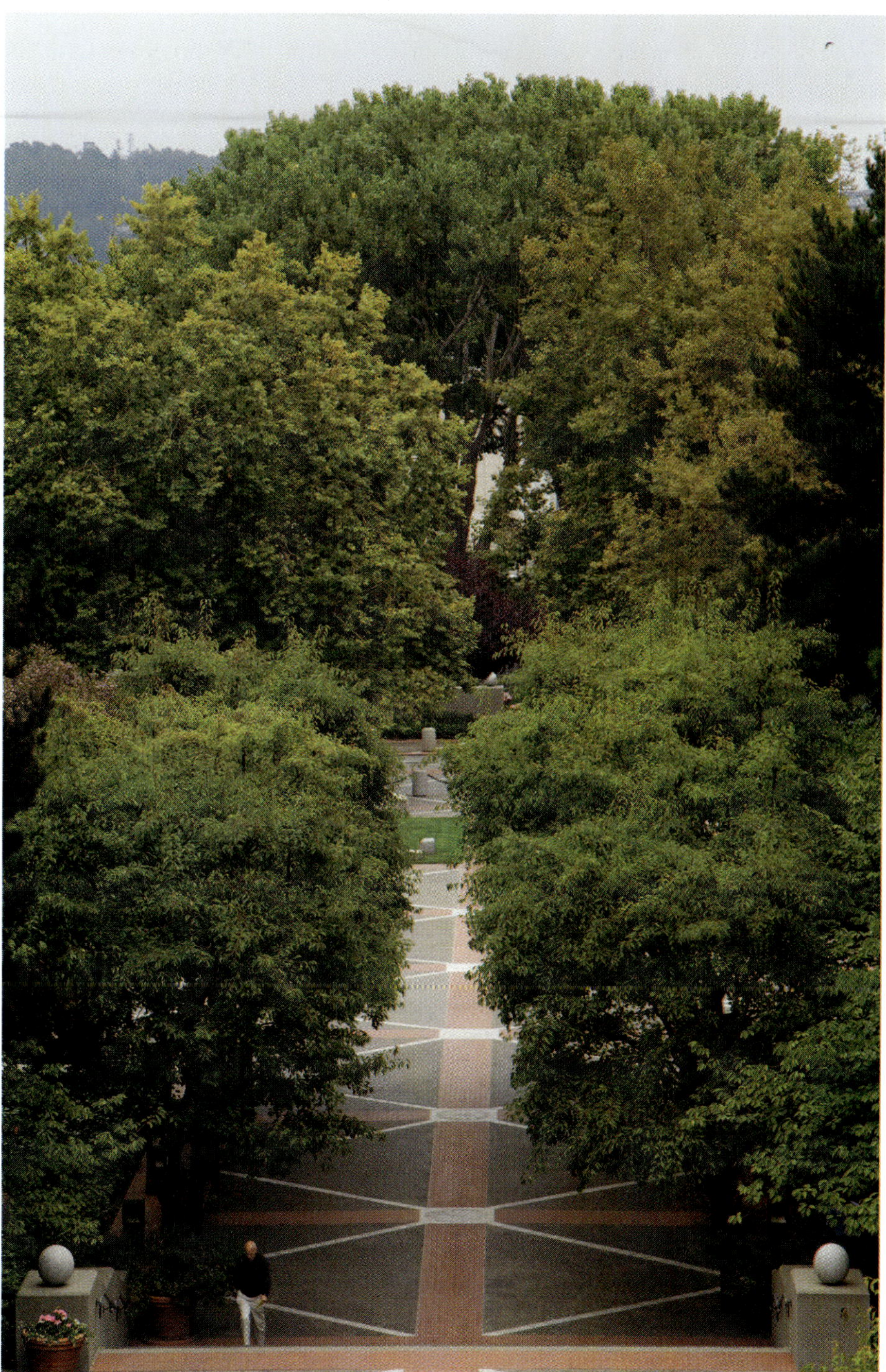

View from stairs out onto Levi's Plaza.

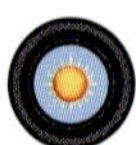 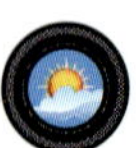 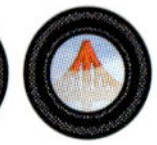

When to shoot: morning, afternoon

Presidio Graveyard

Formally known as the San Francisco National Cemetery, this spot where the dead reside has fabulous views contrasting an eerie repetition of row after row of nearly identical tombstones. Located in the Presidio of San Francisco, which is now part of the Golden Gate National Recreation Area, the graveyard is open to traffic, which means you can drive your car through the gate, even though it looks as if access is restricted. In 1863, the U.S. Congress passed the National Cemeteries Act, which set aside 13 parcels scattered throughout the country to bury war veterans. In 1884, the site was officially declared a cemetery, which covered 9 acres of the Presidio. It was the first national cemetery on the West Coast. As the cemetery has grown over the years, the army has instituted many improvements, including building a concrete rostrum and a chapel and remodeling the lodge. Today, the cemetery occupies around 28 acres, the same as it had in 1932, when the last expansion occurred. In the '60s, the army wanted to make the cemetery larger, but concern over environmental damage stopped them. Thirty-thousand people are buried here.

The Shot

If you go uphill from behind the lodge, which is on the west end of the cemetery, you'll get a great view of San Francisco Bay. When the fog comes in the view of the Golden Gate Bridge is obscured, but the fog enhances the view, especially if it fingers into the bay as a strip of smoky gray. If you wait for passing boats, they can provide an added feature in the bay part of the photo. The divisions going from bottom to top in the frame are clearly marked by contrasting colors—the whites and beiges of the tombstones, the red of one of the building's roofs, the trees' deep green color, the deep blue of the water, the blue-gray of the fog, the brown of the mountain, and the light blue of the sky. I shot this picture with a relatively narrow aperture to keep the entire frame sharp.

The Shot

This shot was taken near the top of the hill, which is in the south end of the graveyard. To get there, you take the road from the entrance southwest and make the first left to go up the hill. You'll pass thousands of graves that seem to all look the same, which is what makes this place so photogenic and provides for some great repetition of objects in photographs of the place. The most interesting element of this graveyard is that you can frame the tombstones in myriad ways, each giving them a different hue and shadow depending on how the light hits them. I framed this shot so that you see the faces of the tombstones. When printed at full size, you can easily read the names and dates.

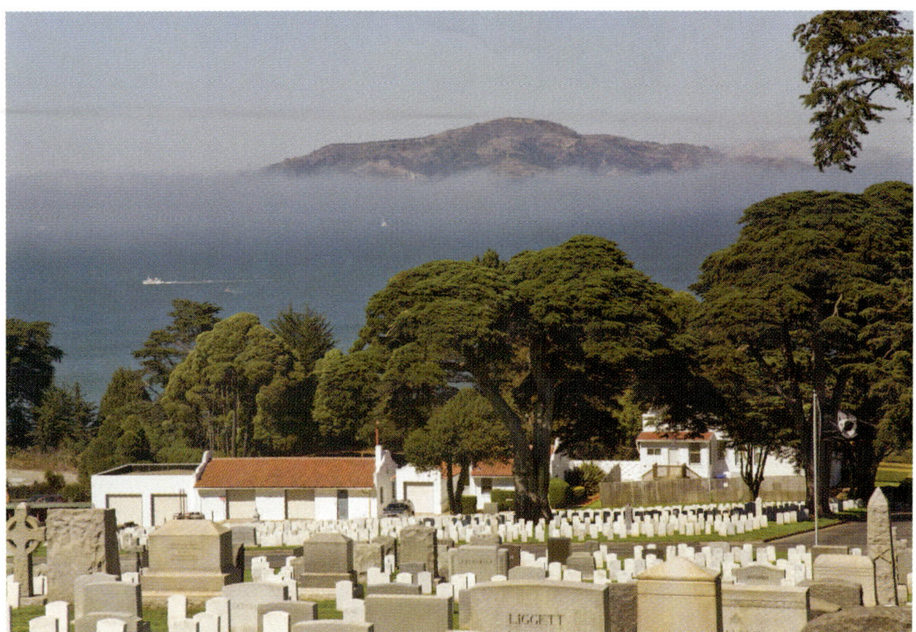

Focal length 98mm; ISO 200; aperture f/10; shutter speed 1/200; August 4:08 p.m.

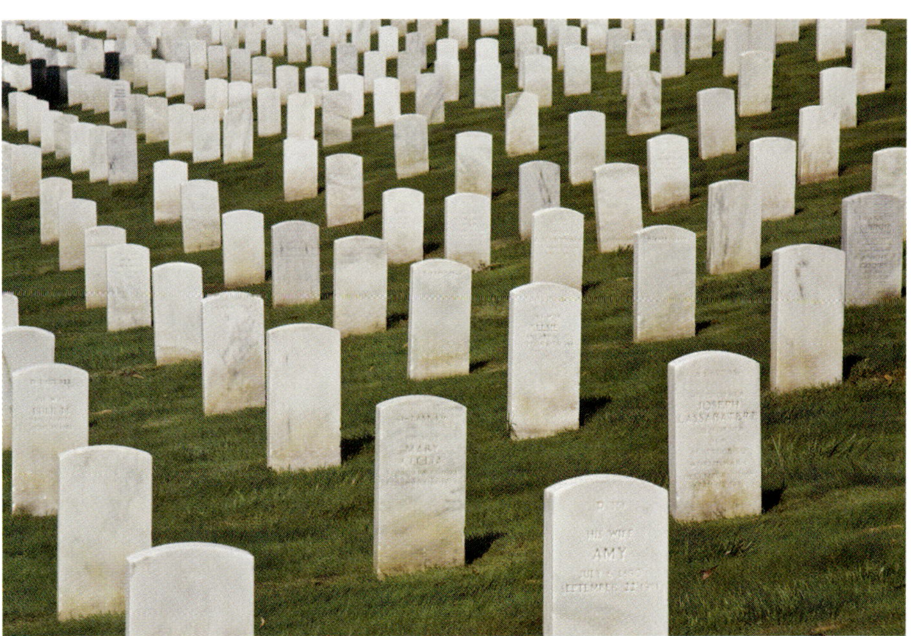

Focal length 105mm; ISO 200; aperture f/10; shutter speed 1/500; August 4:14 p.m.

Getting There

The San Francisco National Cemetery is at 1 Lincoln Boulevard.

To get there using mass transit, from downtown (Fremont and Market), take the 38 Geary and get off at Geary Blvd and 25th Avenue. On the southeast corner of Geary Boulevard and 25th Avenue, catch the 29 bus and get off at McDowell Avenue and Cowles Street. Walk south on McDowell Avenue and turn left on Patten Road, which turns into Lincoln Boulevard.

If you're driving, from the North Bay, take 101 South to the 25th Avenue exit. Merge onto Merchant Road and turn left on Lincoln Boulevard.

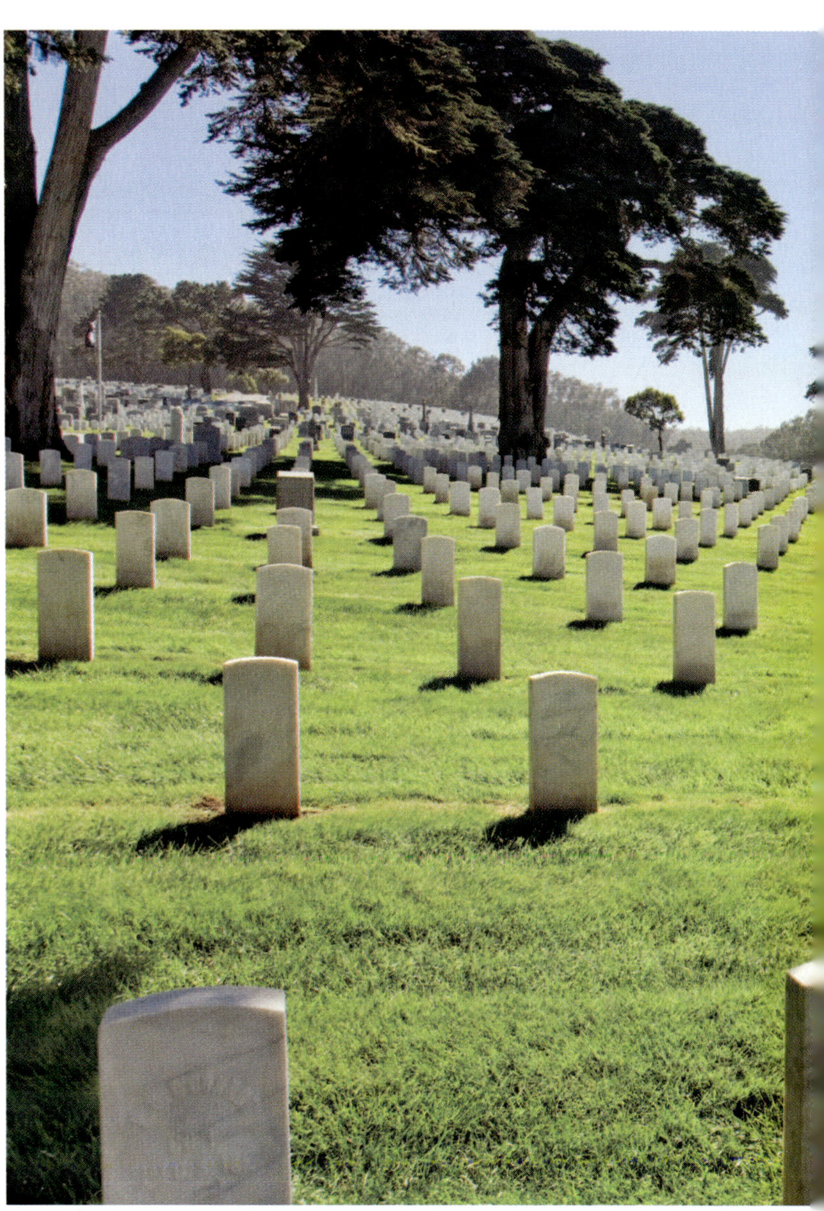

From the East Bay, take 80 West to the Fremont Street exit. Keep right at the fork, then turn left at Folsom, left at the Embarcadero, left at Broadway, right on Van Ness, and left at Lombard Street (which is still called 101 North). Exit at Gorgas Avenue and make a left on Halleck and a right on Lincoln Boulevard.

From the South Bay, take 101 North to exit 434A (Mission Street). Follow the signs for 101 North, which will take you to Van Ness. Make a left at Lombard Street (which is still called 101 North) and exit at Gorgas Avenue. Turn left on Halleck and right on Lincoln Boulevard.

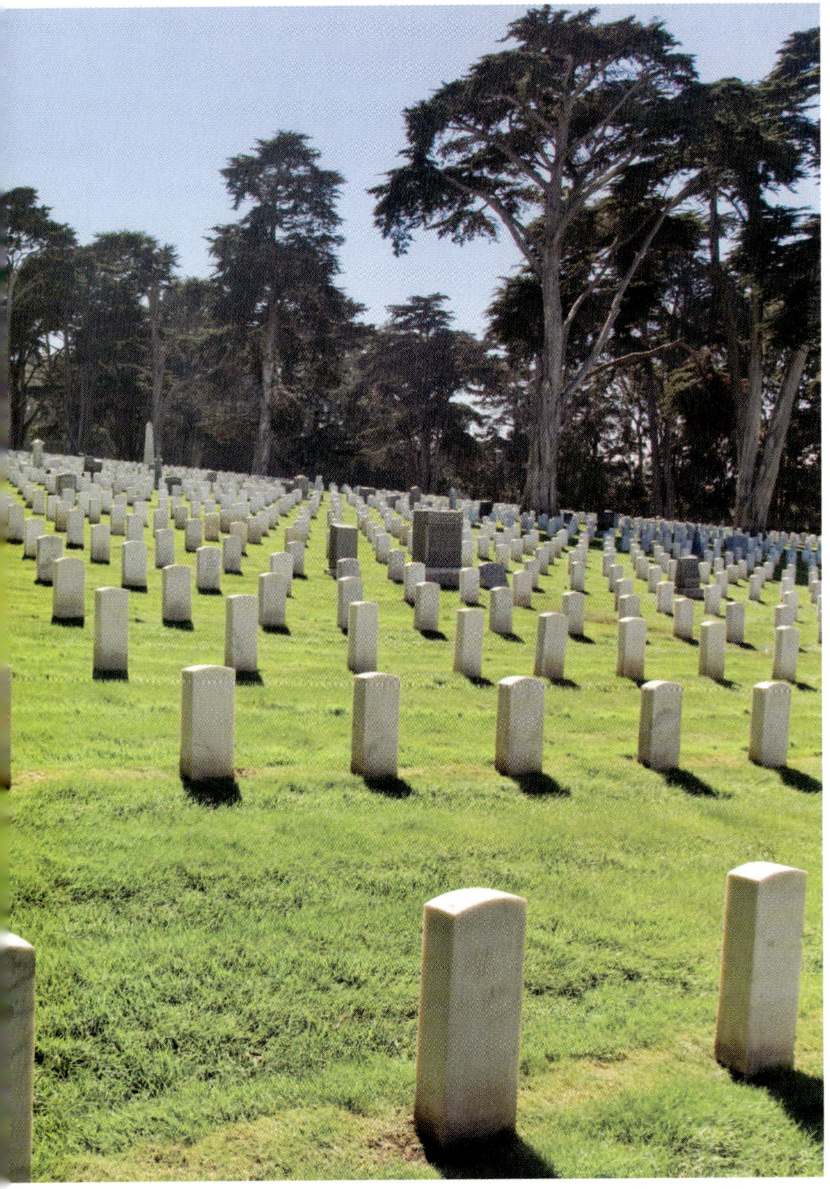

Gravesites from a wide angle.

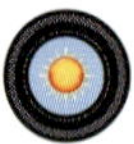 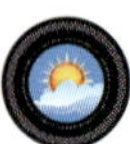

When to shoot: morning, afternoon

Musée Mécanique

To be sure, San Francisco has some great museums—places where you can discover classic art, natural history, and hands-on science. Most require an admission fee, which can be steep when they play host to important exhibitions. There is one museum—the Musée Mécanique—however, that's free and located right at the edge of the Fisherman's Wharf tourist area. While it might not be the "greatest" museum in San Francisco, it certainly is fun, and the photo ops can be your very own blasts from the past. The museum has a collection of more than 300 coin-operated penny arcade machines. Edward Galland Zelinsky started the collection in the early 1930s. As a boy, Zelinsky won some motor oil at a Bingo game. He sold the oil and bought his first penny skill game. He had his friends play the game and saved the pennies he earned to buy more equipment. Through the years he continued with his hobby, with his collection growing so big that it now occupies an entire hall right on San Francisco Bay. The museum has a great webpage at www.museemecaniquesf.com. The museum is open from 10:00 a.m. to 7:00 p.m. Monday through Friday and from 10:00 a.m. to 8:00 p.m. on Saturday and Sunday.

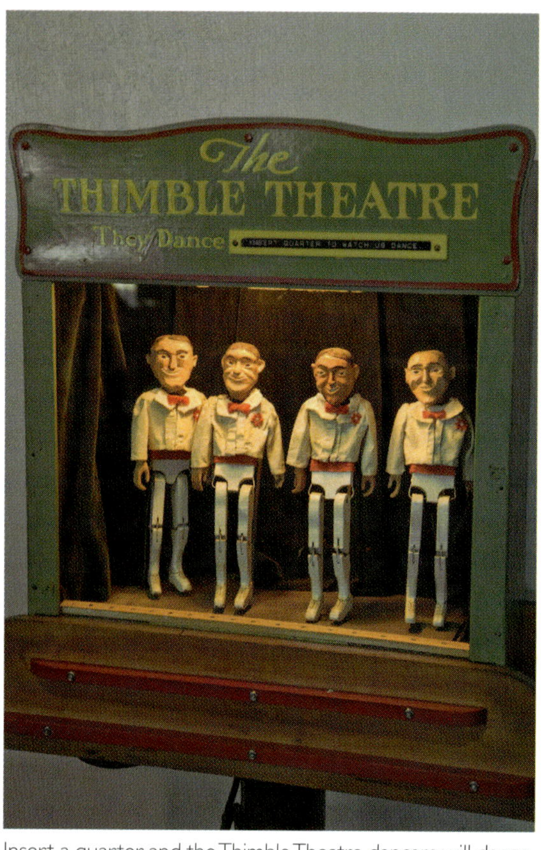

Insert a quarter, and the Thimble Theatre dancers will dance.

The Shot

The camera settings for this image are unusual for an indoor shot. Usually you would probably set your ISO speed higher to help eliminate blur, even at the risk of getting noise. That wasn't the case here because the focus point was aimed at the larger figure in the background, an area with additional, uniform lighting. I also used a wide aperture, which narrowed my depth of field, keeping the sharp area centered on the background figure. The resulting soft focus of the foreground figure almost gives the feeling that he's not only crying, but also shaking a bit. Last to note is the glass issue. The figures are surrounded by glass, so you have to assess the reflection before you shoot. Look for a couple of angles with the least amount of extra reflection. Take a few different photos and pick which one comes out best.

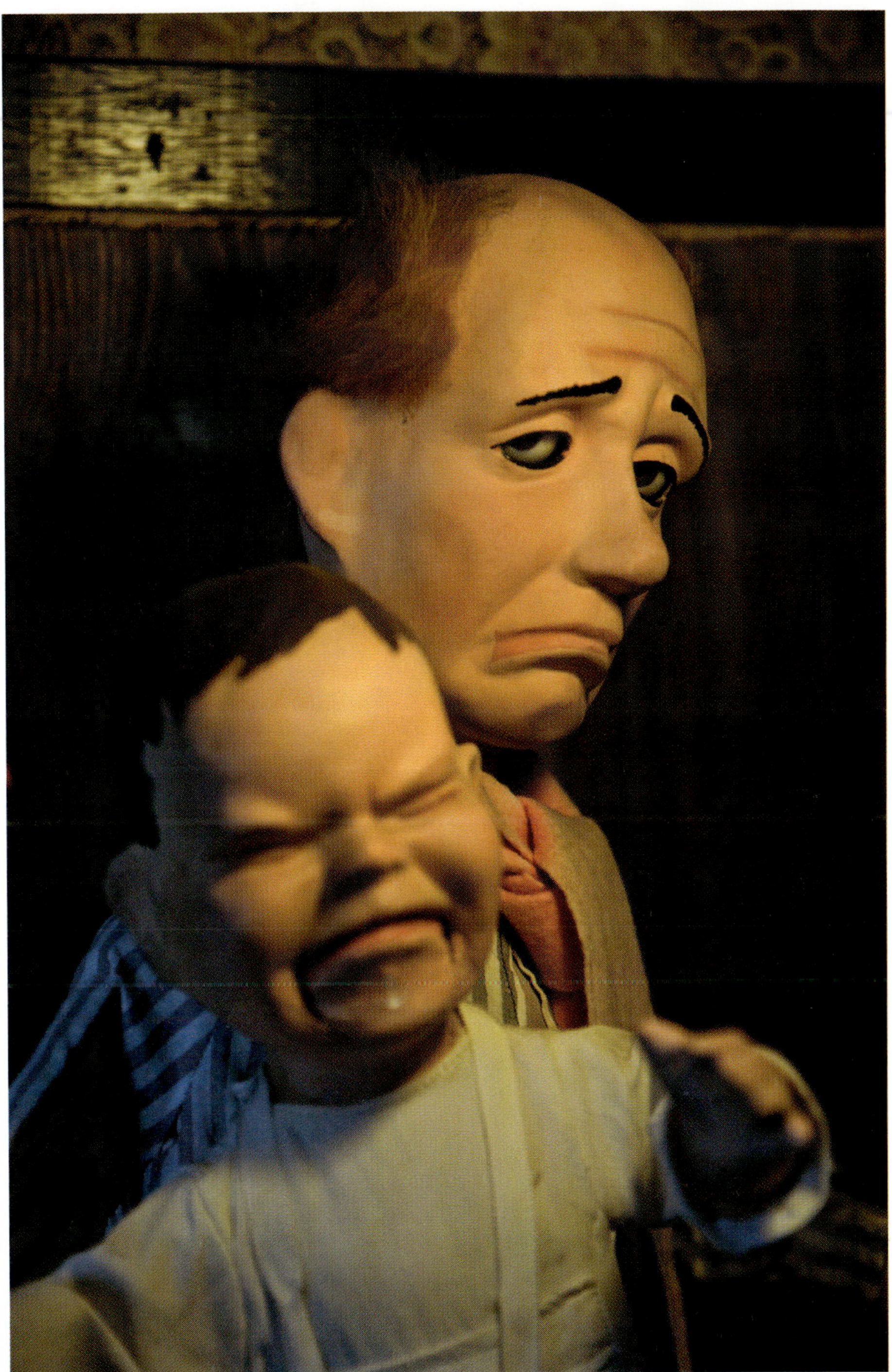

Focal length 80mm; ISO 200; aperture f/4; shutter speed 1/50; August 10:30 a.m.

The Shot

This type of picture has to be my favorite to take because it's so easy. Backlit signs are naturals for photographs; they take to the sensor like butter. There's enough light that you don't get blur from camera shake, especially when you're shooting in Av mode with aperture values from f/5 to f/8. Just hold your camera up and take a few shots straight on. As far as the content of the photo, it's about as retro as you can get. The text includes both script and manuscript, both in sans serif fonts (without "sticks" at the ends of the letters). The cartoon harks back to the days when Iran (then Persia) was a U.S. ally as well as a popular tourist destination. Also of note in this photo is that the plastic upon which the image is superimposed has an orangish tone that makes it look antiqued, which, to be sure, it is.

Getting There

The Musée Mécanique is at Pier 45 Shed A at the end of Taylor Street.

To get there using mass transit, from downtown, catch the F line, which stops at the Ferry Building and lets you off at Jefferson and Jones Street. From there, walk one block on Jefferson and then make left on Taylor and proceed to the end of the street.

If you're driving, from the North Bay, take 101 South. Make a slight left onto Lombard, a left at Van Ness, a right at North Point, a left at Mason, and a left at Jefferson to Taylor.

From the East Bay, take 80 West and exit at Fremont Street. Keep right at the fork and turn left on Folsom Street and then left on Embarcadero, which turns into Jefferson; proceed to Taylor.

From South Bay, take 101 North to 280 North. Exit at King Street, which turns into the Embarcadero, which turns into Jefferson; proceed to Taylor.

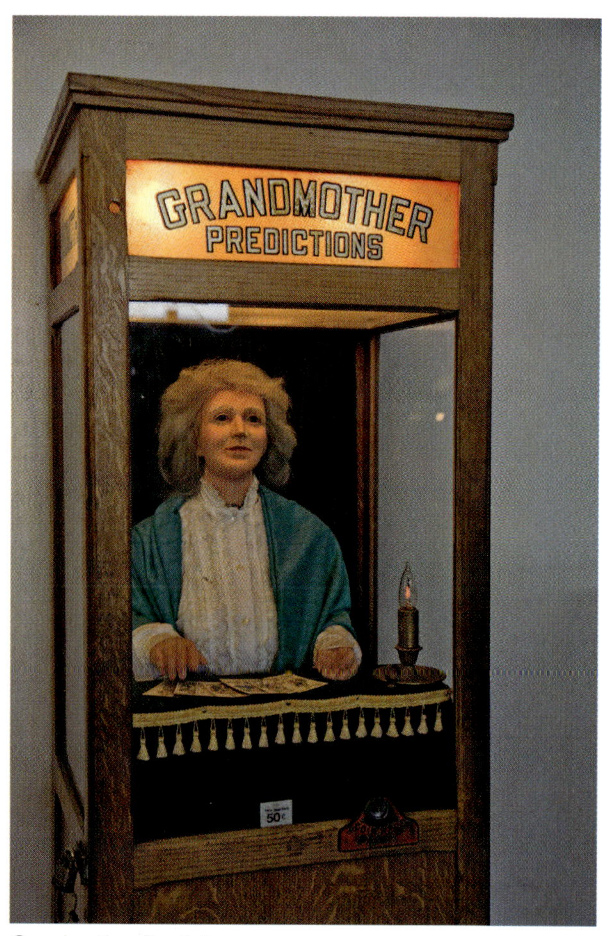

Grandmother Predictions.

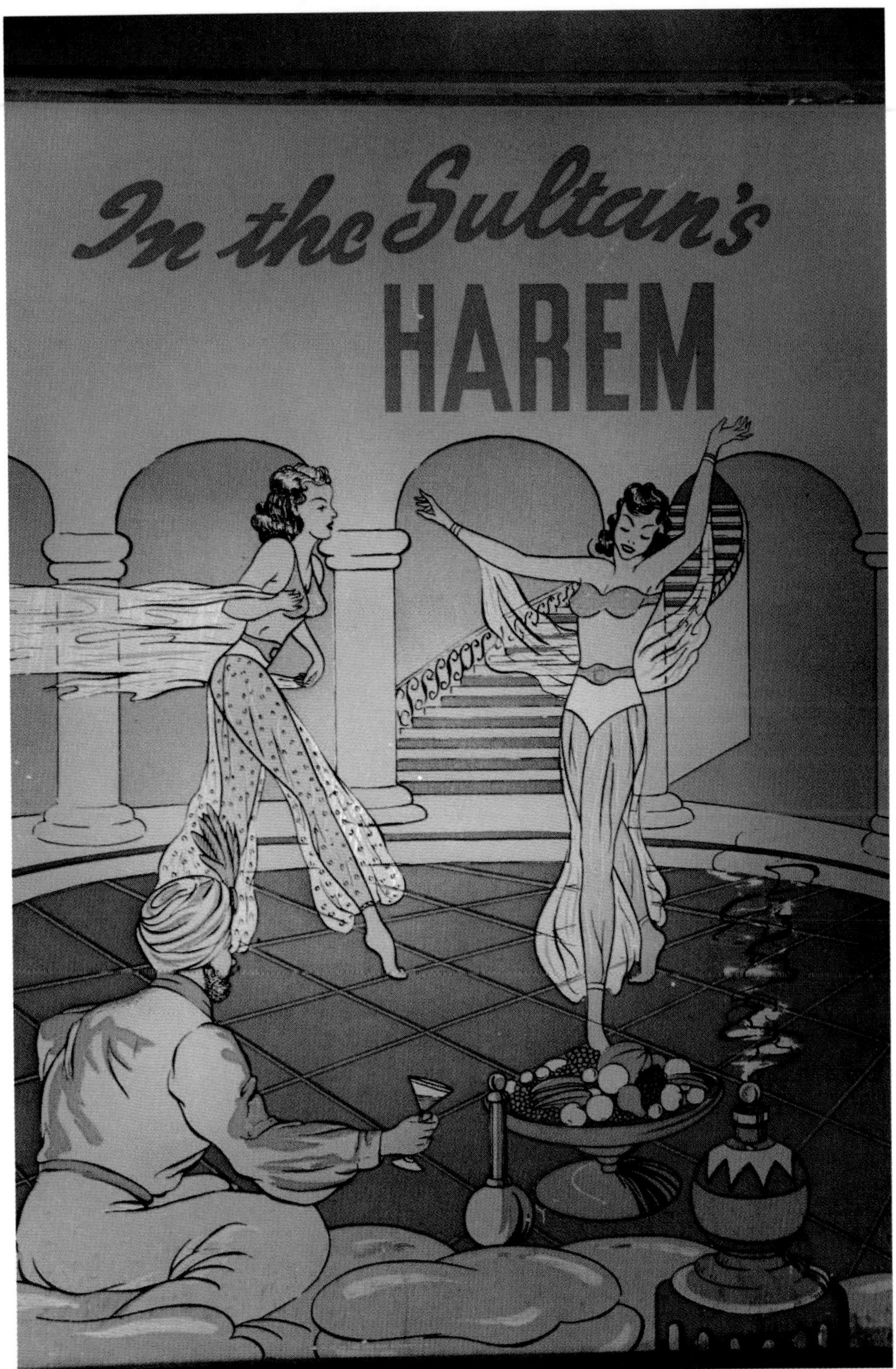

Focal length 73mm; ISO 200; aperture f/5; shutter speed 1/125; August 10:51 a.m.

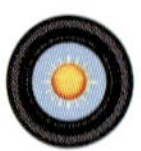 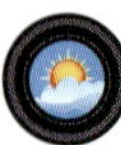

When to shoot: morning, afternoon

Clement Street

Filled with an eclectic mix of Asian fare and other multicultural dining and shopping options, Clement Street isn't a normal destination for tourists. The street runs 44 blocks and is dotted with a variety of businesses, which are housed in one- and two-story structures. The part of the street with the highest concentration of businesses and street life runs from Arguello to about 10th Avenue. There's another area around 25th Avenue that's busy as well. The neighborhood is similar to Chinatown except it's more diverse, with a population that speaks nearly 25 languages. You'll find most everything here that you'd find in Chinatown—roasted duck, dim sum, and Chinese herbs—and then some. In between a plethora of Asian restaurants are businesses that range from used bookstores to funky cafes.

The Shot

Often acknowledged as the best independent bookstore in the Bay Area, Green Apple Books has been around since 1967. It's housed in a pre–1906 earthquake building. The bookstore is just to the west of the northeast corner of Clement and 6th Avenue. This photo was taken from the south side of the street at a slight angle. The man walking across the street at the bottom-left corner of the frame adds some depth to the photo. He also helps to keep the bookstore the center focus of the image as he's walking toward it. Since the picture looks out onto a row of stores on the street, there's no need to narrow the aperture to lengthen the depth of field. In this shot, it's the relatively far distance between camera and subject that allows for uniform sharpness with a wide aperture.

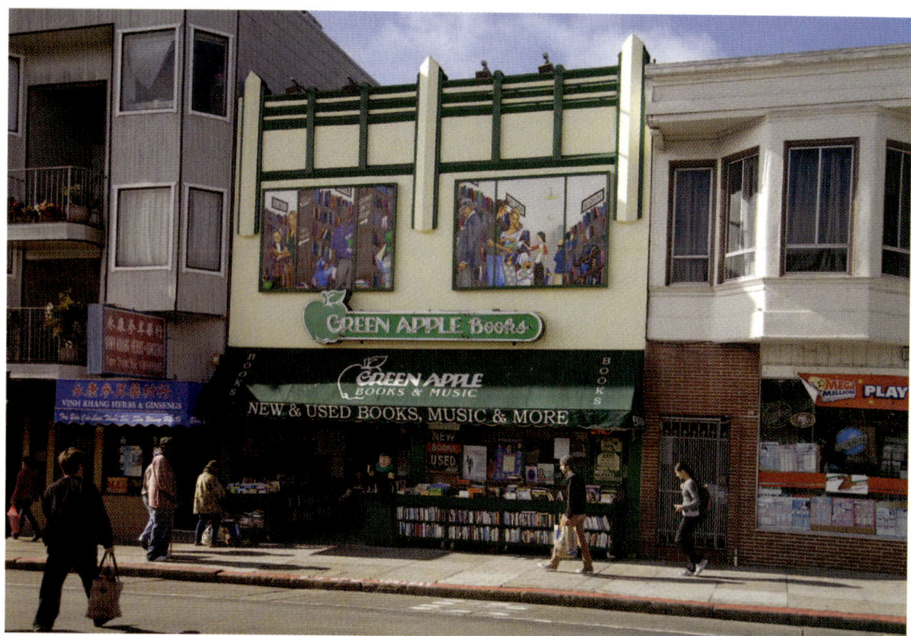

Focal length 35mm; ISO 200; aperture f/4; shutter speed 1/1600; August 4:22 p.m.

The Shot

This is a view of the north side of Clement between 4th and 5th Avenues. This part of the neighborhood has some of the most colorful buildings. I took the shot pointing my camera to the northwest. I angled the shot to include the sky, which was partially covered by the fog that was coming in from the Pacific Ocean. This shot also includes some of the neighborhood's Asian flavor. Right in the middle of the shot is a green sign with Chinese characters. This shot has an interesting perspective in that there are three distinct parts of the photo—the sky with the fog, the row of buildings with the cars, and the surface of the road. Each offers a good contrast with the others. Something else worth noting is the rooflines of the buildings. Each has a different shape, color, and pattern. The backlit signs and awnings have text in different languages, which leaves viewers who aren't familiar with the languages wondering what the signs say.

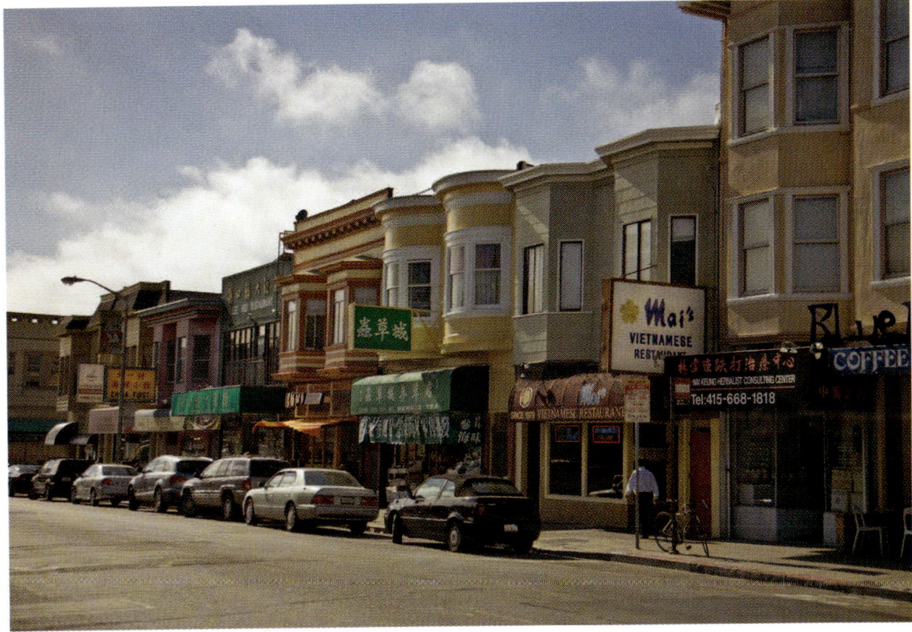

Focal length 45mm; ISO 200; aperture f/4; shutter speed 1/2000; 4:45 p.m.

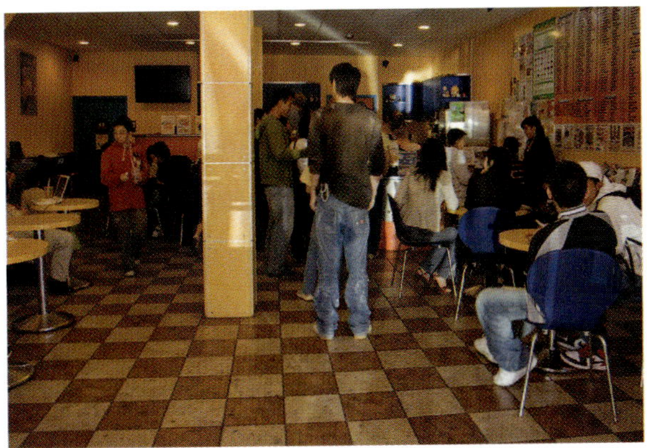

Inside a Clement Street cafe.

Getting There

The busiest part of Clement Street is between 5th and 6th Avenues.

To get there using mass transit, from downtown, catch the 38 Geary along Market Street. Get off at 6th Avenue and walk one block north to Clement.

If you're driving, from the North Bay, take 101 South and exit at 19th Avenue. Make a right on California, a left on 14th Avenue, and a left on Clement.

From the East Bay, take 80 West to exit 1B to merge onto 101 North to exit 434B toward Fell Street/Octavia Boulevard. Merge onto Octavia and make a left on Fell, a right on Divisadero, a left on Geary, and a right on 5th.

From the South Bay, take 101 North to exit 434B toward Fell Street/Octavia Boulevard. Merge onto Octavia and make a left on Fell, a right on Divisadero, a left on Geary, and a right on 5th.

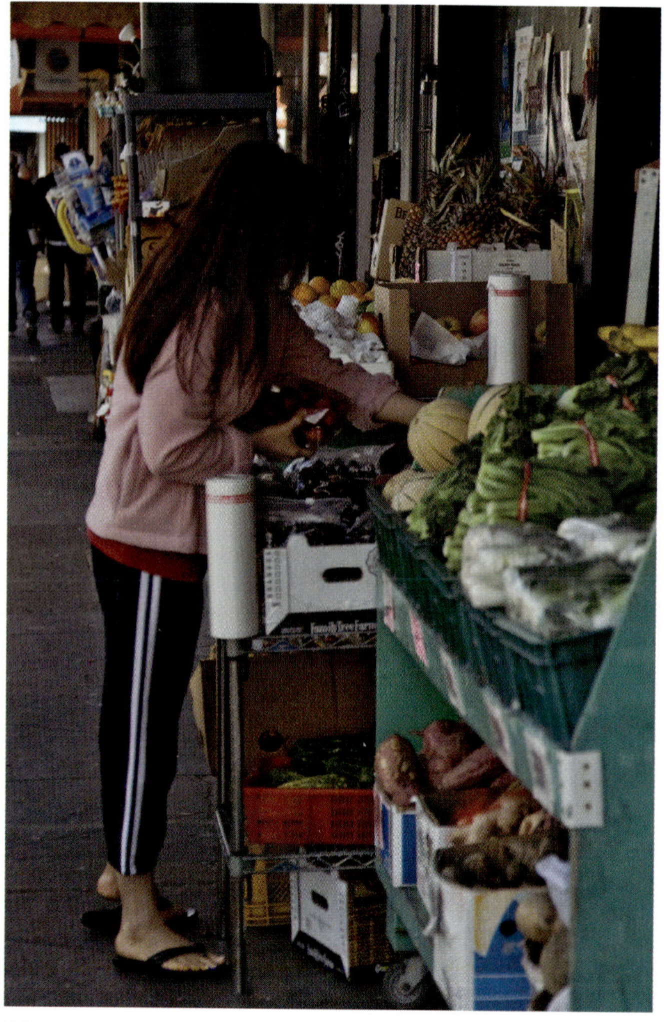

Woman looking at produce.

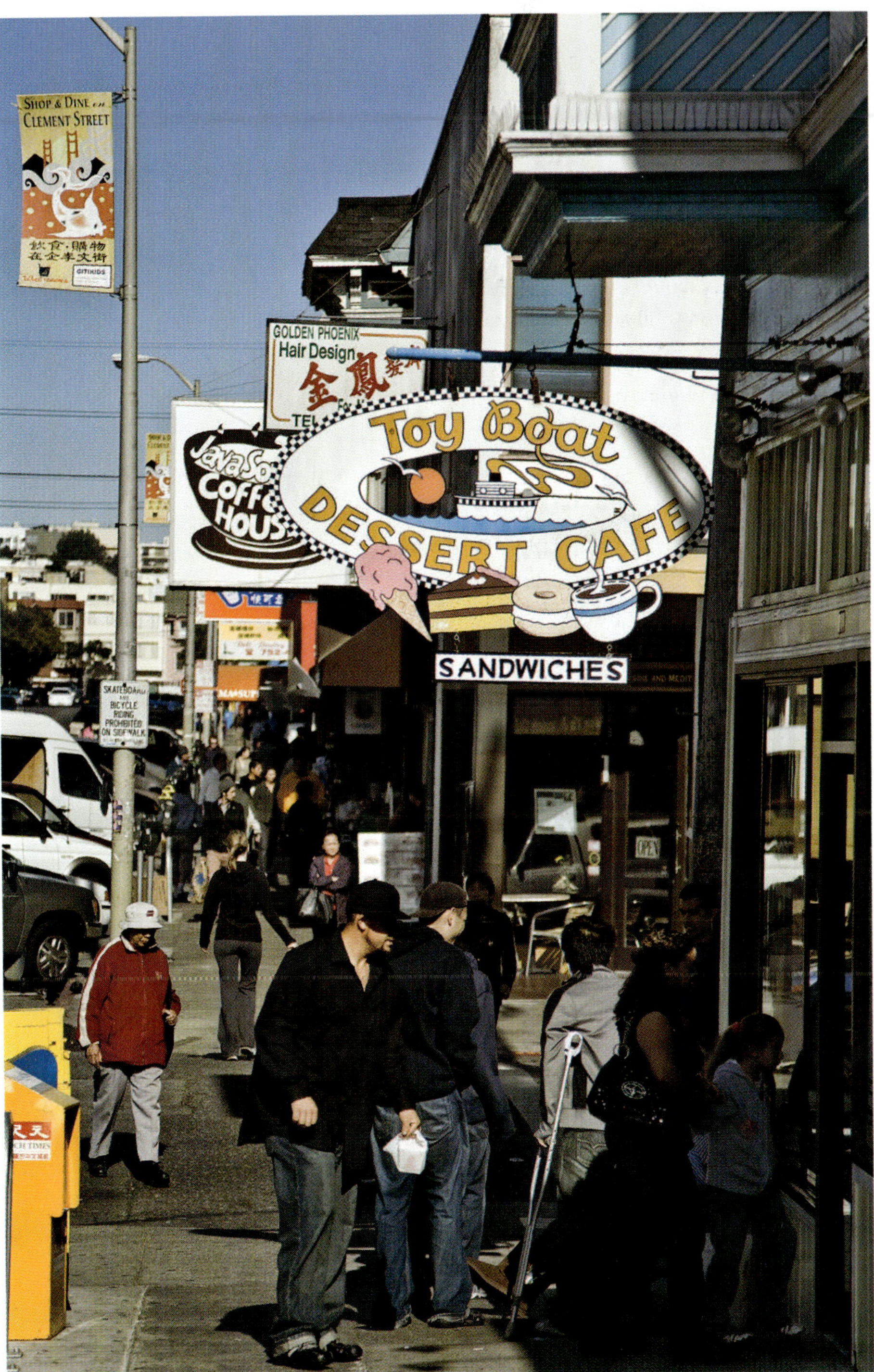

Busy street scene at Clement and 5th Avenue.

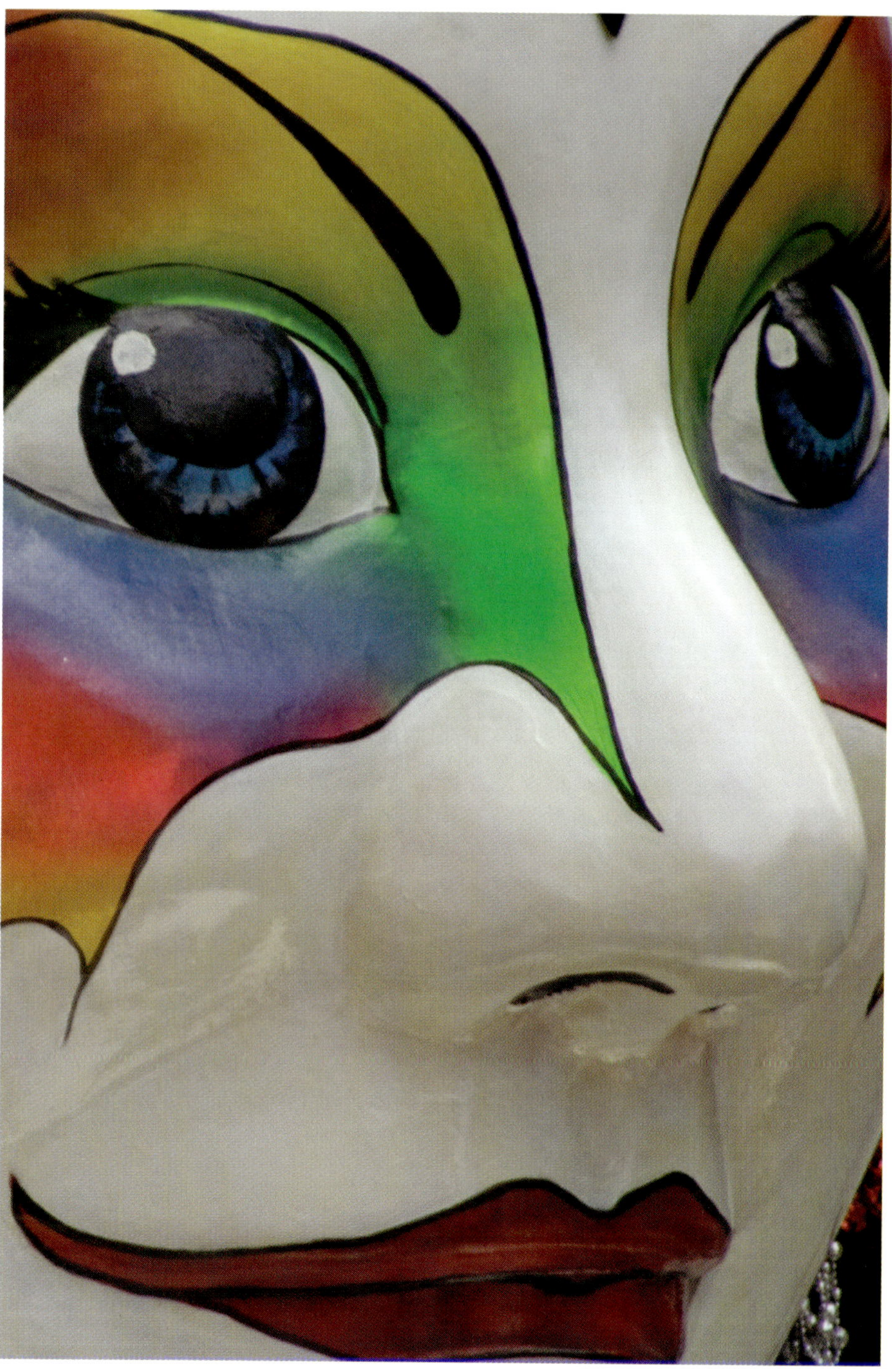

Index

A

B

C

D

E

F

J

K

L

M

N

O

P

Q

R

S

T

U

V